**Islamic Terrorists Attack World Trade Center Towers on
September 11, 2001**

9/11

STEALTH JIHAD

AND

OBAMA

ROHINI DESILVA

To order additional copies of this book, contact:
Xlibris Corporation
1-888-795-4274
www.Xlibris.com
Orders@Xlibris.com
118491

This Book is Dedicated To

Andrew Breitbart

Who inspired so many of us with his great vision and brilliance in pioneering journalistic uses of the Internet and Social Media; his unlimited energy and his abiding commitment to free speech for all; his antipathy towards the tyranny of liberal orthodoxy and political correctness; his great courage in confronting and exposing hypocrisy; his fearless defense of those unfairly targeted; his insistence on fairness in the media; his willingness to fight for fundamental American values; and his belief that Freedom of Speech does not belong solely to big media corporations, but rather that it belongs to every one of us.
You will live forever in the hearts and minds of your admirers.

Surely he recognizes deceivers;
And when he sees evil, does he not take note?

—Job 11:10-12 (NIV)

Acknowledgements

This book could not have been written without the support and inspiration of a great many people. First of all, I owe many thanks to my husband Mark, who helped me crystallize my thoughts, reviewed and critiqued what I had written and had endless patience helping me with various aspects of computer use.

Second, I owe thanks to those who pioneered Conservative Speech. To Andrew Breitbart, who believed that our Constitutional Right of Freedom of Speech does not belong solely to big media corporations, but rather belongs to every one of us and who fought the concept of political correctness relentlessly; to Glenn Beck, whose predictions about Obama's destruction of America, that seemed so far out a mere three years ago, are now coming true; to Sean Hannity and Judge Andrew Napolitano who have tirelessly exposed fraud and corruption within the government; to Joseph Farah whose World Net Daily is one of the most informative websites, if you want to know the news that the New York Times does not think is fit to print; and to Rush Limbaugh, that great communicator and defender of Individual Liberty and Conservative Causes, without each of whom none of us would have the courage to speak out.

Third, I owe thanks to those who are facing death threats, litigation, media blackouts and severe political pressure for their attempts to speak out or disclose secrets that Obama is hiding. Representative Peter King who is under so much political pressure to remain silent. Sherriff Joe Arpaio, in particular, has faced death threats from many anonymous sources and a direct death threat from an Obama supporter, litigation from Obama's DOJ, and endless political pressure. Despite all this, he and his Cold Case Posse, headed by Mike Zullo, have persevered.

Fourth, I owe thanks to all those who have risked their lives to let us know the dangers of Militant Islam. Pamela Geller, who has championed the cause of poor Muslim women who are beaten and even subject to "Honor" killings; Richard Spencer, who has called out warnings on his *Jihad Watch* website; David Horowitz and his Front Page Magazine team, who have told us of Militant Islam's takeover of European and American institutions and others who publish web sites such as *Militant Islam Monitor* and *Bare Naked Islam*. To Geert Wilders, Ayan Hirsi Ali, Dr. Wafa Sultan and others who have been threatened with death and paid a big price for speaking out. To Dr. Zudhi Jasser and Professor Muqtedar Khan who have tried to modernize and moderate Islam and bring it into the 21st Century.

I also owe thanks to my Pastor, Dr. Mark Brewer, whose brilliant series on *The Book of Amos* (NIV) inspired me to conquer my fears and speak out. To the many members of the Armed Forces who have given up their lives in this conflict. Compared to what they have sacrificed for our country, my fears are trivial. To my many friends, including Shachar Peled and Heather Branch, who provided me with leads and ideas for this book. To Jay Jacoby, who did many of my illustrations and also to Jerry Breen and Gary Cornell who did other great illustrations for me. To Tim Davis, Raegan Carmona and Alex Rawls, who helped me obtain illustrations and photos. To Carla Cobar and the rest of the staff of Xlibris, who gave me excellent service and support so this book could get published. To Alyssa Mae Fabiosa and the marketing services staff at Xlibris, Mary Victoria Falzarano and to Dave Desko, whose brilliant marketing will explain why you need to read this book. And to my friend, Rita Barrett, who encouraged me to keep going at a time when I was ready to quit. Without these, and many others who prayed for me, and helped and inspired me, this book would not have been written.

—Rohini DeSilva

Preface

Want to know why I wrote this book?

We immigrants bear a great responsibility for America's slide into Socialism. Once, immigrants came here and kissed the ground in gratitude. They wanted to forget where they came from. They were proud to become Americans. They did not ask for handouts. They only asked for the opportunity to work hard. But the millions of us who have come here more recently have taken America completely for granted. We have come here from Mexico and poorer countries, to take advantage of its economic opportunities and become rich someday. Even those from Saudi Arabia, China and richer countries have come here to have their babies, so someone in the family will have citizenship. They have used the safety and security of America as their insurance policy so they can always come here if there is trouble at home. Even the U.N., which undercuts and criticizes us at every turn, has arranged for its workers to get green cards after working here for just two years! And America has demanded nothing in return for all of the security, riches and benefits she has given to us.

We all come here, but our loyalties remain in our "home" countries. We socialize within our own ethnic enclaves; speak our own languages; eat our own ethnic foods; send our money back "home;" go "home" for weddings and the holidays and plan to go "home" when we retire. Whenever we go back "home," we spend our money lavishly; far more than the locals can afford; priding ourselves on how successful we are.

Meantime, over here, we earn a great living; send our kids to the best schools; buy the biggest houses and cars; and live the American Dream. We pretend we were actually living a better life back "home," but somehow, magically, now live in the United States.

We never ask ourselves, if it is so much better back "home," why are we living here? We know that over here, rapacious politicians and bureaucrats do not harass us. Over here, the government does not prevent us from educating ourselves and earning whatever our talents deserve. But we never bother to learn about the great American traditions or its unique Constitution.

We have never even read the Bill of Rights and do not understand that its sole purpose was to act as a check on government; to prevent the American government, its politicians and its bureaucrats from doing to us here, what is done to us back "home." Most of our college-educated kids seem to know only one section of the Constitution and seem to believe that the First Amendment exists to allow them to mouth off about Republicans and run down our Country. It never occurs to us that all we are doing is taking and that we are giving nothing back to our adopted country.

And now, as the Socialists who are in power are tearing this country limb from limb, we do nothing to defend her. We don't speak out about the flaws in the countries we have left behind; how few freedoms are available there; how much discrimination takes place over there; and how much corruption we dealt with back "home." We don't talk about how great America is. How much freedom it has given us. How we are free to pursue our own happiness without interference by government bureaucrats. Instead, we scornfully condemn America for past wrongs to Native American Indians and African slaves, that were no different from what we did in the not so distant past (and in some cases still do) in our "home" countries—the maintenance and support of caste systems, the discrimination against various ethnic and religious groups; the slaughter and cruelty of the Partition of India, the Killing Fields of the Khmer Rouge and the Disappeared of Argentina. Need I go on? Need I go back more than 100 years to the even greater cruelties and barbaric practices of our "home" countries? No. Compared to our "home" countries, America is truly the Land of the Free and the Home of the Brave.

We don't discuss these things even with our own kids. So when our kids are finished with University; one and all, they return as flaming liberals, running down this country with every breath; advocating Socialist solutions to every problem; and screaming about discrimination at every turn, discrimination that is truly petty compared to what we left behind. And we stay silent. Hoping someone else will defend this country. And that somehow, this country will not become poor and corrupt like the countries we have left behind. I believe that the time has come for us to speak out and defend our Country and save it from slipping into a Socialist quagmire.

I grew up in a Third World country and watched as Socialists came into power by pandering to the unions, demonizing the rich and promising the poor they would be looked after. Once they came into power, they changed everything and transformed the country.

Like heat seeking missiles, they went after whatever made the existing upper class powerful, with the sole aim of neutralizing them and bringing them down. They only cared about power and control. They did not care that they also brought down the economy of the country. The greatest wealth of my native country was in land. They nationalized private agricultural land holdings and subdivided them into small plots, which they gave to their supporters. Compensation for these lands was set at valuations roughly 20% of existing values. And the actual compensation was not paid for 15 or more years. They instituted a wealth tax, ostensibly to prevent people who had inherited their wealth from keeping it and to make them share it with the poor. So whoever was once rich because of land ownership or inherited wealth, now became poor. In case some few remained rich, at one time, Socialists raised the marginal tax rate to as much as 90%.

They nationalized the private school system, one of the finest in Asia at the time, with a 93% literacy rate; and converted it into a public education system, purportedly to equalize opportunity so everyone could get the same education. But they, of course, sent their kids to the finest private schools in England or France, paying for them with foreign currency that was extremely scarce and expensive but available to the connected. Everyone else, of course, got mediocre education. They stopped teaching in English, the universal language which unified Tamil and Singhalese ethnic groups and which allowed our children to get any job they wanted abroad. The teachers who failed to educate in school during the day, conducted class for pay in their homes after school. And the demand to learn English was so great that the classes overflowed from the teachers' homes into the garden; and had to be conducted over loudspeakers. Meantime, the Socialists required all school education to be conducted in the native language, spoken only by a few million people. And they reserved all government jobs for those who could speak the native language, thus shutting out the English speakers and those minorities who spoke a different language; and causing extreme bitterness between the two ethnic groups that later spilled out into a Civil War that lasted for 30 years.

The Socialists encouraged union militancy. Virtually every "grievance" was a cause for strikes that lasted for months. Workers in related companies were required to strike in solidarity with the first. No one crossed picket lines for fear of violence. "General strikes," where everyone went on strike, became common; bringing the economy to a standstill each time. The Socialists adopted and enforced union rules that made it impossible to terminate any worker. They proclaimed so many holidays, and mandated so much vacation and sick leave, that employers had to hire two people for every job. They promulgated a series of regulations that made it virtually impossible for any private company to make a profit. In fact, even if a company was in bankruptcy, it was still required to keep its workers on its payroll.

They terrorized and nationalized private corporations in virtually every sector of the economy; vastly expanded the role of government; and provided government jobs in the newly nationalized company to their supporters. They required permits for virtually everything. And the government bureaucrats, aka the "permit wallahs," who controlled the issue of those permits; viewed their role as the gatekeeper who would keep the gate locked at all costs. So, in order to get a permit, the corporation would have to pay "baksheesh" or make under-the-table payments to the bureaucrat. And the only way the corporation could stay in business was by co-operating with the Socialists; putting a Minister's cousin, nephew or other relative on their Boards; and making sure all donations went only to the Socialist's party. If they openly supported the opposing party, their businesses would be nationalized. In at least one such instance, a private business was bankrupted by constant strikes and union demands. Then it was taken over and handed to the union leaders!

Everything, even matters under litigation, became politicized. It no longer mattered whether one was right or wrong. All that mattered was whom you knew. And there were two sets of rules. If you were a supporter of the party in power; then you could do anything. If you were not a supporter, you were out of luck.

As each election neared, it would be obvious that the economy had gone south, the infrastructure was crumbling, the buses were not running on time and food had become scarce. Furthermore, though the rich had become poorer; the poor remained poor. The only real change was that the Socialists had gotten richer.

Sometimes, if the Socialists were losing badly, they instigated general strikes by the unions. Things would magically get out of hand. Violence would increase. The leader of the government would declare Martial Law, impose a curfew, and very regretfully intone that elections had to be postponed until the security situation returned to normal. This meant that the opposing party would have wasted money and energy running for elections, which would no longer be held as scheduled. And the Socialist leader would get an extended term of office. But sooner or later, elections would have to be held. But the economy would still be in a shambles.

And so, the Socialists would suddenly get religion and appear at various Temples. And they would offer yet more benefits—free rice, free sugar. But there wasn't enough to go around and rice, sugar and other staples had to be rationed. You would need to exchange a coupon to get your weekly allotment of rice and sugar. And the Socialists would demonize the rich once again. And once again, they would profess their undying love and care for the poor.

Need I go on? It seemed unbelievable that this could happen in America, the richest country on Earth. But I can see the pattern being repeated here. And now, three years after the Obama Administration's professed love for the poor, you can see it for yourself. Our economy is in a shambles; our poor are poorer than when he came into office; people have lost their jobs and their health care coverage; people have lost their homes; home values are underwater; gas prices have more than doubled; and Obama has to rig the numbers to pretend that people have found new jobs.

As so, I decided to write this book. But the more I thought about it, the more confused I became. Obama is a brilliant politician who does only what he chooses. If he chooses not to do something, even something he promised, like giving gays or illegal immigrants more rights, he won't do it. So, I knew that when he did something, it was intentional. But while saying the opposite, why was Obama doing so many things that were destroying our economy? Even if he were totally focused on keeping power like a Socialist; why would he do so many things that were bringing our country to its knees? Why was he constantly going before Arab Dictators who gave their people no rights, who wouldn't even allow Christians or Jews in their country and who threatened to annihilate Israel; and yet apologizing for our country as though it was

America that was doing something wrong? There was something more Obama was doing. Something not quite American. Something sinister and malevolent. But I couldn't quite put my finger on it.

I knew Obama had been a Muslim and that his father and stepfather were practicing Muslims, while he mother had been just a free spirit. All his 6 siblings are still Muslims. In the Madrassah he attended, kids were taught only the *Qur'an* and *Shari'ah* law. They learned only in Arabic. The clever ones, and Obama was surely among them, learned the *Qur'an* in a few years.

I knew he had roomed with two Muslim foreign students at Occidental and possibly registered as a foreign student and went under the name Barry Soetoro. I knew he had gone to Pakistan for a couple of years at a time when American citizens were not allowed to travel there. But all these details were deliberately kept fuzzy by the media. In this Internet age, when more information is available than ever before, how is it that we have a President about whom we know so little?

I also knew that once Obama was a Muslim, he could not convert, i.e., commit the Muslim crime of Apostasy, without being liable for the Muslim death penalty. And yet, he claimed to have become a Christian. But that was in Reverend Jeremiah Wright's America-hating, Jew-hating "church" which was anything but Christian. This caused me to suspect his bona fides as a Christian.

But why did it matter if he was still a Muslim? There were two reasons: Muslim rulers all rule as Dictators, collecting all of their country's wealth, giving their subjects no rights and no freedoms, and keeping their subjects in poverty, totally dependent on their ruler. The other reason was that a Muslim ruler would impose *Shari'ah* law, which because it treated women as slaves, executed gays, banned music and concerts and even banned pets; was diametrically opposed to our U.S. Laws. This caused me to worry about what Obama would do to us.

I looked around at Europe and realized that Islamists had almost converted Europe into a Caliphate. Islamists have sent their shock troops of vast numbers of illegals into Europe where they exercise their religious right to have four wives and many children and claim welfare and benefits for all of them. With this incentive they have produced large numbers of children in

European countries that have negative birth rates of the native population. Inevitably, as the Militant Islamists openly boast, Muslims will overtake the native European populations with their numbers. Even now, we can see this in the cities of England where, as the Muslims approach a majority, they commence marching, protesting and demanding more accommodation to their *Shari'ah* laws and even parallel legal systems for them to follow.

Once I reviewed Orthodox Islam, I realized that *Shari'ah* law was an integral part of being a Muslim. And I recognized that Muslims were obliged to follow every aspect of *Shari'ah* and ignore any other laws, including the laws of the countries that took in the Muslims. The results have stunned those Europeans who have followed what is happening. Muslims are totally disregarding the laws and traditions of Europe and, using violence and threats, are slowly converting European countries into Muslim ones.

Once I realized that Europe is being transformed, it became obvious that Obama's plan is to do the same thing here. Not openly, but stealthily. No matter how you looked at it, there was no escaping the conclusion. Take a look at what he has done.

Why has he completely banned domestic oil drilling wherever he has the power to do so, while proclaiming that the country is producing more oil under his administration than any other? Why has he prevented deep sea, and even routine undersea drilling in the Gulf, off the East and West coasts and in the Arctic sea and put hundreds of thousands out of work; while subsidizing deep sea drilling in Brazil? Why has he eliminated coal as a source of American energy, by refusing to open federal lands for coal mining and promulgating rules that make it impossible to open up a new coal plant or ever repair an old one? Why has he canceled the Keystone pipeline that would have given us thousands of jobs and a friendly nearby source of energy years into the future? Did he not realize this made us even more dependent on Middle Eastern OPEC oil? Of course, he did. *(He's brilliant, right?)*

Meanwhile, the sleight of hand is to promote the development of Green Energy. But even as America pours billions into this effort, the Green Energy contribution to our energy needs is now, and into the foreseeable future will be, miniscule. Look behind the curtain and you can see that the only practical result of Green Energy is crony capitalism, where Obama rewards his supporters with billions in public funds; the money "disappears" and Green Energy companies go bankrupt one after another.

Why has Obama run up $6 Trillion in federal debt in three years; while the 43 previous Presidents had run up only $10 Trillion in debt in all the previous 233 years of our country's existence? Why, after promising to go through the budget line by line to eliminate wasteful spending, does Obama have virtually no cuts, but has hundreds of billions of new programs and a big new entitlement that will generate hundreds of billions more of deficits. Doesn't he realize he is bankrupting the country? Of course, he does. *(He's brilliant, right?)*

Why is he demonizing the rich, taking away private property, taking over 20% of our economy with his Obama Care and constantly fighting to raise taxes and take under his control, more and more of the country's private wealth? Why is he encouraging the poor to remain poor and dependent on him so he could be their benefactor; exactly like Muslim rulers do?

Why is he saying he was fighting the "good war" in Afghanistan, while announcing a date of withdrawal; and making rules of engagement that handicap our military and guarantee a defeat for us? Why is he returning Gitmo terrorists to Afghanistan and sending the radical Sheikh Yousuf al-Qaradawi to negotiate with the Taliban for what amounts to our surrender? Why did he ignore the freedom fighters in Iran even as they cried out to Obama for help and were gunned down by the Mullahs? Why is he endlessly pleading with Iran to talk with us about its nuclear program, even as it proceeds to develop its bomb and promises to annihilate Israel? Why is he standing by and talking while Iran's puppet state Syria slaughters its own people who are seeking freedom? All the while assuring us he supported freedom for all. I knew he was originally a Muslim. But he claimed he was now a Christian. But what he was doing merely benefited Muslims. Whose side was he on?

Why was he saying he was deporting illegals, while suing Arizona for doing the same thing and ignoring all the sanctuary cities that were acting as a magnet for illegals; knowing all the while that Muslim Terrorists were infiltrating through our Southern border? Why is he insisting on building a Mosque in the shadow of the World Trade Center knowing full well it was a Victory Mosque celebrating the conquest of America? Why is he allowing Mega Mosques to be built throughout the heartland? Why is he converting our refugee assistance program into one that imports Somali Muslims, the most violent and barbaric of Muslims, into this country; while failing to bring in Christian Copts or Christian Iraqis, Nigerians and Chinese who are being slaughtered or oppressed? Why is he celebrating Muslim religious holidays in the White House and avoiding celebrating Christmas by running away to Hawaii during Christmas time?

Why has he issued orders that all government workers, including our soldiers going into battle, cannot say Christian prayers because they are "offensive;" while allowing Muslims to pray on the streets in Manhattan and have their Mosques use loudspeakers to blare out their call to prayer in Detroit, Dearborn and other cities across America? Why is he listening to the advice of his many White House Islamic Advisors and insisting that Islamic Terrorists not be called "Islamic Terrorists?" Why is he telling us we should be more like Europe even while Europe is going into bankruptcy, in large part because of its exploding illegal Muslim populations that take, but won't work and don't give back? I began to see a pattern here too.

Why is he violating the Catholic's Constitutional Right to Freedom of Religion and dictating doctrine to the Catholics, supplanting the Pope; and issuing commands that Catholics must violate their conscience and pay for contraception and abortion pills for their workers? Why does he speak with the greatest respect for Muslims and the Muslim religion? Why does he claim he is a Christian while actively denigrating Christianity and labeling Christians "Terrorists?"

And then, . . . it dawned on me. He is not a Christian at all! He is a Muslim!! The only way to explain what he is doing is to understand that everything he is doing, he is doing to further one overarching goal—the pursuit of *Stealth Jihad* against this great country!

As so, this book came into being. I hope you will enjoy reading it; that you will consider the great danger facing our country; and that you will speak out and do all you can to protect what is, undoubtedly, the greatest country on earth.

Rohini DeSilva
July 2012

Part I of IV

How the Media Helped Hide Obama's Secrets &
Tricked You into Voting for him

Table of Contents

Introduction

Part I of IV

How the Media Helped Hide Obama's Secrets & Tricked You into Voting for him

Introduction

Listen to Obama explain his Muslim Faith and read the details:

http://www.youtube.com/watch?v=Dc3PzHKCVGM&feature=player_embedded#!
http://conservapedia.com/Barack_Obama%27s_Muslim_Heritage
http://conservapedia.com/Muslim_agenda_of_the_Obama_administration

Admit it. You already had great doubts about Obama. But two of the most powerful groups in America—the Media and the Islamists—tricked you into voting for him. In this Part I, I will show you how the Media helped hide Obama's secrets and tricked you into voting for him. In Part II, I will explain Islam and show you how Islamists have tricked Europeans and pursued a Stealth Jihad to convert Europe into Eurabia. In Part III, I will show how Muslims are tricking you and pursuing a Stealth Jihad right here in America. And in Part IV, I will tie these threads together and show you what Obama is doing to our country. I trust you will have the courage to face what your instincts tell you is true.

This is serious stuff; so don't waste my time and yours screaming about "racism." Obama is not an American Black. His American half, through his mother, is White and the other half, through his father, is African and Muslim. And don't talk to me about "Hate" and call me an "Islamaphobe" either. First, make up your mind: either it is OK to be a Muslim or it is not. If a Muslim is the same as a Hindu, a Buddhist, a Jew or a Christian; then it is not "hate" to say Obama is a Muslim. If, on the other hand, (a) Islam is not a religion but rather a very dangerous religious/political/military ideology, and its Qur'an commands all true Muslims to do Jihad against us and destroy us; and (b) in Muslim countries, non-Muslims are persecuted for practicing their religion and forced to live like Dhimmis, aka slaves or serfs; then it means extreme danger to you and our country. But it is still not "hate." Just as the Park Service doesn't "hate" grizzlies but simply warns you about the dangers; so it is with me. I don't "hate" Obama or Muslims. But I am warning you, because it is imperative that you figure out for yourself whether or not Obama is a Muslim, as I say he is; so you will watch what he is doing, and realize he is destroying America.

Also, don't tell me that 1.2 Billion Muslims are going to rise up to attack me. Of those 1.2 Billion, half are women. And they couldn't possibly want to remain as they do now, being totally subservient to men, and being subject to genital mutilation, rape and "honor" killings. Then, there are the vast numbers of decent and moderate Muslims who have escaped from the strictures of Orthodox Islam and are living in non-Muslim controlled countries. They want to get along with everyone; have no desire to "kill the infidel," like orthodox Muslims do; or be subjugated by Orthodox Muslims. Then, there are those Muslims who are neither radical Orthodox nor even more radical Salafist, living in Muslim countries, who have participated in the Arab Spring, and who are crying out, and even dying, to get our American freedoms for themselves. None of the above groups, which constitute the vast majority of those 1.2 Billion, would want to silence people like this writer. In fact, it is in their interest that the extremists be exposed. It is only the extremist and radical Orthodox Muslims that seek to destroy those with an opposing point of view. Today, these extremists profess to speak for the moderates; but they will destroy the moderates as soon as they get the opportunity; just as the rulers in Syria and Iran are killing the moderates within their borders.

Chapter I

What do you know about Obama? . . . Nothing at all!

You knew absolutely nothing about his personal and professional life; and nothing about his eligibility, his brilliance, his socialism or his religion in 2008. So, when you last voted for him, you knew nothing. **And you know nothing even today**!

The last election was a triumph of Media marketing over substance; promoting Obama as the "American Idol." He bounded onto the stage with his great, practiced smile and used the reverb to bring power to his voice as he read from his teleprompter, what someone else had written for him. And the Media assured us *"He was the most brilliant man living!" "The world would love us now!" "The only way America could redeem itself of its sin of slavery was by electing a black man!"* Women fainted. Others lined up for hours "to collect some of Obama's stash" and believed he would make them rich. The excitement reached fever pitch. Like a giddy teenager, you fell for the good-looking dude who promised "Hope!" and "Change!!" And you handed over to him our country, its great traditions and its enormous wealth.

So . . . did you enjoy it as he held up America as an object of scorn and ridicule by his constant apologizing on our behalf for sins we have supposedly committed? Are you happy with the way Obama has kept his promises? Remember he said he was a uniter not a divider? He has divided our country into so many different segments that you can hardly call us Americans any more. Blacks vs. whites; Latinos vs. whites; women and those who "war" on them; Catholics vs. abortion proponents; Gays vs. all others; liberals vs. conservatives; rich vs. poor. Do you like having his SEIU thugs going to people's homes with bullhorns and placards and terrorizing their kids and their wives? Do you like having thugs stabbing cops and marching around warring on the rest of us, as they did recently in Chicago? Do you like it that your media won't even show you images of those thugs?

So, . . . are you yourself better off now than you were 3 years ago? Haven't your gas prices more than doubled? Isn't your grocery bill going through the roof? Aren't your electricity and heating bills skyrocketing? Do you like being poor and dependent on Obama to get you some money? Do you like looking around for food stamps or some government program, which will help you survive? Do you like meeting friends who have lost their jobs and are about to lose their homes? Isn't your own home underwater? Or do you have your house at all? Have you and your kids got decent jobs? Of course not!

Just like an abused and battered woman waiting for her man who is "working late" yet again; you too wait for Obama to fulfill his promises. You listen to the lies he says even as you can see he had been drinking again, or shooting up again; or from the rumpled shirt, that he has cheated on you again. As the election nears, there is a choice you have to make. Are you going to kneel down and beg him, *"Lie to me one more time so I can believe you"*? Or are you going to say, *"Enough!! I deserve better than this!!"* . . . ?

Lie to me One More Time
So I can Believe You!

© First-Amendment-Rights.com

**Enough!!
I Deserve Better than This!!**

You know absolutely nothing about his personal life: You read Obama's book, *Dreams from my Father*. But Obama's close friend and neighbor, the terrorist Bill Ayers, claims he wrote this book, making it a work of fiction.[1] You do know that his father and his stepfather were practicing Muslims, while his mother was a free spirit. You know that Obama attended a Madrasah, which is a religious school that teaches only the *Qur'an* and *Shari'ah* law and only in Arabic. You do not know of any of his past girl friends or his relationship with his parents or his relationships with his various stepsisters and stepbrothers. In fact, he has at least 6 step-brothers and sisters, **all of whom are Muslim**; Abon'go Malik 'Roy' Obama, 'George' Hussein Onyango Obama, Auma Obama, Mark Obama Ndesandjo, Maya Soetoro and Lia Soetoro. The media, which tracked Herman Cain's every move as far back as 20 years ago, has been unwilling to interview even one of these siblings to ask about their relationship with Obama.

Nor has the Media been willing to disclose any of the details of his dealings with his personal mentor, communist Frank Marshal Davis; his fundraiser Tony Rezko, now jailed for fraud; his relationship to his longtime friend, neighbor, fellow professor, and communist Weather Underground terrorist Bill Ayers and his wife Bernadine Dohrn; or his relationship to the America-hating Anti-Semite Jeremiah Wright, who was his "Pastor" for 20 years in a hate-filled, completely racist "Church" that is definitely not Christian. Or even something as mundane as Obama's medical records. Even the lowest ranking member of the Armed Forces handling sensitive matters would be required to obtain a Security Clearance.[2] But Obama, our highest-ranking member, our Commander in Chief, could not get even this basic Security Clearance because this requires disclosing personal history, including birth records, and school records; disclosing personal medical history, including Obama's admitted use of cocaine and other drugs;[3] disclosing foreign country residencies; and disclosing associations with people such as Frank Marshall Davis, Bill Ayers and Bernadine Dohrn, who have expressed virulently anti-American beliefs and also expressed desires to overthrow the government.[4] **Knowing all of these facts, the JournoList Media has actively hidden all of Obama's personal life from you.**

© 2008 Jerry Breen www.newbreen.com
The Men Behind Obama

You also know absolutely nothing about Obama's professional life: Obama himself profoundly disrespects our country by refusing to let us see or disclose his original birth certificate, his adoption records, his passports as an Indonesian and as an American, who paid for his trips to India and Pakistan, the dates and the names of his elementary schools in Indonesia and Hawaii, his SAT's and his LSAT's, his college records at Occidental. Whether he was enrolled as a Muslim foreign student Barry Soetoro, and why he roomed at Occidental with two Muslim foreign students. His GPA and records at Columbia and Harvard, the name of the person who funded his education at Columbia and Harvard, his Harvard Law Review articles or any writing sample. The nature of his position at the University of Chicago, the titles and content of his lectures and scholarly articles at University of Chicago and his Illinois Bar Association records. How much did he earn at University of Chicago for what he did? Before she dialed back in 2006 when Obama ran for President, and while she was not entitled to practice law, what did his wife Michelle do for the $307,000 per year job she held at the University of Chicago Medical Health Center?[5] **Is he our President or is he our Ruler who doesn't have to answer to the people?**

Chapter 2

So, how did Obama get elected?
The Media-Hollywood Mafia Complex,
the most powerful group on Earth,
Tricked you into voting for him

They constantly yap about "taking the money out of politics". But, in fact, they themselves make the most money out of politics! Every single candidate, and every Super Pac, has to pay tribute to them for ads!! If you don't advertise, you would be totally at the mercy of the Media. They could use puff pieces to build you up. Or they could destroy you. They'd make up polls to show you are losing when you are not. *Ad Nauseam* repetition of "bombastic," "baggage" and "unhinged" and Newt is toast!! Sheen dissed his gay producer and was instantly fired! It was then "discovered" he was a drunk, a cokehead and a womanizer!! And, as they say, "He will never work in this town again!" Ditto Mel Gibson. Everyone in Congress is terrified of them. In fact, the Media Mafia is more powerful than the President, the Congress and the Judiciary combined; and far more powerful than Halliburton and any other corporation that they constantly revile.

And definitely, they are the richest 1% in existence! They have used their power to give themselves tax breaks and exemptions from IRS scrutiny. They rake in billions on their movies, but claim they didn't make a profit and never pay a penny in taxes!! They are also totally biased. For instance, large numbers of the New York Times' staff are homosexual and virulently anti-Christian. But they hide their bias as they push an extremist gay agenda and sneer at Christians. They are welcome to express their opinions. But they should call their programs "ABC/NBC/CBS/CNN Opinions" or "All the Opinions fit to Print" rather than "News." But they pretend to be unbiased and honorable journalists even as they destroy anyone who opposes them. What sense does it make to give them First Amendment protections to keep lying to and manipulating the American people and operate as a Mafia?

The JournoList Conspiracy: Here is how they worked then, and continue to operate now. First, hundreds of prominent journalists from Time, Newsweek, the Associated Press, Reuters, the Washington Post, New York Times, Politico, Bloomberg, Huffington Post, PBS, a large NPR affiliate in California, Hollywood big shots, professors and other liberals created a top-secret, password-protected website, the JournoList.[1,2,3,4] They used this website to plan and coordinate their attacks on Republicans, whom they unfailingly called *"Racists!"* or *"Hatemongers!"* They resort to omissions, distortions and exaggerations. Another favorite tactic is to "discover" some trivial matter the target spoke about and scream: *"The whole world is offended by what you said!"*

The conspiracy continues even today. In a brilliant expose, Tucker Carlson of Daily Caller[5] has shown how David Brock and his Media Matters operate. First of all, Media Matters gets it money from various George Soros affiliated groups. Media Matters staffers actually worked with the White House to take down Obama's "enemies," aka conservatives. To co-ordinate strategy, Media Matters' staff had weekly meetings with White House officials, and followed up with meetings with progressive organizations. Over 50 researchers would be assigned to dig up dirt on a target. Others would write thousands of emails, purporting to come from actual people, complaining about the target. Yet others would send emails and make phone calls to the advertisers demanding they pull their ads, and make threats that if they didn't, the company itself would face an advertising campaign against them. Next, Media Matters staffers actually wrote the copy for prominent liberal journalists—MSNBC anchors and executives, Greg Sargent of the Washington Post, James Rainer of the LA Times, Eugene Dobbs, E.J. Dionne, and many more. And following instructions from Obama, their chief targets are Fox News and Rush Limbaugh, who remain under constant attack. Among their biggest successes were Don Imus, Lou Dobbs and Glen Beck, all of whom Media Matters got fired. Then, there was Dr. Laura and Judge Napolitano whose advertisers Media Matters also targeted, so that they too had to give up their shows. For all of these, Media Matters wrote fake emails and made fake phone calls to their sponsors and advertisers pretending that the public was opposed to them. Advertisers and sponsors panicked and withdrew their advertising. This was media terrorism at its worst. And all the while, Media Matters, this most uncharitable entity, acting as the hyper-partisan arm of the Democrat Party, enjoyed tax-exempt status as a politically neutral "charitable corporation!" They also used the JournoList to act in concert to conceal the truth about Obama. **They were then, and remain today, a vast left-wing conspiracy whose main purposes are to destroy our First Amendment Freedom of Speech and protect Obama.**

© First-Amendment-Rights.com

JournoList Media doing the Bidding of their Boss, Obama

Their trick is to copy Goebbels; endlessly repeating lies, extending the envelope of our credibility with each repetition, until we believe things we would never have believed earlier. Then, and now, the media ignores news that is not pro-Socialist like they are. *(Think. Have you ever read or heard anything positive about a true Christian or Conservative?)* Next, they present a vigorous defense of their man Obama. Lots of puff pieces. No enquiry whatsoever about the truth. Actually no journalism; just party propaganda; like Pravda, Xinhua News or North Korean "news." Next, they present their position as the "cool" and "tolerant" one, which you emulate. In fact, Obama recently scolded the Media, claiming they were giving too much credence to conservative explanations for their positions and treating them as being worthy of consideration, but I do not think they need to change much to adhere to his wishes. Finally, like a pack of hyenas, they go after anyone who says anything they oppose. They mock, sneer and make fun of their target. Once you laugh along with them at us, they've got you ready to believe anything they say about their victim. Ad Hominem attacks? Allegations of Racism? All O.K. They jeer at anyone opposing them by calling them racists, homophobes, bigots, crackers, hayseeds, hicks, rednecks, right wing extremists or, absolutely the worst epithet, Evangelicals; "clinging to their guns and religion" as Obama so famously sneered. Don't believe me? Check out the examples below:

Watch the Media Trick You:

(i)   **Democrats:** At Chappaquiddick, **Ted Kennedy** drove a young girl into the river and left her to drown. He remained a drunk and a womanizer. **Bill Clinton** was a serial adulterer. He raped Juanita Broderick; used his position of power to demand sexual favors from Katherine Wiley; seduced a young subordinate, Monica Lewinsky; and committed perjury in court over his sexual harassment of Paula Jones. But the Media pretended each of these was an isolated incident, and not a pattern of disgusting behavior. **John Edwards** was a consummate liar. He dragged his dying wife to his campaigns so he could pretend he was a caring, loving husband. Meanwhile he was producing a child with a mistress and stating it was his aide's child. **Barney Frank**[6] was a foul-mouthed bully. He installed his husband at Fannie Mae, gave him a six-figure salary and millions in bonuses; while he intimidated and bullied anyone who tried to probe the malfeasance at Fannie Mae. This malfeasance ultimately caused the global financial crisis and huge numbers of Americans lost their homes. One of Barney's previous boyfriends dealt drugs and another ran a prostitution ring out of Barney's home. Barney was, and is, a total disgrace to the Gay Community. Yet the media's PR machine has presented all the above as great liberal lions who had great policies and compassion for the poor!! And you were tricked into voting enthusiastically for these dregs of human society! Think . . . Can you name one specific policy these guys espoused that has turned out to be socially and economically good for America?

(ii)   **Republicans:** Contrast this to the way the Media Mafia treats Republicans. **Sarah Palin**[7] was brutally attacked by the Media. The media spent millions flying 200 lawyers to Anchorage to spend four weeks to try to dig up dirt on her. But they found nothing. Then, they sent some Sleazoid to move right next to her home so he could invade her privacy by eavesdropping on every word she spoke and peering into her daughters' bedrooms both day and night. He found nothing. Then the Media sought to make Mrs. Palin the lead example of "violent" speech, not giving a single example of actual violent speech, but instead using insinuations and distortions of what she actually said; all the while totally ignoring countless examples of violent speech on the left. But the constant attacks and talk of "her huge unfavorable ratings" made her decide not to run. Removing her from the political stage as a possible opponent to Obama in 2012 was one of the JournoList Mafia's biggest victories. The media also mercilessly hounded **Herman Cain**, an American black, taking him out before American blacks realized Cain was far better for them than Obama. Three Dung Beetles, (co-incidentally all from Chicago and all with bankruptcies and previous sexual harassment charges against others) crawled out of the sewer long enough to hurl accusations at Cain. Two crawled right back. The third, who crawled out of Axelrod's apartment building (same difference!) accused Cain of groping her. The media actually wanted us to believe she was penniless; but still had money to fly from Chicago to Washington to ask Cain for a job. Whereupon he assaulted her!! But no racism here, no Sir-eee!!.

Watch Hollywood Manipulate You: When someone mentions "Sandusky" I am sure you puke in disgust. Yet, Michael Jackson allegedly slept with young boys. But he should be excused *"because he was like a child,"* we were told. Woody Allen slept with his adopted underage daughter while he was living with her mother. *"But it didn't really count,"* we were told, *"because he was not married to the girl's mother and the girl herself was adopted anyway."* Roman Polanski raped a 13-year-old girl. *"But that is ok,"* we were told, *"because the girl has said she has forgiven him!"* I could go on for pages, but you get the point.

The Media arouses our emotions and uses prurient sexual titillation to get us to part with our money and drive us to accept more and more perversion as normal. And we go along, wanting to appear "cool" and "open minded." Long ago, the Media used their great creative talent to produce uplifting films, which people enjoy even today. But now, they are totally biased against patriotic Americans. Do they ever depict a Christian as a good and honorable person? Of course they don't. And, if a good Christian does become the subject of a movie, all indicia of their Christian values are expunged from the story before it is turned into entertainment. They could make movies about the great sacrifices made by our courageous soldiers risking their lives for our country; and sometimes, to save their fellow soldiers from certain death. They could make a wonderful movie about the courage of Egyptian women. Lara Logan, a CBS reporter, was stripped naked and brutally raped by a violent mob of Egyptian men who had believed she was Jewish. But a group of vulnerable and defenseless Burka-clad Muslim women had the courage to disregard the extreme danger to themselves, surround Lara Logan[8] and whisk her away to safety.[9] How much play did this story get in the New York Times?

Instead, the Media enjoys exercising their raw power over us to force us to "enjoy" depressing, disgusting films. Consider the garbage they are showing us.[10] In *Three and a Half Men*, the promo (seen by children of all ages) showed a naked Kutchner dangling his penis in front of two kids who looked about 10 years old. We only saw his naked back, but the children were in front of him with their eyes glued on his genitals as he bounced up and down. When we complain about this vulgarity, no doubt we will be told: *"It is O.K. because the actor wore a nude body suit!"* Then consider the movie *"Shame,"* depicting a man indulging in grossly obsessive and perverted sex, watching extreme porn (which we get to see too), sleeping maniacally with prostitutes, girl friends and whoever. *"This is not sexual perversion,"* we are told. *"It is merely an addiction, for which we should show great sympathy and understanding."* Finally consider the ultimate in depravity, *"The Skin I live In."*[11] Banderas, (who should know better), is the plastic surgeon father who kidnaps the guy who raped his daughter, cuts off his genitals and grafts a face onto him; making the rapist looks exactly like Banderas' daughter. Then Banderas proceeds to rape his "daughter," having violent sex with her/him and using dildos to cause maximum pain. No doubt, we will be called upon to accept and make excuses for all this garbage. Polanski and/or Woody Allen will soon be given Lifetime Achievement Awards at the Oscars. And Banderas will, no doubt, receive an Oscar for "brilliant acting."

Take *"50 Shades of Grey."* This best seller, about to be made into a movie, depicts a "virgin" who falls for a Sadomasochist and then descends into all kinds of Sadomasochitic sexual perversion. Once you remove the excuse that she was a "virgin," what do you have? Pure, unadulterated porn. Next, take "*The Dark Knight Rises.*" This was marketed as a "dark" movie thriller. In fact, the "*Joker*" and the other protagonists were all pure evil incarnate, whose evil was shown in excruciating, mind-numbing detail. Heath Ledger, who depicted the *Joker*, took his own life. And it spawned a copycat, who dyed his hair orange, wore the same disfiguring makeup, marched into the sold out midnight screening of the latest *Batman* movie, and did, in real life, exactly what the Joker did in the movie. It was so like the movie that when the gas canisters exploded, some in the audience thought it was a publicity stunt! But this was real. The murderer used double-barreled shotguns to kill 12 people, including a six-year-old child, and injure over 50. Did Hollywood take any responsibility for inducing unstable, fragile minds to copy their mayhem in actual life? Of course not. The blame was instantly deflected onto the Tea Party. And various groups interested in taking away our Second Amendment Rights called for "gun control." How about a call for "Hollywood Control" to prevent them from marketing extremely violent or sexually perverted movies? Oh No!! That would violate their First Amendment Rights!! *(For those who are unclear on the concept, the Second Amendment comes right after the First Amendment. And if you cannot prevent exercise of the First Amendment, you cannot prevent exercise of the Second Amendment either!! And stop complaining about the perversion and debasement of our culture. It is you who are pouring poison into your mind and destroying your soul. It is you who are inducing Hollywood to make these movies by spending your money going to see the garbage they produce and making them billionaires!)*

Look what has happened to our Public Square. A Cross? A Manger? "*No! No!! It violates the Separation of Church and State! It simply cannot be allowed! It is offensive to some people!!*" But naked men performing oral sex on each other in the middle of the street at Gay Pride parades? "*Absolutely fine. We are a tolerant people!!*" Mosques blaring the Muslim call to prayer five times a day? "*Fine! We must respect their religion!*" Church bells calling Christians to worship? "*Oh, they are violating the noise ordinances and disturbing their neighbors!*"

We Americans need to recognize we are being force-fed spoonsful of raw sewage. First we are called upon to admire the little bits of Arugula or

Artisanal Cheese ("*the brilliant acting*" "*the great direction*" "*the wonderful photography*" "*the powerful and disturbing message*") we find in the sewage (like "*The Skin I Live In.*") Then, slowly, gradually, we are led to believe the sewage is really tasty. The end goal is to have us not only agree to eat the raw sewage, but also say it tastes really good!

We are tricked into thinking we are being "cool" and "open minded" and definitely more "*sophisticated*" than those ignorant hicks who object to these perverted TV shows and movies. In fact, we are totally controlled by the media, which is leading us down the path to perdition. Just like child molesters, they are grooming us into accepting the unacceptable. If the media tells us black is white or the sky is green, we agree wholeheartedly. And now, there is no line, be it of sexual perversion or of simple decency towards a political opponent, which we will not cross. We make excuses for the inexcusable. We sneer at those who don't agree with us. We have lost our conscience and our morality. Ultimately, we will lose our ability to think and to make decisions for ourselves.

Chapter 3

Four great frauds are being perpetrated on us by Obama and completely concealed by the Media: First, His Eligibility; Second, His Brilliance

The Media bullied us constantly and told us that the whole world hated us because of George Bush. Using Goebbels' strategy, this was repeated endlessly. So, we elected Obama as President, mainly so we could prove to the whole world that we were not racists, and that we were "cool" and "open minded" enough to vote for a black, any black. **But look at the frauds being perpetrated on us:**

Eligibility: Obama's eligibility has been challenged[1] in at least 100 court cases throughout the country[2] and Obama has spent millions defending these cases. But there has never been a single hearing. Each case has been dismissed on the grounds that the plaintiff has no standing to bring the case. Not a former or current military officer, not a rival for the presidency or an elector, not a State Representative, not a tax payer, not a relative of Obama and not an ordinary citizen. Lt. Col. Dr. Terry Lakin[3] was actually court martialed and jailed for refusing what he considered unlawful orders issued by Obama whom he believed was not a lawful President. He was not allowed to present any arguments or call any witnesses or subpoena any documents. And a statement of these facts was deleted from Wikipedia.[4] According to the various courts, including the 9th Circuit, **no one on earth has standing to ask questions about Obama's eligibility**. The 9th Circuit further held that it was too late to investigate alleged election fraud, because Obama had already been inaugurated![5] (If we apply this rationale to Bernie Madoff, it would be too late in investigate that fraud and Madoff should be allowed to keep whatever assets he bought with the money he stole!!) A Hawaiian Judge has even said the public is not entitled to view Obama's Birth Certificate because of privacy concerns.[8] (But Obama's Axelrod got Obama's Republican rival Ryan's divorce records unsealed a week before Obama's Illinois Senate election![6])

© First-Amendment-Rights.com

100 Lawsuits and Still No Birth Certificate!

Sheriff Joe Arpaio has worked with 6 investigators lead by Mike Zullo, who interviewed hundreds of experts. He stated that the long form birth certificate Obama had provided was not a copy of a document; but rather a computer generated forgery.[7] In the most recent hearing in April 2012, in New Jersey, Obama's attorneys insisted that a birth certificate was not necessary to prove eligibility in New Jersey[8] and that even Mickey Mouse could be placed on the ballot.[9] In June 2012, in Florida, even though he was already the President and was running unopposed in the upcoming election, Obama's attorneys claimed they do not have to prove eligibility because he was not yet the Democrat nominee for the 2012 election![10]

The Judiciary is actively preventing any investigation. They could call for opposing experts to present their findings and then render a decision. They could order Hawaii to turn over the original birth certificate. They could order Occidental to turn over Obama's school application to see if he applied as a foreign student. But they refuse to act. Similarly Congress

37

could hold hearings as to Obama's eligibility. But they won't act either. Perhaps the Judiciary and Congress are all terrorized. Or perhaps they see political gain in supporting Obama; or political peril in opposing him. Perhaps they are counting on the JournoList press to keep matters hidden. And true to form, anyone who wants to verify Obama is eligible to be President is sneered at by the JournoList and called a pejorative "Birther." And no doubt, the JournoList will eventually tell us: *"It doesn't really matter if Obama was ineligible. He has already been President for so long, we should just forget about it."*

Whatever their motivations, both the Judiciary and Congress have now rendered themselves irrelevant. If Obama can flaunt a forgery in lieu of an actual Birth Certificate, and neither of the other two supposedly co-equal branches of government is willing to challenge him and exercise their duty of "Checks and Balances;" then they cease to exist as independent branches of government. And our Government gets transformed into a Dictatorship, with Obama as its head.

**Former System of Checks and Balances
in the American Government—Circa 1787-2008
Three Co-Equal Branches: President, Congress and Supreme Court**

As for us, the American public, why should an ineligible President be allowed to lead our country; spend trillions (mostly on his cronies—the Solyndra's, the Bankers and the Union guys); put us into debt; and spend another bunch of millions gadding about on Air Force One to get himself re-elected? **If he is ineligible, he should be impeached.**

Brilliance: The JournoList also told us that Obama is the most brilliant man alive, who could solve all problems and unite the country. And there was no need for us to ask to see his grades at Columbia or Harvard or even at Occidental. We hadn't seen any articles he wrote as Editor in Chief of the Harvard Law Review or as a Constitutional Law Professor. Nor had we heard any speech he made without a teleprompter telling him what to say. Based solely on the JournoList's assurance of his brilliance; and knowing full well that Obama had never run even a small business or held a management level job in the private sector; we elected him President, to manage the finances of the greatest country on earth. We were told we should be like Europe. And sure enough, just like Europe, we are sinking into a morass of debt! $16 Trillion and rising by the minute! Just check out the debt clock.[11]

By now, it should be obvious to one and all that Obama is not only not brilliant, but he is totally incompetent and does not care a whit about the suffering of ordinary Americans. **Even as Obama spends more in 3 years than all the other 43 presidents combined and raises the debt from $10 trillion to $16 Trillion; and still cannot produce jobs;[12] the JournoList continues to assure us:** *"It would have been much worse if not for Obama!"*

Chapter 4

The Third Great Fraud being completely concealed by the Media: His Socialism and the Massive Corruption of the Obama Administration

What do you know about Socialism?

Is Obama just like Robin Hood?

© First-Amendment-Rights.com

**Socialism does not mean Obama will take from the rich
And give to the poor!**

No! No!! Cut the romantic music!! Delete that naïve notion you have that Obama will take from the rich and give to poor little you. **You are <u>not</u> going to get richer! That is <u>not</u> how Socialism works**.

In 2008, would the majority of us have elected a Socialist/Communist? Of course not. Watch the JournoList distract us by attacking the messenger and concealing the truth: When Joe the Plumber asked if Obama was a Socialist who planned to redistribute income; Joe was ferociously attacked. We were told, *"Joe is poor, he didn't pay his taxes, he is merely a plumber, he is uneducated, and not an Ivy Leaguer, you see; so you should ignore him."* **By now, you should realize that the more viciously that the JournoList attacks, the bigger the secrets they are hiding for Obama.**

Obama's Harridan-in-Chief, Elizabeth Warren, had listed herself as "Cherokee" in order to get herself an affirmative action position at Harvard. Now she says her great, great, great grandmother was Cherokee. But when challenged, she refuses to discuss this further or explain why, if she can't prove she is Cherokee, she ever listed herself as one. In short, Elizabeth Warren has also been proved to be a fraud; except that she does not have the Media in her back pocket. Congress refused to confirm her as Obama's consumer advocate czar. Now she is running as Senator for Massachusetts. She shrieks that no one in America owns anything, no matter how hard he has worked, because he uses roads and infrastructure built by *"The People."* Everything belongs to *"The People"*—meaning Warren, and by extension, Obama. And we'd better vote them in so they can do "more for us"—(actually, do more for themselves!) . . . . Obama echoed her Marxist view when he said, in his July 17th speech, that *"if you've got a business (meaning any privately owned business)—you didn't build that. Somebody else made that happen."* **How are Warren and Obama different from Communists?**

Massive Green Energy Loans to His Cronies: 80% of the $20.5 Billion in the Energy Department's Stimulus loans for "green energy" went to Obama's top donors. This is how it worked: First, Obama flew about the country on Air Force One (at our expense) chanting, *"Green Energy!" "Green Energy!!"* and persuading the people that green energy could supplant oil and gas. Then, he instructed his DOE to give funds to his supporters. To ensure this was done, friends of the supporters were installed at the DOE (and paid for by us). Essentially, the program operated as a slush fund, giving massive amounts of our money to companies owned by Obama's supporters who had made large contributions to Obama's various campaign committees.

Scientists and economists, who could assess the viability of the projects and make sure that taxpayer's funds were not wasted, did not make the DOE's decisions. Instead, political operatives, such as Steve Spinner, who was on the Obama Campaign's National Finance Committee and a top bundler himself, and others connected with the grant recipients, advised the DOE. *Note how the Media failed to tell us of this blatant conflict of interest!* Various Democrat Senators and Congressmen also brought pressure on DOE to make grants to favored recipients. At the time the DOE loans were made, many of these recipients were already unable to pay their bills and had Junk Bond credit ratings and/or had seriously flawed business plans; meaning they could not have obtained funds in the open market.

Nevertheless, the DOE gave our taxpayer money to them in the form of "Loans" or "Loan Guarantees." What a Federal Loan Guarantee does is assure the creditors that the money they loan would always be paid back; if not by the borrower, then by the taxpayers. Therefore, even though they knew the companies were likely to fail, financial institutions were willing to lend. This, in turn, caused the value of the company to rise tremendously. Once the company share price rose, the principals would sell off their shares and make tremendous profits. Subsequently, the company itself would falter and frequently go into bankruptcy. Others who remained would pay themselves massive "retention bonuses" as their companies filed for bankruptcy. Them companies would go belly up, and we, the taxpayers, would be left on the hook to pay off the 'Loan Guarantees."

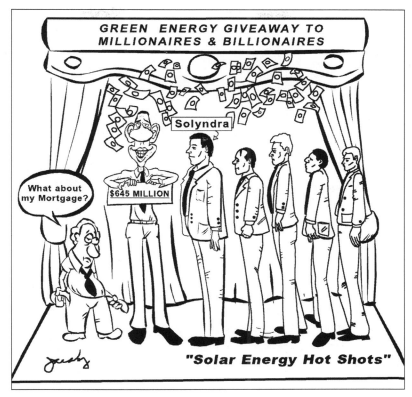

Socialism means Obama's Millionaire and Billionaire Cronies Collect Millions and Billions of our Money!

The Fraud & Corruption in the Green Energy Program: Peter Schweizer's great book *Throw Them All Out*[1] lists the recipients of Green Energy grants. Do any of these people listed below look like they need taxpayer money?

- **$529 Million to** support **Al Gore** for **Fisker Automotive's A123 systems**;
- **$1,400 Million to** support **Robert F. Kennedy, Jr, with Larry Paige, Sergei Brinn** and two other Google Execs for **Bright Source**;
- **$275 Million to** support **Larry Paige, Sergei Brinn** and two other Google Execs for **Solar City**;
- **$465 Million to** support **Larry Paige, Sergei Brinn** and 3 others for **Tesla Motors**;

- **($2.14 Billion in total for the multi-Billionaire Google owners);**
- **$4,700 Million to** support **Ted Turner and Paul Tudor Jones,** for **First Solar;**
- **$115 Million to** support **Larry Summers** and others for **First Wind;**
- **$1,500 Million to** support **Eric Redman & Laura Miller** for **Summit Texas Clean Energy, LLC;**
- **$2,199 Million to** support **Seth Waugh** for **Solar Trust of America;**
- **$737 Million to** support **Michael Froman** for **Solar Reserve;**
- **$291 Million to** support **Vinod Koshla** for 3 different projects; and
- **$2,500 Million to** support **BP & Rio Tinto** for Hydrogen Energy.[2]
- **$10 Million award to** support **Phillips** for an "affordable" LED light bulb, which costs $50.00 per bulb!

Funding Wasteful Projects that are now Bankrupt: Sharyl Atkinson[3] of CBS News has reported that 12 companies that received a total of $5.8 Billion from the DOE are now in financial trouble and that 5 of these have already filed bankruptcy:[4] Essentially, $5.8 Billion of our hard-earned dollars have gone . . . . **Poof!!**

- **$535 Million for George Kaiser and Solyndra:** $535 million went to Solyndra,[5] headed by George Kaiser, an Obama bundler, even though the company was failing at the time. The company is bankrupt; and in strict violation of federal law, Obama allowed Kaiser and other shareholders to recoup their investments before the taxpayer.[15] 1100 workers are laid off, and the money is gone! . . . **Poof!!**
- **$118 million of Obama's Stimulus funds for Ener1,**[6] a car battery maker, with 1,400 employees, laid off its workers and filed for bankruptcy on Jan 27, 2010 . . . . **Poof!!**
- **$43 million for Beacon Power,**[7] which had a CCC—Junk Bond rating when the loan was given, also laid off workers and filed for bankruptcy in October 2011 . . . . **Poof!!**
- **$400 million for Abound Solar**[8] owned by **Pat Stryker,** one of **Colorado's wealthiest people, an Obama bundler and a huge Democrat contributor whose Bohemian Companies has given**

nearly $500 million to Democrats and Obama between 2008 and 2012. Abound Solar was a solar module maker which Obama promised would create over 2000 construction jobs and over 1,500 permanent jobs. But it actually created only 425 jobs, laid off 300 or 70% of those, and declared bankruptcy in February 2012. Meantime, Stryker's Bohemian Companies gave over $500 million to Democrat organizations and Obama and the $400 million we gave to Abound is gone! . . . **Poof!!**

- **$433 Million for Ron Perelman and Siga Technologies:**[9] $433 Million went to Siga Technologies, controlled by Ron Perelman, one of the world's richest men and another Obama donor. Siga received a no-source, no-bid, no-questions-asked contract for a smallpox pill, which had never been tested, which would be effective for only 2 years, and which cost $255 a dose; to be used in case the existing smallpox vaccination, costing $3 a dose, was not effective against smallpox; which was eradicated in 1978! And $433 Million is wasted![10] . . . . **Poof!!**

- **$1.2 Billion from the DOE for Sun Power,[11] approved hours before the program expired on September 30, 2011**. This loan was strongly pushed by Rep George Miller III (D-Calif)[12] and lobbied for by his son, George Miller IV. [20] The same day, Sun Power received a $100 million contract from the Navy to provide electrical power to the Naval Air Weapons Station China Lake, California, beating out 12 other proposals. And also received American Recovery and Reinvestment Act or "stimulus" funds for it to install solar panels on 90 public schools in Rep. George Miller III's congressional district. But when it received the loan, it owed more than it was worth and it had announced it was building its factory in Mexicali, Mexico! And it would only produce 15 jobs in the US. Essentially our "loan" cost us $80 Million per job! The Loan was announced in April 12, 2011. Six weeks later, on May 24th, Sun Power's CEO exercised options to acquire 428,343 shares of Sun Power at $3.30 per share, $18 less than its trading price. France's Total purchased 60% of Sun Power at a value 60% over market price. Then, the CEO sold 428,084 shares at $23.24, receiving approximately $11 million and making a profit of $20 per share or approximately $9.5 Million. As of October 2011, Sun Power faces a number of lawsuits from various investors, including Retirement Funds, for fraud and deceit; its debt of $820 million is greater than its market capitalization of $800 million; and the Stock is now down to about 20% of its value when CEO Warner sold his shares! . . . . **Poof!**

- **$98.5 Million for Nevada Geothermal Power**[13] was strongly pushed by Senator Harry Reid, (D-Nevada) even though it couldn't even pay its bills. According to its auditors, it now faces multiple defaults! . . . . **Poof!**

- **$50 Million grant from State of Massachusetts plus land plus infrastructure and $3 Million from DOE for Evergreen Solar.** Bankrupt! . . . **Poof!**

- **$500,000 grant from DOE for SpectraWatt**, which paid $745,000 to 4 top executives; borrowed millions it has not repaid; and declared bankruptcy![14] . . . **Poof!**

- **$10 Million prize to Phillips**[15] for creating an "affordable" LED bulb that actually costs $50.00! . . . **Poof!!**

- **$700,000 to Prof K. Hammond of Northwestern University to create Joke-Telling Computer software.**[16] More than enough to pay off many people's mortgages! . . . . **Poof!!**

- **$873,000 to Teach African Men to Wash their Penises:**[17] This grant went to UCLA "researchers" to reduce HIV by teaching African men how to wash their penises after sex . . . . **And Plouffe!!** **Help Obama explain this one!!!**

Folks, you cannot make this up!

Even the Solar Plants that could be operational have been stalled by foreseeable Environmental & Native Indian Tribes' Objections: The Obama Administration has gifted 21 million acres of public property, more than the area of Los Angeles, Riverside and San Bernardino counties put together, for "green energy" projects. Far more than it has for oil and gas exploration over the last decade.

NextEnergy Resources' $1 billion Genesis Solar Project, being built with an $825 million loan guaranteed by federal taxpayers and located on BLM land 200 miles east of Los Angeles, was fast tracked by BLM. But it has been derailed by discovery of Sacred Indian bones and artifacts. NextEnergy officials say that Genesis would not have moved forward with this project if they had known of these obstacles because the economic damage is severe. Meantime, the Native Americans state that even though the remains are outside the boundary of the construction, the project is part of a "living spiritual world" and Genesis has "disrupted the peace of our ancestors and our relationship with the land. There is no mitigation for such a loss." *Checkmate! Project derailed!! (Note also how Sacred Indian relics and even "the living spiritual world" surrounding Native Indians' sacred relics is given great respect; with no discussion whatsoever about Separation of Native Indian Church and State!!)*

Pattern Energy's Ocotillo Wind Project, which would build 112 turbines each 450 feet tall across 12,500 acres of BLM land, has also been stalled by objections from Indian Tribes.[18]

Bright Source Energy's Ivanpah Solar Project consists of 173,000 solar mirrors, each the size of a garage door, set in a circle around a water tower 460 feet high on six square miles within 3,500 acres of land inside the Mojave National Wildlife Preserve. Computers focus the mirrors onto the water tower and heat the water to more than 1,000 degrees. This creates steam, which will drive the generators to create up to 370 megawatts of power, enough to drive 140,000 homes during peak hours. *(But, of course, this is only during daylight hours when the sun shines. All you liberals will have to rely on traditional energy at night when you need to power up your computers, your server farms, your air conditioners and switch on your lights!)*

The 3,500 acres of land was donated free of charge. The Federal government provided $1.8 billion in federal loan guarantees, $45 billion in federal tax credits and other grants. California provided property tax exemptions and $90 million of sales and use tax exemptions. It also gave a grant of $70 million funded by a ratepayer surcharge. The private investors, the Google owners, Morgan Stanley and CalSTERs, essentially got a tax shelter and contributed only small amounts of their own money.

The project would hire 1,000 unionized workers for two to three years during construction. But after that, it would only hire 80 workers.

The cost of producing solar energy is three times as much as the cost of traditional energy. And the ratepayer would have to pay up to 50% more for solar energy derived from renewable sources.

This project was also fast tracked, with the federal environmental officials working in secret with the energy company and leading environmental groups such as the Sierra Club, Defenders of Wildlife, the Natural Resources Defense Council and the Center for Biological Diversity.

Animosity has been sparked between these leading environmental groups and local groups who view the big groups as having sold out. Jeffrey Lovich of the US Geological Survey said they scoured published research looking for environmental analysis of the project. They found just one minor paper. Essentially, he said, no one knows what will happen to the wildlife in the Mojave after the project goes on line. Larry LaPre, a BLM wildlife biologist, has said that while some aspects of the project have been carefully thought out, other approaches are "complete nonsense," like BrightSource's notion that "gentle mowing" of barrel cactus, which take over 100 years to grow into even a small cactus, is an acceptable practice!

The project has involved the flattening of thousands of acres of desert in which there were 900 species of plants and 300 species of animals. Barrel cactus plants, which take 100 years to grow into even a small plant, were lopped off at the top to fit them under the solar mirrors. Endangered desert tortoises were relocated, resulting in as many as a third of them dying. Birds have vanished. Insects have been fried in the heat of the mirrors. What birds or insects remain will be burned to a crisp whenever they approach the solar mirrors. And this will result in massive loss of pollinators, so that many plants will not be able to reproduce.

A huge plume of heat is rising up from the water tower, and the Federal Aviation Administration is concerned about radar interference. The Marines have asked for more information about the glare produced by the vast carpet of solar reflectors.[19] Other environmentalists are concerned about the ill effects of heating up the desert floor to such a degree.

The public has donated the land. The taxpayer is on the hook for the federal loan guarantees. The federal taxpayer has provided federal tax credits and other grants; the California taxpayer has provided property, sale and use tax exemptions and the California ratepayer has paid an energy surcharge of $70 million. The California ratepayer will also pay a 50% surcharge for the electricity this plant produces. This project will hire only 80 workers at $15 *million dollars per worker. Various endangered species are being killed. Bird and insects are being fried. And Obama will fly around the country chanting "More Taxes! I need more Taxes!" to make up for the $45 billion in tax credits he has given to this project, wasting yet more of our money. Somebody explain to me how, exactly, did the public benefit from these projects?*

Obama's Green Slime Racket: Algae is the green slime that causes stagnant water to stink to high heaven. An Alga is a simple plant life that needs carbon, hydrogen, oxygen and nitrogen to grow. Coal is the remains of long dead plant life, so it is full of the ingredients needed to grow algae. It is burned to create the products Algae need to grow. But Obama hates coal.[20] As he said in January 2008, if somebody wants to build a coal plant, they could; but it will bankrupt them, because he is going to be charging them a huge sum for all the greenhouse gases that will be emitted.

Kathleen Sibelius hates coal too, so much so that she vetoed a major "green energy" project because it used coal![21] Sunflower Electric and Tri-State Generation and Transmission Association wanted to spend $3.8 billion to expand **Sun Power's Holcomb Power** plant to create algae based biofuel. The companies had gone through extensive hearings and litigation[22] to reach this point. Several community leaders spoke about how the proposed new facility would help their area. The two proponents told the hearing how the carbon-enriched biomass could be dried and processed into solids and oils; fed back into the power plant as renewable fuel; and processed into biodiesel. The carbohydrates could be fermented into ethanol and the protein used as feed and fertilizers for crops. Most of the water could be recycled and used in the coal plant cooling system or returned to the reactor for additional algae growth. But the Sierra Club, various other Clean Energy organizations and various religious groups such as the Sustainable Sanctuary Coalition and Presbyterians for Earth Care opposed this project. In 2009, as governor of Kansas, Sibelius vetoed the construction[23] because it would have to burn coal to produce nutrients for the algae and she wanted to "reduce greenhouse gas emissions."

One can only conclude that the proponents of the Holcomb expansion must have been Republicans and/or that they failed to hire T.J. Glauthier as their advisor. Check out T.J. Glauthier's influence below. Soon thereafter,

Obama decided to "invest" $510 Million in biofuels;[24] essentially giving our money to his contributors and cronies. He also has made various other government departments purchase this biofuel at exorbitant prices. Senator McCain said that the Navy has spent more than $400 per gallon on roughly 20,000 gallons of algae-based fuel for testing. A 2010 University of Virginia study found that though algae-based biofuels offer a higher level of energy output than other sources of biofuels; their production results in significantly more environmental degradation. Obama has caused numerous coal plants to close and prevented drilling for oil, both of which are already economically viable. But Obama has insisted on giving our money to his friends[25] He now touts Algae as the "fuel of the future," even though it will take 15 years or more to become economically viable without government subsidies:

- $25 Million in Stimulus Funds to Paul Woods, for **Algenol**;
- $105 Million to Jason Pyle of **Sapphire Energy**. Pyle has donated exclusively to Democratic campaigns, candidates and committees;
- $21 Million to **Solarzyme**. TJ Glauthier was a strategic advisor to Solarzyme and also a member of the Obama's transition team, who also happened to work on the energy section portion of the 2009 stimulus bill. Solarzyme and Glauthier have donated at least $360,000 to Democrats since 2007. Obama issued an executive order that the U.S. Navy spend $12 Million to purchase 450,000 gallons of biofuel, priced at $15.00 per gallon, an estimated 4 to 7 times the normal cost of regular jet fuel;
- $10 Million to **EnerNOC** which, with Glauthier on its Board, got a DOE contract despite being underbid by competitors; and
- $6.7 to **SunRun**, also with Glauthier on its Board.

Benefitting His Cronies and Destroying American Jobs by Canceling Projects:

- **The Keystone Pipeline & Warren Buffet:**[26] The Keystone pipeline was under environmental review for years and would have carried oil from our neighbor Canada to Houston and created at least forty thousand direct jobs and hundreds of thousands of related jobs. Recently, Obama stopped the Keystone Project. Without this oil, we become even more dependent on Obama's buddies in OPEC. Also without this pipeline we are forced to use Burlington Northern

Santa Fe Railroad to transport the oil. Obama's sanctimonious buddy **Warren Buffet** spent $26 Billion to purchase 77% of BNSF shares in 2009, paying a premium of 31% over its then closing price. Coincidence? Payback? Or worse? *What did Buffet know and when did he know it?*

- **Deep Sea Drilling & George Soros:**[26] Obama issued a 6-month moratorium on oil drilling in the Gulf after the BP blowout, even though there was nothing to indicate that there were any problems with other deep sea drilling or with non-deep sea drilling. The American Petroleum Institute estimates that we have U.S. resources to generate nearly 160,000 new, well-paying jobs and $1.7 trillion in revenues to federal, state, and local governments, with $1.3 trillion from offshore drilling alone. Within 48 hours after the moratorium, Petrobras, the Brazilian deep-water drilling company, contacted Laberde Marine, which owned 33 semi-submersible rigs and/or drill ships. The owners begged their Louisiana Senators and Governor Jindal to get the moratorium lifted so they would continue to work here. Jindal did all he could to save jobs in his area. Each drilling rig supported over 1,400 jobs. The Gulf provided 30% of our national domestic oil production. But, as you recall, Obama refused. While the Obama administration was shutting down off shore drilling in the Gulf and other US coastal waters; our Ex-Im Bank was supporting deep water drilling in Brazil with a $308 million dollar loan guaranty for Petrobras (the Exxon Mobil of Brazil) consummated in the Spring of 2010. And, when Obama went to Brazil in April 2011, he had nothing but support for Brazil's deep water drilling and promised that the United States would be supportive customer for a "stable" source of energy in our hemisphere *(Take that, Canada!)* The drilling rigs went to Petrobras, in which **George Soros** owned over 3 million shares worth $881 million. Obama actually promised to buy more oil from Brazil. The price of gas, which we Americans have to pay, has nearly doubled in the last three years. And Petrobras and George Soros, the chief sponsor of Obama, have benefitted. Soros claims he sold his shares before Obama helped Petrobras. But Soros owns so many inter-related corporations,[28] he could have transferred title without necessarily losing any profit.

Pretending Green Energy can Replace Traditional Energy is a favorite Obama tactic: Among Obama's czars, was the self-avowed communist radical and Black Nationalist, Van Jones.[29] Van Jones was a Bay Area radical agitator who was a committed Marxist-Leninist-Maoist, waging war on the capitalist system and the police. He was also a member of STORM, a radical organization in the Bay Area. Van Jones is a classical community agitator, using race as a means of working up minority groups against the majority. In one such speech, he said to the Native Americans, *"No more broken treaties. No more broken treaties! Give them the wealth. Give them dignity. Give them the respect that they deserve. No justice on stolen land. We owe them a debt."* To the immigrants, he said *"What about our immigrant brothers and sisters? What about people from all around the world who we're willing to work out in the fields, with poison being sprayed on them, poison being sprayed on them because we have the wrong agricultural system and then we're willing to poison them and poison the Earth to put food on our table but we don't want to give them rights and we don't want to give them dignity and we don't want to give them respect?"* *"The white polluters and the white environmentalists are essentially steering poison into the people of colored communities."*[30] Van Jones was in charge of green energy. Van Jones and Energy Secretary Stephen Chou were the ones who handed out billions of our money to Obama's cronies for green energy projects such as the Solar and Green Slime projects that failed.

Tilting at Windmills: Obama is also much in favor of windmills. Have you observed how Obama presents his arguments for his point of view and explains how his opponents are wrong? He sneers and jeers at them! Obama openly mocked skeptics of his proposals to promote alternatives to fossil fuels, comparing them to those who argued against Christopher Columbus' voyage to America: *"If some of these folks were around when Columbus set sail, they probably must have been founding members of the Flat Earth Society. They would not believe that the world was round.*[31]

But, of course, Obama was dead wrong. Windmills do not work. What you need to know about electricity is that it does not go off somewhere into a storage facility and wait for us to turn on a switch and demand electricity. Electricity has to be produced as and when there is demand for it. The essence of a windmill is that it will not follow demand. Rather, it will work only if and when the wind blows. So, by definition, wind is an unreliable source of electricity, working only about 20% of the time. If you want a stable supply of electricity, then you have to provide all windmill projects with back-up electrical generators. These generators will produce electricity for the 80% of the time the wind does not blow. *And liberals can pretend they are using Obama's beloved "alternative green energy."*

Each windmill rises at least 252 feet in the air, with three blades each 140 - 300 feet long. Each turbine is rated to generate up to 2.1 megawatts of power. They generate electricity when the wind blows. But the wind blows only part of the time, and not necessarily when we need the electricity. Therefore, wind turbines generally operate at only 20% efficiency, compared to 85% efficiency for coal, gas and nuclear power plants. Even worse, wind power frequently drops to nothing, just when the demand for electricity is greatest in the early evening. And winds howl at night, generating lots of electricity, when there is no demand.

But Obama has set up Renewables Obligation Certificates (ROC's), which force the grid operator to pay the wind farm operator for putting power onto the grid, whether or not the grid could use the electricity.[32] *Another Obama redistribution scheme—get traditional energy companies, which don't vote for Obama, to subsidize "green energy" windmill owners, who do vote for Obama!* A 2008 report by the Department of Energy's Energy Information Administration reported that in 2007, while the average subsidy per megawatt hour for all energy sources was $1.65, the subsidy for wind and solar was about $24 per megawatt hour.[33] And Obama provided $2.3 Billion in tax credits to create "high-quality" green jobs.[34] The Administration has also fast tracked wind farm approvals off shore in the eastern states. They have shortened the environmental review process and are seriously considering requests for federal loan guarantees and tax credits for wind farms from various developers including Google Inc.[35] If you recall, the Google owners, being poor and unable to fund projects themselves, also obtained over $2 Billion in funding for various solar projects.

In 2011, **Minnesotans** ended up paying $70 million more than they needed for electricity because of "green energy" mandates, according to the Minnesota Rural Electric Association. Taxpayers already pay a high price to subsidize wind energy through billions in federal grants, loan guarantees and tax credits that prop up the wind industry, according to the Minnesota State News. The Minnesota State Legislature directed electric utilities to purchase one out of every four kilowatt hours from renewable energy. As the recession caused demand for electricity to drop, the prices of traditional energy also dropped. But Minnesotans were stuck purchasing unnecessary wind power at huge premiums.[36] **Massachusetts** has a requirement that its utility purchase 27.5% of the output of the offshore Cape Wind project. While natural gas prices are declining, Massachusetts's customers will be compelled to buy electricity from the wind farm at four times the current rate.[37] **California** also has a 20% "renewable energy" requirement. And Californians are wondering why our electricity rates are going up!!!

But Obama knew of, and ignored, an early 2009 study by Spanish Professor Gabriel Calzada Alvarez, Ph.D., of **Spain**'s alternative energy program that showed Wind Energy was a total loss. Green jobs created were temporary 90% of the time; and each green job required $752,000-$800,000 in government subsidies. Wind industry jobs cost even more, $1.4 million each in subsidies. And for each green job gained, 2.2 to 4.27 other jobs were either lost or not created in other industries. Electrical costs rose 31%, taxes rose 5% and government increased.[38] Spain's unemployment rate rose to 18% at least in part because of the spending on green jobs that did not materialize and the raising of taxes required to support the spending. **Calzada's report went on to forecast that the U.S. could lose 6.6 million jobs if it followed Spain.[39]** *But, of course, Obama followed Spain and we now have double that amount of unemployed to show for it. But, you see, the unemployment is the fault of the rich, or perhaps even George Bush.*

Britain's experience was the same as Spain's. A new analysis of wind energy supplied to the UK National Grid in recent years had shown that wind farms produce significantly less electricity than had been thought, and that they cause more problems for the Grid than had been believed.[40] **Danish** researches at the Center for Politiske Studier came to the same conclusion: "*It is fair to assess that no wind energy to speak of would exist if it had to compete on market terms.*[41]

Radical Activists control the Obama Administration: Obama's administrators actually banded together with the Center for American Progress (CAP) a George Soros funded entity headed by John Podesta and other environmentalists, to plan how to discredit and/or conceal these reports. As the IDB editorial states, this was a shameless politicization of what should be a professional bureaucracy. It shows how influential radical activists and trade lobbyists are in the Obama Administration.[42]

Around September 2011, Obama went to a $25,000 per plate fundraiser hosted by **Tom Carnahan** of Missouri. Carnahan's energy development firm Wind Capital Group received $108 Million of our tax money to develop a wind farm called the **Blue Grass Ridge Wind Farm**.

See how it works? Obama gives his cronies our tax money for worthless projects. He ignores reports from other countries showing it does not work and that it will cause severe job loss. He also deliberately shortchanges our Treasury by giving his cronies tax credits so they do not even pay taxes. Then, having deliberately wasted all this money, Obama will, of course, run around the country chanting, "The rich are not paying their fair share of taxes!"

Wind Farms kill Birds: If all this has not got you mad enough, consider the effect Wind Farms have on birds. Wind turbines do not all move at the same time. Sometimes, one moves. Other times many move, but not necessarily those adjacent to each other. The spinning of the turbines are totally random and they can spin at up to 200 mph. Visualize yourself as a raptor that follows a rabbit or squirrel into the stationery turbines. Suddenly, one, then another, starts spinning. Is it any wonder the bird will be chopped up? Rush Limbaugh was right, so many years ago, when he referred to a Wind Farm as a Condor Cuisinart. That is exactly what they do.

Wind turbines have been killing almost 70 Golden Eagles each year at California's Altamont Pass, 20 miles east of Oakland, California. A 2008 study estimated 2,400 raptors, including burrowing owls, American Kestrels and red tailed hawks, as well as about 7,599 other birds, nearly all of which are protected under the Migratory Bird Treaty Act, are being killed every year by the turbines at Altamont.

But nothing was being done. According to Mr. Glitzenstein, who petitioned the U.S. Fish and Wildlife Service to take action, "It's absolutely clear that there's been a mandate from the top" echelons of the federal government not to prosecute the wind industry for violating wildlife laws. Finally, the Sierra Club and Defenders of Wildlife have filed a lawsuit to block two more proposed wind projects, North Sky River and Jawbone, due to concerns about their impact on bird populations. [43]

There are similar problems at **Pine Tree** and **North Sky River** wind farm projects located in the Tehachapi Mountains, just north of Los Angeles. The wind blows strong, and the spring migration of birds, tanagers, warblers, orioles, grosbeaks, vireos and flycatchers, flow like rivers low to the ground, and get decimated by the turbines. This is also a critical area for federally protected eagles and condors, which fly high, swoop down on prey and also get caught to the spinning turbines. An expert on raptor ecology, who has been working with raptors since 1989, says that he has never found a dead eagle outside of wind farms. And to find so many dead eagles inside the wind farms, 8 dead eagles at Pine Tree alone, is beyond the pale.

The liberal solution, like all liberal solutions, is to tax people more and waste yet more money on "solutions" that do not work. The "solution" being attempted here is to install avian radar detection units, which sell at about $500,000 each. These supposedly shut down the wind turbines when they detect incoming birds and start up again as quickly as possible. Apparently, they work best in flat, uncluttered land devoid of trees and bushes, which would prevent identification of the bird. For an additional couple of hundred thousand, they could add a telescopic video attachment, which could discern an eagle from a turkey vulture. (*God knows why they need to know!*) The DWP now plans to test a $3 Million radar system designed to sweep the horizon, vertically and horizontally, for large birds.[44]

Can you think of anything sillier? Anyone who spends a few hours at desolate areas where the wind blows would know that these areas are frequented by protected species of birds. Even in my own urban home, hawks and migrating eagles enjoy riding the thermals when the wind blows. How come they didn't realize that installing turbines that spin at 200 mph would decimate the birds? What is the point of the turbine, which only works when the wind blows, if you have to shut it down when birds are flying around because the wind is blowing? And can you bring a turbine whose blades are spinning at 200 mph to a sudden halt without damaging the turbine itself and possibly bringing down the entire turbine, blades and tower? And they are supposed to start up again after the bird leaves. What is the bird supposed to do? Say, *"OK, I am leaving now?"* And are we going to cut down every single tree or bush in the hundreds of acres of the wind farm so the *"Detection System"* can work? And what is the point of *"discerning between an eagle and a turkey vulture?"* And do you seriously think any of those expensive *"detection systems"* can actually prevent bird deaths? The turbines spin at over 200 mph. How come nobody has considered the speed at which birds swoop down on their prey? The Golden Eagle and Duck Hawk have been estimated to clock 165-180 mph when diving after prey. Even mourning doves, ducks and geese can reach speeds of 55-60 mph.[45]

How is anything going to shut down the turbines in time to stop killing the approaching birds? *Obama is such a brilliant man. He would never have wasted so much of our taxpayer money on such idiotic schemes like wind turbines. It must have been Bush's idea!*

Problem:
200 mph Wind Turbine slaughtering birds diving in at 150 mph.
Liberal solution:
Extract millions from Taxpayer for "solutions" that won't work.
Conservative solution:
If you must do something idiotic, at least, do it cheap!

Let me give you a conservative solution. Let's put stop signs around the wind farms so the birds will know to stop and not go into the wind farms. This would be just about as effective as the liberal solution, but cost far,

far less. My even better and totally brilliant conservative solution involves copying Obama and focusing like a laser on jobs! It consists of hiring the unemployed to hang around the wind farms and use some of the SEIU's bullhorns to scare the birds away. If the SEIU insists, I will let them use my signs as placards. We would solve the unemployment problem and also save the birds. And thus, we would kill two birds with one stone!

Of course, the unions would demand air-conditioned huts for the people to rest in, special gear for them to wear and specially cooled drinks. Then, we would need Administrators to supervise the Supervisors who supervise the Workers. Then, we would have to provide 12 weeks' vacation, health benefits and massive pensions. And the unions would say it is too hot and windy for an 8-hour shift, so we would have to hire two sets of workers for each job, essentially 6 workers per 24-hour shift. Then, we would have to send air-conditioned buses into the inner city to bring in the workers. Once we are done with accommodating the union's demands, we would spend as much money on labor as we save from generating electricity from the wind farm. So, as always happens whenever militant unions get involved, we would have to shut down the wind farms. But Obama wouldn't let that happen. Obama would jet around the country on our dime shouting, "We need more Taxes!! Everybody must pay their fair share!!" . . . . But don't ever say I didn't try. to solve the problems caused by Wind Farms and save the birds too!

Oil and Gas Producers & Electricity Grid Operators have been fined millions: Over the past two decades, the federal government has prosecuted hundreds of cases against oil and gas producers and electricity producers for violating some of America's oldest wildlife-protection laws: the Migratory Bird Treaty Act and Eagle Protection Act. A violation of either law can result in a fine of up to $250,000 and imprisonment for two years. [46] In August 2011, US Fish & Wildlife (FWS) officials spent 45 days flying around North Dakota in a helicopter looking for evidence that birds were landing on the open waste pits of petroleum producers in North Dakota. *(Nobody bothered about the huge cost of joy riding around in helicopters for days on end!)* They found 28 dead bids, mallards, gadwalls and a sandpiper. They forced the oilmen to pay $1,000 per bird. Pacific Corp, a Wyoming utility, had to pay $10.5 million in fines after 23 golden eagles and other protected birds were electrocuted. FWS even tried to fine a little Virginia girl for 'illegally possessing" a woodpecker she had saved from a hungry cat.[47]

But though they kill a great many more birds, there have been no prosecutions against Wind Farm owners. Instead, Obama is fast tracking approvals for wind farms in the ocean, where even more migratory birds will be flying. *(And where we won't be able to see the birds being killed!)* Today, the FWS estimates that wind turbines are killing over 330,000 birds. By 2030, with more than 100,000 turbines expected to be operation, it estimates that annual bird mortality rates will exceed 1 million. These numbers could be much larger because bird carcasses are almost immediately eaten up by other wild life. However, in April 2012, the FWS reversed course. *(Not because of political pressure, Oh No!)* FWS issued a fact sheet stating, *"We anticipate issuing programmatic permits for wind, solar and other energy projects. Permits may authorize lethal take that is incidental to an otherwise lawful activity such as mortalities caused by collisions with rotating wind turbines."*[48]

"Lethal Take" according to Obama's people, is the euphemism for federally approved slaughter of eagles. *It could also be a synonym for what Obama is doing to us, taking our money and destroying our economy! You will also note the disparate treatment. If you are a traditional energy company, or even a little child, FWS will fine you. But if you are an Obama crony cleaning up on taxpayer money, FWS will issue an authorization for "Lethal Take" of endangered birds!*

A mere 3 years later, it is obvious that Joe the Plumber was right and that Obama is a Socialist/Communist! (Someone explain to me the difference. I think a Socialist is a Communist-in-Waiting, waiting until he has amassed enough power to become a dictator and crush the people.) All this money doled out to fund cronies of Obama who are Millionaires and Billionaires who could readily afford to fund those projects themselves; to fund his conies' wasteful projects which are now bankrupt; to fund his cronies' Green Slime projects which are not commercially viable; to cancel projects which would be viable to benefit his cronies financially; and to fund wind farms which are also not commercially viable; is more than enough to create jobs for all of us in America and pay off all our delinquent mortgages!! None of the projects listed above have benefitted our people or given them jobs. Yet, Obama keeps asking for more money to "help the poor" but actually, to give to his cronies.

This is why big government is so dangerous. The more money Socialists take from corporations or from us private individuals; the more they give to themselves and the more corrupt they become. Obama is not really opposed to trickle-down economics. He just wants to dictate who gets the money at the top before a fraction of trickles down.

And we need to revise our definition of Socialism. Contrary to the romantic Robin Hood-like notion that everyone has; **Socialism does not mean** Obama is taking from the rich and giving to the poor. **What Socialism really means is that Obama is taking from the rich and the middle class and giving to himself and his cronies.**

Meantime, our jobless remain unemployed! Our middle class slides down into poverty. And the poor remain poor!!

Chapter 5

The Fourth Great Fraud being completely Concealed by the Media: Obama's Religion

So we come to the key question: Is Obama a Muslim?[1] The second anyone raises questions about Obama's religion, the JournoList media attacks him ferociously and protects their guy Obama: *"He can't help it if his parents made him a Muslim!"* *"He is a devout Christian in Jeremiah Wright's Church—and never mind that Wright is not really a Christian and really an America-hating anti-Semite!"* *"That is so racist of you!"* *"You hate black people!!"* But, at the same time, they assure you Islam is a "religion of peace," just like the other religions, Judaism, Christianity and Hinduism etc. If this is so, what is so "hateful" about saying Obama is Muslim?

Why Islam is so dangerous: In 2008, would we have elected a Muslim? Of course not! We would have recoiled in horror at the implications of having a Muslim head of state. We don't want a Muslim ruler who will take away all freedom from their own people;[2] persecute our Christians;[3] [4] destroy our churches;[5] force us to remove our crosses[6] because they are "offensive,"[7] and merely a "small body on two wooden sticks" as the leader of the Union of Muslims in Italy, Abdel Smith, said when he forced Italy to remove crucifixes from its schools;[8] cover up our women in Burkas and flog them if they dare to even drive;[9] hang our gays;[10] and even destroy all our dogs and pets[11] because Muslims consider them "unclean"!!![12]

**A Muslim Ruler will require that Women wear a Hijab.
Women must be fully covered in public and cannot even drive.
They must wait for a relative to drive them everywhere!**

A Muslim Ruler will ban Gays!

A Muslim Ruler will ban Pets!
A British Agency cravenly apologized to Muslims for "offending"
them by putting a picture of a German Shepherd puppy on a
postcard mailed to the public!

In fact, as documented in Part II, Islam is not a religion, but a religious/cultural/political/military ideology that seeks to destroy us. **And what is dangerous about Islamic rulers[13] is that they rule like communist dictators, using Islam and *Shari'ah* law to bully, intimidate and terrorize the ordinary Muslims in their countries**.

© Mohamed Kadri/Xinhua Press/Corbis
A Muslim Ruler subjugates his people
The Arab Spring Uprisings spread from Algeria throughout the Middle East
Ordinary People died trying to get some of our American Freedoms.

We have seen how all, including even Obama, must bow to the King of Saudi Arabia.[14] Muslim rulers are rich beyond imagining because they own everything. Ordinary Muslims have no money, no hope and no freedom. They have to be lowly supplicants, begging the great king to give them a job or some money to live. *(Just like we have to beg for our unemployment benefits and our welfare checks.)* 60% of the Saudis are below 20 years of age and 40% of them are unemployed but 90% of all workers are foreigners. 40% of Saudis live on less than $1,000 a month. A young woman who dared to drive her own car was jailed. A young man who made a film showing the grueling poverty in Riyadh, and an interview with an Imam who said young girls were being sold into prostitution, was arrested. Over a million Saudis use the Internet and a great number of them use Facebook. They can see what freedoms we enjoy.[15] They are sick being serfs. They want to be like Americans. This is why they are risking their lives protesting and there is an "Arab Spring"[16] or uprising, in every Middle East country.[32] Even as we speak, thousands of Syrians are being slaughtered by a Muslim dictator. In fact, the whole world wants to come to America. Everyone wants the freedom to pursue his own happiness. He dreams of having the freedom to have a wife and a family; own a car and a home; work hard; start his own business and even become rich; without being controlled by an all-powerful government.

If Obama were a Muslim, through his government, he would end up owning everything; and we would end up like the Syrians; dirt poor, and fighting and dying to have a semblance of freedom. And he would not support Israel, which would end up being encircled and destroyed.

The reason the media is doing its best to prevent us from discussing Obama's Muslim Faith is that they don't want Americans to understand the connection between Obama being a Muslim and how he would rule as a Muslim ruler.

Did Obama Really Give Up Islam? If he really converted, why has Obama never explained what was better about Christianity than Islam? Why has he never said anything about the epiphany that caused him to finally seek out Christianity when he was in his early thirties? How come Obama can't find anything good to say about Christianity? And he says nothing bad about Islam? He is very anxious to prevent any negative stereotype of Muslims;[17] but does not hesitate to criticize Christians. Remember his famous sneer about Christians, "clinging to their guns and religion?" Obama knows the entire *Qur'an* by memory but cannot even quote a well-known Bible verse accurately. He actually calls himself "his brother's keeper"!! *(Perhaps an appropriate mistake. In Genesis 4:9 (NIV), Cain tries to hide the fact he killed his brother Abel by saying, "Am I my brother's keeper?" Obama is killing America and hiding the fact!)* And Obama has never quoted the 23rd Psalm or John 3:16. Why not? When Obama slipped and referred to "my Muslim Faith;"[18] Stephanopoulos hurriedly corrected Obama. Why? Obama said the Muslim *Adhan* or Call to Prayer is "one of the prettiest sounds on earth at sunset;"[19] and, according to NY Times reporter, Nicholas Kristoff, recited it in flawless

Arabic.[20] But the NY Times scrubbed the Kristoff interview from its website. Why?

In his inaugural address, Obama said: "We are a nation of Christians and Muslims, Jews and Hindus and non-believers," astonishing everyone by his inclusion of Muslims, who had never been part of our History. In his speech in Turkey, he said, *"Though we once were, we are no longer a Christian nation. (Surprise!).*[21] *We are a Jewish nation, a Muslim nation, a Buddhist nation and a Hindu nation and a nation of non-believers."* [22] This is standard Obama doublespeak. First he expands the concept of a Christian nation to include all other kinds of religions, no matter how small. In so doing, he obscures that fact that this is still a predominantly Christian nation. It is just like saying "Water is not really water. It includes all kinds of particulates, bits of dust, grass, and other sediment. So it is not water." And it is also a way of getting us accustomed to thinking of Muslims as mainstream Americans. In 2009, he cancelled the National Day of Prayer,[23] ostensibly because it could offend atheists; and didn't care that cancelling it did offend Christians. In 2010, he omitted reference to the Creator[24] when he quoted from the Declaration of Independence. His first post-inaugural interview was an exclusive with an Arab station, Al-Arabiya TV. He explained to Hisham Melhem why Muslims have to be treated with great respect, *"I have Muslim members of my family. I have lived in Muslim countries."*[25]

He cancelled the Boy Scout's 100-year celebration[26] and started a tradition of having a very expensive and grand White House *Ifta*r dinner at *Ramadan,* inviting various Muslim leaders and praising Muslims to the hilt. He said, *"Muslims have always been part of our American family."* He remembered the *"heroes who rushed to help . . . including proud and patriotic Muslim-Americans." "Muslims-Americans were first responders . . . For these past 10 years, Muslim-Americans have helped to protect our communities as police and firefighters. Across our federal government, they keep our homeland secure, they guide our intelligence and counter terrorism efforts . . . Muslim-Americans help to keep us safe."* [27] While ladling on the syrupy praise, he never said a word about Muslim terrorists who caused massive destruction and death on 9/11.[28]

He claimed that his having an *Ifta*r dinner was reprising Thomas Jefferson's "*Ifta*r dinner" 200 years ago! In fact, Thomas Jefferson merely postponed a dinner for 2 hours so the Muslim Ambassador could eat. At the time, Thomas Jefferson was negotiating with a Muslim Ambassador to prevent further Barbary Coast attacks by Muslim pirates.[29] *(Even 200 years ago, Muslims were behaving like Barbarians!)* Meantime, Obama has canceled the Annual Christmas Dinner at the White House for 3 years running;[30] choosing instead to spend Christmas Day vacationing in Hawaii.

Obama has flagrantly violated our Constitutional guarantee of Free Exercise of Religion. He has launched a frontal attack on the Catholic Church[31] and demanded it violate a central tenet of their religion. First, he asserted that because they receive money from him, they must do as he says. And provide, either directly or indirectly, free "reproductive health" services, *(by which he means abortion services),* to all women at their churches, their hospitals and their schools. Obviously, if the Catholic Church does any accommodation on this point, it ceases to exist as the Catholic Church.

The second prong of his attack was to divide and splinter Catholics by sneering that many Catholic women want birth control services and do not obey Catholic teachings anyway; essentially suggesting that Catholics rewrite their Doctrines to accommodate his beliefs. Thus he separated Catholics into conservatives who won't support him and will obey their church; and liberal women who will genuflect to Obama and his sacrament of abortion and death, vote for him, and put their loyalty to him and their greed to get "free" birth control pills; before their loyalty to their church. He has also violated the beliefs of the 70% of Americans who oppose abortion and the killing of unborn babies, by insisting that everyone pay for unlimited abortions for everyone. Couple this with his support for killing living babies born of botched abortions, [32,33] and you have a man truly obsessed with death. This violation of the Constitution's Free Exercise of Religion is not the action of a Christian President. Nor is it the action of any President who intends to obey the oath he took to uphold our Constitution.

© First-Amendment-Rights.com

Our New Founding Father re-writes Our Constitution

When people began to realize how flagrantly Obama was violating the Constitution, they were shocked and Obama's poll numbers began to fall. But Obama's JournoList army rushed out to defend him and attack anyone who criticized him. Working with the Democrats, they distracted the public with talk of Sandra Fluke who demanded free contraception from Georgetown, a Jesuit Law School. They further distracted everyone by attacking Rush Limbaugh for criticizing her.

And in the ensuing brouhaha, people lost sight of the key problem:

By asserting that he has the right to say what kind of First Amendment Rights we Americans can have, Obama has totally changed our Constitution. He didn't merely violate it. He actually rewrote it. If Obama can exercise this kind of unlimited power, then our Supreme Court and the rest of our Judiciary are irrelevant. And Congress becomes irrelevant too. In short, Obama becomes a Dictator.

And any minute now, he will take the place of the Pope in suggesting what other adjustments in Doctrine the Catholic Church should undertake. And become the Titular Head of Protestant and Jewish Denominations in suggesting how they too should rewrite their religious teachings. For instance, if Obama's notion of "public health" trumps Religion; what is to prevent Obama from demanding that people not go to church or synagogue but instead, go for exercise? After all, working out is better than sitting in a pew and becoming obese! And Obama pays for people's health services, doesn't he? And can't he extend his "public health" power to encompass the notion of the "public interest" too? After all, he owns everything and pays for everything. Because it so offends Muslims, can he not ban the eating of pork? And because it offends Muslims[34] and also because pets mess public parks which Obama pays to have cleaned; can he not ban us from having dogs?[35]

But Obama never suggests any change in Muslim doctrine. Instead he shows the most profound respect for it. He doesn't demand that Muslim women be required, or even allowed, to remove their burkas; even though virtually all of them would like to do so. And it would be in keeping with our Equal Protection clause to provide Muslim women with the same rights as non-Muslim women and all men. Instead, he always supports Muslim Orthodoxy. He has actually agreed to let Muslim women wearing Burkas pat themselves down at security check points in airports;[36,37] instead of demanding that they comply with federal law and be subject to TSA pat-downs. **Do you still insist Obama is a Christian who is following our Constitution?**

If he really did convert to Christianity, he would have been killed: We now know Obama was a devout Muslim when he was young, and worse, we can't pinpoint when, or if, he ever converted to Christianity! And we know that if anyone gave up his Muslim faith and converted to Christianity, he would be deemed a *Murtad*, or Apostate, and he would have been killed![38] In February 2012, 23-year-old writer Hamza Kashgari of Saudi Arabia tweeted something that Muslim clerics considered offensive. Saudis sent 30,000 Tweets in one day demanding Kashgari's trial for apostasy; his newspaper was ordered to stop publishing his articles; his photo and address were posted on line; various Facebook posts offered money to whoever killed him; and out of sheer terror, even his friends denounced him. Kashgari fled the country. But the Saudi police pursued him across the globe and, working with Malaysian authorities, picked him up at the Kuala Lumpur airport and returned him to Saudi Arabia where he faces the death penalty for apostasy. Kashgari, who merely said something deemed insulting, is going to face trial and execution for Apostasy.[39] Right now, Iran is planning to execute

Pastor Youcef Nadarkani,[40] who converted from Islam to Christianity. As recently as June 2012, some brave man was able to capture on his cell phone, a video of a young Tunisian whose throat was cut because he had converted to Christianity.[41] But Obama, who has supposedly converted to Christianity, thereby committing the ultimate Apostasy against Islam; is alive and well, and entertains Orthodox Muslims at the White House all the time. **So, do you really believe he has converted from being a Muslim and become a Christian?**

Obama's Homeland Security has issued a broad and sweeping "Threat Assessment" against Christians, Right Wing Radicals & Returning Veterans:[42] Apparently, anyone who objects to the economic downturn, the current political climate and Obama's socialist policies is a potential terrorist whose opinions are based on "hatred of particular religions, racial or ethnic groups." Meantime, Obama has prohibited the use of the words "Islamic Terrorists" for people who actually committed terrorist acts. Even Nidal Hassan, who stood on a table, shouted "Alahu Akbar" and slaughtered 13 unarmed soldiers, is not a "terrorist," but merely suffered from "pre-traumatic stress syndrome" caused by his having to go to Iraq, and this was actually a mere case of "workplace violence."[43]

Obama denounces our Constitution and praises Islam's *Shari'ah* laws: As you will see, Obama is gradually turning America into a Caliphate and imposing *Shari'ah law* on us. He assures us there is no conflict between *Shari'ah* and our Constitution. But this is a blatant lie. *Shari'ah* treats women as chattel and subjects them to "honor" killings;[44] beheads gays;[45] and considers people of other faiths as *infidels* who should be exterminated.[46] Obama has also taught that our Constitution is so flawed, it should be re-written. Presumably by him as our New Founding Father! Slowly, gradually, we are being prepared for the day when we will accept that *Shari'ah* is better than our Constitution.

Obama is also destroying our dreams with his constant tax increases, his disastrous economic policies and his regular attacks on every industry that is prospering without him; and converting us into *Dhimmis*[47] aka slaves or serfs: Soon, there will be no independent middle class. They are losing their homes, their savings and their jobs. Everyone is becoming poorer and more dependent on the Government for jobs and/or benefits. Already, more than 50% of us are totally dependent on Obama and his government and must bow before him and must vote for him.

Ultimately, most of us will become poor and totally dependent on Obama. He started off as the popularly elected head of our government, but is slowly become our Ruler, issuing edicts to us from on high. Soon, we will all be forced to prostrate ourselves before him (and vote for him) if we want our government-sponsored jobs and benefits to be continued. Obama will have transformed America, exactly as he promised. And we will no longer be a free people.

Chapter 6

Questions for the Media

You will soon be going all out, attacking this book and every criticism of Obama, in order to get this President re-elected and this country converted into a *Shari'ah* compliant Caliphate like Saudi Arabia, Syria or Iran. But before you don your war paint; answer the following questions:

(a)   How many Hollywood movies can you screen in *Shari'ah* compliant countries?
(b)   How many gays live in peace as gays in *Shari'ah* compliant countries? and
(c)   What kind of treatment is provided to those with AIDS in *Shari'ah* compliant countries?

The answers are none, none and none. **Can you live with what you are going to do?**

Question for You:
Think about what you have just read and answer the Question

Look at the vast amount of information that has been hidden from you by your current media. And consider how dishonest and deceitful they have been. When the JournoList starts up with its usual chant to cover up for Obama: *"This book is full of Hate." "The writer hates Obama because he is black;"* remember that when the Park Service tells you to watch out for Grizzly Bears; it doesn't "hate" the bears. It is simply warning you. So it is with this book. There is no "hate" for Obama. This book is just warning you.

Do you still think we are not being fed a bunch of crap? I know that we are. Though we think we are being "cool" and "open minded"; we are actually under the complete control and domination of the JournoList Media-Mafia. Even when this country is sinking into the mire, the media tells us. *"This is Bush's fault and not the fault of the man running the country*"! And it contradicts itself with: *"And the country is doing fine!"* And, many of us still swallow this shit!!

In fact, you know absolutely nothing about Obama's personal and professional life; and nothing about his eligibility or his religion, even today. Are you still going to be a giddy teenager, never checking what he is doing to this country and voting for him because of his looks?

There is a conflagration that is burning up our Constitution, our Freedom and our way of life. It is coming closer and closer to you. And someone is shouting, "Fire!" But the JournoList will use its usual technique of finding some little thing wrong; and distorting and inflating it to cast doubt on everything that has been said: *"It's all a bunch of lies and exaggerations!"* And the JournoList will castigate the messenger: *"He's just a liar! A bigot! And a racist!!"* And then the JournoList will soothe you with: *"You are too sophisticated to believe that quack."* And contradict itself with: *"Besides, the fire is just burning your neighbors. It is nowhere near you!"*

The burning question is:

Will you believe the JournoList and wait in a trance until You and your country are burned to a crisp?
Or
Will you wake up and shout "Good God!! There really is a fire!"... ?

Part II of IV

What is Islam? How Islamists have pursued *Stealth Jihad* in Europe

Table of Contents

Introduction

Part II of IV

What is Islam?
How Islamists have pursued
Stealth Jihad in Europe

Introduction

Listen to Obama explain his Muslim Faith and read the details:
http://www.youtube.com/watch?v=Dc3PzHKCVGM&feature=player_embedded#!
http://conservapedia.com/Barack_Obama%27s_Muslim_Heritage
http://conservapedia.com/Muslim_agenda_of_the_Obama_administration

Admit it. You already had great doubts about Obama. But the two most powerful groups in America—the Media and the Islamists—tricked you into voting for him. In Part I, I showed you how the Media tricked you and helped hide Obama's secrets. In this Part II, I will explain Islam and show you how Islamists tricked the Europeans and pursued a Stealth Jihad to convert Europe into Eurabia. In Part III, I will show how you Islamists are tricking you by pursuing a Stealth Jihad in America. And in Part IV, I will tie these threads together and show you what Obama is doing to our country. And I trust you will have the courage to face what your instincts tell you is true.

This is serious stuff; so don't waste my time and yours screaming about "racism." Obama is not an American Black. His American half, through his mother, is White and the other half, through his father, is African and Muslim. And don't talk to me about "Hate" and call me an "Islamaphobe" either. First, make up your mind: either it is OK to be a Muslim or it is not. If a Muslim is the same as a Hindu, a Buddhist, a Jew or a Christian; then it is not "hate" to say Obama is a Muslim. If, on the other hand, (a) Islam is not a religion but rather a very dangerous religious/political/military ideology, and its Qur'an commands all true Muslims to do Jihad against us and destroy us; and (b) in Muslim countries, non-Muslims are persecuted for practicing their religion and forced to live like Dhimmis, aka slaves or serfs; then it means extreme danger to you and our country. But it is still not "hate." Just as the Park Service doesn't "hate" grizzlies but simply warns you about the dangers; so it is with me. I don't "hate" Obama or Muslims. But I am warning you, because it is imperative that you figure out for yourself whether or not Obama is a Muslim, as I say he is; so you will watch what he is doing, and realize he is destroying America.

Also, don't tell me that 1.2 Billion Muslims are going to rise up to attack me. Of those 1.2 Billion, half are women. They couldn't possibly want to remain as they do now, being totally subservient to men, and being subject to genital mutilation, rape and "honor" killings. Then, there are the vast numbers of decent and moderate Muslims who have escaped from the strictures of Orthodox Islam and are living in non-Muslim controlled countries. They want to get along with everyone; have no desire to "kill the infidel," like orthodox Muslims do; or be subjugated by Orthodox Muslims. Then, there are those Muslims who are neither radical Orthodox nor even more radical Salafist, living in Muslim countries, who have participated in the Arab Spring, and who are crying out, and even dying, to get our American freedoms for themselves. None of the above groups, which constitute the vast majority of those 1.2 Billion, would want to silence people like this writer. In fact, it is in their interest that the extremists be exposed. It is only the extremist and radical Orthodox Muslims that seek to destroy those with an opposing point of view. Today, these extremists profess to speak for the moderates; but they will destroy the moderates as soon as they get the opportunity; just as the rulers in Syria and Iran are killing the moderates within their borders.

Chapter 1

What do you know about Islam?

You know almost nothing except that, according to Bush, they practice a "religion of peace;" and according to Obama, "they are just like us," and "there is no conflict between Islam and the U.S. Constitution." Nothing could be further from the truth. The U.S. Constitution and *Shari'ah law* are diametrically opposed to each other.[1,2] Obama, who was once a practicing Muslim, and who taught U.S. Constitutional law, certainly knows better. Obama is practicing *"Taqiyya,"* deliberately lying to the American people.

Islam is a religion, a legal system and a political/military ideology all merged into one set of laws, *"Shari'ah Law,"* which every true Muslim must follow: Islam and *Shari'ah* law cannot be separated from each other. Islam <u>is</u> *Shari'ah. Shari'ah* law consists of the *Qur'an*, the word of the Prophet Mohamed (comprising 114 *Sura* or chapters); and the *Sunnah*, (the Way of the Prophet, as recited in the *Hadiths* or reports of Mohammed's life by people who knew him personally). Muslims believe that because *Shari'ah* is the word of their God, Allah, derived from the *Qur'an* and the *Sunnah*, it is not optional. To violate *Shari'ah* or refuse to accept its authority is to commit rebellion against Allah. All practicing Muslims are required to combat those who violate *Shari'ah*. And no Muslim is permitted to obey any law of any country which contradicts *Shari'ah* law. In short, *Shari'ah* dictates every aspect of life, and all law, to a practicing Muslim and also that *Shari'ah* is the supreme law they must follow; supreme over all other laws. *"And whoever desires a religion other than Islam, it shall not be accepted from him, and in the hereafter he shall be one of the losers"*—*Qur'an, Sura* 3.85.

There is no such thing as "Separation of Church (Mosque) and State" in Islam. The fatal mistake Westerners make is to believe that Islam is merely a religion and try to understand its influence on Muslims as they would understand the influence of Judaism or Christianity on Jews or Christians: Islam itself does not seek any accommodation with Western Religions. There are no churches or synagogues in Saudi

Arabia and the Saudi Grand Mufti has called for the destruction of
all churches in the Middle East.[3] Islam's political/military aspect is
intertwined with its religious aspect. And its political ideology is at war
with the West. We must realize that once we agree that an American
can be a good orthodox Muslim; we have also automatically agreed he
is entitled to follow *Shari'ah* law. And where *Shari'ah* conflicts with our
US Constitution; *Shari'ah* must rule and our Constitution must be cast
aside. This necessarily creates two sets of laws, *Shari'ah* for Muslims; and
the U.S. Constitution and its laws for non-Muslims. **And we end up
accommodating, and even defending, a "religion;" which is actually
an ideology that is at war with us and which seeks to destroy us**.

True Islam conflicts with our Constitution in virtually everything:
It is truly absurd to permit Rep. Keith Ellison to place his hand on
the *Qur'an*, (which itself declares Islam is the supreme law), and take
his oath to uphold our Constitution, (which states our Constitution is
the supreme law). The *Qur'an* conflicts with our Constitution in the 1st
Amendment's Establishment of Religion, Free Exercise of Religion and
Free Speech clauses; the 5th Amendment's Due Process clause; the 6th
Amendment's right to impartial jury trials, right to confront a witness,
and right to an attorney; the 7th Amendment's right to Trial by Jury; the
8th Amendment's prohibition of Cruel and Unusual Punishment; the
13th Amendment's abolishment of slavery; the 14th Amendment's Equal
Protection Clause and, of course with Article VI itself which states that
Our Constitution is the Supreme Law of the land. Should he win again;
how will Obama take his oath? On the Bible or, as Obama calls it, on
the "Holy *Qur'an*"?

**True Islam is a violent and barbaric religious ideology, stuck in
the dark ages**: The most controversial issue of the day is whether
Jews have the right to be in Israel. The answer is found in the *Qur'an*
itself, which documents that Jews were in the Middle East, in Mecca
and Medina, Saudi Arabia, even before Mohammed was there! See if
you see a foreshadowing of Nazi death camps here: *"Then the Apostle
(Mohammed) went out to the market of Medina and dug trenches in it.
Then he sent for them (the Jewish tribe at Medina, the Bani Quraiza) and
struck off their heads in those trenches as they were brought out to him in
batches. . . . There were 600 or 700 in all, though some put the figure as
high as 800 or 900. . . . This went on until the Apostle (Mohammed) made*

an end of them."—*Hadith* Vol, 1, Book 2, Number 25, *Sira,* p463-4. *"Allah's Apostle (Mohammed) said, "The Hour {of the Last Judgment} will not be established until you fight with the Jews, and the stone behind which a Jew will be hiding will say. "O Muslim! There is a Jew hiding behind me, so kill him."*—Volume 4, Book 52, Number 177; Narrated by Abu Huraira. *"Fight and slay the pagans wherever ye find them, and seize them, beleaguer them, and lie in wait for them in every stratagem of war."*—*Sura* 9:5. Here is what is done to infidels who resist Islam: *"Their punishment is . . . execution, or crucifixion, or the cutting off of hands and feet from the opposite sides, or exile from the land."*—Sura 5:33. Muhammad also burned out eyes with hot irons—*Hadith* vol. 1, no. 234, and deprived people of water until they died—*Hadith* vol. 8, no. 796.

Shari'ah law itself directly commands all Muslims to perform these barbaric acts: *"It is He {Allah} Who has sent His Messenger (Muhammad) with guidance and the religion of truth (Islam), to make it superior over all religions even though the Mushrikun (non-believers) hate (it)"*—Qur'an 9:33. *"O Prophet! Strive hard against the unbelievers and the hypocrites and be unyielding to them; and their abode is hell, and evil is the destination."*—Qur'an 9:73. *"And (as for) the man who steals and the woman who steals, cut off their hands as a punishment for what they have earned, an exemplary punishment from Allah; and Allah is Mighty, Wise"*—Qur'an 5:38

There is no such thing as "moderate" Orthodox Islam. Early moderate verses are abrogated by later violent ones: Prophet Mohammed wrote the entire *Qur'an* himself. His word and the *Sura* constitute *Shari'ah* law and every syllable of it must be obeyed. However, according to accepted Islamic practice, his prior peaceful passages, written in Mecca when he was among people of other faiths; are abrogated by his subsequent more violent passages, written in Medina, after he conquered all unbelievers. But the verses are not listed in chronological order. Muslim scholars have identified which were written earlier and which were written later. As it says in the *Qur'an* 2.106 *"Whatever a Verse do, we (Allah) abrogate and cause to be forgotten. We bring a better one or similar to it. Know you not that Allah is able to do all things?"* All Muslims, including Obama, know that the prior peaceful passages are abrogated—exactly like a lower court ruling that was overturned by the Supreme Court. A frequently quoted verse is: *"There shall be no compulsion in religion"*—Qur'an 2:256. But this is from the Meccan period and is abrogated by subsequent violent verses from the Medina period. Therefore, all Muslims who quote early "peaceful" passages written in Mecca, and say the *Qur'an* does not require them to commit violent acts, are not telling the truth.[4,5]

"To understand what a Muslim really means, it is necessary to listen to them in Arabic . . . There is no organized Islamic movement in America that is peaceful . . . They are all jihadist movements . . ." says Walid Shoebat,[6] a former Muslim, in an eye opening video. *"Those who practice true Islam practice misogyny, censorship, anti-Semitism, homophobia, wife-beatings, beheadings, honor killings, pedophilia/child "marriages," murder infidels, etc. This is evil, and Islam sanctions every bit of it, . . ."* a former Muslim writes.[7] Also see David Horowitz's *Front Page Magazine;*[8] Robert Spencer's *Jihad Watch;*[9] Pamela Geller's *Atlas Shrugs;*[10] *Militant Islam Monitor*[11] or *Bare Naked Islam.*[12] These very few who speak out are risking their lives. We owe them a huge debt of gratitude.

There is also no such thing as a "moderate" Orthodox Muslim, contrary to what many Americans believe: Orthodox Islam,[13] as exemplified by Prophet Mohamed's own words in the Qur'an and by the Saudi Wahhabi Islam, is a violent and militant Islam with which a true Muslim is not allowed to disagree. It is this radical Wahhabi Islam that is being preached in virtually all of the thousands of mosques being built by the Saudis and others in America today.

Non-Radical, Moderate Muslims face many problems: There are a great many moderate non-radical Muslims, many of whom I count as my friends. However, the media and the Islamists always lump moderate and decent Muslims in with Radical ones. But this is merely a political ploy, using moderate Muslims as a cover to advance Militant Islam's own goals. Moderate Muslims obtain absolutely no benefit from being allied with the Wahhabis. If the Wahhabis prevail, the Moderates will be exterminated.

There are a great many Moderate Muslims who reject the violent political/military ideology of Islam; seek to isolate and follow the religious aspect of Islam; and also live in Western countries with their freedoms and culture. But they face many problems. *First*, they face discrimination from Militant Muslims who do not consider them to be "true" Muslims because Moderates reject aspects of the *Qur'an* with which they disagree.[3,6,7] *Second*, they face discrimination from Americans because Americans are rightly concerned that any Muslim could be a terrorist. If we fail to monitor Muslims, we expose ourselves to terrible consequences, like the 9/11 attacks. They must understand that just as we could not distinguish between good Germans and Nazis; we cannot distinguish between Moderate and Militant Muslims, especially when Moderates remain silent. *Third*, Moderate Muslims face a terrible dilemma. If they speak out about the barbarity of Wahhabi Islam, they and/or their families here and abroad will be subject to terrible repercussions and even death. But if they remain silent, and Wahhabi Islam takes over America; it is their families that face the worst consequences. Their wives and daughters will be forced to wear the hijab and become second-class citizens; their sons could become radicalized; their gay children will be killed; and even their pets will be destroyed. In short, they will be compelled to revert to the Islam from which they have fled.

They deserve our sympathy and our prayers. We ourselves lack the courage to speak out. So we cannot demand that the Moderate Muslims speak out. Yet they need to have the courage to discuss with their Imams how to bring Islam into the 21ˢᵗ Century. Or perhaps join groups such as Dr. Zuhdi Jasser's Muslim Liberty Project , Professor Muqtedar Khan or Professor Salim Mansoor and try a reformation like Martin Luther did. They must do this for their own sakes, for the rest of us and for America itself.

Orthodox Muslims can never assimilate into our culture: The *Qur'an* requires them to live apart; obey *Shari'ah* laws; and never be friends with non-Muslims. *"Let not the believers take the unbelievers for friends rather than believers; and whoever does this, he shall have nothing of (the guardianship of) Allah, but you should guard yourselves against them, guarding carefully; and Allah makes you cautious of (retribution from) Himself; and to Allah is the eventual coming." Qur'an, Sura3.28. "They desire that you should disbelieve as they have disbelieved, so that you might be (all) alike; therefore take not from among them friends until they fly (their homes) in Allah's way; but if they turn back, then seize them and kill them wherever you find them, and take not from among them a friend or a helper."—Qur'an, Sura 4:89. "Surely Allah has cursed the unbelievers and has prepared for them a burning fire"—Qur'an, Sura 33:64, "O you* *who believe! Do not make friends with a people with whom Allah is wroth; indeed they despair of the hereafter as the unbelievers despair of those in tombs."—Qur'an, Sura 60:13.*

We assume that Orthodox Muslims wish to assimilate into our culture; that Islam is a religion just like ours; and that we should accommodate it under the 1st Amendment's Free Expression of Religion. But Islam is not only a religion, but also a culture and a political/military system, each inextricably intertwined with the other. And it is unyielding in its opposition to the West.

Muslims are using "Being Offended" as a political Tool to further *Jihad* against us: As you will see below, Muslim culture is completely incompatible with ours. Virtually everything Western "offends" them. This is proven by how often Muslim mobs march around rioting, looting and "protesting" some "offense" in Europe and in Britain. (*Of course, they could not march around, riot and loot in their home countries. If they did, they would be shot. Exactly like those who remain in those countries, such as Syria, Egypt, Iran, Saudi Arabia, Libya etc., have been shot.*) Nevertheless, once they get to the West, they actually consider themselves superior to us; and the rest of us *Haram,* or sub-human. A Muslim will not get the death penalty if he kills a non-Muslim—*Qur'an 4:89.* Militant Muslims will never assimilate and, in fact, are conducting a carefully orchestrated campaign to convert Europe into Eurabia. The illegal immigrants sent to European countries and to America, are part of their advance shock troops, setting up a beachhead for either a *Stealth Jihad,* or a violent one. If you don't believe me, watch this:

http://www.youtube.com/watch_popup?v=pOq1gJzJ8cM

***Taqiyya:* Muslims are explicitly instructed to lie to non-Muslims.** *"Taqiyya"*[14] or lying, deceiving, tricking or intimidating infidels like us is the accepted form of behavior for Muslims. In contrast, the Western ethos holds one should not lie and lying in our courts is a punishable offence called perjury. A good example of *Taqiyya* is when Islamists quote *"There shall be no compulsion in religion"*—*Qur'an 2:256.* But they are deliberately giving the wrong impression. Under the doctrine of Abrogation or Naskh,[15] this early verse from the Mecca period has been cancelled out by other intolerant verses of the Medina period that have been quoted above.[9] Another great example of *Taqiyya* is when Obama reassures us that there is no conflict between Islam and our laws!! As you will see, *Shari'ah* is in total conflict with our Constitution. It is typical of a Muslim to lie and deceive other people as Obama has done. Another great example of *Taqiyya* is when Muslims assured European Authorities they were a "Religion of Peace." They explained away Islamic terrorist acts saying they were "isolated incidents." They constantly argued they should not be discriminated against because they were just like people of other religions, trying to live a peaceful life and assimilate into the host country. But as soon as the Muslims obtained a majority in any European City or in the Tower Hamlets in London, they put up signs saying *"Shari'ah Zone,"* and prevented anyone who does not follow all the strictures of *Shari'ah* law from entering. Because of their use of *Taqiyya*, the only way one can judge Islamists is by what they have done, not by what they say. And what they have done, as soon as they obtained a majority of the population, is throw away all pretense of democracy and impose autocratic Islamist rule on everyone, including non-Muslims.

Jizya: **Muslims believe they, and their proxies, have the right to collect "Jizya," i.e. Blood Money or Taxes, from *Dhimmis,* Non-Muslim slaves, in exchange for allowing them to live**: *"Fight those who do not believe in Allah, nor in the latter day, nor do they prohibit what Allah and His Apostle have prohibited, nor follow the religion of truth, out of those who have been given the Book, until they pay the tax (Jizya) in acknowledgment of superiority and they are in a state of subjection."*—*Qur'an* 9:29. In Sura 9:29, the *Qur'an* sets out the amount of taxes Muslim overlords are to collect. **The purpose of *Jizya (taxes)* is not only to collect money, but also to humiliate the *Dhimmis* (slaves), and to emphasize the superiority of Islam**.

Despite their constant complaints about discrimination against them, Muslims do not hesitate to discriminate against people of other religions, such as Jews, Christians, Zoroastrians, Hindus, and Buddhists, that they subjugate by *Jihad* or war. When they conquer another group of people, they enforce the Contract of *Jizya* against these people, whom they consider *"Dhimmis"* or slaves.

For centuries, Christian, Jewish and Zoroastrian peoples of the Middle East, North Africa and much of Europe suffered under the oppressive strictures of Dhimmitude. Muslims had conquered the Byzantine Empire in 638 A.D. and cut off access to Jerusalem. The Crusades were launched only in 1095 to regain access to Jerusalem and re-conquer Spain. Muslim apologists pretend that Jews and Christians lived in peace and harmony under Moorish rule in Spain. But the apologists do not mention that the Moors permitted Non-Muslims to rise only because they needed their administrative skills. They also do not mention that when Non-Muslims were allowed a measure of freedom, Muslims rose up and slaughtered hundreds of *Dhimmis*, mainly Jews. **Essentially, therefore, *Dhimmis* lived like slaves in the Antebellum American South. <u>Their only choices were to be killed or to live as *Dhimmis*, paying *Jizya* and working for their Muslims overlords.</u>** *(Sounds just like what is happening to us here, doesn't it?)*

The payment of *Jizya or* blood ransom, which has to be paid by all who refuse to convert to Islam; was done in a public ceremony designed to humiliate and impress upon the people that they had been conquered and often involved blows to the head or neck. This ceremony signified that their life and belongings were protected; and the "free" non-Muslim had ratified the compact that assured them protection. In short, the payment of Jizya was an honor bestowed upon the conquered people, as a just compensation for not being slain by the merciful conqueror.[16] *Remember this the next time you hear Obama demonizing the hard-working successful people and humiliating them by jeering at "the rich" in America and demanding that they pay more Jizya or taxes to him.*

This Contract of *Jizya* had a number of other restrictions, which formed the discriminatory system of *Dhimmitude* imposed upon non-Muslims. (*No Freedom of Contract here!*) The vanquished non-Muslims could not bear arms. (*No Second Amendment rights here*!) No church bells were allowed. There were restrictions concerning the building and restoration of churches, synagogues, and temples—for the most part, once destroyed, a church, synagogue or temple could not be rebuilt. (*No Free Exercise of Religion here either*!) There was inequality between Muslims and non-Muslims with regard to taxes and penal laws. (*No Equal Protection here*!) A Muslim court would refuse to hear the testimony by a Dhimmi.

(*No Right to Confront an Accuser or Right to prove one's innocence!*) Jews, Christians, and other non-Muslims, including Zoroastrians and Hindus, were required to wear special clothes. (*Yet another discrimination by a group that won't allow our TSA or our FBI to do its job because they claim it "discriminates" against Muslims!*) Overall, non-Muslims were subject to humiliation and abasement. It is important to note that these regulations and attitudes were institutionalized as permanent features of the sacred Islamic law, or *Shari'ah*. Islam manifests itself as a political ideology, not merely a religion, when its teachings are followed on these and other prominent and enduring features.[17]

Muslim Apologists pretend Islam is a "religion of peace": Muslim sophists, and non-Muslim *Dhimmis* (slaves) who support them, explain away the barbaric "honor" killings of women as *"just a cultural practice."* They also claim that reports of other barbaric Islamic practices, such as beheadings, stonings, floggings, executions, etc. are the exaggerations of some extremist right-wing media. Alternatively, they claim these are isolated acts of a few, crazy individuals; or of some fringe group of "fundamentalists," "extremists," "fanatics," or "Islamo-fascists." None of this is true. **What is going on today is the practice of true Orthodox Islam, exactly as it has been practiced from the time of Mohammed.**

Muslims war with everyone: They war with their fellow Muslims of other sects, with ordinary Muslims of the same sect in their own countries, with non-Muslims and they also war against their own Women: Muslims have killed more fellow Muslims than any that have been killed by any Western power. Between half a million and one million Muslims were killed by the Muslim Army in East Pakistan, now Bangladesh, in 1971. In the Algerian civil war in 1992, more than 150,000 Muslims were killed by their fellow Muslims. Sudan's Janjaweed Muslim militias have killed hundreds of thousands of fellow Muslims.[18] Right now, Shiite Muslims in Pakistan are being killed by Pashtuns. The Hazaras are being murdered by Pashtuns in Afghanistan.[19] Muslims kill other Muslims with impunity in Iraq and Afghanistan. In Iraq, the Shia majority is killing Sunnis. Syria's Bashar Assad, an Alawite Muslim affiliated with Iran's Shiites, is killing Sunni Muslims. The Middle East Dictators of the Arabian Peninsula are all Sunnis, who are depriving their Shia Muslim majorities of their rights. Muslim Dictators oppress and even kill Muslims of their own sects in countries such as Saudi Arabia, Yemen, Algeria and Libya.

As I will detail below, Muslims are warring with and slaughtering Christians in Egypt, Kenya, Nigeria, Ethiopia, Sudan, and virtually all countries in Northern Africa. They have burned churches and discriminate against Christians even in Indonesia, supposedly a model of democracy.[20] They are now killing Christians and expelling them from Iraq. They do not permit any Christians or Jews to exist in Iran, Saudi Arabia and other Middle Eastern countries. They are demanding that Christian not practice their religion in European countries and have forced the removal of crosses from schools in Italy. Muslims are in constant conflict with Hindus in India and they have been fighting with Indians over Kashmir since independence in 1948. Muslim groups, the Uighurs, are warring with the Chinese. And Muslim Chechens are warring with the Russians. 160 Militant Imams have even infiltrated tiny Sri Lanka, in which only 8% of its 20 million population is Muslim. The imams came in as tourists but were actually preaching a virulent form of Islam. Fortunately, the Sri Lankan government had the good sense to deport them.[21] The Maldives, an archipelago of beautiful tropical islands with an almost 100% Muslim population, has not been so lucky. In 2008, it finally overthrew a dictator who had ruled for 30 years. But the democratically elected President Nasheed was overthrown in a 2012 coup by Mohammed Waheed, a member of the Adhaalat party affiliated with the Muslim Brotherhood.[22] Now, it is moving to enforce *Shari'ah* law, shut down the beautiful resort hotels, end all flights to Israel, stop the sale of alcohol, prevent massages and ban mixing of the sexes.[23]

As far as I have been able to discover, there is no country on earth where a majority Muslim population has lived in peace and harmony with a non-Muslim population. Even when they do live in relative peace and harmony as a minority; once their numbers increase, the militant Muslims take over and inflict their *Shari'ah* rules upon the non-radical Muslims and the communities they live with.

Worst of all, as will be detailed below, all Muslims, including those in Europe, treat their women as chattel, practicing polygamy, female genital mutilation, pedophillia, which they call child "marriage" and killings of women, which they call "honor" killings. Watch these two videos and see for yourself:

http://www.youtube.com/watch?v=vOIbgd5qcrg&feature=related
http://atlasshrugs2000.typepad.com/honor_killings/

Any non-Muslim who still believes Islam is a "religion of peace," can readily verify this. He, or better still, she, should try to make any positive statement about any other religion in Ramallah, Riyadh, Islamabad, or anywhere in the Muslim world. He had better write his last Will and Testament before he does so, because he would instantly bring down extreme violence upon himself!!

With Muslims warring with other peoples throughout the whole world, against their fellow Muslims and even against their own women; there is no possible way anyone can claim that Islam is a "religion of peace." Anyone who asserts that is either a fool or a knave.

It is the duty of all observant Muslims to wage *Jihad* against us and set up the Caliphate worldwide: *"Allah's Apostle (Muhammad) was asked, "What is the best deed?" He replied, "To believe in Allah and His Apostle. The questioner then asked, "**What is the next (in goodness)?**" He replied, "**To participate in Jihad (religious fighting) in Allah's Cause**"*—Vol 1, Book 2, Number 25; Narrated Abu Hurair.

Every Muslim has the duty to wage *"Jihad,"* which means the war or struggle against non-Muslim countries to establish the religious/cultural/political/military ideology of Islam. Militant Muslims had sent 161 Imam on tourist visas even into tiny Sri Lanka, which only has 20 million people and only an 8% Muslim population, which was living at peace with people of other cultures. The aim of these Imams was to rabble rouse and commence a *Jihad* against the other ethnic groups. When it was discovered that the Imams were members of Tablighi Jamaat and preaching a militant Islam, the government had the good sense to deport them.[24] Otherwise, even Sri Lanja would have been made part of the "Caliphate." The *"Caliphate"* consists of countries controlled by Muslims that observe *Shari'ah* law;[25] where non-Muslims like us are either killed; or subjugated to live in a state of *"Dimmitude"* or slavery, and pay *"Jizya"*[26] or taxes, to our Muslim overlords.

Using *Stealth Jihad*, Islamists are spreading *Shari'ah* law throughout the world: As can be seen below, *Shari'ah* law in being spread in Africa, in Europe and now, in America too. The goal of *Jihad* is to subjugate the target country and make it a *Shari'ah* compliant Muslim Caliphate where the native population will work as *Dhimmis* (slaves) and pay *Jizya* (taxes) to support the Muslim population. Europe is a good example of *"Stealth Jihad"* in action, where the means used is not outright war; but rather, *Stealth Jihad,* a slow and gradual process that operates under the radar, but which accomplishes the same goal of subjugation of the native people.

Chapter 2

Europe's Socialist Leaders have facilitated *Stealth Jihad* against their own Countries

Europe's leaders have helped Islamists pursue *Jihad,* resulting in the conversion of European States into Muslim-controlled States: European Socialists have made unforgivable mistakes in how they have dealt with mostly illegal Muslims. Socialists allowed unlimited numbers of illegal Muslims into their countries so they, the Socialists, would get votes. These Socialists did not realize that, eventually, when Muslims had sufficient numbers, as they have in Tower Hamlets in London, they would vote out the Socialists themselves. The Socialists allowed these illegal Muslims and others to immigrate without verifying they were fleeing persecution and not merely seeking better economic conditions. They did not require that these people learn the host country's language and assimilate. Instead, the Socialists provided unlimited welfare benefits without enforcing any cut-off date or any requirement that they obtain work. They permitted Muslims to practice Islam without recognizing that Islam did not grant basic human rights to women, gays, non-Muslims or even moderate Muslims. And worst of all, they permitted Muslims to practice their "religion" without realizing that this meant Muslims would practice *Shari'ah* and refuse to follow the host country's laws. And because *Shari'ah* is completely different from Western Law; European countries have ended up with two sets of laws and two sets of communities; one for Muslims and another for non-Muslims. To reverse these mistakes, these countries would have to resort to civil war. Obviously, they cannot do that because to fight radical Islamists, they would need to awaken the spirit of the native Europeans, which they themselves have spent years breaking. Therefore, I believe these mistakes are now irreversible.

An overview of how *Stealth Jihad* works: First, Muslims sent hordes of illegals into various European cities. Once these illegals got their welfare and other benefits; they brought in more illegals. The host countries usually had a system of "family reunification." And this enabled the illegals to bring in more Muslims whom they claimed were their parents, siblings or their wife and children. But, under *Shari'ah*, they could have as many as four wives. Sometimes, they divorced the existing wife, went back to a Muslim country and brought in a replacement wife. Other times, they brought in a "nanny" for their children or a sick relative, whom they would later "marry" in a *Nikah* ceremony in their local Mosque, thus avoiding having to register the marriage with the authorities. At other times, the "nanny" would simply disappear into the community and be entitled to receive welfare and other handouts. In all European countries, whichever technique they use to hoodwink the authorities; Muslims practice polygamy, having many wives and taking welfare benefits for all their wives and their many children.

Britain's case is typical of all European countries. Britain has had laws against bigamy and polygamy since 1604. The punishment is up to 7 years in prison. But, because of *"political correctness,"* the authorities have been unwilling, or unable, to deal with the exploitation of Britain's laws by illegals. Britain officially recognizes only one wife; but since it has determined to accommodate the "cultural sensitivities" of Muslims; they don't ask questions about second or third wives. Instead, they simply treat these extra wives as single mothers who are entitled to housing benefits and other benefits for themselves and their kids. Each of these wives would have many children, each of whom is also entitled to benefits. Benefits for a man living with his harem are large. For each wife, the man gets $16,230 for spouses through income support, housing and child benefit of $1,623 for the first child and $1,135 for each additional child. But if he moves each wife out to a separate house, then she is entitled to a house with a separate room for each child. As he has more children, they get to move into an even larger taxpayer subsidized home. And the full housing benefit alone in some parts of London can reach as high as $171,900.[1] Two Muslim women, Baroness Flather and Baroness Warsi, a coalition cabinet member, have spoken out about the failure of British authorities to address the issue of polygamy and the attendant frauds on the welfare system. They point out that the children grow up angry and confused; with a father they rarely see because he has so many wives to visit. And they believe that polygamy is destroying families and the social structure of the country.

To an impoverished Muslim woman coming from a country like Bangladesh, Morocco, Yemen, Pakistan and even Turkey; being the second wife to a Muslim in a European country, which would provide all these benefits; is truly like coming to paradise. She does not care at all about European laws; that European authorities do not recognize her status or that native British are paying taxes to support her. All she cares about is that she gets her benefits from those authorities. She acknowledges only *Shari'ah* law, under which she is deemed married and her status secure. And therefore, there is an unlimited supply of potential "wives" willing to come to Europe.

For the Muslim man, this is better than paradise. He can have sex with as many women as he likes. But he has no financial responsibility for any of them, or for any children he sires. In fact, the more children he sires, the more money he gets and he also gets to move into a bigger house. And, under his *Shari'ah* law, he is the master of all of them. This penniless and frequently uneducated man, who came from a Muslim country where he was totally subservient to a Muslim Dictator, is now the rich lord of his extended family. But he owes no fealty to the European Country or the native Europeans that provide for him, his wives and his children. And he will not obey their laws. He obeys only *Shari'ah* law and subjects himself only to his local Muslim leader or Imam who, he believes, got him his benefits.

Essentially, the British are paying hostile men from another country, with a hostile religion antithetical to British culture and traditions, to come into their country and breed and overwhelm their welfare systems. Even worse, they are paying welfare to hostile Muslim men to hang around with nothing to do other than to denigrate and abuse the host country!! But, because of the Authorities' adherence to their political ideology of *"multi-culturalism"* and *"diversity"* (and of course, their desire to get votes!), they refuse to discuss these issues. Officially, British authorities say there are 1000 polygamous relationships. But social workers who are of the same culture, and who deal with these groups of people, estimate there are at least 20,000 Muslim men living in polygamous relationships in England.[2] As more Muslim men enter into these relationships, it becomes the norm in Muslim majority areas. And the Muslim population, heavily dependent on welfare, grows exponentially.

And as they achieve large numbers in any area; they commence demanding more and more accommodation to their beliefs; which are diametrically opposed to the beliefs and culture of the native population. If they do not get what they want; they resort to marches, intimidation and violence.

For the native European taxpayer, this has become a nightmare because they have to work and pay taxes to support all these people. Once again, Britain's plight is illustrative. Native British people watch with despair as their country, with its great Christian traditions, is turned upside down. If they speak out, Muslim apologists use the standard techniques they have used to begin the conquest of Europe. First they attack the messenger: *"He is a liar!! He is an Islamaphobe!!"* Next, they appeal to the liberals of the host country: *"You are much more sophisticated than those yokels!!"* *"Let us have some inter-faith dialogue!"* *"Diversity!!"* *"Multiculturalism!"* *"Tolerance!"* *"Our culture is compatible with Western values!"* *"You know Islam is a religion of peace!!"* Then, they offer votes to the Socialists in exchange for receiving benefits and for Socialists' agreeing to subjugate those who oppose Islamic practices. And finally, if persuasion fails; they instigate their mobs to riot and terrorize the Authorities of the host country.

When the authorities began cooperating with the Militant Muslims, it became tantamount to a death sentence for their countries. They embarked upon this course of cooperation with the Muslims over the vigorous protests of their native population, which objected to changing their laws and their country's traditions; and to paying such high taxes to support so many illegal immigrants who took so many benefits. So, on one side, there were the Socialists who for political reasons, cooperated with the Muslims and on the other side, there were the conservatives.

In order to curry favor with what they perceived to be a new bloc of voters, the Socialists began the practice of denouncing the opposition with epithets such as *"Nativists" "Xenophobes" "far right," "extremists"* and *"intolerant,"* etc., and demanding obeisance to *"Multiculturalism"* *"Diversity,"* etc. They instituted *"political correctness"* on the social order in their countries, insisting that every culture was equal to every other culture. According to them, a group of impoverished and uneducated illegals who had come to their country not speaking the language, not being able to read, having no concept of personal hygiene, and no concept of Western Culture and Traditions; was exactly the same as a local European. In so doing, they denigrated their own culture. For instance, in 2006, Sweden's newly elected Prime Minister, Fredrik Reinfeldt, said: "*The core Swedish is only barbarism. The rest of the development has come from outside.*" In 2002, Mona Sahlin, now the party leader of the Social Democrats controlling 35% of the votes, said: "*I think that what makes so many Swedes envious of immigrant groups is, you have a culture, an identity, a history, something that binds you. And what do we have? Mid-summers' eve and such ridiculous things.*" The party leader of the Center Party, who is in the current government coalition, said the following: "*It is really not the Swedes that built Sweden. It was people that came from abroad.*" **Remember this the next time you hear Obama running down our country and its traditions and telling us that we have to "change" so we can have "hope!"**

In Britain, because authorities have embarked upon a policy of accommodating the Muslims' beliefs; they have forced their native populations into silence and submission. In other parts of Europe, Islamists have gone even further and made the legislatures pass "Hate Speech" laws, which punish the native Europeans with steep fines and jail terms if they speak out.

As Muslims started committing crimes, the authorities became defensive when the natives criticized them for failing to act; and also fearful of repercussions from violent Muslim mobs if the authorities tried to take any action against the criminals. As a solution to their dilemma, they began pretending that crimes committed by Muslims were done by some amorphous "Asian" gangs. But as Muslims practiced more of their own customs, ignored the laws of the host country and began to overwhelm the host country's economy with their financial demand for welfare and benefits; the authorities began to realize that they were losing their country.

But if they objected to any Muslim practice or behavior, the mobs rioted and intimidated the authorities. And always, acting like pincers, the Militant Muslims, posing as "moderate" Muslims wearing Armani suits, were there with their lawyers, using the native European law to argue for more "tolerance;" claim that each violent incident was an "isolated one" and that the whole Muslim community should not be blamed for that one incident. Arabs have unlimited money because the West is forced to buy their oil. They can buy PR people, the media and spokespersons. They have powerful attorneys who will sue anyone who disagrees with them. Finally, death threats can be organized, as was done to Geert Wilders, Ayan Ali Hirsi, and others.[3] This is common practice in Muslim countries, as has been demonstrated by the case of 23-year-old Hamza Kashgari, a Saudi columnist.[4] The British authorities do not have the legal resources; the PR machines or the will to counteract these sophisticated Militant Muslims.

So, step-by-step, the authorities, squeezed by their fear of the mobs on one side and the legal arguments of the quasi-Moderate but actually Militant Muslims on the other, have been forced to accommodate more and more of the Muslims' practices. They are forced to turn a blind eye to polygamy and child "marriage." They are forced to pretend spousal abuse and "honor" killings do not occur. They are forced to pretend the first wife is not being ill-treated and discarded for the second wife. They are forced to allow schools to teach the *Qur'an*. They are forced to ignore polygamy and to support a man, his four or more wives and his many children. They are forced to tolerate Muslim ghettos where no outsider can go without fear. There are forced to provide legal services to those Muslims who become terrorists because they are all on welfare. And, in the ultimate irony, they are forced to support the very people who conspire against their country. The Muslim Radicals who conspired to blow up London's transportation system in 2005, and the clerics who preach a violent *Jihad* against England, Anjem Choudary, Abdel Rahman Saleem and Abu Hamza, were all on welfare and, in addition, all of them were cheating the system![5] Remember this technique. The two groups, the mobs and the highly educated "Moderate" but actually Militant Muslims work in concert. One group riots and terrorizes the populace and the authorities. The other group then comes forward offering excuses and platitudes and assures the authorities that they really are a peaceful people. Very stealthily, the Muslims acquire a majority in some area. The minute they do so, all talk of "democracy" and "tolerance" goes out the window. Shari'ah law is enforced and non-Muslims are beaten and chased out of what has become "their" area. You will see this pattern all over Europe and Great Britain; in Jenya and in Nigeria; and in America too.

To an outsider; it is obvious that these Authorities are forcing their countries to commit suicide. But the authorities continue to insist that the native people support the immigrants no matter how badly they behave. Why? Elementary, my dear Watson. The Socialists cannot admit they have made a mistake. If they do, they will get voted out of office and lose all their perks and their power. So they keep plugging away, wasting their country's money, destroying its heritage and its social structure and dooming it to a certain death.

This subjugation of native Europeans by European authorities has facilitated the Islamists' goal of *Jihad*, or war and conquest, against Europe. And voila!! Without having to resort to war, *Stealth Jihad* has achieved the Islamists' goal.

Chapter 3

Europe is almost part of the Caliphate now

In major cities throughout Europe, the Muslim populations have reached a critical mass enabling them to set up "No-Go" zones, which function as microstates governed solely by *Shari'ah* law; and enforced solely by Muslims. The host countries' Courts are powerless to enforce their laws in these "No-Go" zones because the law-breakers cannot be caught or, if caught, will not talk. And they are unable to provide even the most basic services such as police, fire fighting and ambulance services. The police are assaulted and their police cars are burned if they enter those areas. In these "No-Go" zones, Muslim gangs regularly harass local non-Muslim residents. If the locals call for help, the police cannot respond. In fact, to cover up their powerlessness, the authorities now use euphemisms and misleading phrases to try to conceal the extent of Muslim crimes. For example, police regularly refer to Muslim crimes as being committed by amorphous "Asians," which could mean Indians, Philippinos, Burmese, Malaysians or even Japanese. In this way, they avoid keeping statistics of actual Muslim crimes. And because the police can't/won't respond, non-Muslims are fleeing, converting these areas into 100% Muslim-controlled enclaves. This, in turn, leads to the adjacent areas being at risk and those non-Muslims fleeing. And on it goes. Combined with the astronomical birthrate amongst Muslims; (An official U.K. statistic of 7.2 children per Bangladeshi woman in Tower Hamlets alone!); a negative birthrate among native Europeans; and the fact whites are fleeing; these countries are quickly turning into Muslim-Controlled Caliphates.

Geert Wilders[1] estimates that Europe will be 25% Muslim within the next decade. Amsterdam, Marseille and Malmo are already 25% Muslim. In a great many other cities, over 50% of the under-18 population is Muslim. Paris is now surrounded by a string of Muslim ghettos, the banlieues; where their kids rioted for months on end, and over 100 cars were burned each night. Many state schools in Belgium and Denmark serve only halal food.

European welfare systems are redistribution mechanisms, taking money from the skilled and educated Europeans in order to give it to non-skilled newcomers from the Third Word. Because of this and virulent anti-Semitism, Jews are fleeing in record numbers.[2] It has been calculated that of 100 twenty-year-olds in France, 70 have to work and pay taxes to support their own aging population and also the 30 young Muslim immigrants who are unskilled, do not speak the language and depend on welfare. And young skilled native Europeans are fleeing. Europeans in general are also fleeing. Since 2004, there was more emigration of ethnic Germans and Dutch citizens out[3] of those countries than there were immigrants moving in.

Gays are beaten up in Amsterdam. This is in keeping with the *Qur'an,*[13] Two young gay Iranian boys slept with another boy. This was called a "rape." The two, aged 16 and 17, were imprisoned for 2 years until they were over 18. Normal hanging requires a drop of at least 8 feet to ensure the neck is broken. But these boys were hung from a truck, which ensured they would not die immediately, but only die after prolonged suffering.[4]

In some cities, like in **Brussels, which is 20% Muslim**, 2 police cars have to respond—one to handle the emergency, and the other, to protect the first police car. **German** "No-Go" zones are proliferating at an alarming rate. In the **Netherlands**, a court forced the release of the list of 40 "No-Go" zones that the authorities, because of fear of retribution, had denied existed. In **Gothenburg, Sweden,** more than 15 police cars have been destroyed. And large swaths of the city of **Malmo**, with its 25% Muslim population, are "No-Go" zones. As **Malmo** based Imam, Adly Anu Hajar, has triumphantly announced, **"Sweden is the best Islamic state"!**[5]

© JP Laffont/Sygma/Corbis
Muslims assert Dominance:
"Prayers" on Streets, Montmartre, Paris

France[6] used to have a strict policy of Separation of Church and State and forbade the teaching of religion in schools. Authorities have now banned headscarves and face covering veils in public. But there are 751 "No-Go" zones in France, (known euphemistically as Zones Urbaines Sensibles "ZUS", meaning Sensitive Urban Zones), in which over 5 million Muslims live and in which the French writ does not run. Muslims arrive in buses and trains to pray. They demonstrate their power by taking control of the streets and sidewalks; thereby blocking off all businesses, and sealing off non-Muslims in their homes and offices. Marine Le Pen, the recently elected leader of the conservative National Front, likens this to the Nazi occupation. Nikolas Sarkozy, worrying he will lose the coming Presidential election, says immigrants need to melt into the French society and should not have ostentatious prayers in the streets in France. But the authorities in the 18th Arrondissement, near Montmartre, are so stupid that they believe the problem is one of lack of space, and hope to "solve the problem" by spending $32 million of public money and building larger mosques for the Muslim population!

The Muslims can never assimilate. After receiving training in Pakistan and Afghanistan's terrorist training camps, Mohamed Merah,[7] a young French-Algerian citizen, killed 7 people in Toulouse—3 soldiers, a Rabbi, his two sons and a little girl, all of whom he executed at point blank range, while videoing the whole event for publication. **This inability to integrate and the complete hatred for any other than his fellow Muslims demonstrates that Muslims cannot assimilate into western countries. And those that encourage more Muslim immigration do so at their own peril.**

© Bebeto Matthews/ /AP/Corbis
Muslims assert Dominance: "Prayers" in front of Milan's Cathedral

Italy[8] has its own problems. For years, they ignored their illegal Muslim populations. But they provided welfare and benefits to them, and even to their multiple wives. Now that Muslims have enough numbers, they are exerting their power. They march around "protesting" about something or another. Then, miraculously, they arrive at some Catholic Basilica exactly at the moment they have to pray. Equally miraculously, they produce prayer mats and kneel to pray in the Piazza, right in front of the Church. Recent "prayers" in front of the Duomo in Milan, in Venice and even in Rome[9] have sparked outrage amongst the local public. Ordinary people are smart enough to realize the Muslims are showing their contempt for Christians and demonstrating their intent to take over the country. But the Hoi Polloi have been unable to find a solution to the problem. And the Archbishop of Milan is idiotic enough to assert, "everyone has an inalienable right to pray"!!

Belgium has ceded its four major cities to Islam: The graffiti in Brussels make it clear: "Welcome to Belgistan!" Abu Imran, head of *Shari'ah* for Belgium, a major Muslim organization in Brussels, is quite clear about the fate of Europe and the world. *"Shari'ah will be implemented in Belgium and throughout the world. . . . There is no difference between Shari'ah and Islam. They are inseparable . . . Democracy is the opposite of Islam . . . We will replace Belgium's laws with Shari'ah. It is Allah who says what is allowed and what is not. . . . There is no such thing as a Democratic Muslim . . . A Muslim who says he is against Shari'ah is impossible . . . ."* Sam van Rooy,[10] who edited an 800-page analysis of Islam by various major intellectuals in Europe called *"Islam—Critical Essays on a Political Religion,"* says that Islam is a fascist religion. That the danger is that Islam has its religious aspect, which causes people to fail to recognize the danger of political Islam. According to him, Belgium will be Muslim in 20 years. He says that already, four major cities, Brussels, Rotterdam, Antwerp and Amsterdam, have large, aggressive and very fast growing Muslim populations. He says in Brussels, Islam is the biggest religious group and worries about what will happen to his country once Muslims become a majority. Abu Imran agrees. He is certain Belgium will be Muslim by 2020. *"If the unbelievers want to match us, then they have to take four wives and have lots of children. Otherwise, we will be the majority by 2020."* You must watch this video yourself:

http://www.youtube.com/ watch?feature=player_embedded&v=SbMnA3uO9As

Sweden has big problems too: Approximately 5% of the Swedish population is Muslim. They reside mainly in Stockholm, Gothenburg and Malmo. In Rosengård in the southern city of Malmö, about 30-40% of the populations are foreigners, mostly Muslim immigrants. There are similar areas in the second largest city of Gothenburg and all over the country.

Kent Ekeroth, the international secretary for the Sweden Democrats, which opposes Muslim immigration, says the government does everything it can to stigmatize his party by calling them "racists" etc. Swedish elections require voters to take a "Ballot Paper" belonging to the party for whom they want to vote. But the government elections workers regularly "forget" to display the papers of the Swedish Democrats, claim they ran out of them, have difficulty locating them etc. and thus prevent people from voting for the Swedish Democrats. The media ignores their presence. They are not invited to TV sponsored debates. They are not invited to schools though other political parties are invited. He says homes of his party members have been attacked with an axe in a door, their windows smashed, threats sprayed on their doors and their cars have been burned. They themselves have been attacked with tear gas, baseball bats, knives and stones, had glass bottles thrown at them and been bullied in the streets by gangs. *Keep this in mind, next time you are called a "racist" by Obama or his supporters.*

Crime rates are skyrocketing. Muslim immigrants are grossly over-represented when it comes to violent crimes such as rape, assault and the like. People from the Middle East and Africa are, for instance, five times more likely to commit rape or assault than the rest of the population. There have been riots in Islamized territories such as Rinkeby close to Stockholm. Police were attacked with stones. Firefighters were prevented from stopping the arsons that the immigrant gangs had started.

Islam is now the second official religion in Sweden, after Christianity. Muslim unemployment rates are more than four to ten times as high as for natives. What this means is that very large majorities of the Muslim population are on the dole!!

But the Swedish Socialists have tried to appease the Muslims by adapting to their demands. The Socialist government supports Islamic schools and in order to further Muslim integration into Swedish society, has established a Swedish Islamic Academy to train Imams.[11] Nothing can be sillier than this policy. The Swedes in power do not seem to know that *Taqiyya* or lying and deceit is an authorized form of Muslim behavior. Or understand that Muslims do not honor Swedish law, but rather obey only *Shari'ah* law. The authorities do not speak Arabic. The newly trained Imams will promise to teach the virtues of democracy and then preach a virulent hatred for the host country. How does the Swedish government plan to find out what the Imams are actually doing?

Pork meat has been withdrawn from some schools in Sweden. The Muslim holiday Ramadan, which lasts for a month, has been introduced in a school north of Stockholm. Separate bath times for men and women have been put into effect in the southern city of Malmö. Also in Malmö, the Social-Democratic mayor, to cater to his Muslim constituency, went so far as to issue a boycott against a tennis match between Sweden and Israel![12]

An Iranian immigrant to Sweden expressed astonishment at his new country's policies: "In Sweden my family encountered a political system that seemed very strange. The interpreter told us that Sweden is a country where the government will put a check into your mailbox each month if you don't work. She explained that there was no reason to get a job." Immigrant benefits costs Sweden at least 40 to 50 billion Swedish kroner [approximately $7 billion] every year and has greatly contributed to bringing the Swedish welfare state to the brink of bankruptcy.[13]

Sweden has now started a project, entitled "*There's no place like home*" ('Borta bra men hemma bäst'), designed "to allow immigrants the opportunity to better understand the options and possibilities available to help them return to their home soil." Plans call for the party to distribute 10,000 "goodie bags" filled with USB memory sticks, DVDs, and other information in various languages about how to apply for repatriation grants. As David Wood has posted: *"life as an unemployed immigrant in Scandinavia beats life under the Taliban any day of the week. No one wants to leave freedom for Shari'ah. (Instead, they want to convert free countries to Shari'ah states! Go figure!)"*[14] *Here we have yet another silly liberal "solution" that will not work. Why on earth are the authorities giving USB memory sticks and DVD's to people who have come from a country where the electricity supply, if available, is totally unreliable and where the populace is unlikely to own or even be able to use a computer?*

Britain's Muslim problems are worst of all: A dramatically increasing Muslim population has now overwhelmed what was once a predominantly Christian country. Once they have sufficient numbers, Muslims separate themselves from the others and seek to preserve their Islamic identity and protect themselves from what they call "the satanic values of Britain." The Rt. Rev Michael Nazir-Ali,[15] the Bishop of Rochester, a Pakistani convert from Islam, and the Church's only Asian bishop; fears that unlimited Muslim immigration is diluting the Christian nature of Britain. He also fears that the Christian Church will be disestablished within a generation, breaking a 6-century-old bond that has existed between the Church and the State since the Reformation. Bishop Nazir-Ali says very few of these Muslims have been integrated into British society. He asserts that people of a different race or faith face physical attack if they live or work in these communities, which are dominated by a strict Muslim ideology. David Davis, the shadow home secretary, has accused Muslims of promoting a kind of "voluntary apartheid" by shutting themselves off in closed societies and demanding immunity from criticism. He notes that different legal systems for people of different religions will promote divisions between communities.

Abu Izzadeen, recently freed from prison for funding terrorism, described how he wants to impose *Shari'ah* law on Britain and convert it into an Islamic Emirate. 3 million, or over 5% of the British population, are Muslims; and their number is increasing rapidly. There are 25 areas with large Muslim populations, including parts of **Manchester, Bradford, Dewsbury, Leicester** and **Luton**, which are listed by British Authorities as areas of extreme violence.[16] Abu Izzadeen says Muslims are going to take over these areas and that they will be patrolled by thousands of Muslim youth who will "enforce" *Shari'ah* laws.

14% of **Walthan Forrest**, 25% of **Newham** and 33% of **Tower Hamlets** are Muslim. Tower Hamlets is mostly Bangladeshi and, **if you count only under 16's, over 50% of the population is Muslim.** These three areas have over 100 Mosques. White residents have been ethnically cleansed out of large parts of Tower Hamlets, East London.

The entire infrastructure of Britain is changing.[17] Britain is now the main center for Islamic Finance outside the Muslim world. There are 85 officially recognized *Shari'ah* courts in Britain handling everything from divorce, marriage and property rights to petty criminal offenses. Across London, 24 Islamic primary and secondary schools that teach thousands of children are allowed to teach Islamic studies.

© Peter Marshall / Demotix/Demotix/Corbis
Muslims assert Dominance: Britain's Shari'ah Controlled Zones

In both Muslim majority and non-majority areas in several boroughs of London, England, large posters have appeared. The signs warn the public they are entering a *Shari'ah*-controlled zone,[18] where no alcohol, drugs, smoking, gambling, music, concerts, gays, porn, prostitution or free mixing between the sexes will be allowed.

Tower Hamlets[19] now has a Muslim Mayor. Massive vote rigging has been alleged. Extremist Bangladeshi Muslim preachers, called the "Tower Hamlet Taliban" regularly issue death threats to women who refuse to wear Islamic veils. Street advertisements deemed "offensive" are vandalized. Gays are threatened and beaten. If they complain, they are accused of fueling "Islamophobia."

© sinister pictures / Demotix/Demotix/Corbis
Muslims assert Dominance: Veils are mandatory for women in The Islamic Republic of Tower Hamlets, London

These areas are now worse than Bangladesh itself. Unemployment is around 50%. The UK Government estimates a birth rate of 7.2 children per Bangladeshi female,[20] which is reputed to be the highest in the developed world, possibly the highest in the entire world! In contrast, the Bangladeshi birth rate in Bangladesh itself is only 3.2! A large number of spouses come from Bangladesh, get citizenship automatically upon marriage, and then have the right to import yet more impoverished Bangladeshis into the U.K.

Since Britain has tacitly acknowledged the right of a Muslim male to marry 4 wives; this gives each Muslim male the opportunity to import 4 wives and produce a potential 28 or more children! And the British taxpayer keeps supporting them.[21]

When radical Salafist, Anjem Choudary was asked why he was demanding *Shari'ah* controlled zones in Britain and why he didn't go to a *Shari'ah* law country if he didn't like the people in Great Britain; he replied, "*Who told you . . . that Great Britain belonged to you? The country belongs to Allah!*[22] *If I were to move to the jungle, I would not live there like the animals.*"

Britain Authorities are now *Dhimmis*, actively promoting Muslim Ideology and concealing Muslim crimes: British Authorities are so intimidated by Muslims that they give in at every turn. Muslim mobs regularly march in protest around London making demands and getting *"insulted"* by something a non-Muslim said or did. Muslims are even offended over the Olympic logo which they claim spells out *"Zion"*! In fact, they had even devised a plan to build the largest Mosque in the world as part of the 2012 Olympics. But this was stopped because of public outcry. However, the massively expensive Olympic infrastructure, paid for by British taxpayers, is going to be handed over to Muslim authorities in Tower Hamlets once the games are over. British authorities are also exquisitely sensitive to Muslims. They have even refused to ban Islamic schools from beating their pupils for fear of *"upsetting Muslim sensitivities."*

The British authorities also actively conceal the vast number of crimes Muslims commit against native British people: Rape against British women[23] is an almost daily occurrence. And Muslim gangs rape lone men. Two such rapes of men took place recently in Manchester. The police, as usual, stated: *"this is very rare"* and listed this as a crime by amorphous *"Asians"* in their weekly reports of Muslim perpetrated street rapes."[24] In May 2012, nine Muslim men were convicted of organized rape and sex trafficking of underage white girls. These incidents had been reported since 1991, but the authorities had ignored them. According to Ann Crier, a former member of parliament, the authorities were *"petrified of being called racist and so reverted to political correctness."* As Melanie Phillips, a journalist has said, *"in politically* *correct Britain, no criticism of religious or ethnic identities is allowed, and so, the child rape industry was allowed to continue with repeated failures to prosecute.*" In sharp contrast to this, a 42-year-old white secretary was recently jailed for 21 weeks for having gone into a tirade about how the authorities are allowing immigration and multiculturalism to destroy British civilization.

A former American military intelligence officer, Tim Larkin, who was also a martial arts expert, wanted to teach self-defense in areas where there had been Muslim-native British riots. But the Home Secretary denied him a visa on the grounds that he would be teaching violent self-defense, which is unwelcome in Britain and "not conducive to the public good![25] In short, the police won't protect the native British people, or even their little girls. And it doesn't want anyone teaching them how to defend themselves either. And they are paving the way for Militant Muslims to take over their country. *Remember this, the next time Obama tries to take away your Second Amendment rights and when Obama and Holder try to explain why they started the "Fast and Furious" plan in the first place.*

17 year-old apprentice baker Daniel Stringer-Prince,[26] - was attacked on February 5, 2012, when he was in a Muslim controlled area near **Asda, Manchester**. Daniel suffered a fractured skull, broken cheekbones and 2 fractures to his eye socket. He may lose this eye. His friend Kavan suffered a broken nose. They were passing a kebab store when a Muslim inside threatened them with a knife and indicated he would slice their throats. The boys ignored the threat and walked on. But a gang of 8 Muslims emerged from the shop and beat them savagely as they tried to get inside a relative's home.

The worst part of this story is that the British Authority, Det. Insp. Dave Moore, tried to pretend it was just an attack by some amorphous "Asian" gang. He said, "I do not want anyone to jump to conclusions about this." In fact, British Authorities did not want to face the retribution of Muslims if they called it what it was—Muslims enforcing *Shari'ah* and preventing non-Muslims from entering "their" areas.[27] Any wonder that native Europeans flee areas controlled by Muslims?

There is an epidemic of rapes of European girls and women by Muslim men: Under *Shari'ah,* when women are raped, they are deemed to be prostitutes and it requires the word of 4 independent witnesses to substantiate their claim of rape—*Qur'an* 4:15-16. Similarly, when men are raped, they are deemed to be homosexuals. The Islamic punishment for either a woman or for a man who is raped is the death penalty for the victim.[28]

Throughout Europe, Muslims are insisting the women deserve it because they are "exposing" their bodies—meaning their bodies are not fully covered in Burkas—and are raping European women. Norway has an epidemic of rapes, all committed by Muslims.[29] Even in Britain, 400 underage white girls[30] have been drugged and raped by Pakistani Muslim gangs who insist that all white girls are prostitutes because they don't wear the Hijab. Last year, even as they celebrated the overthrow of Mubarak and their "freedom," Egyptian men surrounded and brutally raped what they claimed was "uncovered meat"—CBS reporter Lara Logan![31]

Europe is bankrupting itself paying *Jizya* to Muslims and doesn't even realize it: Europe is taxing their own citizens to pay outrageous welfare and benefits to mostly illegal Muslims who hate their host country and will never obey its laws. For instance, polygamy is a crime. But under *Shari'ah*, Muslims claim they have the "religious" right to marry up to four wives. So we have truly absurd results. While a native British man would be jailed for polygamy; a Muslim will receive benefits for 4 wives and 4 families if he produces a paper showing the "marriage" took place in a Muslim country which recognizes polygamy!![32] Soon, this will extend to "marriages" taking place in a British Mosques. Little wonder the native populations are outraged.

Norway pays *Jizya*: According to a University of Oslo study, "non-Western immigrants" are ten times as likely to be on social assistance as native Norwegians. In **Germany,** Muslims are four times as likely to be receiving welfare as non-Muslims.[33] **Norwegian** (Oslo) imams preach brazenly that Muslims should *expect* such welfare benefits and *feel justified in supplementing them by stealing from stores* as a form of *Jizya*[34] extracted from their infidel "host" societies, even though these societies have not yet submitted themselves to Islamic Law! *Remember this when we come to a discussion of gangs who are busting into pubic places in Chicago and into a Nordstrom's in Portland. They call themselves a "flash*

*mob," steal whatever they see and justify it on the ground that it is "owed"
to them.*

Welfare & Benefits Costs are Exploding: These burgeoning European
Muslim communities are consuming disproportionate amounts of state
sponsored welfare benefits. For example, **Danish** Muslims comprise 5%
of the population, yet they receive 40% of the governmental outlays.[35]
Norway[36] just arrested 100 Somali Muslim families for welfare fraud.
Britain[37] provides massive benefits: welfare, income support, disability
living allowance, careers' allowance, jobseekers' allowance, housing
benefit, council tax benefit, tax credits and child benefits, to name a few.
In Britain, a Muslim man can claim up to $4,800 a month in support
for his four wives and $1,575 a year per child. 10 Muslim families cost
British taxpayers $1.5 million per year[38] in just housing benefits. Some
collected rent of over $3,200 per week, the equivalent of a mortgage for
a $2.3 million house! In **Swede**n, Ayan Abdulle lived in Gothenburg
and collected benefits. When Sweden stopped her benefits, she moved
to Britain. Using false names for 5 of her 6 kids, she collected benefits
in both the true and the false names. In 6 years, she collected more
than $400,000 in benefits.[39]

Polygamy and Benefits Fraud go hand in hand across the continent.
Last year in **France**, a polygamous Muslim and father of 17 children
was charged with welfare fraud when authorities discovered that "two
of his companions lived in Dubai for a year while continuing to receive
welfare benefits worth 10,000 Euros ($13,161)." In 2005, the UK
Telegraph reported that the governor of Pakistan's Sindh province had
received **British** state benefits of around £1,000 ($1,608) a month for
ten months, plus the rent for a northwest London house. Muslim leader,
hate preacher and Islamic law proponent Anjem Choudary, has boasted
about receiving £25,000 ($40,200.00) a year in benefits, explaining that
the money "belongs to Allah."

The council house occupied by the wife and eight children of England's
most infamous convicted hate preacher, the hook-handed Abu Hamza,
received a £40,000 ($64,320) "makeover paid for by taxpayers." His
children are British-born, the *Daily Mail* reported, "meaning they are
entitled to support from the state, which would continue even if Hamza

is extradited." This support has included close to £700 ($1,125) per week in rent, benefits, and allowances.

Four weeks after the July 7, 2005, bombings in London, four explosions disrupted the city's public transportation system once more. British authorities subsequently discovered that the Muslim radicals involved in the attack had collected more than £165,000 ($265,321) in benefits, aided by multiple addresses and national insurance numbers. Two of them originally won asylum in Britain by using forged passports and false names.

Abu Qatada, the terrorist sometimes referred to as "Osama bin Laden's ambassador in Europe," was found guilty of plotting to plant bombs during millennium celebrations in Jordan. After his release from prison in 2008, he was granted £150 ($241) a week, or £8,000 ($12,887) a year, in "incapacity benefits" for a bad back, despite later being photographed on the anniversary of the July 7 London bombings, wearing a knapsack and carrying groceries. Along with publishing that photo, the *Telegraph* revealed "Qatada's[40] family is understood to be claiming around £47,000 ($75,576) a year in benefits. £500 ($804) a week in child benefits for the four of his five children under 18, £210 ($337) for income support, £150 ($241) for incapacity benefit and £45 ($72) in council tax benefit, along with a council home worth around £800,000 ($1,286,407)."[41]

Chapter 4

Traditional Western Cultural Practices are prohibited by Islam and Traditional Islamic Practices are Abhorrent to Westerners

Shari'ah **considers Dogs and other pets "unclean"**[1] **and Muslims want dogs banned**[2] **from public places in Europe**: British banks have banned piggy banks[3] because they offend Muslims. Muslims constitute 12% of **The Hague** and are now pushing for dogs to be banned from the city. In **Lerida, Spain**, where Muslims are 20% of the population, they want local officials to regulate the presence of dogs in public spaces and ban them from all public transport, so the dogs don't "offend" Muslims. When the city refused to acquiesce, more than a dozen dogs were poisoned in Sep 2011 alone. Many dogs have been killed in the **Cappont and La Bordeta** districts, which are heavily populated with Muslims. In **Britain**, blind passengers are being ordered off buses and refused taxi rides if they bring their guide dogs. Police sniffer dogs are not allowed to come in contact with Muslims. Some dogs actually have to wear leather booties, so they do not cause offense to Muslims! In British prisons, Muslims prisoners are given fresh clothes after sniffer dogs search their cells. In **Tayside, Scotland**, the Police department used a German shepherd puppy as part of a campaign to publicize its new non-emergency phone number. But then, it cravenly apologized for featuring the puppy because it was potentially offensive to the city's 3000 Muslims!

Not Shari'ah Compliant: In Muslim controlled areas Pets are banned!

Shari'ah **explicitly authorizes discriminating against, enslaving and/ or murdering Women, Gays and non-Muslims—***Hadith* **vol. 4, no. 260:** *"In Saudi Arabia, following a tradition of Muhammad, who said that "two religions cannot exist in the country of Arabia," non-Muslims are forbidden to practice their religion, build houses of worship, possess religious texts, etc. Non-believers or atheists in Muslim countries do not have "the right to life"; all the major law schools, whether Sunni or Shia, agree that they are to be killed. (Muslim doctors of law generally divide sins into great sins and little sins. Of the 17 great sins, unbelief is the greatest, more heinous than murder, theft, adultery, etc.) Slavery is recognized as legitimate in the Koran. Muslim men are allowed to cohabit with any of their female slaves, and they are allowed to take possession even of married female slaves. One does not have the right to change one's religion if one is born into a Muslim family. Here is how the great commentator Baydawi sees the matter: "Whosoever turns back from his belief, openly or secretly, take him and kill him wheresoever you find him, like any other infidel. Separate yourself from him altogether. Do not accept intercession in his regard." And here are the punishments in store for transgressors against the Holy Law: amputation, flogging, crucifixion, and stoning to death."* [4]

Muslims practice slavery to this day: Blacks and Arabs are two distinct ethnic groups. The Arabs are Semites and will never respect Blacks. Muslim Arabs have always owned and/or traded black slaves.[5] While Western nations discontinued this practice, Arab slavery continues to this day.[6] Arabs are exterminating or enslaving blacks in Sudan and

Mauritania. It is estimated that 20% of Mauritania's population is used as bonded labor akin to slavery. In Saudi Arabia, in 1940, slaves constituted approximately 20% of the population. *Have you ever wondered why Obama, who constantly reviles all Americans because some Americans once had slaves; never complains about Arabs having slaves even today?*

Even today, many of the Saudi's 5.5 million foreign workers, particularly their domestic staff, both women and young boys, are treated like slaves.[7] It is fairly common for Muslim masters to burn maids with hot irons, smash their teeth and rape or kill them. Quite a few maids leap to their death from upper stories to escape rapes or beatings. Muslim authorities are mainly concerned with the inconvenience and expense to the Saudi masters to find replacements; and do not indict or jail the Muslim miscreants. Popular Muslim preacher Abu Ishaq al-Huwaini has boasted that Islam allows Muslims to buy and sell conquered infidel women, so that "when I want a sex-slave, I go to the market and pick whichever female I desire and buy her."[8]

Nearly 1.4 million Sri Lankans, mostly maids, work in the Middle East. In August 2010, 50-year-old L.T. Ariyawathi returned from Saudi Arabia with 24 nails embedded in her hands, legs and forehead[9] She said she had to work continuously from dawn to dusk and when she wanted to take a break, they inserted the nails as punishment. "The woman heated the nails and gave them to her husband who hammered them in," Ariyawathi said. "When I shouted in pain, their (seven) children would show me a knife and threaten to kill me." Doctors removed thirteen 2" nails and five needles from various parts of the woman's body. But the remaining ones, in her hand, were not removed immediately because of fear of serious nerve and arterial damage. This barbarism is not unusual. In August 2010, another Sri Lankan maid, Balasubramaniam Shashikala, aged 22, was admitted to a Saudi Hospital. She said they had heated nails and driven them into her body. Doctors discovered 7 nails inside her body.[10]

Under *Shari'ah law*, there is no such thing as "Equal Protection Under the Law for all", as provided in our U.S. Constitution: Under *Shari'ah*, Muslims consider Jews, Christians, Hindus, Buddhists, (and even the Secularists/Atheists who support Muslims), "*Haram*" or dirty and not quite human. Non-Muslims, known as infidels, are not entitled to equal treatment under their law. Did you know that Britain now allows British Muslim cops to refuse to protect British Jews?[11]

Our Constitution gives all people, men and women, equal rights. In contrast, *Shari'ah* law gives men virtually absolute power over women. *"Men are the managers of the affairs of women . . . Those you fear may be rebellious—admonish; banish them to their couches and beat them"—Qur'an, Sura* 4:34. Polygamy is outlawed in the U.S. But Muslims believe in marriage to as many as four wives. We have extensive laws covering Matrimony, Dissolution and Child Support. But their men can divorce a wife by merely saying *"Talaq"* or "I divorce thee" three times—*Qur'an,* 2:229. The Qur'an endorses wife beating—*Qur'an* 4:34. Under *Shari'ah,* a woman's testimony is half that of a man's—*Qur'an* 2:282. Women do not have equal property rights to men. Inheritance rights of women are half those of men—*Qur'an* 4:176. Sexual relations with a child is the crime of pedophilia in the U.S. But it still exists in Saudi Arabia, which is still trying to ban the existing practice of child "marriage" to children as young as 10.[12] Their women must remain covered with a hijab.—*Qur'an* 24:30-31. *Qur'an* 33:59. Women received the right to vote only in 2011 but it is not clear for what they can vote. They still cannot drive, but must wait, like children, for a family member to take them to and from any trip they want to take.

**Shari'ah Complaint Saudi Women must wait
for a Family Member to drive them**

Gays are subject to death. Adultery in punished by stoning to death. *"The Jews {of Medina} brought to the Prophet a man and a woman from amongst them who have committed (adultery) illegal sexual intercourse. He ordered both of them to be stoned (to death), near the place of offering the funeral prayers beside the mosque."*—Volume 2, Book 23, Number 413; Narrated Abdullah bin Umar.

Arab Spring happened because under *Shari'ah*, there is no "Equal Protection" for even ordinary Muslims: A King or a Mullah rules every Middle-Eastern country with an iron fist; exactly like a Communist Dictator; using Islam and *Shari'ah law* to subjugate their people. Ordinary Muslims live like serfs. Can you name any one of the "57 States" controlled by Muslims where the ordinary man has freedom like in America? You can't.

Unemployment in Yemen was over 30%. Mohamed Bouazizi was trying to earn a living selling produce. He had endured years of official corruption and harassment where government officials would constantly ask to see his permit and demand payment. On Dec 18, 2010, an official slapped him in the face, confiscated his scales, tossed aside his goods, and, in an ultimate insult, spat upon him. When he went to the city to complain, they ignored him. He had reached his breaking point. Shamed, frustrated and humiliated by his treatment by government officials, he doused himself with paint thinner and set himself on fire. Why do you think he did this? Because he had no hope for a better future. Just grinding poverty and humiliation at the hands of a Dictator and his cronies.[13] Why did 5 unemployed men set themselves on fire in Rabat, Morocco in January 2012? In Iran, over a million young people rose up in 2009, begging for help and calling out "Obama! Obama!" But Obama ignored them[14] and a great many of them were killed. Why do you think there was an uprising called the "Arab Spring"? Because thousands of ordinary people in Arab countries such as Iran, Tunisia, Egypt, Libya, Yemen, Bahrain and Syria are ready to die, and thousands have already died, to get the freedoms we enjoy in America!![15]

The Judeo-Christian precepts "Thou shalt not Kill," "Thou shalt not covet they neighbor's wife or goods," etc., are applied by us to all people, irrespective of race or creed. But, to Muslims, these precepts do not apply to non-Muslims: *"Then . . . , kill the Mushrikun* *{unbelievers} wherever you find them, and capture them and besiege them, and prepare for them each and every ambush"*—The Verse of the Sword: *Qur'an* 9:5. Muslims can kill Jews or Christians with impunity, rape their women and take over their property—*Hadith,* vol. 4, no 260. In fact, most Jews have already been chased out of Muslim countries. And the Christians are being slaughtered and raped.[16] As Obama pulls our troops out of Iraq, Iraqis are exterminating Christian Iraqis.[17] Today, Egyptians are burning churches[18] and killing the 10% minority Coptic Christians who have lived in Egypt since the first century, before Mohamed was even born! The Muslims believe they are entitled to get rich by stealing the property of the Copts.[19] In Northern Nigeria's Muslim-controlled Kano province, the Boko Haram are burning Christian churches.[20] Once churches are destroyed or damaged, Muslims will never allow them to be rebuilt or repaired. 219 Christians have been killed in January 2012 alone. Now, 3 Million Igbo Christians are fleeing the Boko Haram.[21] Kenyan Muslims are killing Kenyan Christians.[22] Obama and Muslim leader, Raila Odinga, both belong to the Kenyan Luo tribe. Odinga claims Obama is a "close personal friend." When Odinga lost the Kenyan Presidential election in 2007, his tribe went on the rampage, burning down 600 odd churches, many with people inside. Obama was instrumental in forcing the Christian Kenyans to share power with the Kenyan Muslims[23]

© SAYYID AZIM/AP/Corbis

Obama with his fellow Luo Tribesman, Muslim Leader Raila Odinga Campaigning in Kenya

115

A woman is subject to an "Honor" Killing for merely living like an ordinary Western woman: A woman is deemed to have "dishonored" Islam by having a non-Muslim boyfriend, refusing to cover her face, asking for a divorce, or even refusing to "marry" her rapist. There are over 17,000 "honor" attacks per year[24] in Britain alone. Even the famous British star, Afshan Azad, who played Padma Patil[25] in the Harry Potter series, was beaten by her father and threatened with death by her brother, for dating a Hindu boy. You must watch this heart breaking video.[26] And check out these pages on Atlas Shrugs.[27] You will weep as you see the beautiful faces of young Muslim women who have been murdered. And, if you can stomach it, scroll down to see the faces of those who have been burnt or mutilated.

These "Honor" Killings occur even in America![28] Note how many of these killings take place because the woman is "too Americanized." This alone is proof that American values and Islamic values are diametrically opposed to each other. On Christmas day, 2011, a Muslim man dressed himself up as Santa Claus, went to his brother-in-law's home and killed his estranged wife, his daughter, his son, his 2 in-laws and their daughter because his wife had asked for a divorce.[29]

Aasiya Hassan was beheaded by her husband. Muzzammil Hassan founded Bridges TV to counter the negative perceptions of Muslims. However, when his wife Aasiya asked for a divorce, he beheaded her.[30] Mina and Sarah Said wore makeup and has Christian boyfriends. Their father took them for a ride in his taxi and shot them dead.[31] Noor al-Maleki, aged 20, was a beautiful young woman who went to college and had great dreams. She fell in love with an American Iraqi. Her father arranged a marriage for her with a man in Iraq and she refused. Her father drove over the mother of her boyfriend and her. The older woman was seriously injured. But her father ran over his daughter Noor a second time and killed her.[32]

Under *Shari'ah*, 4th and 5th Amendment Rights are not available to us: None of our constitutional protections are available to us when facing Muslim justice. Vigilante street justice and "honor" killings are acceptable. A Muslim will be forgiven for murder of an apostate, an adulterer or a highway robber—*Qur'an 3:85*. A Muslim will not get the death penalty if he kills a non-Muslim—*Qur'an 4:89*. A local Imam will issue a *Fatwa* or regulation, authorizing punishment of a non-Muslim. The non-Muslim will not even get a hearing, leave alone an attorney, the right to confront his accuser or any of the protections we offer to our people, and even to Muslim terrorists who kill our soldiers!

There are over 85 official *Shari'ah* courts in Britain and many unofficial ones in other European Countries: British courts officially sanction Britain's *Shari'ah* court decisions. *Shari'ah* courts are made up of Muslims elders. Women are not equal under *Shari'ah* law. Women cannot marry outside their faith. Even if they marry a Muslim and need a divorce, property is not divided equally. The wife does not get her own attorney. Usually, she is pressured to give in to whatever the elders recommend. Once she signs a consent form, it is filed with the British court as proof that the divorce is final and that proper financial settlement has been made.

In other European cities, *Shari'ah* tribunals operate inside Mosques. They operate behind closed doors and mete out justice, bypassing the official courts of the host country. Rapes and "honor" killings tend to be ignored because the Host country cannot get inside the Muslim enclaves to obtain evidence and no one will act as a witness.

Chapter 5

There is no Free Speech under Islam
Free Speech bans to appease Muslims
have spread to Europe and even to America

No one can speak against Islam because there is no such thing as "Free Speech" in Islam: Saying anything against Islam; or even anything perceived by them to be against Islam; subjects you to death. "Allah's Apostle Mohammed said: *"I have been ordered (by Allah) to fight against the people until they testify that none has the right to be worshipped but Allah and that Muhammad is Allah's Apostle, . . ."—Hadith* Volume 1, Book 2, Number 24; Narrated by Ibn Umar. *"And fight them until there is no more Fitnah (. . . worshipping others besides Allah) and the religion . . . will all be for Allah alone [in the whole of the world]"—Qur'an* 8:39.

In Europe, there are two sets of Free Speech laws: One set of laws for Muslims, who have free speech rights, and can say anything they like against Europeans. And another set of laws for Europeans, who are treated differently. Europeans still have free speech when it comes to talking about themselves; but they cannot say anything against Muslims. Muslims riot and pillage whenever they are "offended." No one is allowed to speak out about the danger of Islam. The few who do are either killed by Muslims or sued by their own governments for "inciting hatred."

In the **Netherlands**, Ayaan Hirsi Ali, a Somali refugee who became a liberal Dutch parliamentarian, had been fighting for women's rights. She made a film, called "Submission" with Theo Van Gogh, depicting the terrible way women are treated by Muslims. Theo Van Gogh's throat was slit and his body sliced up by a Muslim who objected to the film.[1] Hirsi Ali[2] was forced out of parliament by the Dutch. She then fled to America. Geert Wilders is in the crosshairs of Muslims for his outspoken denunciation of Islam's effects on European culture. Wilders says that Islam is a violent religion that is fundamentally altering the culture and taking Holland and the rest of Europe back into the dark ages. He also produced a film *"Fitna."*[3] He has been threatened with death, sued in his home country, banned from Britain and declared persona non grata by an American Hotel where he was scheduled to speak.

In **Denmark**, there is no free speech either. An increasing numbers of stories were being self-censored by journalists who are afraid of Radical Islamists. In 2005, *Jyllands Posten,* became concerned that no one was willing to illustrate a book about Mohammed and it commissioned 12 cartoonists to draw cartoons of Mohammed, which it also published. Death threats were issued against all 12[4] and they were forced to go into hiding. Militant Muslims also threatened to bomb the offices of *Jyllands Posten.* Muslims rioted all over the world. People were killed at Bagram AFB. Danish embassies in Syria and Lebanon were attacked. The Norwegian embassy in Syria was set on fire. And riots spread all over the Muslim world. As one protester proudly informed the BBC: ***"They want to know whether Muslims are extremists or not? Death to them and to their newspapers!"*** [5]

The authorities are now so afraid of Muslims that they have passed laws making "hate speech" a crime. All that is needed for conviction is for someone else (read, a Muslim) to feel "threatened, insulted or degraded." And there is no defense to Libel. One is not allowed to prove the truth of what one says. Laars Hedegaard, an author, pointed out the barbarity of Islam:[6] *"Without trials, Muslims are authorized to kill Muslims who have left Islam; Muslims who have been guilty of fornication must be stoned to death; over 20,000 women are subject to "honor" killings each year; 50,000 Muslim girls in Germany are subject to genital mutilation; hundreds of thousands of little Muslim girls are sold into "marriage" with older men."* For stating these facts, **which he offered to prove were true**, Hedegaard was prosecuted and convicted. Meanwhile, a prominent Imam had stated that *Shari'ah* would be instituted as Denmark's official legal regime when there were sufficient Muslims in Denmark. As Hedegaard pointed out, this *"threatened, insulted and degraded"* a vast number of Danes, but the public prosecutor had not brought suit against the Imam.

In **France,** Islamists made death threats against the editor, fire bombed the offices and took down the website of *Charlie Hebdo,* a French satirical magazine because they announced that Prophet Mohammed was going to be a guest editor of the magazine for a week. At least in France, the authorities defended the free speech rights of the Magazine.[7]

There is no such thing as "Free Speech" even in America: Even in America, we now have two sets of laws. One set for Non-Muslims and the other for Muslims. Essentially, Muslims create a separate set of laws for themselves by their violent and barbaric responses, such as death threats, killings, beheadings and riots, to the exercise of free speech by anyone else. As a result, our authorities censor us. And we ourselves are terrorized and remain silent. As the NY Times would so indignantly remind us with respect to any form of speech, (except speech against Muslims); this is chilling our free speech and destroying our democracy!

Eric Alan Bell spoke out against the massive Mosque being built in Murfreesboro, TN. CAIR labeled him an Islamaphobe. Islamic blogs picked this up and printed his name and photo and hinted he was an "enemy of Allah." He believes his life is threatened.[8] Molly Norris, a Seattle cartoonist,[9] merely suggested that we eliminate threats of death by having an "Everybody draw a cartoon of Mohamed Day." She has received so many death threats she has gone into hiding. And Obama's FBI won't protect her. Dr. Wafa Sultan,[10] a psychiatrist and a Syrian-American citizen who spoke out against Islam, has also been forced to go into hiding.

Pastor Terry Jones,[11] who threatened to burn the *Qur'an* in response to the proposal to build the 9/11 Victory Mosque, also received death threats. His mere threat set off mobs of violent Afghanis in Mazar-i-Sharif, who killed seven UN workers and beheaded two. General Petraeus strongly condemned Jones saying it put American lives in danger. Obama also issued a strongly worded condemnation. The New York Times, on April 2, 2011, castigated Rev. Jones and spoke tenderly of Muslim hurt feelings as follows: *"Afghanistan, deeply religious and reflexively volatile, has long been highly reactive to perceived insults against Islam"*!

Nobody pointed out that this was pure Muslim barbarism! The New York Times, that great defender of everybody's First Amendments right to burn the U.S. Flag; to expose Military secrets; to disclose the home addresses of covert CIA agents; to promote putting cow dung on a painting of the Virgin Mary; to promote taxpayer funded "art" of the crucifix in a jar of urine, etc.; was "shocked" anyone would dare to exercise free speech rights by thinking of burning a *Qur'an!*

Obama has insisted that our soldiers leave Afghanistan precipitously and to that end, he has insisted that our soldiers partner with, and train, Afghanis. In February 2012, there was another *Qur'an* burning crisis.[12] Radical terrorist prisoners had defaced their *Qur'an's* by writing messages to each other on them and on other material handed to them. Authorities feared the prisoners were plotting an attack and ordered the American soldiers to burn the incendiary documents. These inadvertently included some *Qur'ans*. Of course, someone informed the mobs, who rioted, burned down various buildings and killed 30 people, including 6 of our soldiers. Two of those were officers were shot by our supposed Afghani "partners" inside the secure compound. All the senior officers of the Administration apologized profusely to the Afghanis. Obama himself wrote a personal letter of apology! Now, the Obama administration states it has identified 5 soldiers involved in burning the books and it is planning to bring them to trial. And it refuses to say whether or not our solders will be handed over to the Afghans. If they are, of course, our soldiers will be tried under *Shari'ah* law, with no Constitutional protections whatsoever, and, for burning a *Qur'an,* they will be subject to the death penalty.[13] Meantime, Obama has not been able to find any of the people who killed our 6 soldiers! Nor has he demanded that the Afghanis locate the miscreants and punish them!! Or even apologize to us!! Needless to say, no apology or assistance in finding the murderers of American soldiers has been forthcoming.

In sharp contrast to all this great respect for the *Qur'an*, Obama himself directed the U.S. Army itself to burn Christian Bibles.[14] The Bible had been translated into Pashtun and Dhari by some missionaries and sent to Afghanistan. A soldier had handed them out. Obama's Justice Department found out and ordered that the Bibles be burned; and that Lt. Col. Mark Wright discipline the solder because it *"could be perceived that the US Military was trying to convert Muslims."* They said the Bibles could not have been shipped back because they may have returned through other channels and that *"might give the impression"* that Obama's U.S. Government was distributing Bibles! *Does this sound to you like a Christian President who is concerned about Christianity or even about the welfare of our American soldiers?*

Chapter 6

Islamic Apostasy Laws mandate
Death for those who convert

Once you are a Muslim (like Obama was), you cannot ever convert to any other religion (like Obama says he did): If he ever did convert, he would be a *Murtad* or Apostate, subject to the punishment of death—*Qur'an 9:29; Hadith, Vol. 4, No 260*. In addition to killing infidels like Jews and Christians, Muslims are also commanded to kill any Muslim who dishonors Islam; especially one who converts.[71] Right now, the Saudis have forced the repatriation of a Saudi columnist Kashgari, who had tweeted something clerics considered blasphemy and believed it showed Kashgari had left the Muslim faith. Kashgari now faces the death penalty. As recently as June 2012, some brave man was able to capture on his cell phone, a video of a young Tunisian whose throat was cut because he had converted to Christianity.[1] There is no way they would allow the President of the United States, who was once Muslim, to ever convert to Christianity.[2]

See the tricks Muslims play: We cannot call anyone a Muslim Terrorist if there is even one moderate Muslim who is not a terrorist!! But most "moderate" Muslims, who are perfectly decent people, tacitly co-operate with the terrorists by their silence. If they have family, terrorists will kill them. These "moderates" make it impossible for us to distinguish between the fanatics and themselves. And by not paying closer attention to all Muslims; we make it more likely we will suffer the consequences of terrorist acts. So, they should not complain of discrimination. Every German who co-operated with Nazis was held responsible. And, just as we didn't have to stop fighting Nazis because there were some good Germans; we don't have to give up our fight against Terrorist Muslims because of the "Moderates."

Our politicians' failure (or refusal) to understand Islam has resulted in complete confusion in our dealings with Muslims: The political/military ideology of Islam seeks to dominate and destroy us. They will never assimilate culturally either. Without our Constitution there would be no First Amendment. But while our Constitution's Article VI, Supremacy Clause dictates that our Constitution transcends all other laws; *Shari'ah* law dictates theirs is the supreme law. So when we accommodate their "religion", we automatically accommodate their political/military system that seeks to supplant ours.

Essentially, Muslims are using our 1st Amendment rights as a shield to hide behind while they advance their goals; and also as a sword with which to destroy our Constitution. Of what use is our 1st Amendment Rights if we no longer have a Constitution that grants 1st Amendment Rights to us?

Chapter 7

Think about what you have just read and answer the Question

Look at the power of the Muslims. Listen to Obama and the Muslims say theirs is the "Religion of Peace." Consider what you have found out about the barbarism of Islamic law; and their behavior. Consider how they have never assimilated, but rather, created two parallel societies with two different sets of laws within the countries that took them in. And see how Europeans have been tricked. Look at the vast amount of information your current media has hidden from you. And see how they have tricked you. Consider how Obama told you that there was no conflict between *Shari'ah* and our Constitution. After you read this, isn't it obvious he was lying to the American people?

Muslims want Europeans to obey their laws, become slaves or *Dhimmis* and pay tribute or *Jizya* to them by supporting them; while they do not bother to work and produce unlimited numbers of children by up to four wives! They have almost succeeded over there. If we don't pay attention, what has happened in Europe is what is in store for us in America.

When the JournoList and the Islamists start up with their usual criticisms; remember that when the National Park Service tells you to watch out for Grizzly Bears; it doesn't "hate" the bears. It is simply warning you. So it is with this book. There is no "hate" for Obama or for Militant Muslims. This book is just warning you.

There is a conflagration that is burning up our Constitution, our Freedom and our way of life. It is coming closer and closer to you and someone is shouting, *"Fire!"* But the JournoList, the Islamists and Obama will use their usual technique of finding some little thing wrong and inflating it to cast doubt on everything that has been said: *"It's all a bunch of lies and exaggerations!"* And they will castigate and threaten the messenger: *"This book is full of Hate."* *"She's just a liar! A bigot! And a racist!!"* *"The writer hates Obama because he is black!"* *"The writer hates Muslims!"* *"She is an Islamaphobe!" "She has insulted Islam!!"* And then they will soothe you with: *"You are too sophisticated to believe that quack."* And contradict themselves with: *"Besides, the fire is just burning your neighbors. It is nowhere near you!"*

The burning question is:

Will you believe Obama, the Islamists and the JournoList and wait in a trance until you and your country are burned to a crisp?
Or
Will you wake up and shout "Good God!!
There really is a fire!" . . . ?

Part III of IV

Militant Islamists are exerting tremendous power in America

Table of Contents

Introduction

Militant Islamists are exerting tremendous power in America

Introduction

Listen to Obama explain his Muslim Faith and read the details:
http://www.youtube.com/watch?v=Dc3PzHKCVGM&feature=player_embedded#!
http://conservapedia.com/Barack_Obama%27s_Muslim_Heritage
http://conservapedia.com/Muslim_agenda_of_the_Obama_administration

Admit it. You already had great doubts about Obama. But the two most powerful groups in America—the Media and the Islamists—tricked you into voting for him. In Part I, you understood how the Media tricked you and helped hide Obama's secrets. In Part II, you understood Islam and how Islamists tricked the Europeans and pursued a Stealth Jihad to convert Europe into Eurabia. In this Part III, you will understand how Islamists are tricking you by pursuing a Stealth Jihad in America. In Part IV, I will tie these threads together and show you what Obama is doing to our country. And I trust you will have the courage to face what your instincts tell you is true.

This is serious stuff; so don't waste my time and yours screaming about "racism." Obama is not an American Black. His American half, through his mother, is White and the other half, through his father, is African and Muslim. And don't talk to me about "Hate" and call me an "Islamaphobe" either. First, make up your mind: either it is OK to be a Muslim or it is not. If a Muslim is the same as a Hindu, a Buddhist, a Jew or a Christian; then it is not "hate" to say Obama is a Muslim. If, on the other hand, (a) Islam is not a religion but rather a very dangerous religious/political/military ideology, and its Qur'an commands all true Muslims to do Jihad against us and destroy us; and (b) in Muslim countries, non-Muslims are persecuted for practicing their religion and forced to live like Dhimmis, aka slaves or serfs; then it means extreme danger to you and our country. But it is still not "hate." Just as the Park Service doesn't "hate" grizzlies but simply warns you about the dangers; so it is with me. I don't "hate" Obama or Muslims. But I am warning you, because it is imperative that you figure out for yourself whether or not Obama is a Muslim, as I say he is; so you will watch what he is doing, and realize he is destroying America.

Also, don't tell me that 1.2 Billion Muslims are going to rise up to attack me. Of those 1.2 Billion, half are women. They couldn't possibly want to remain as they do now, being totally subservient to men, and being subject to genital mutilation, rape and "honor" killings. Then, there are the vast numbers of decent and moderate Muslims who have escaped from the strictures of Orthodox Islam and are living in non-Muslim controlled countries. They want to get along with everyone; have no desire to "kill the infidel," like orthodox Muslims do; or be subjugated by Orthodox Muslims. Then, there are those Muslims who are neither radical Orthodox nor even more radical Salafist, living in Muslim countries, who have participated in the Arab Spring, and who are crying out, and even dying, to get our American freedoms for themselves. None of the above groups, which constitute the vast majority of those 1.2 Billion, would want to silence people like this writer. In fact, it is in their interest that the extremists be exposed. It is only the extremist and radical Orthodox Muslims that seek to destroy those with an opposing point of view. Today, these extremists profess to speak for the moderates; but they will destroy the moderates as soon as they get the opportunity; just as the rulers in Syria and Iran are killing the moderates within their borders.

Chapter 1

Let's face it. On 9/11,
the Islamic Terrorists won and Americans lost!

We have to acknowledge that we suffered a devastating defeat on 9/11. Islamic Terrorists won and America lost. And our current political leadership has ensured that we continue to lose. Islamic terrorists have been at war with America since 1993[1] when they first attacked the World Trade Center with a truck bomb. The mastermind of that attack was Khalid Sheik Mohamed, who also masterminded the 9/11/2001 attacks. Between 1993 and 2001, Islamic terrorists had attacked American interests four other times; bombing the Khobar Towers in 1996; bombing two of our embassies in Nairobi, Kenya and Dar-es-Salaam, Tanzania in 1998; and bombing the U.S. Navy Destroyer, the Cole, in 1997. But America did not take these attacks seriously.

In fact, President Clinton's administration did the opposite. In 1995, President Clinton's Deputy Attorney General, Jamie Gorelick,[2] taking into account the 4th Amendment rights of the suspects, issued instructions that created a "wall of separation" between the FBI and the CIA, and prevented them from exchanging information on counter-terrorism investigations. These instructions prevented FBI agents in Minneapolis from informing the CIA about suspected terrorists learning to fly planes but not wanting to learn how to land them. And Gorelick's instructions also prevented us from discovering the 9/11 plot in time to stop it. The 20th hijacker, Zacarias Moussavi had been detained on an immigration violation, and his computer contained details of the 9/11 plot. But the FBI was not allowed to search this computer. As with all liberals, Gorelick's focus was on protecting the rights of the criminal suspect; and not so much on protecting the rights of the American public. And this mistake cost us dearly.

The Jihad against us began anew on 9/11. The World Trade Center towers, each 110 stories high, were symbols of the might, power and success of America. It is no co-incidence that they were targeted for destruction. Nor is it a co-incidence that the date used was 9/11. As you will see later on, Muslims use symbols to communicate. Destroying the World Trade Center on 9/11 was clearly a statement that they will destroy the symbol of our pride in our country and make us beg for mercy and call 911 for help.

© Sean Adair/Reuters/CORBIS
3000 of our people were murdered on 9/11

Osama bin Laden sent 20 Islamic Al Qaeda terrorists, 15 of them from Saudi Arabia, to hijack four planes. One terrorist was arrested, but the rest of them continued the attack. Two of the planes were flown into the World Trade Center Towers. One was flown into the Pentagon. The other was on its way to Washington, D.C. but was forced down in Pennsylvania when the passengers attacked the hijackers. Over 3000 of our people were killed.

Tony Gutierrez/epa/Corbis
The World Trade Center Towers were reduced to rubble

Do you remember what it was like? Those in their early twenties and under may have been too young to comprehend what happened. But for the rest of us, the events of that day are seared in our memory. Hundreds died on impact as the planes, fully loaded with gasoline for the cross-country trip, crashed into the two buildings at 525 mph, essentially acting like missiles. The buildings were set on fire. Smoke and flames poured out of the tops of the towers. Some people rushed up to the roof believing helicopters would rescue them. But helicopters could not withstand the fires or the winds. At first, people in the South Towers were told not to worry, that there was only a stray plane that had struck the North Tower. But half an hour later, the South Tower was also attacked. Firefighters went up the stairs carrying their heavy hoses and equipment to try to bring the fires under control. But chaos reigned as paper and pieces of the buildings streamed out all over the area. There was thick smoke and fires all around; it was totally dark; debris was falling all around them; and there was no possible way the firefighters could have put out those raging fires. They walked people down over 80 flights of stairs to the ground and then went back up to get more victims. Think about it, the buildings were on fire and in danger of collapse. Yet, risking almost certain death, those firefighters climbed back up to try to save more people! Do you have that kind of courage? I don't. We owe them an enormous debt of gratitude for what they did that day.

The first groups that came out were relatively unscathed. Later groups were severely injured and burned. Some groups stayed in the plaza, only to be killed as the buildings collapsed. The South Tower collapsed first, less than an hour after the impact. The North Tower fell an hour and a half after it was attacked. Over a billion tons of steel collapsed in a dust cloud that could be seen for miles. The Twin Towers dragged down one other building and damaged many more. More than a million people had to be evacuated from lower Manhattan.[6] FDNY had deployed 200 units, over half of its units. More than 400 firefighters were deployed when the buildings collapsed. Of those, 343 firefighters were killed, together with 60 police officers.

But easily the worst possible thing happened above the points of attack, on the upper floors. 1355 innocent people were trapped in the North tower, which took an hour and a half to collapse. Do you remember those harrowing moments? Black smoke billowed out of the upper windows. Desperate people stood by the windows waving their shirts trying to get our attention, trying to tell us that they were trapped inside, praying that someone would come and get them. Some had crawled out and were holding onto the mullions, trying to escape the heat inside. Fires were burning just below them. Elevators did not work. Staircases could not be used. Helicopters would not come.

As the fires kept rising, the heat was becoming intolerable. The smoke was so thick they could not breathe. Ceilings were falling, floors were collapsing and the buildings were beginning to shake. Many made their last cell calls to their loved ones. Some tied tablecloths, drapes and even shirts onto their wrists is a desperate hope that those would act as some sort of parachute. And then, over 200 people did the only thing they could do; they jumped out of the buildings. They were conscious as they fell at nearly 150 miles per hour. And one after another, they crashed onto the concrete below, and their bodies smashed into bits.[3]

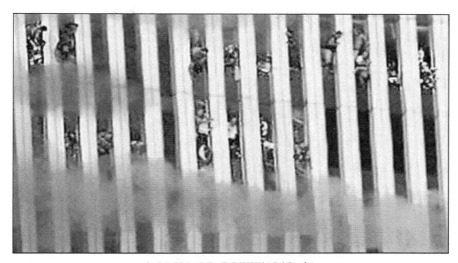

© RICHARD DREW/AP/Corbis
**Over 1300 people were trapped in the North Tower and
Many were forced to Jump to their Death.**

Osama bin Laden and his supporters were jubilant. And Palestinians danced in the streets celebrating our loss.[4] At first, our own people mourned deeply. But as the years went by, politics took over. As the overwhelming majority of Americans supported the war on Terror, it became clear that allowing Americans to be overtly patriotic redounded to the benefit of Republicans.

And Democrats commenced denigrating the attempt by George Bush to fight Al Qaeda. Criticisms and outright mockery of George Bush went on non-stop for years in all the major media. In fact, there had never been such blatant attempts to undermine us during a time of war. They mocked the war in Iraq saying it was "blood for oil" and even as our troops fought, Harry Reid claimed, "This war is lost". Hillary Clinton[5] said that she had to "suspend disbelief" as General Petraeus informed Congress of the success in Iraq. The left-wing New York Times gave a big discount for a full-page ad by the anti-war group Move On calling General Petraeus "General Betray Us."[6]

And Obama and his other leftists insisted that Iraq was the wrong war; that the "good war" was in Afghanistan. But this lasted only until he actually had to fight in Afghanistan. Now that he is in the "good war," he has decided not to fight, but rather to withdraw our troops; return the captured terrorists to Afghanistan; and send a radical cleric to try to "make peace", aka negotiate surrender, with the Taliban![7]

© CHIP EAST/Reuters/Corbis
The 9/11 Cross was found in the rubble

As rescue workers combed through the wreckage desperately looking for anyone who might still be alive; Frank Sillecia discovered, still standing amidst the total destruction, a 20 foot steel beam in the shape of a cross.[8] For the thousands who had prayed and paid homage to our dead there; the Cross became a powerful symbol of hope. People scratched their names on the Cross. They knelt in the rubble and prayed there. Pastors and Priests said mass there.

Our public officials consider themselves "tolerant." As you will see later on, they permit Muslim prayers that block the public streets. They permit gay sex during gay pride parades on public streets. But our oh-so-tolerant public officials believe that all Crosses must be removed from all public spaces because the Cross is "offensive" to atheists, Muslims and leftists; and it supposedly "violates the separation of church and state!" They insisted that this Cross be removed. It is truly a national disgrace that, in a country where the vast majority of the people are Christian, any Cross is deemed so "offensive" that it must be removed. It actually took 10 years of litigation before we were allowed to install the 9/11 Cross[9] in the 9/11-memorial museum!

Related to that has been the attempt to prevent us from remembering and honoring our dead on 9/11. TV stations have stopped showing photographs of the Trade Centers burning or collapsing. Sophists have said that any attempt to remember 9/11; or the agony of those who had to choose between being incinerated or jumping out of the burning buildings; amounts to *"exploitation." "It is too distressing,"* they say. Of course, these same sophists have no problem with us seeing extremely violent movies that depict made-up horrors. It appears that what really bothers these people is that 9/11 actually happened. It is not make believe. **Islamic Terrorists, obeying Allah, did murder 3000 innocent civilians on 9/11.** And one has to wonder if, by preventing us from remembering who did this to us and why; this is another attempt at *Stealth Jihad*. But we must always remember, lest it happen to us again.

On the 9th anniversary, Obama himself tried to change the nature of the 9/11 remembrance by announcing a "Day of Service and Remembrance,"[10] as though 9/11 was just another bake sale day or Girl Scout cookie sale day. Contrast this to Franklin Delano Roosevelt's speech about Pearl Harbor "December 7th 1941—a day which will live in infamy."[11] On the 10th year commemoration, Obama politicized the event by including only left-leaning pastors. Obama wanted to be the one who said the prayers for us Christians. As so, Obama and Mayor Bloomberg excluded conservative Christian Clergymen and Christian prayers.[12]

Obama imagines that every law-abiding group is comprised of terrorists.[13] He thinks that Christians; gun rights advocates; opponents of abortion, illegal immigration and big government; Tea Party supporters; and even returning Veterans who have just fought for our country; are all terrorists. His DHS issued a "threat assessment" report on April 7, 2009, just before a countrywide series of Tea Party rallies, warning of "Right

Wing Extremism" and stating it would be working with State and local partners to protect America from the dangers of "rightwing extremist radicalization." Obama's Muslim Advisor on his Advisory Council on Faith-Based and Neighborhood Partnerships, Eboo Patel, seeking to minimize what Islamic Terrorists did, likened Al-Qaeda to Christian "totalitarians" in the US. and Jewish "totalitarians" in Israel.[14] On July 4, 2012, the Department of Homeland Security published another report on Terrorism. Americans "suspicious of centralized federal authority and reverent of individual liberty" are "right-wing extremists." Also included are "religious" groups. In short, all religious Christian conservatives and those who believe in limited government are terrorists.[15]

But Obama has never referred to the actual terrorists as Islamic Terrorists. In fact, he has ordered the FBI to purge all references to Islamic Terrorists in counterterrorism training manuals because the material was in *"poor taste"*, employed *"stereotypes"* or presented information that *"lacked precision."*[16] After meeting with Islamic operators, the FBI was pressured to purge all references to *"Radical Islam"* from all of its documents because this was *"offensive"* and *"racist."*[17] This kind of political correctness makes it impossible for our counterterrorism officials to operate successfully. The main purpose of Obama's review was to purge material that linked terrorism with mainstream Islam. But, as you yourself have seen in Part II of this book; it is mainstream Islam itself that demands that its adherents wage *Jihad*, or terrorism, against us! In a foreword to a book titled *Muslim Mafia: Inside the Secret Underworld That's Conspiring to Islamize America*, Rep. Sue Myrick (R-N.C.) warns us, *"Since the 1960s there has been a concerted effort on the part of radical Islamists to infiltrate our major institutions. Front groups of terror now operate openly in our country, comprising a network of support for jihadists."* Last year, Myrick alleged that Hezbollah was planting operatives among illegal immigrants entering the U.S. through Mexico.

In fact, Obama has been full of praise for Muslims: *"In the past 10 years, Muslim-Americans have helped protect our communities as police and firefighters... Across our federal government, they keep our homeland secure, they guide our intelligence and counter terrorism efforts... Muslim-Americans help to keep us safe."*[18] Obama, who was once a Muslim, certainly knows of the threat of Islamic terrorists. One has to question how Obama's actions in labeling Christians and other law abiding groups as terrorists;

and refusing to recognize actual Islamic Terrorists as terrorists; serve the better interests of Americans.

With the constant propaganda of the Main Stream Media Mafia and Obama's pressure on various government departments to downplay the threat of Islamic Terrorism; our people have begun to lose sight of the dangers we face. And so, our anguish has been forgotten and the determination to rebuild has been dissipated.

At first, we were determined to rebuild the towers, taller than ever . . . to show the terrorists that they cannot defeat us. But all we have managed to accomplish in 10 years is two reflecting pools occupying the space where the two towers stood and a memorial museum. As far as I can determine, there is no statement in this complex, *"This atrocity was committed by 19 Islamic Militants obeying Allah and waging Jihad against America."* There are video depictions of some of what happened. But there is no video in a continuous loop showing the airplanes striking the towers and what happened thereafter. I've gone through their web site and can't find mention of even the 9/11 Cross.

To me, the reflecting pools only depict fires burning, resignation, calm acceptance, deep sorrow and surrender to our fate. If an asteroid had hit and 3000 people had died, this same memorial would be quite appropriate. There is a lot missing. I don't see outrage at the intentional horror inflicted on us; the wanton destruction of our buildings; and the injustice of murdering 3000 innocent civilians. I don't see the determination to fight to defend our country. Why could we not have a picture of the firefighters as they worked? Why can we not have holographic images over the pools depicting the Trade Centers being hit and collapsing?

And 10 years later, while we don't seem to have either the money or the will to rebuild those Towers or ones like it. However, Saudi Prince bin-Talal, working with Bin Laden Construction (Osama's father's company), plans to take just 36 months to build the world's tallest building in Jeddah![19]

As you can see, by ignoring the actual terrorist attacks on us before 9/11 and by setting up roadblocks to successful FBI and CIA interaction; we allowed the terrorists to succeed on 9/11. But now, once again, we are sugarcoating the threat and setting up roadblocks to prevent our FBI and CIA from discovering terror threats against us. By not even allowing us to see images of the Trade Centers collapsing and the people jumping out of the towers; and by calling it a "Day of Service," Obama is trying to make us forget it ever happened. By chattering on and on about supposed "Christian Terrorists" and refusing to call the actual terrorists "Islamic Terrorists," Obama is trying to obscure who the actual terrorists are. If we don't know who our enemy is, how are we going to fight them? If Obama really means to protect Americans, why is he doing this?

Americans have spent Billions on Security at home: After 9/11, we have spent countless billions for security for our public facilities, our ports, airports, courthouses, State and Federal Buildings. The U.S. Government and State Governments have been forced to hire untold government workers, with attendant costly union protections, pensions plans and other benefits, for the ATF, the FBI, the TSA and other security agencies and parallel state agencies. Keep in mind that the TSA is an entirely new agency, formed after 9/11, because private sector airlines and local government authorities were no longer willing to shoulder the responsibility and the potential liability associated with running airport security. Even our private office buildings now have to spend billions for both electronic pass card systems and security personnel. The new Freedom Tower is costing more than $3.8 billion to build, double the cost of Dubai's Burgh Khalifa, the world's tallest tower, which cost only $1.5 Billion. The extra costs are mainly for security features such as a heavily reinforced, windowless podium and a thick core of concrete and steel around its elevator shafts. All these costs to the Port Authority of NY & NJ have translated into higher bridge and tunnel tolls and reduced spending on transportation infrastructure.[21] Because of the 9/11 terrorist attacks, our whole economy was, and is, under severe stress, possibly leading to our current economic crisis.

The average Iraqi 40-year-old looks 10 years older than his American counterpart due to the enormous stress they regularly undergo.[20] But now, we too are constantly on edge, waiting for the next terrorist attack. And this stress is extremely damaging to all of us.

We have spent billions and lost countless precious lives fighting wars in Iraq and Afghanistan. And Obama is ensuring we lose these wars. He cares more about "innocent" or not-so innocent Muslim civilians than he does about our own soldiers. He has imposed politically correct rules of engagement on our troops that virtually ensure that more of them will get maimed or actually die. We lost 66 of our service members in June 2011 alone.[21] Our President has precipitously withdrawn forces from Iraq to placate his liberal political cronies and is converting a victory, which brought Democracy for the Iraqis, into a defeat. The excuse offered is that the Iraqis refused to agree to continuing the arrangement where U.S. troops would not be subject to Iraqi jurisdiction, but the Iraqi position was the result of Obama's decision to offer a fig leaf continuing presence of 10,000 forces that was of no interest to the Iraqis and did not justify conceding the jurisdictional point to the U.S. As usual with the Obama Administration, the negotiating position is established to guaranty failure. Obama is also unable (or unwilling) to obtain a victory in Afghanistan. In fact, he has just appointed the radical Sheikh Yusuf al-Qaradawi to negotiate with the Taliban to ensure a humiliating withdrawal and defeat for Americans![22] And, in any event the Taliban, knowing that American forces will be neutered in 2013 and gone by 2014, is not negotiating seriously with us. First they refused to allow the Karzai government a seat at the negotiating table, and then they broke off negotiations. . . . **Can anyone argue with a straight face that we won the war on terror?**

Chapter 2

Obama is continuing *Stealth Jihad* by using the TSA itself to defeat us. The TSA is primarily focused on humiliating and controlling Americans

All terrorist attacks in the past 15 years have been committed by Muslim Men:[1] For a Muslim, killing infidels like us is part of their religion, as has been documented in Part II by numerous direct quotes from the *Qur'an. (Christianity does not call on us to kill people. So please spare me the garbage about Timothy McVeigh's 1995 bombing. He is as much a Christian as Hitler, Lenin, Stalin or Pol Pot was. And wasn't Janet Reno, who sent in tanks against American citizens in Waco, Texas and killed 80 Branch Davidians, including 27 little children, a Secularist like you?)* **There have been no terror attacks by non-Muslims against Muslims, though Obama constantly refers to Tea Party members as "terrorists."**

Muslim men have committed all the terror acts in the U.S. in the past 15 years. Of these, there have been 32 attacks during which they have killed 54 people. A radical jihadist group responsible for nearly 50 terror attacks is operating 35 terrorist training camps in the U.S.[2] The terrorists include Naser Abdo, the would-be second Fort Hood jihad mass murderer; Khalid Aldawsari, the would-be jihad mass murderer in Lubbock, Texas; Muhammad Hussain, the would-be jihad bomber in Baltimore; Mohamed Mohamud, the would-be jihad bomber in Portland; Faisal Shahzad, the would-be Times Square jihad mass-murderer; Abdulhakim Mujahid Muhammad, the Arkansas military recruiting station jihad murderer; Naveed Haq, the jihad mass murderer at the Jewish Community Center in Seattle; Mohammed Reza Taheri-Azar, the would-be jihad mass murderer in Chapel Hill, North Carolina; Ahmed Ferhani and Mohamed Mamdouh, who hatched a jihad plot to blow up a Manhattan synagogue; Umar Farouk Abdulmutallab, the would-be Christmas airplane jihad bomber; Abdel Hameed Shehadeh, the would-be terrorist from Staten Island, and, of course, Nidal Malik Hassan, who stood on a table shouting *"Alahu Akbar"* while he assassinated 13 unarmed soldiers at Fort Hood. Many others like them have plotted and/or committed mass murder in the name of Islam and motivated by its texts and teachings—all in the U.S. in the last couple of years and all of them Muslim men.[3]

Why is Obama searching all Americans and not focusing on searching Muslim men? Despite the fact that Muslims are responsible for 100% of the terrorist attacks against Americans; Obama and his TSA insist on searching everyone. Obama's theory on TSA searches is beyond absurd. For instance, if you want to find some spinach, would you commence your search in the meat section of the grocery store, then scrutinize the cereals and then examine the liquor section? Won't you go straight to the vegetable aisle? Why? Because you don't have the time to waste. If there is a credible bomb threat in Wall Street; do you expect the FDNY to go to Harlem, and then check out the East Side and West Side, so that people living in lower Manhattan won't feel discriminated against? Once there, should they search a black, a yellow, a white, a brown, etc. to make sure no one is "profiled"? Why not? Because, obviously, they won't have time and resources to waste! But Obama refuses to give greater scrutiny to Muslim men because, as he indignantly reminds us, he doesn't want to "profile Muslims and violate their civil rights" by inflicting special searches on Muslim men. Of course, Obama does not display the same love and attention to our civil rights; because he insists on inflicting those same intrusive searches on all of us!

If the main point is to find the terrorists; then Obama should look where they are most likely to be—among Muslim men. If, on the other hand, the purpose of the TSA is to exert power over all Americans; why then, Obama will search and humiliate everyone!! As I said in Part II, this humiliation of the people they oppress and subjugate is, of course, totally in keeping with the cultural practices of Orthodox Muslims.

Through the TSA, Obama has asserted enormous power over all of us. And, as Obama trains them to be more and more aggressive towards Americans and violate our rights with impunity; Obama is creating the "civilian army" which he promised to create when he ran for office. If you recall, he said he would double the size of the Peace Corps and quadruple the size of AmeriCorps and the size of the nation's military services. Do you recall his chilling pledge? "*We cannot continue to rely on our military in order to achieve the national security objectives we've set. We've got to have a civilian national security force that's just as powerful, just as strong, just as well-funded."* [4] And Americans lose once again.

As the TSA becomes more unionized, the TSA will focus less on finding terrorists; and more on protecting their own jobs, benefits and pensions. But Obama wins big. He creates his civilian army with a bunch of poorly educated people who could not otherwise obtain jobs with the same pay and benefits. So they will always remain loyal to him and vote for him. Another benefit to Obama is that those 85,000 TSA members are unionized and pay dues to the Unions, which rebate money to Obama and his various campaign committees. If each union worker pays just $25.00 a month, then the union gets $25 million a year of tax-free money for Obama to play with.

These TSA agents now wear blue uniforms with gold badges, exactly like the police. They call themselves "officers" though they do not have the training of even a security guard. In March 2012, Obama's DHS purchased 450 million new bullets,[5] which offer "optimum penetration for terminal performance." For simpletons like you and me, this means that the snub nosed bullets can pass through barriers and will expand upon impact to inflict maximum damage inside our bodies. DHS is also calling for bids on 175 million rounds of rifle ammo and in March 2012, this was increased to 450 million rounds.[6] In March 2012, Obama issued an Executive Order that authorizes him, through the DHS to take control of private property without due process in the case of an emergency.[7] The National Defense Authorization Act gives Obama the right to detain any American without a warrant, formal charges or any reason other than declaring the person a threat to the nation. On July 6, 2012, Obama issued an Executive Order on National Security Communications, which gives him the right to take over all forms of communications facilities, including private facilities, that he deems necessary.[46] In April 2012, it was disclosed that the DHS had ordered 2,717 Mine Resistant Ambush Protected vehicles (MRAP), which would be distributed to "hot" areas of the country.[8] In June 2012, it was disclosed that the FAA is clearing the use of drones, armed and unarmed, over American airspace by law enforcement officials.[9] In March 2012, President Obama authorized himself to declare Martial law in a national emergency. After this, the federal government has the authority to take over every aspect of American society: food, livestock, manufacturing, industry, energy, transportation, hospitals, health care facilities, water resources, defense and construction.[10] Taken individually, the above items seem relatively benign. But taken together, they seem pretty sinister.

Last I checked, we were not in the middle of a civil war, so I am not clear why the Homeland Security needs all this power and ammunition; unless, perchance, Obama plans to go to war with us?[11] The TSA has also added more drones to patrol the border.[12] A Texas county police department has purchased drones that can carry and fire weapons, which can be controlled by a remote operator using a game console.[13] Obama did order the execution in Yemen, of an American citizen, Anwar al-Awlaki,[14] using drones without obtaining any warrant or having any judicial hearing. He has also refused to disclose the memo discussing what legal authority, if any, he had for this act. We have Obama's assurances that the ammunition and weapons will only be used by the TSA in a manner that will not violate our constitutional rights. Do Obama's promises reassure you?

We do not have unlimited resources to search each and every person. Yet, the TSA insists on treating innocent Americans the same as Muslim men. Take a look at those that Obama's TSA searches—Senators, toddlers in wheelchairs, dying women, nuns. We have a TSA that feels up men's testicles and penises; fondles women's breasts and vaginas; demands that breast prosthesis be removed; molests little children and asks handicapped children who are unable to walk to remove their braces and walk!! It strip searches 85-year-old women; and demands that 97-year-old women remove their adult diapers so they can be "properly" searched. What is the TSA's plan when a girl is wearing a sanitary napkin? And what if the girl is wearing a tampon? And if they send the girl to the toilet to remove these items, won't she be disposing of the so-called "bomb" too? The TSA fines anyone who refuses to allow his genitals to be examined and touched. But, while checking grandma and a child, it exempted a Muslim man.[15] It scrupulously examines Catholic Nuns.[16] Though, of course, Muslim women are always exempt and permitted to inspect themselves![17] **And, after all these intrusive searches, the TSA has never found a single terrorist! And Muslims the world over are laughing at us!**

How the TSA's "pat down" search works: Nothing is more humiliating and degrading for a man than to have to present his genitals for examination by a total stranger. Once the government has every American lining up and humbly presenting the most private and sacred parts of their bodies for uneducated strangers to examine, it has thoroughly defeated the nation. For those who have never had the "privilege" of having an euphemistically named "pat down" search; it should be noted that this does not stop at the top of the thigh, but rather, extends into a woman's or young girl's vagina! And extends into checking the testicles and penis of a man. And, in keeping with its policy of non-discrimination, the TSA does hire lesbians and gays who could be doing these "pat downs." A man has to be searched by someone of the same sex. I wonder, what about sexual orientation? Can a man refuse to be searched by a gay guy? If so, then who should search him?

The TSA uses its Arrest Power to force us to submit to searches that violate our 4th Amendment Rights: When they are humiliating a passenger and someone else films the abuse, the person filming is ordered to stop, or else be subject to arrest. One kid was actually arrested for writing the appropriate section of the Fourth Amendment on his torso. The part that says: ***"The right of the people to be secure against unreasonable searches shall not be violated!!"***[18]

© Jack Kurtz/ZUMA Press/Corbis
**Travellers remind the TSA that it is violating
the Fourth Amendment!**

The TSA uses its "pat down" power to humiliate Obama's political opponents: Don Rumsfeld has two titanium hips, so the TSA decided he had to be given a total "pat down"; even though it knew full well that Don Rumsfeld couldn't possibly be a terrorist.[19]

Senator Rand Paul,[20] a prominent Tea Party supporter and vocal opponent of TSA searches and therefore, an "enemy" of the administration and its TSA; was flying to DC to speak at the March for Life rally, another "enemy" of Obama, the staunch abortion supporter. Apparently, the TSA officials can cause the alarm to go off even without an actual security event. The TSA obviously knew Rand Paul was a Senator and not a terrorist. But, out of sheer spite, they set the scanner to indicate there was something on the Senator's leg. The Senator showed his leg had nothing in it and offered to go through the scanner again. But the TSA refused and insisted the Senator have a full body "pat down." When the Senator refused the "pat down," the TSA detained him and prevented him from making any phone calls. When the Senator came out of detention room to call and let his people know he was going to miss the fight and was unable to speak at the rally, the TSA threatened to arrest him! Finally, he rebooked on another flight and went through the same machine again. And this time, this same machine showed nothing!![37] After the fact, the TSA claimed that the Senator was combative. When security tapes proved this was untrue; they claimed there was a "glitch" in the scanner. **This clearly demonstrates that the TSA has the ability to trigger alarms and create the need to search people, even Senators. And furthermore, that the TSA is totally unprofessional, and uses its searches as a political tool to humiliate Obama's political opponents.**

TSA screeners are corrupt. They let drug couriers through without screening: Using code words "white girl," "green bay packers" and "crystal" for cocaine, marijuana and methamphetamines, a former TSA employee in LAX organized TSA screeners to meet with drug couriers. In exchange for bribes, these TSA agents allowed the couriers to get through their machines and smuggle their drugs.[21] If this were a private corporation or the TSA under Bush, the head of the organization would be excoriated for allowing malfeasance. But now, because it is a government department headed by a Democrat, we are being informed, "*This is an isolated incident*" and the matter will be dropped. The question really is:

What precautions is the TSA taking to ensure their screeners don't take bribes to allow a terrorist to smuggle bombs on board?

Take a look at the "Terrorists" they terrorize: The TSA has been totally inhumane in whom they choose to search.

(a)   **Can a toddler in a wheelchair** with a cast on his leg possibly be a terrorist?[22] According to the TSA, he could be, so he must be forced to stand up so he can be searched, even though this causes tremendous pain and distress to him and his parents. And, the parents are forbidden to take any pictures!

(b)   **They demand handicapped kids remove their leg braces and walk:** No exceptions are made for even handicapped children. The TSA actually demanded that a developmentally disabled little 4-year-old boy who could not walk without leg braces, must remove his braces and walk through the scanner!![23]

(c)   **They search the elderly in wheel chairs:** Then there is the case of the 97-year-old frail, 105 lb. grandmother needing a defibrillator and in a wheelchair.[24] She was dying on leukemia and could barely walk. She was flying to see her family in her final days. The TSA checked the wheelchair and then decided to give her a full body "pat down" which took over 45 minutes. In sheer terror, she soiled her diaper. Then, they demanded her daughter take her to the rest room and remove the diaper because they couldn't do a "proper search" or else, she couldn't fly at all. Think about this. **If the TSA had the faintest notion that this dying woman was carrying a bomb, why did they send her off to the rest room, where she could have disposed of the "bomb"?** It is obvious that they sent her off because they knew there was no bomb. But they were determined to humiliate and terrorize this poor dying woman anyway. In true doublespeak, the TSA defended itself saying they couldn't exempt any group of people, and that they "resolve security alarms in a respectful and sensitive manner"!

In another similar case, a 107 lb. 85-year-old woman, Lenore Zimmerman,[25] using a walker, was concerned that the microwave radiation in the naked body scanner would interfere with her defibrillator. The metal bar of her walker caused a gash in her leg and caused blood to flow, soaking her sock. According to Mrs. Zimmerman, the TSA did not treat the bleeding, but instead took her to a private room and strip-searched her. And she missed her flight. As the TSA euphemistically referred to it, "TSA screening . . . is designed to treat all passengers with dignity, respect and courtesy . . ."[41]

Nadine Hays was arrested, charged with battery, handcuffed and strip searched over applesauce;[26] even though she explained that her 93 year-old mother required the applesauce to take her medications. The caretaker, who wanted to vouch for Nadine, was ordered to stand back while they searched and fondled Nadine's senile and confused mother off-camera.[27]

(d)   **They grope women and it is truly disgusting.**[28]

(e)   **They demand breast cancer survivors remove their prosthesis:**[29]
A breast cancer survivor was required to remove and show her prosthetic breasts and was not allowed to retrieve documentation showing the serial numbers of her prosthesis and the phone number of her doctor.

(f)   **They grope little children.**

(g)   **They even inspect Catholic Nuns.**[30]

(h)   **But they exempt Muslim women and men**:
Muslim women can inspect themselves.[31] According to CAIR's advisory, Muslim women wearing a hijab can only be examined at the head and neck areas. As for the rest of the body, the Muslim woman will be given gloves and allowed to pat herself down. Then, the gloves would be examined for chemical residue.[45]

And Muslim Men need not go through the body scan machines:[32] The Fiqh council of North America has issued a fatwa prohibiting observant Muslim men from going through the body scan machine because it is a violation of Islamic teachings for men or women to be seen naked by other men or women: *"Islam highly emphasizes modesty and considers it a part of the faith."* And of course, the Obama Administration will honor the sensitivities of Muslims. It is unclear whether they will require Muslim men to go through a "Pat Down." And you and I will never find out because they TSA does not have to show us its rules!!

But Orthodox Muslim women can inspect themselves!

(i)   **And you will be detained and accused of being a racist if you complain of the preferential treatment of Muslims**: On Feb 29, 2012 in England, David Jones, creator of the cartoon character Fireman Sam, remarked on the ease with which a Muslim woman completely covered by a hijab was able to pass through security without even showing her face. Apparently, a woman is taken into a private room if they want to inspect her, but this woman was not. He himself had been stopped and searched because he had an artificial hip. As he put his scarf and belongings in a tray, he joked "If I was wearing this scarf over my face, I wonder what would happen."[33] A Muslim security guard overheard this and claimed she was deeply distressed by this "insult." The security personnel demanded he apologize. But he insisted his remark was not racist. He simply wanted everyone to be treated equally. But he was told, "we live in a different time and some things are not to be said." He was detained for an hour until he finally conceded that someone "could" have been offended. As he said, "Something like George Orwell's 1984 now seems to have arrived in Gatwick airport. . . . What I underwent amounts to intimidation and detention." **As you can see, now we are not allowed to even remark on disparate treatment. We have to accept that we are second-class citizens, and submit, exactly as though we were already being ruled by Muslim Rulers!!**

Whole Body X-Ray Scanners are Dangerous:[34] Rapiscan's backscatter X-ray machines,[35] used to take pictures of a person's naked body, are "virtual strip searches" because they reveal the outlines of the person's whole body, including their private parts. Though the TSA says the operator can only see an outline, in fact, images of the naked body are available on TSA computers and there are numerous instances where TSA personnel have been caught watching them. There have been numerous complaints about passengers being ogled or subject to inappropriate remarks by TSA officials. Rapiscan lobbied the Obama administration very heavily and is now the only supplier to the government. In 2011, it received $300 million in stimulus funds to supply 250 x-ray machines and 264 millimeter-wave scanners. By 2012, the TSA intends to more than triple this amount to install 1,275 of these machines and make them their primary screening tool. If a passenger refuses to go through the scanner, he will be subject to a very intrusive and humiliating full body search. And so, passengers will comply with instructions to go through the X-ray scanner.

A far worse consequence of their use is that these machines violate a long-standing principle in radiation safety—that humans shouldn't be X-rayed unless there is a medical benefit. If these were medical devices, they would have been subject to extensive testing by the FDA. But only Rapiscan itself has tested the TSA's machines. In May, 2010, a team from UCSF consisting of a cancer specialist, a molecular biologist, biochemists and biophysicists wrote to John Holdren, Obama's Science and Technology Czar, stating that these machines, which concentrate the radiation on the skin, could lead to a whole host of cancer-related problems: mutations and melanomas or skin cancer; immune system problems, breast cancer, effects on a baby in utero and even in little children. Dr. David Banner of Columbia has stated that the radiation produced by these machines is 20 times higher than the official estimate. Physics Professor Peter Rex at Arizona State agreed and stated his concerns that one of these machines could malfunction causing unsafe amounts of radiation on one area of the body. In June 2012, the TSA attempted to rebut these studies by asserting that the findings of its latest "scientific study" showed there was little risk to people. However, the author of the study did not test the actual machines. She merely drew "scientific" conclusions from scanner radiation data released publicly by the TSA itself![36] Now, the TSA worker's union itself has complained about the safety of its workers. And the TSA has supplied dosimeters to measure the radiation levels of TSA workers at over 100 airports across the country.[37] Meantime, Rafi Sela, the leading Israeli Airport Security expert, remarked that these machines are relatively ineffective at disclosing material hidden in the groin area and in body cavities; and that Israel does not use these machines. **What is the point of all this, except to humiliate our people?**

Obama asserts he has the right to strip search everyone: Now, Obama's DOJ has gone a step further and told a Federal Appeals Court that the Department of Homeland Security has the authority to literally strip search Americans inside airports[38] if it views that "it is necessary in light of the ever-evolving threats." The DOJ attorney insisted that, despite the clear violation of the Fourth Amendment Rights of the American public, the judges shouldn't "hamstring the agency."

The VIPR program now extends searches to subways, trains, ports and highways: Obama's TSA has also commenced a security check program known, curiously, as the VIPR program (Visible Intermodal Prevention and Response program) at subways, train and cruise ship ports,[39] according to Nico Melendez of the TSA. And it has further extended this program by doing its VIPR program on Highways.[40] As the TSA said "Where is a terrorist more apt to be found? Not on an airplane—more likely on the interstate." *Note: The TSA does not use this theory to search Muslim men. If it followed its own logic, it should ask itself, "In which group is a terrorist more apt to be found?" and the answer, of course, would be "among Muslim men!!"* In Tennessee, the TSA conducted a test program stopping trucks on highways. During their random inspections, they used bomb and drug sniffing dogs. The TSA acknowledged it did not have any specific threat, meaning no "probable cause" for conducting these searches. And it did not obtain a warrant. If they can search airports, subways, trains and even highways, they can search any one at any time.

Essentially, the Obama administration has asserted the right to violate the Fourth Amendment of our Constitution at any time it wishes. So, the TSA can seize and fondle your daughter as she returns home alone at night, and neither she nor you would be able to complain! Officially, the TSA agents are "helping" the local police, but, in practice, it is the Federal Agents who are in the lead role, and the state police officers are merely in a helping role. And so, very quietly, the Obama Administration has also usurped the police powers of the State, thus violating the Tenth Amendment too.

Obama, like the Stasi, now wants us to inform on one another: Even as they commenced this program, they commenced another, the First Observer Highway Security Program, which called upon all drivers and passengers to inform the police if they see something suspicious—"Say something if you see something." In short, exactly like the East German Stasi program, people are being called upon to inform about each other. The only difference is that in East Germany, 1 in 7 people was an informer. In America, we haven't reached that stage yet.

Courts give State Workers, Welfare Recipients, Prisoners and even Gitmo terrorists more rights: In sharp contrast, State Workers and Welfare recipients have more rights than you and I. A Florida court just held that the Governor had no right to order state workers to submit to random drug searches because it constituted an unreasonable search and seizure in violation of the Fourth Amendment. There is a similar challenge to a requirement that people receiving welfare take random drug tests. And the ACLU is confident Florida courts will strike it down just as a court in Michigan has done on the grounds that such "searches" violate the Fourth Amendment.[41] American prisoners have more rights than airplane passengers. From 1984, all the way to 2010, the 9th Circuit had held that it was a violation of the Fourth Amendment to strip search incoming inmates without probable cause![42] And court cases about unconstitutional searches of inmates or their visitors are still pending in various courts. An army of civil liberties attorneys including the ACLU, took one such case all the way to the Supreme Court. Unfortunately for the ACLU, a recent Supreme Court decision has held that people subject to arrest, even for a minor offense, can be strip searched before being taken into jail[43] because people have tried to smuggle prohibited items into jail. Even Gitmo Terrorists' attorneys assert that strip searches are humiliating, am invasion of privacy and a violation of the Fourth Amendment.[44]

However, not a single one of the great and patriotic defense attorneys who defend the rights of criminal suspects and Gitmo terrorists has ever bothered to defend the innocent American public from unreasonable TSA searches. It appears that, for Obama and his supporters, the Fourth Amendment exists to protect Muslim women and men, terrorists, criminals, state workers and welfare recipients. *As for the ordinary people of America, you are not even at the bottom rung of the ladder. You don't exist at all! Remember that, the next time Obama assures you he loves you.*

SPOT does not spot anyone: The TSA's counterterrorism "specialists" have a special program called "Screening of Passengers by Observation Techniques," known as SPOT.[45] They are specially trained (and, no doubt, given extra pay,) to watch travelers who pose potential security risks and who indicate stress, fear or deception. But on at least 23 different occasions, they failed to detect 16 separate *jihadi* operatives who moved through target airports. One such terrorist pleaded guilty to providing support to Somali terrorists. Another pleaded guilty to providing al Qaeda support. Others have been tied to the 2008 Mumbai bombings, plots to attack the Quantico Marine base, the New York City infrastructure and an attack by a Pakistani trained American jihadi on an Afghani base.

But SPOT, in addition to not spotting a single terrorist, cost us $211 million in 2010. And Obama wants to spend another $232 million in 2011 to subsidize 3,350 SPOT personnel and provide another $30 million or so for the unions and Obama to spend.

To summarize, we have a TSA that is used by Obama as a political tool to embarrass and humiliate his Republican political opponents. Obama has instructed the TSA to humiliate, grope and fondle our people and exempt orthodox Muslim women and men from searches. Obama has asserted the right to strip search anyone at any time and extended this right to trains, ports, highways, and subways and, obviously, once he decides to extend this, to passenger cars. He makes us go through Rapiscan machines, which emit dangerous

x-rays and even the TSA's own workers are complaining about their negative effects. To add insult to injury, the TSA has never caught a single terrorist! It is obvious that the main purpose of this program is to give Obama power over his American subjects.

Chapter 3

The Flight 93 Memorial & The 9/11 Victory Mosque Were planned by Islamists to Celebrate their Victory and to Humiliate America

It is common practice for Muslims to celebrate victories of their Jihad by building mosques on top of Christian churches, Jewish synagogues or Hindu temples.[1] In 630 AD, Muslims captured Islam's holiest city, Mecca, and erected a mosque at the *Ka'aba*—the site of a building reputedly built by the Patriarch Abraham. The great mosque at Cordoba was built over the Christian Church of St. Vincent. The eighth century *Al-Aqsa* Mosque rests on the site of the destroyed Jewish Second Temple in Jerusalem. The Ayasofya Mosque was built over the Byzantine Christian Hagia Sophia Basilica in Istanbul. And the Umayyad Mosque in Damascus was constructed over the remains of what was once the Church of St. John the Baptist. Other well-known mosques include the Bari mosque in India, the Fethiye Camii in Turkey, the Qutub Minar in Afghanistan, the Asqa Mosque in the Hague (formerly a Synagogue), and of course all in Israel: The Al Asqa Mosque/al-Haram ash-Sharif, the Mosque in Tomb of the Patriarchs, the mosque attached to the Rambam shul (Hurva), to name just a few well known examples. And there are plenty more examples from all around the world.[2]

Muslims use symbols to represent their ideas: Why did they attack us on "9/11"? Obviously they wanted to symbolize that America is now in trouble and calling for help. Why did Abdulmutallab pick Christmas day to try to light his panty bomb? Why did Mohamed Osman Mohamud pick Christmas to try to kill people celebrating the lighting of the Christmas tree in Portland, Oregon? Obviously, they did this to inflict maximum harm on Christians and also to mock Christians. Why did someone throw a shoe at President Bush? A shoe would have trod on feces. It is symbolical of something extremely unclean. By throwing a shoe at our President, the man intended to show maximum contempt for the President <u>and</u> for all the people of America. Of course, the American liberals, those idiots who don't understand other cultures, cheered because they thought that the attack was directed solely at Bush!

Consider how Muslims have handled the Flight 93 "Memorial":[3,4]

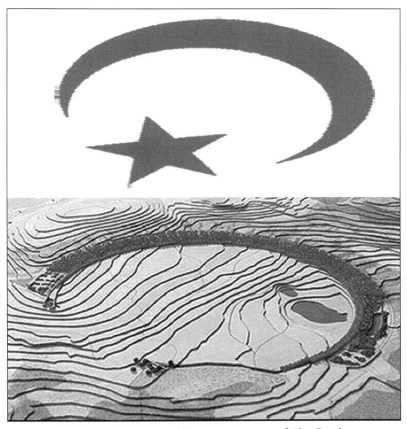

© Composite image and caption courtesy of Alec Rawls,
author of *Crescent of Betrayal: Dishonoring the Heroes of Flight 93*

**The Muslim flag is in the photo on top and
The Flight 93 Memorial is below.
The resemblance is obvious**

© Composite image and caption courtesy of Alec Rawls,
author of *Crescent of Betrayal: Dishonoring the Heroes of Flight 93*

**This "Tower of Voices" is actually a Minaret with a Crescent
on top, facing Mecca and symbolizing the Muslim "Heaven."
Steel cylinders are the 40 murdered Americans, hanging below
the Crescent, never reaching "Heaven," presumably in "Hell."**

The so-called Flight 93 Memorial is a complete sham.[5] It is full of
Muslim symbols and is designed to be the world's biggest open-air
Mosque, complete with crescent shaped perimeter and minaret. The
whole structure is designed to resemble a Muslim flag with a red crescent
made up of red maples and a 93-foot tall crescent topped tower set at the
exact spot where the Muslim star would appear.[6] There is a wall opposite

the Red Crescent with 44 memorial glass blocks. But there were only 40 murdered passengers and crew. The other 4 are inscribed "9/11." Thus, they are also symbolically memorializing the 4 terrorists!

Inside the tower are 40 steel cylinders representing the 40 murdered passengers and crew, symbolically hanging under the crescent. The crescent represents the Muslim Heaven. The 40 murdered Americans are hanging below the "heaven", presumably in "hell." (But note, there are no 4 extra steel cylinders representing the terrorists in "hell" here.) If you bisect either of the two crescents, you point to within 2 degrees of Mecca.

The main entrance is from the back. As you stand in the doorway provided; you are bound to weep and bow down in sorrow at what was done to your fellow Americans. And, guess what? You will be bowing down <u>and facing Mecca, exactly like a devout Muslims would.</u> Symbolically, you will be bowing to, and worshiping, Islam. **And Muslims the world over will be laughing at you!**

The architect Paul Murdoch actually calls the design the "Crescent of Embrace" and the 93-foot tall crescent-topped spire that stands where the Muslim star would stand, the "Tower of Voices." The Crescent and Star are the symbols of the Muslim World. In fact, the Muslim equivalent for the Red Cross is the Red Crescent. There is no possible way the architect was unaware of these facts. Yet he pretends there are no Muslim symbols at all. It is obvious that this quisling has either already received money from Muslim interests or hopes to get commissions in the future. He should be required to return all fees he received. For intentional infliction of emotional distress, he should be sued by all family members of those who died and by the public. And for collaborating with the enemy in a time of war and furthering *Jihad*, he should be charged with treason and given the electric chair!

Despite numerous complaints to the National Park Service, this project is going forward. The traitors who approved this waste of $60 million of taxpayer money should be identified and fired.

If it had included a single Christian Cross, people would be shrieking *"Separation of Church and State!" "It offends someone!"* and the Cross would have been removed. But despite the fact that the Crescent is also a religious symbol; it clearly offends a great many people; and it also denigrates our country; the two Crescents remain!

Given that Muslims use symbols to represent their victories over other peoples; it is obvious that **we Americans will be laughed at for being so ignorant and downright stupid that we allow our Flight 93 memorial to be used to commemorate the Muslim victory over us!!**

The 9/11 Victory Mosque: Imam Faisal Abdul Rauf plans to build a mosque in the shadow of the World Trade Center Towers.[7] He obtained permission in a few weeks.[8] Why was this permission ever given? Muslims pray 5 times a day. They use loudspeakers to broadcast their prayers. And this is what they say: *"Allah is great! I bear witness that there is no god except Allah! I bear witness that Mohamed is the messenger of Allah! . . ."* Did no one consider it would be an outrage to have this prayer broadcast over the spirits of 3000 innocent people who had been murdered in Allah's name?

You can see the powerful influence of Islamists in the speed with which the permission was granted. Christians have no such luck. In addition to making us litigate for 10 years to get permission to install the 9/11 Cross; 11 years later, the St. Nicholas Greek Orthodox Church that existed prior to 9/11 has still not received permission to rebuild!

In America, Rauf says he is a man of peace and wants inter-faith dialogue. He says (as does Obama) that the U.S. Constitution is *Shari'ah* compliant. (Note the phrasing—Both Obama and Rauf do not say that *Shari'ah* is compliant with our Constitution; they say the Constitution is *Shari'ah* compliant. They both clearly intend to tell us that *Shari'ah* is more important than the U.S. Constitution.) Our leaders reassure us that there is no real clash of civilizations; that Rauf is a true moderate who wants to get along. But Rauf is two-faced. In Egypt, he says he has no intention of having any dialogue with us.[9,10] Furthermore, Rauf says that *Shari'ah* can and will be established, even in Democratic countries. Even his books change titles: The American title: *"What's Right with Islam Is What's Right with America"* becomes, in Malaysia: *"A Call to Prayer from the World Trade Center Rubble: Islamic Dawa* (proselytizing) *in the Heart of America post-9/11.* [11] Once this mosque, or any other, is installed, no one on earth can ever take it down without a major battle with all 1.2 Billion Muslims.[12,13]

Rauf's associate Sharif El-Gamal, was a mere waiter in 2002. But by 2008, El-Gamal had approximately $5 million to purchase the mosque property. He also had an additional $45.8 million to purchase a property on 31 W 27th Street.[14] Our media has shown no interest whatsoever in finding out how El-Gamal got $50.8 million dollars.

Rauf is strongly supported by President Obama, our "Christian" president! Rauf is also strongly supported by Mayor Bloomberg. Follow the money. Bloomberg's businesses are heavily invested in mid-east oil producing countries and Bloomberg News is doing a joint venture with Prince Al-Waleed, to be called Al-Arabiya.[15] Rauf actually has the gall to ask for taxpayer subsidies for his Mosque cum Inter-Faith Conference Center. But, as you now are aware, uncovered women will never be allowed in there. And there will never be a Christian or Jewish Prayer offered inside that building.

The mosque was originally named the Cordoba Mosque. Once enough Americans figured out that the original Cordoba Mosque represented the Muslim conquest of Spain,[16] and therefore the new Cordoba Mosque obviously symbolized the Muslim conquest of America; the name was changed to Park 51 Mosque. Rauf's aim in building the 9/11 Mosque is to celebrate a Muslim Victory over America. He is using Taqiyya to deceive us. **Why are we co-operating in our own humiliation?**

Islamic influence is clearly behind the Flight 93 memorial and the attempt to build the 9/11 Victory Mosque: The traitor-architect Paul Murdock was clearly currying favor with Islamists when he designed his "Crescent of Embrace" as an open air Mosque, supposedly to "memorialize" Flight 93. And as for the 9/11 Victory Mosque, isn't it obvious that Muslims were funding the waiter Sharif El-Gamal with $50 odd million to buy properties in New York? Muslims celebrate their conquests by building mosques over the buildings of those they have conquered by *Jihad*. Isn't this an example of *Stealth Jihad?* Knowing this, why did so many of our leaders, including Obama, support Imam Rauf? Isn't it obvious Islamists exert a powerful influence on our leaders? What kind of Christian American President would agree to have Islamists celebrate the conquest of America this way?

Chapter 4

Destroying our Christian Heritage by Stealth Jihad Is another way of Destroying America itself

There is an all out assault of Christianity and Christians in America today. There are also two related arguments made to denigrate America. That the Christian founders of America "stole" the land from Native Americans and that America's Constitution was written by "dead white Christian males who were slave owners."

The whole purpose of this assault is to destroy our heritage and tear out the roots of Christianity from America. Once this is done, America is left defenseless. America and its traditions can then be redefined to include all forms of social deviancy. They can be redefined to include all forms of Communism, Marxism, Socialism and/or Fascism. American values can also be redefined to say that both Christianity and Militant Islam are consistent with our Constitution. And so, America can be easily destroyed. *Don't believe me? You should trust me by now to know that I don't say what I can't prove! Anyway, let's take a look.*

America and Christianity are inextricably intertwined. Our Constitution embodies Christian principles. It was Christians of various denominations fleeing religious persecution in Europe who founded all of the 13 original States that became America. All 13 supported and endorsed a denomination of the Christian religion for hundreds of years and this is enshrined in the constitutions of many State governments even today.[1] It was Christian pastors who led the fight against British imperialism and King George. Some of these Christian pastors gave up their lives to obtain Freedom and Independence for America. It was Christians who led the fight to end slavery, which had been brought to America by the British.[2] Among those who fought to end slavery were a great many leading white Christians and also many black Christians, among them a leading black Christian, a former slave, Richard Allen.[3] *Why haven't you been told about this? Glenn Beck told you. But liberals will never let you know that Blacks and Whites fought together to eliminate slavery. Once Blacks find out, Blacks can't be roused up by Liberals to hate*

Whites and always vote for Democrats; and Liberals cannot dismiss our Constitution by saying it was written by rich white slave owners!!!

There is actually no such phrase as "separation of church and state" in our Constitution. There are two phrases dealing with religion in the First Amendment of our Constitution: *"Congress shall make no law respecting an establishment of religion, or prohibiting the free exercise thereof."* Government shall not "establish a religion," meaning the government shall not establish one single Christian denomination, such as the Roman Catholics, and decree that every one of any other denomination will be persecuted like they were in Europe. And the government shall not prohibit the "Free Exercise of Religion," meaning the government shall not use its might and power to take away the people's right to practice their religion as they wish.[4] The 10th Amendment was added to the Bill of Rights in 1791 because many of the founders, Patrick Henry, Samuel Adams, Thomas Jefferson and others, feared that the Constitution would eventually lead to a strong, centralized, federal power which would destroy the individual liberty of the People. The 10th Amendment states: *The powers not delegated to the United States by the Constitution, nor prohibited by it to the States, are reserved to the States respectively, or to the people.* In fact, the entire US Constitution and the Bill of Rights were enacted to prevent the Federal Government from oppressing us and exercising its vast power over us.

Those who want to destroy America by destroying Christianity have played a very subtle game with us. First, they redefined the teachings of Jesus Christ to include Communist/Marxist/Socialist/Fascist principles under the guise of "Social Justice." Jesus asked us to give to the poor. "Giving" is a voluntary act. Christians and Conservatives give more to the poor than any other group in America even though, in general, Conservatives are considerably poorer than Liberals.[5] Obama asks us to "give" to him and his government. This is not a voluntary act. We don't "give." He "takes." Like the recently upheld ObamaCare, these penalties are taxes, which force us, under penalty of jail, to surrender our money to Obama. There is a massive difference between the two. And, as I showed you in Chapter 3 of Part I, Obama has taken from us and given to his "green energy" cronies. Not to the poor, who remain poor. In fact, blacks have become poorer than they were before Obama came into power.

Second, there is an attempt to dilute the concept of Christianity, tricking well meaning people who believe in "interfaith dialogue" and "tolerance" into replacing the moral standards of Christianity with a moral relativism that says "anything goes" and "why can't we all just get along." Under this theory, Christian beliefs are given equal weight with beliefs that are repugnant or unacceptable to Christians and which do violence to their faith. Remember when we discussed how the Media was forcing us to be "tolerant" of more and more sexual perversion? And how we, wanting to appear "cool" "sophisticated" and "tolerant," were accepting all forms of sexual perversion?

Refusing to be "tolerant" is hard, much harder than just sliding down an easy path to "acceptance" and "tolerance" of anything and everything. People will abuse you and mock you for being "intolerant." Good Christians are faced with a dilemma. They want to be "tolerant" and "inclusive" and find it hard to draw the line beyond which they will not "tolerate" any more.

Abortion For instance, where does your Christianity end and the mother's "right" to an abortion begin? When the baby being aborted is 3 months in the womb? 6 months? Or just before birth? For Obama, the baby is not a baby even if it is born alive after a botched abortion! He actually voted to allow the abortionist to throw the baby in the dumpster.[6] Yet he calls himself a Christian. *Would you? Or do you realize you have to draw a line somewhere?*

Gays: Christians tolerated gays. But now, extremist gays are asserting that speaking out against gays is a "hate crime" and this bill was signed into law by Obama in 2009.[7] According to Rev Donald Wildmon of the American Family Association, this law criminalizes the Bible and uses the threat of federal prosecutions and long jail sentences to silence Christians from expressing their Biblically-based religious belief that homosexual conduct is a sin.[8] *Did you intend that your tolerance of gays be extended to the point that you yourself are silenced? Now that it has, can you do anything about it? Or, perhaps, was your "tolerance" not the right thing to do?*

Militant Islam: Well, the same principle applies to Militant Islam too. At some point, we have to decide whether we are Christians or whether we are merely a nation of "The Tolerant." At some point, we have to stand up for our Christian beliefs!

Smart Islamists know it is hard for us to take a stand. So they use the argument "Not all Muslims are bad Muslims, so you can't say that there are any bad Muslims." This argument coaxes us into accepting all the evil that orthodox Muslims practice. *(If you have any doubts that their practices are evil, go back and read Part II again! Then tell me that it is acceptable to murder a woman because she wants a divorce, or murder a young girl because she wore make up, or hand over a 10 year old little girl for "marriage," or hang a gay because he is gay or kill a puppy because it is "unclean!")*

I know that many of you believe you should not tell other people how to live their lives. But then, what happens to our laws? What happens to our principle of equal treatment under the law? Is murder a crime? *What are you going to do if your Muslim neighbor is beating his wife black and blue and threatening to kill her? What are you going to do if his little daughter says he is going to kill her because she has a Black/Latino/Christian boyfriend? Are you going to let him kill his wife or daughter because you are "tolerant" and "don't want to tell him how to live his life?" Or are you going to call the cops and expect them to arrest and jail him? What if the "unsuitable" boy friend is your teen aged son? Are you going to be "tolerant" and wait until he is killed too?* We need to have one set of laws. And we need to be proud of the laws that we have. They have served the country well during the past 200 years, so much so that America, starting from nothing, has overtaken all the other civilizations of the world.

"Toleration" only works one way – we tolerate them, they stone us: Worst of all, just as they did in England, the minute Muslims get a majority in any one American city, like Dearborn, Michigan, they stone and attack Christians who venture into "their" territory.[9] All talk of "tolerance" and inclusiveness" goes out the window! Too late, we realize that their demand for "tolerance" was just a trick, *Taqiyya,* that they played on us in order to get control over us. And the Islamists' Stealth Jihad advances into yet another country. This time, into America!!

Christianity is diluted and extinguished: And very gradually, Christianity itself becomes indistinguishable from any other religion; or from Atheism; or from extremist environmentalism; or from the extreme

163

animal rights crowd who insist all animals are the same as humans; or from all forms of extreme homosexuality, including the notion that a child can have three lesbian mothers;[10] or from pedophilia, which is now being normalized and defined as "intergenerational sex;"[11] or even from Militant Islam, which authorizes female genital mutilation, killing of women, pedophilia euphemistically called "marriage", the killing of gays and the extermination of pets; and which considers people of other faith as *"infidels"* who should be annihilated.[12] All of these have to be encouraged in the name of "diversity;" all have to be "tolerated." All are deemed equally good. And we Christians have to "tolerate" all of it.

Because of "political correctness" no one can say anything is bad or evil. However, Obama considers Christianity itself to be a source great evil and of potential terrorists. As I have shown you before, on 7th April 2009, Obama's TSA had issued a "threat assessment" against Christians, Right Wing Radicals and Returning Veterans.[13] On July 4, 2012, it issued another "threat assessment" where "Conservatives" and "religious people" who are "suspicious of centralized federal authority and reverent of individual liberty," must be watched.[14]

Why are Christians and Christianity such a "threat" to Obama? Christians are a threat because they will prevent the takeover of America by Obama and his Islamic allies. Destruction of a people's religious identity and heritage is a common Islamic practice.

Islamists destroyed the Bamiyan Buddha Statues: The Taliban used explosives, tanks and anti aircraft weapons to blow up the 4th Century Bamiyan Buddha Statues, one 175 feet and the other 120 feet tall. The entire world reacted in shock and horror at this wanton destruction. Why was this done? The people in Bamiyan were not Buddhist any more. But these statues represented their identity. This is what they would rally around when attacked by their enemies. Bamiyan was the base of the Taliban opposition, the rebel Northern Alliance led by ousted President Rabbani. As Professor W.M. Rathje of Stanford said, how could the Taliban better destroy and humiliate their opponents than by destroying their heritage?[15]

Islamists destroy the heritage of every country they conquer: Today, Islamists are destroying the ancient heritage of the **City of Timbuktu in**

Mali. Timbuktu, with a majority of Sufi Muslims who believe in Saints, had one of the oldest libraries and was famous as the center of Islamic learning since the 15ᵗʰ century. At it zenith, Timbuktu had 100,00 residents, 25,000 of whom were students attending its university. The tombs of their saints were just adjacent to the 14th-Century Djingareyber mosque. This had been designated a World Heritage Site. An Al Qaeda connected Salafist group, Ansar Dine, seized control in April 2012. They intend to impose Shari'ah law, which deems these ancient artifacts idolatrous. Since then, they have destroyed many of the centuries-old shrines and tombs to Islamic saints, revered by the Sufis. They have destroyed the sacred door of the 15ᵗʰ Century Sidi Yahia mosque. And they are destroying the library.[16]

The Cordoba Cathedral/Mosque: When the Moors conquered Spain, they deliberately built a Mosque on the site of the Cordoba's Cathedral. When Amr Bin al-As, Prophet Mohamed's companion, conquered it in AD 641, he had the great library of **Alexandria, Egypt** destroyed. [17] Now that the Muslim Brotherhood controls Egypt, prominent Muslim clerics have begun the call for the demolition of **Egypt's Great Pyramids**, which Salafists deem a "symbol of paganism."[18]

Nobody has tried to remove Buddhist Statues from Sri Lanka's public square: Sri Lanka was originally populated by the Veddahs, an aboriginal people. Then, Buddhism was brought to Sri Lanka. One could say Buddhism conquered the Veddahs and "stole" their land, just as leftist critics of Americans allege Americans "stole" the land from Native Indians! Now, there are Buddha statues in public places all over the country. Some incredibly beautiful, some enormous, the largest being over 46 feet long and carved into a mountainside. There was a thirty-year civil war between the Sinhalese, mainly Buddhists, and the Tamils, mainly Hindus. Despite all the atrocities that were committed against each other, it never occurred to anyone to demand that the Buddha statues be taken down because they were "offensive." and "discriminated" against those of other religions. No one even thought of bombing those religious symbols. For hundreds of years, Buddhists, Hindus, Christians and Moslems have lived together in this tiny country. They all accept that Sri Lanka is a Buddhist country. No one finds Buddhist customs "offensive" and tries to remove them from the public square.

Nobody talks of Separation of Native Indian Church and State in connection with Sacred Native Indian relics: Sacred Native Indian Bones are given more respect than the Christian Cross. When bones are discovered on federal land, all construction is halted out of respect for sacred Indian bones. Nobody says they are "offended" because of the favoritism being shown. Nobody calls for the "Separation of the Native Indian Religion and State." The Genesis Wind Farm project may be shut down because of discovery of sacred Indian bones.[19] The Fallbrook construction project may also be shut down because of discovery of Sacred Indian bones.[20]

Nobody talks of Separation of Mosque and State: Obama celebrates Ramadan and has grand *Iftar* dinners in the White House. The Pentagon celebrates *Ramadan*. The Justice Department defends the right of a Muslim teacher to take time off to go to Mecca. It defends the right of Muslims to build a Mosque in Murfreesboro, Tennessee even though they had not obtained proper permits. A Judge has just postponed a Military Trial of Gitmo terrorists out of respect for the month of Ramadan and their holy religion! Muslims block the streets of Manhattan to "pray." Nobody is jumping up and down shrieking about "Separation of Mosque and State." The ACLU and Americans United have no problem with any of these.

"Separation of Church and State" is just a trick. *Taqiyya,* **being used to destroy Christianity in America:** When you consider how Liberals in America permit Sacred Native Indian bones and artifacts to be displayed and honored in public lands all over the country; and how they tolerate Muslim expression of their faith in public; it is clear that the issue of "Separation of Church and State" in America is merely an excuse to single out and destroy Christianity. Nobody else tries to destroy the religious heritage of the people of other countries. For example, Hindus in Sri Lankans made no attempt to destroy Buddhist statues in their country even though there was a 30-year civil war between the two groups.[21] It is only the Islamists, in an alliance with Socialists/Communists, who seek to remove Christianity out of America. And they are doing so in order to take away our identity as a nation and to humiliate and destroy America itself.

Americans United, headed by Ayesha Khan, and the ACLU, headed by Ramona Ripston, bring the lawsuits that destroy our Heritage. Ramona Ripston's husband, Stephen Reinhardt, who headed the 9ᵗʰ Circuit Court of Appeals, imposes their wishes on us. The ACLU is constantly claiming to be "offended" by Christian crosses and the Ten Commandments and demanding that they be removed. Working closely with them is Americans United for the Separation of Church and State, represented in public by Barry Lynn. What we don't see is the name or face of their Director. She was once an ACLU attorney and now works for Americans United. It is she who directs their litigations against everything Christian. Her name? Ayesha Khan.[22] *You want to guess what her religion is? And who is funding her to attack Christian religious symbols at every turn?*

Working closely with her is the ACLU itself. In California, Ramona Ripston heads the ACLU. The most outrageous decisions against Christianity in particular, and America in general, are issued by the 9ᵗʰ Circuit Court of Appeal, once headed by Stephen Reinhardt. Why is this relevant? Because, unknown to the general public, the two of them have been married for years. She brings the lawsuits destroying America, its Heritage and its Traditions. As Chief Judge, he made us obey the ACLU's wishes on everything. Even recently, California voters overwhelmingly approved Proposition 8, the ballot proposition banning gay marriage. Ramona Ripston's ACLU brought suit to overturn the will of the people. Her husband Stephen Reinhart was one of three judges on the panel of the 9ᵗʰ Circuit and he dutifully overturned Proposition 8![23] ,[24]

Removal of American Symbols of Identity and Pride began with the Supreme Court's Authorization of Flag Burning: In 1968, a Vietnam war protestor burned his draft registration as a symbol of protest against the war. The Supreme Court said that was not protected by the First Amendment.[25] But in 1989, when another protestor burned the American flag as a protest against the war, the Supreme Court held that the First Amendment protected this. The Court said that the State of Texas could not criminally sanction flag desecration in order to preserve the flag as a symbol of national unity.[26] This great triumph for Liberals was engineered by none other than the ACLU, represented by its board member, William Kunstler.[27] Kunstler's other great successes include representation of the Black Panther Party and representation of Obama's friend William Ayers' Weather Underground terrorist organization.[28] It was this Flag that represented our Country. Our soldiers marched into battle carrying this flag. Our dead soldiers' caskets are draped with this flag to show our utmost gratitude for the sacrifice made by our soldiers. It is the symbol of our identity and the rallying cry that helps us unite to defeat America's enemies. And a bunch of leftist attorneys who represent terrorists were able to convince the Supreme Court that people should be allowed to spit upon our flag!!

This disrespect for our National Flag has now been carried to the extreme: Burning the American flag or displaying it under the Mexican flag[29] is a common practice when illegals march demanding more rights.[30] In a Denair, CA middle school, an American kid was not allowed to have an American flag on the back of his bike because it could stir "racial tensions."[31] California's schools have commenced the practice of allowing kids of Mexican heritage to celebrate Cinco de Mayo by waving Mexican flags. Some students at Morgan Hill Unified School District decided to show their patriotism by wearing American flag T-shirts and bandannas. The two wearing bandannas were ordered to take them off. Three students wearing the American Flag T-shirts were sent to the principal's office where they were told to either wear their T-shirts inside out to cover up the American Flag, or go home. As their attorney said, *"students who wish to show their pride in another nation's heritage should not have their speech protected more than those who celebrate America."*[32]

Christian Symbols like the 10 Commandments are being removed: There has been a spate of decisions against Christianity. Alabama's Chief Judge Roy Moore had placed a granite monument at his courthouse engraved with the 10 commandments. The ACLU and Americans United were the lead plaintiffs demanding that the 10 commandments be removed. Ultimately, a Federal judge ordered it removed and also ordered that the State be fined if the 10 commandments were not removed. Judge Moore refused and was stripped of his Judgeship. He was also sued by the ACLU and Americans United for $550,000, which they claimed was the cost of their lawsuit against him.[33] The ACLU also sued to remove the 10 Commandments from a display included in a "Foundation of American Law and Government" display. The reasons given were that one Board member had acknowledged he was a Christian and motivated by his beliefs. And one student had complained that the posting of the Ten Commandments *"made him feel like an outsider because the school is promoting religious beliefs I do not share."*[34]

Crosses are being removed: What did the Islamists do in Bamiyan, in Timbuktu, in Egypt and in the rest of the world to the heritage of their enemies? Well, they are dong it in America too.

(a) The Cross on Mount Soledad, which is a war memorial, is 43 feet high, had stood there since 1913 and can be seen from the freeway. It is now seen as "offensive" to other religions and atheists and also an "unconstitutional" violation of the "Separation of Church and State" (which is not listed anywhere in the Constitution which was written by religious Christians!) Congress actually passed a law, which removed the land where the cross stood from the public domain and handed it over to the Department of Defense. But a lawsuit was brought, of course, by Ramona Ripston's ACLU.[35] And the trial judge ruled it can be seen from far and it was offensive. After over 15 years of appeals, Ripston's husband Stephen Reinhart and the rest of the 9th Circuit confirmed it should be removed by sending it back to the trial judge who had ruled it must be removed. An appeal to the Supreme Court was rejected in June 2012. So now, it will have to be removed, per the trial court's order.[36],[37]

(b) The Mohave Cross, to commemorate fallen soldiers from World War II. Is 7 feet tall and was erected in 1934 in a remote area inside the 1.6 million acre desert, the Mohave National Monument, belonging to the federal government. One Atheist represented, of course, by Ramona Ripston's ACLU, demanded it be removed and filed suit. In 2003, the government transferred the land where the cross stood to private ownership. But Ripston's husband Stephen Reinhart and his 9th Circuit said the transfer itself showed "favoritism" for Christianity and ordered the cross removed.[38] (*No discussion whatsoever about the "favoritism" and outright conflict of interest shown by a wife bringing a lawsuit which a husband then decides in her favor!! And then awards her attorney's fees too!!*) Pending appeal from this decision, the VFW covered the cross in plywood! In 2010, the Supreme Court held that the cross could stand. Since then, vandals have gone into the desert and destroyed the cross.[39],[40] *Note well this sequence of events. You will see it later on in this book. And you will see it in practice as the election nears: Liberals demand something* *and harass their opponents with multiple lawsuits. If they lose, magically, "vandals" or "street thugs" appear and obtain for the Liberals what they did not get through their lawsuits.*

(c) The Providence Rhode Island Cross: There is a small cross on the median of a highway saying "God Bless America." Humanists have objected because this is seen as an attempt to evangelize Christianity. They want the cross removed.[41]

(d) The 9/11 Cross: This Cross was found in the rubble of 9/11. It took 11 years of litigation to get permission to bring back the cross to the 9/11 site. Even now, there is scant mention of this Cross in the literature about the memorial. 12 years later, completion of the memorial itself has been halted over a money dispute between the Port Authority and the private foundation that raised money to build the memorial. Obama has not stepped in to provide the money needed. But our Christian President, Obama, has been actively promoting the construction of the 9/11 Victory Mosque at the site of this horror so that Muslim prayers can be heard 5 times a day wafting over the souls of our dead.[42]

Individual Christians are being ordered to violate their Christian beliefs: Christians were ordered to stop handing out Christian literature at an Italian festival in **Buffalo**, **NY**, even though other groups were allowed to hand out their literature.[43] A **New Mexico** court has ordered that a couple of devout Christian photographers must agree to photograph a Lesbian commitment ceremony even though gay marriage was illegal in the state. They were fined $7,000.[44] A Christian T-shirt company refused to print the **Lexington, Kentucky** City's T-shirts for their annual gay parade. A discrimination complaint has been filed against them.[45] An atheist has filed a lawsuit against a family owned restaurant in **Columbia, PA** for "discriminating" by giving a 10% discount to Christians on Sundays if they brought in the church bulletin to show they went to church![46] **Ocean Grove Camp Ministry**, a Christian Association in California, was sued for "discrimination" for refusing to allow their hall to be used in a civil commitment ceremony for two lesbians.[47] Citizens of **El Paso, TX** area churches who promoted petitions opposing the city administration's decision to implement benefits for same sex partners after the voters rejected it, are facing jail time for exercising their First

Amendment Rights.[48] The **Minneapolis Special School District** kicked out the Good News Club that had been operating after school programs for 75 years because it was "proselytizing."[49] In **Phoenix, AZ**, the host of a Bible Study group who hosted around 15-20 people in his 4.5-acre backyard was told that he was really a church and had failed to comply with the zoning, building, fire and safety codes. He was summarily found guilty of all these violations and sentenced to jail for 60 days, three years' probation and a fine of $10,000!![50] When the case went on appeal to the 9th Circuit, John Tutelman, the Prosecutor, requested that Defendant Salman's probation be revoked and that he be given a jail term of two-and-a-half years![51]

Christian College Students are being forced to give up their Christian beliefs in order to obtain their degrees: A Christian student in a graduate counseling program at **Eastern Michigan University**, Julea Ward, asked that another student handle the case of a homosexual suffering from depression because she, being a Christian, could not affirm the student's sexual relationships. She was dismissed from the program. Similarly at **Augusta State University** in Georgia, Jennifer Keeton sued last year after being told she had to renounce her Christian faith and take re-education courses to counter her Christian morality or be expelled from a master's program. She was required to undergo "sensitivity training," read up on homosexual issues, attend a "gay pride parade" and report on it. After losing in a U.S. district court, she has appealed to the 11th U.S. Circuit.

Conservative Christian Organizations are being forced to accept Gays as their leaders: In *Christian Legal Society v. Martinez*, the U.S. Supreme Court uupheld the decision by **Hastings College of the Law** at the University of California at Berkeley to eject a Christian legal group for not allowing open homosexuals in leadership positions. Writing for the majority in that case, Associate Justice Ruth Bader Ginsburg said: "Condemnation of same-sex intimacy is, in fact, a condemnation of gay people," and "our decisions have declined to distinguish between status and conduct in this context."[52] **Vanderbilt University** of Tennessee ordered that all groups accept everyone, even if the newcomer does not subscribe to the belief statement of the group. This was clearly aimed at forcing Conservative Christian groups to allow gays to lead their groups. When they refused, they were kicked off campus.[53]

Christian Prayers are not allowed in Schools in America: The School Principal of PS 90 in **Coney Island, Brooklyn** banned "God Bless America" from the kindergartener's graduation "because it is not age appropriate." She replaced it with Justin Bieber's "Baby:" "*Are we an item? Girl, quit playing . . . my first love broke my heart for the first time . . .*" was deemed perfectly fine for 5 year olds to sing! **Judge Biery of Texas** banned the words, "Amen" "Prayer" "Invocation" and "Benediction" from a Texas High School graduation. Any violation by any student would result in the school superintendent being jailed![54]

Christian Prayers are not allowed even at off-campus Events: The ACLU crafted a "Consent Decree" in the **Santa Rosa District, FL**, which threatens school district employees with fines and jail time for even praying over a meal. Teachers are considered to be in their 'official capacity" whenever a student is present, even at a private event. Teachers are not allowed to reply to an e-mail sent by a parent if the parent refers to God or Scripture. Teachers are not allowed to pray, bow their heads, or fold their hands to show agreement with anyone who does pray. The teachers complain they are forced to pray in closets. Michelle Winkler was brought up on contempt charges after her husband, who is not employed by the school district, offered a meal prayer at a private event in a neighboring county. The Pace High School Principal Frank Lay and Athletic Director Robert Freeman were brought up on criminal contempt charges because the ACLU complained that Freeman offered a blessing for a lunch for some 20 adult booster club members![55] At **Cranston High School in Rhode Island**, a single atheist was able to force the school to remove a prayer mural that had been there since the 1960's. The school was also ordered to pay legal fees of $173,000 to the atheist and her attorneys, the ACLU, of course.[56] The school district was advised it would cost them a further $500,000 to appeal the case, so they took down the banner.[57]

Christian Schools cannot be given any Tax money. There have been ongoing battles trying to get little children the chance of a good education in Christian schools. There is no dispute that Christian schools are far superior to public schools in education. *The problem for liberals and Islamists is that Christian schools teach Christian values, like the 10 commandments. And this cannot be allowed!* Also, liberal teacher's unions control public education. If parents were allowed to take their children out of these pubic schools, there would be no one left. In fact, whenever there is an opportunity, parents overwhelmingly ask that their kid be allowed to escape from the inferior education and vile culture of public schools. But liberals have insisted that children remain in public schools, even though over 40% of children in public schools are failing. Little black children in DC public schools, the worst in the nation, were being allowed to obtain $7,500 "opportunity scholarships" to go to private schools. There was a demonstrable improvement in their performance. Once Obama took office, he shut down the program. Congress then revived it. But Obama shut it down again by withdrawing funding for this program in his 2013 budget.[58] You can see that Obama values his teacher's unions and the money he gets from them over teaching the poor children in black neighborhoods.

But Tax Money will soon be used for Islamic Schools: Arabic is being taught in a NY school and now, Representative Andre Carlson of Indiana, a Muslim, has recommended that the *Qu'ran* and Islamic methods be taught in public schools.[59] All of this, of course, takes taxpayer money to fund Islamic religious schools. All 200 2nd through 5th graders at PS 368 in Hamilton Heights will be will be taught Arabic twice a week, the same amount of time allotted to science and music courses.[60] The ACLU and Americans United have no problem with the teaching of Arabic and Carlson's proposal to teach the *Qu'ran* and Islamic values in pubic schools. No anxiety at all about "Separation of Islamic Church and State"!!

Christmas has been banned: There is a complete ban on holiday symbolism in Boca Raton public school buildings. Christmas and Hanukkah will no longer be celebrated in New York's Batavia school district. Secret Santa gift exchanges were banned in elementary school in Newburyport, Mass. A Stockton, CA elementary school has even banned poinsettias, Christmas trees and Santas.

Christmas is banned from the public square, or forced to share the holiday with other "religions" that exist solely to mock Christianity. In Pitman, NJ, they removed a banner "Keep Christ in Christmas." "Remember the Reason for the Season" was removed at Lincoln Southeast High in NE. In Santa Monica, Atheists replaced a 58-year tradition of a Christmas display. In Loudon County Virginia Court House, VA, atheists hung a skeleton in a Red Santa suit from a Crucifix. Another "religious group," the Church of Flying Spaghetti Monsters, swapped baby Jesus for a plate of spaghetti with bulging eyes![61]

Hollywood Constantly Mocks and Sneers at Christians: Remember Andres Serrano's depiction of a Crucifix in a jar of urine? He was dying of AIDS because of his own acts. But he blamed Christians. And his "work of art" was staged in publicly funded Museums all over the United States. Then, there was the depiction of the Virgin Mary covered in cow dung by Christopher Offal, also displayed all over the country in public museums paid for by the taxpayer.[62] Then, there was the Smithsonian paying our tax dollars for David Wojnarowicz's imagery of ants crawling over a crucifix. This guy was also dying of AIDS.[63]

Hollywood never shows a good Christian. According to their propaganda machine, all Christians are bigots, red necks, slave owners and extremists. Add to that Obama's "threat assessment" that Christians are potential terrorists and you get the picture that liberals want to paint about Conservatives. Hollywood's latest is to make a movie that asserts that Jesus is the product of the rape of Mary by a Roman soldier and claim that Jesus' miracles were not real.[64] How about a play "intended to convey a message of tolerance and love . . . . By a student who is committed to protecting and preserving the freedom of thought, speech and expression"? Yes, such pap could never be uttered about anything other than a play that denigrated Christianity. In this case, it is a play being performed in Tarleton State University in Stephenville, Texas the week before Easter. The play by Terrence McNulty depicts Jesus as a gay man, having a sexual affair with Judas. All the apostles are gay. Joseph is an alcoholic wife-beater and Mary gives birth alongside a chorus of moaning men. At the end of the play, Jesus is crucified with the moniker above his head, "King of the Queers." [65] The University of Delaware paid $50,000 (twice the author's going rate) and commissioned a play depicting suicide, date rape, gun rights, the founding fathers and abortion; all from a liberal perspective, mocking conservatives. In it, the author also depicted Jesus as being "very compassionate" and authorizing the lead actress to have an abortion and kill the baby in her womb![66]

Obama has banned prayer in pubic buildings.[67] He has also banned the celebration of Christmas in all Federal and State Buildings.[68]

No Christmas carolers are allowed in Post Offices. In my own Post Office, a teller was ordered to take down Christmas decorations she had put up in her personal workspace. In fact, most post offices don't even carry Christian stamps, even during the season, and what stamps are available marking the season are invariably secular. But you can find *E'id* stamps! No more Christmas lights, trees or Menorahs at the Staten Island Ferry Terminal. The Air Force even apologized for an email promoting Operation Christmas Child, which provides 8 million holiday gifts for poor kids in 100 countries![69] A Christmas card saying "Happy Christmas" cannot be sent by U.S. Congressmen, as per rules issued by the Franking Commission.[70] As detailed above, it actually took 10 years of litigation before we were allowed to install the 9/11 Cross[71] in the 9/11-memorial museum! As they say: *"Separation of Church and State!"* and *"Someone might object!"*

However, Obama's Justice Department sued and obtained $75,000 from a California school district for having refused to allow a teacher to take 3 weeks' leave right in the middle of the school year to go to Mecca, while she was still on probation and while it was not even a Muslim requirement to go at that time.[72] Can you imagine Obama doing this for a Catholic teacher to go to Rome or a Christian or Jewish teacher to go to Jerusalem for 10% of the school year?

The Army is removing all vestiges of Christianity from the Armed Forces. The Word "God" is deemed "offensive," and soldiers are not allowed to practice their faith openly outside the chapels. They are not allowed to pray even before going into battle where they may die, because Christian prayers could be "offensive" to non-Christians.[73]

Christians are actually being stoned by Muslims in Dearborn, Michigan and then charged with Disturbing the Peace!: Muslims, who preach that theirs is a religion of peace, objected strongly to the mere presence of Christians at their 2012 Dearborn Michigan Arab Festival. Christians who peacefully held up signs asserting their Christian faith were verbally and physically assaulted by Muslim mobs with bottles, stones and other objects. And then threatened with further violence and mayhem. You know the end of the story. Did the police arrest the Muslim mobs? Of course not. The police demanded that the Christians move[74] Even though they had not done anything physical but had merely stood there with their placards, and were bleeding from being assaulted, the Christians were charged with a breach of the peace. Thank God, they were acquitted.[75]

If Obama pays even a part of your benefit, then you cannot pray: Senior Citizens' meals at the Ed Young Senior Center near Savannah, Georgia, are subsidized by the Federal Government. Accompanying the federal subsidy are federal rules. If the government pays even a part of your meal, then you cannot pray before eating it!![76] Notice the similarity to the argument he made about forcing Catholics to give abortion pills to everyone. He claimed he had the right to do it because he paid for people's Health Care!! *For those of you who think it is a great thing that Obama is taxing us more and collecting more and more of our money, remember what he is doing. Once he pays for you, he owns you and you have to do as he commands!*

Renaming Good Friday: The **City of Davenport, Iowa** wants to rename Good Friday as "Spring Holiday"[77]

The Very Name of Jesus is deemed "unconstitutional" Volunteer chaplains in the Charlotte-Mecklenburg Police Department (CMPD) can pray, but will no longer be able to invoke the name "Jesus" when they pray. Why? The ACLU, of course, says it is improper to mix religion with the function of state agents.[78] The American Civil Liberties Union and Americans United for Separation of Church and State are celebrating their victory in a U.S. circuit court decision that states even "a solitary reference to Jesus Christ" in invocations before the Forsyth County Board of Commissioners' meetings could do *"violence to the pluralistic and inclusive values that are a defining feature of American public life."*[79]

Remember what I told you when we started this Chapter? That the whole purpose of the assault on Christianity is to destroy our heritage and tear out the roots of Christianity from America? Once they have removed our Flag, Our Crosses, the 10 Commandments and all vestiges of our Christianity and other symbols of our identity from the pubic square; nothing is left. Nothing is left for us to rally around and mount a defense of our country. Even I would not have had the courage to write this book. If we allow this to continue, America will be left defenseless and easily destroyed.

Chapter 5

Islamists are waging "*Stealth Jihad*" and Exerting Enormous Power in America

There are thousands of mosques in the US[1] and the numbers have grown by 25% in the past 5 years.[2,3] A Mosque, a place of worship, always includes a Madrassah, a place of teaching and learning. The majority of these Mosques belong to the Wahhabi Sect, which teaches *Jihad* or violence against Americans.[4] Who funded these Mosques? As you saw earlier, even in Sri Lanka 160 Militant Imams had come in on tourist visas and overstayed their visas to preach militant Islam. How many Militant Imams are preaching *Jihad* in the U.S? Does anybody know? The U.S. is funding trips for Rauf of the 9/11 Victory Mosque, and also funding mosque renovations in 10 different countries.[5] Why?

In the last two years alone, since Obama was elected, 12 major multi-million dollar Mosque projects have been planned throughout America.[6] They are all located either next door to, or directly across from, Christian Churches. It is obvious this is a challenge to Christianity from Islam. (There is no need to check whether Islam is challenging Judaism. Their *Qur'an* requires them to kill the Jews—*Hadith, Vol 4, Book 52 no 177,* narrated by Abu Huraira.)

The Muslim populations living around these mosques are not wealthy enough to support their construction costs; nor do they have sufficient congregants to need such large Mosques. Funding is obviously coming from wealthy Middle East countries like Saudi Arabia, Kuwait, Bahrain and Qatar. The official state religion of Saudi Arabia is Wahhabi Islam, the orthodox Islam discussed above. *Jihad*, the conquering of non-Muslims and their enslavement, is one of the central tenets of Wahhabi Islam. All Mosques include Madrassah's (just like the one Obama attended in Indonesia), which will teach only the *Qur'an* and Islamic precepts, including the practice of *Jihad* against us.

There is a $10 million complex being planned for Atlanta. And other multi-million dollar complexes are planned for Boston, Massachusetts,

Sheboygan, Wisconsin and Portland, Oregon. Three more are being built in the heart of the Bible belt in Tennessee. One is in Memphis, another just outside Nashville and the third in Murfreesboro. The last, a multi-million dollar, 52,000 sq. ft. mosque complex on 15 acres of land, was approved in 17 days without any public debate; while other large congregations' plans take over 18 months to obtain approval. There are only 250 Muslim families here, almost all of whom are working class or on welfare.[7] On May 29, 2012, a Judge found that the Mosque had been built without obtaining proper approvals and halted construction. It should be noted that Obama's Department of Justice filed a brief demanding that the case be dismissed Do you think DOJ would have filed suit to protect a Christian church? And we must still ask the question, how did this happen? Obviously, Muslims are asserting tremendous influence throughout America.[8]

Here again, you can see *Stealth Jihad* at work. Nobody notices the number of mosques going up because they are in different parts of the country. Nobody thinks that these Mosques are preaching *Jihad* against us and training their adherents to fight us. Nobody realizes that Moslems are asserting their power in this country, exactly as if they had fought and conquered us.

Muslims already have infinitely more influence than Christians in America: Muslims block many major streets in Manhattan to pray on Fridays; thereby claiming America for Allah. Hear the call to prayer and see the photos here.[9]

© Bebeto Matthews/ /AP/Corbis
Muslims assert Dominance: Blocking Manhattan Streets for "prayers"

Consider Muslim Power at the U.N.: Obama's "57 States" are all Muslim countries that vote as a bloc and which, together with their supporters in European countries that have very large Muslim minorities, constitute a majority at the U.N. In fact, the Muslim states have now taken to calling themselves the "Caliphate." **Why is America wasting its taxpayers' money by supporting these institutions?**

Muslim power is being exerted all throughout our universities:[10,11] The Council of American Islamic Relations ("CAIR") receives almost 99% of its funding from Islamic countries but does not regiaster as a Foreign Agent or comply with the Foreign Agents Registration Act's requirement to disclose its donors. Nevertheless it is involved in litigating against various American Corporations and it funds the Muslims Students Association ("MSA"). MSA has chapters in virtually all of our Universities.[12,13] Though most students are not terrorists, MSA chapters have nevertheless produced a great many radical terrorists.[14] MSA was indicted in a case where UC of Irvine Moslem students prevented Dr. Michael Oren, Israel's Ambassador from speaking.[15] It also called for Jihad and prevented Dr. Daniel Pipes from speaking.[16] Muslim students also objected to Harvard's honoring Martin Peretz and prevented him from speaking at Harvard.[17]

Essentially, there is mob rule in our Universities. Radical professors accept funding from Arabs and spout pro-Arab propaganda. Administrators promulgate University rules against "Hate Speech," formulate "Codes of Conduct," and demand "diversity" and "tolerance;" to prevent students from speaking out against extremist Muslims. And MSA affiliates use mob violence to prevent others from expressing any contrary opinions. All of the above spread virulent anti-Semitism, anti-Christianism and anti-Americanism on campuses throughout the country. And our children are terrorized, silenced and sandwiched between these three groups. Their choices? Accept pro-Muslim doctrine and become *Dhimmis* like the rest of them. Or speak out; be awarded lousy grades; be called "Islamophobes" and other vile epithets; and live in constant fear of violent reprisals.

After 9/11, Rudy Giuliani refused to accept $10 Million from Saudi Prince Al-Waleed bin Talal.[18] But in 2006, Harvard accepted $20 million from the Prince to fund an Islamic Studies Program. Muslim courses are now offered across 21 departments, programs and schools at Harvard.[19] Harvard is now beholden to Prince Al-Waleed and unlikely to oppose him on anything. Georgetown University's Prince Al-Waleed Bin Talal Center for Muslim-Christian Understanding produces programs with a strong pro-Muslim bias. No criticism of "Honor" Killings; no discussion of conflicts between *Shari-ah* and our Constitution; no lecture series about conflicts between Islam and Christianity; no symposiums on how Middle Eastern rulers should share wealth with the poor in their own countries; no seminars on how to bring *Shari'ah* into the 21st Century here. Instead, John Esposito, head of the Center, plies us with platitudes, using "political correctness" as an excuse to conceal the truth. *Taqiyya* in action! He is regularly featured in the Washington Post, on NPR and other news outlets; sneering at any who raise objections to the barbaric practices of Islamists; and concealing the fact that he is totally owned by the Saudis.[20] **A perfect example of a complete *Dhimmi!***

Muslim tentacles also extend throughout our Justice system: 25% of the top 100 American Law Firms have provided millions in legal services fighting to release Gitmo detainees caught in combat trying to kill our soldiers. They have been working free of charge; deploying armies of attorneys and paralegals; flying attorneys to Cuba, doing very expensive pre-trial work; and conducting endless expensive litigations. Many of the terrorists they helped release went right back to the battlefield to kill more American soldiers. JT Mason of prestigious Paul Weiss was one of those defense lawyers who conspired to provide leaflets to Gitmo detainees advising them how to claim "torture" "Koran burning" and other egregious offenses to Muslim sensibilities. Their excuse? "So they can earn the trust of the Terrorists"![21] Other defense lawyers released the home addresses of our covert CIA agents so their wives and children could be targeted and killed by terrorists.[22] Should they get tax deductions for working free? It is not *"pro bono"* work, which means "in the public interest." It is definitely not in the public interest to support the enemy while we are at war and our children are being killed! Do these sound like patriotic Americans? **Isn't it obvious that these top law firms are drooling over the money they can earn from their rich Arab clients?**

Our Court system has also been compromised: There have been at least 50 cases in American courts involving conflicts between US law and *Shari'ah*. In 27 of those, *Shari'ah* was applied. Usually these cases involved Muslim women and children being denied the Equal Protection they would have been entitled to under US laws.[23] Recently, over 70% of Oklahomans passed a Constitutional Amendment requiring our judges to adhere to our laws and not apply *Shari'ah* law. Justices O'Brien, McKay and Matheson of the 10th Circuit struck it down.[24,25] These judges knew how cruel and inhumane *Shari'ah* laws are and knew they conflicted with our Constitution. **Why did they rule as they did?**

Arab Financial Centers will soon replace ours: Arab sponsored American Universities are training our students in *Shari'ah* financing. (*Check out Ann Barnhardt's blog for a hilarious explanation of Shari'ah financing.*[26]) Al-Waleed's group is also promoting the use of *Shari'ah*, *Sukuk bonds* and *Zakat financing* by various American Financial institutions.[27] **Soon Wall Street will take its money, its well-paying jobs and its tax base, and move to the Middle East!**

Muslim tentacles have also spread throughout our vital businesses: Delta Airlines' Sky Team has been joined by Saudi Arabian Airlines.

Delta now discriminates against Jews and refuses to board Jews at DC and NY airports onto flights that link with Saudi Arabia Airlines.[28] Prince Al-Waleed's Kingdom Holdings owns large percentages of shares in Coco Cola, Pepsi, McDonalds, AOL, Saks, Disney, Apple Computer, Amazon, Citibank, Twitter, Carlyle Group and other major US Corporations.[29] Is it in our national interest that so many of our prized corporations are now owned by the Saudis and other Middle Eastern investment organizations? Shouldn't there be some discussions about the fact that we are dependent on them for our oil, and that perhaps we should not be dependent on them for our financing and also permit them to control our prized businesses?

Muslims own large segments of the Media and can control what we see & hear: Prince Al-Waleed and Financier Jamal A. Khashoggi are building a 24-hour Arab channel with Mayor Bloomberg called Al-Arabiya.[30] As a result, Mayor Bloomberg has become a *Dhimmi,* supporting Muslims at all costs. The NY Police were training their officers in counterterrorism using *"The Third Jihad"* a film created by moderate Muslims, showing that Muslim extremists are bent on establishing a worldwide Islamic regime. Muslim leaders, obviously not "moderate", objected and called it "racial profiling". They demanded that Bloomberg fire his Police Chief.[31] He refused. But Bloomberg ordered the police to stop showing the film.[32] Muslims have put enormous additional pressure on Bloomberg, objecting to post-9/11 police surveillance of their Mosques, bookshops and other Islamic businesses and institutions. Remember that scene in *The Godfather* **w**here every major mob figure was in attendance paying homage to Corleone and the FBI was taking down license plate number of cars parked outside the Corleone family compound to gather information for future use? Was there anything wrong with that? Was it anti-Catholic? Following the exact pattern of mob marches in Europe; Muslims are marching in New York, calling New York a "Police State" and demanding that Bloomberg require the NYPD to stop any surveillance unless there is an "actual threat."[33] **Apparently, 9/11 itself and over 30 subsequent attacks, all by Muslim men, are not sufficient to warrant police surveillance.**

Now Muslim Advocates have filed a lawsuit against the NYPD stating it should not do surveillance on New Jersey Muslims attending mosques that the NYPD has assessed as potential terrorism risks. The obvious goal, which has been successful with respect to federal law enforcement, is to prevent the NYPD from discovering and preventing terrorist attacks. So, even though a Muslim has committed every single terrorist act in the past 15 years; we will copy the TSA and have the idiocy of the NYPD wasting its time surveilling people in Catholic Churches and Jewish Synagogues so the Muslims won't feel "discriminated against." *Of course, those who will pay the price when Muslim terrorists explode more bombs are American citizens like you.*

Farhan Doe, who was rejected because he says gays should be imprisoned, has filed another lawsuit against the NYPD saying he was discriminated against because of his views. This is correct, up to a point. But Farhan comes from a cultural and religious background in which imprisoning and executing gays, stoning women and killing pets because they offend his morals would be his duty as a law enforcement officer. In Muslims countries, it is law enforcement personnel who beat women who have "exposed" their faces and arms, and execute apostates for converting to Christianity. As Daniel Greenfield asks in his excellent article on this point: *"Farhan's lawyer says that his client has the right to believe whatever he pleases, and he has a point. But the question is with enough Farhan's in the political, judicial and enforcement arms, how long will the rest of us have that right?"* [34]

© Mary Altaffer/ /AP/Corbis
Muslims Assert Dominance:
Demand that NY Police stop Surveillance

Muslims own large segments of the Media and can control what we see & hear: Prince Al-Waleed and his companions took a $300 million stake in Twitter, own 90% of Rotana Media Services, own 5% of Apple, own major shares in Time Warner (parent of CNN) and is the second largest shareholder ($8 Billion) of News Corp, the world's second largest media conglomerate, parent of Wall Street Journal, Dow Jones, DirecTV, Fox News and Twentieth Century Fox.[35] Al-Waleed is collaborating with Fox News to produce an Arab News show.[36] It has been alleged that Al-Waleed ordered Fox News to slant its coverage of Muslim riots in France where Muslim youths in the banlieues burned over 100 cars a night for months.[37] *In fact, this entire book contains information that the Mainstream Media Mafia should have informed the American public. Ask yourself, why has the Media concealed all this information from you?*

Arabs clearly control our Politicians & Campaign Consultants on both sides of the Aisle: John McCain tried to hide Obama's Muslim origins by preventing his people from even uttering Barak Hussein Obama's middle name. Who advised him? Why? Do you remember when the media attacked Bush mercilessly for years on end? And no one defended Bush's positions? And the Republicans lost the White House to Obama and both houses of Congress to the Democrats in 2008? Mary Matalin was Bush's campaign director. But it turned out she was married to James Carville, a Democratic political consultant. To ordinary folks like me, she was hopelessly compromised and conflicted and unable or unwilling to defend Bush.

It appears that all Republican consultants are compromised this way. Why else did they advise Mitt Romney to embrace his Romney-Care? "Republican" consultants now tell all Republican candidates that they shouldn't attack Obama personally for what he has done to our country but only discuss his "policies." The current "truth" handed down by our campaign gurus is that Obama is well meaning, but just in over his head. This notion that Obama should not be attacked personally only redounds to Obama's benefit. This way, there will never be a discussion of whether Obama was born in America. And if not, who brought him here and raised him up to be a Senator and then the President? Whether Obama is a Muslim and if he was a Muslim, how a Muslim Ruler would rule America. No one will anyone ever ask why Obama castigates our American "Millionaires and Billionaires" but never mentions Middle East multi-Billionaires who are buying up property and building mosques all over our country. Instead, Republican candidates will be limited to dry discussions of "policy"; which are guaranteed to put the audience to sleep and guarantee a loss for the Republicans! **Why are Republican consultants working to help Obama?**

Why don't we force our Politicians to disclose their holdings of *Shari'ah* complaint funds and their Middle East Oil Investments? We get nearly 30% of our oil from the Middle East. We are borrowing $4 out of every $10 we spend. Our Fed buys 70% of the Treasuries we issue, thus ensuring that our Dollar declines in value and that inflation will rise. In just three years, Obama has added $6 Trillion dollars to the National Debt, which was $10 Trillion when Obama was inaugurated. Our country is sinking into irreversible decline. Yet, Members of Congress are unable to stop spending. Why don't they care? Could it be that Members of Congress and their consultants are invested in *Shari'ah* compliant funds that rise in value as our Dollar sinks? Should Members of Congress have any investments in Middle East countries? Shouldn't they be required to disclose these?

Obama forces American businesses to borrow from Arabs: Obama causes private businesses unsustainable losses by promulgating onerous regulations; levying massive fines; prosecuting time and money consuming lawsuits; and demonizing them all the time. Businesses are then forced to find investors or financiers who will keep them from bankruptcy. And because Obama has bankrupted our banking and financial systems; businesses are compelled to turn to the Saudis for financial support. Once Muslim investors own large chunks of a company; the companies must do as the Muslims command and exist in a state of *Dhimmitude!* This is the classic hunting pattern: **Obama, the pack leader, terrorizes and bankrupts private American Corporations; and drives them right into the maws of his co-hunters, the Saudis.**

Obama ensures OPEC will always have power over us by giving us no alternative except OPEC oil to enable us to meet our energy requirements. Those who have the money get to exercise the power. They buy or bribe to get whatever they want. The rulers of OPEC countries are rich beyond imagining because we pay them over $338 Billion a year for oil. OPEC is advised by Dr. Khalid al-Mansoor. He also arranged for Obama to get into Harvard Law School and either he or Prince Al-Waleed paid Obama's law school tuition.[38,39]

Of course, this explains why Obama groveled to King Abdullah,[40] titular head of Sunni Muslims, bowing deep down from his waist, genuflecting and almost kissing Abdullah's hand.[41] But he treated Queen Elizabeth, titular head of the Church of England, with a complete lack of respect by showing her a breezy familiarity. And in strict violation of protocol, his wife even patted Queen Elizabeth on the back![42] So, where does the Obama family's respect lie?

Obama has repaid his debt to his benefactors a thousand-fold. The only way for us to escape from the enormous power of the Arabs is to become energy sufficient and cease buying oil from the Middle East. We have more oil and gas reserves here in our own country than in any average Middle-East country.[43] But Obama has seen to it that we Americans will always continue to be dependent on OPEC and send them our money. Whenever he can, Obama prevents us from drilling for oil, using fracking to get natural oil and natural gas, using our coal plants, building nuclear plants or having any reliable source of energy; other than foreign oil. He has even stopped the Keystone Pipeline, which would bring us oil from Canada, reduce dependence on OPEC oil and provide us with thousands of jobs!! **Why did Obama do this, other than to repay his OPEC sponsors?**

Chapter 6

Muslims are setting traps for America and Americans

The Drift Nets surrounding Americans: As you have now seen, Americans are being squeezed into poverty, a little bit here, a little bit there. This is making us more dependent on our ruler Obama and his government to provide us with money to live; and is making our country more and more like a Muslim controlled Caliphate.

Muslims are operating exactly like those who use drift nets for deep-sea fishing. These "Walls of Death," made of virtually invisible plastic filaments, extend for many feet down and extend 30-40 miles across the ocean. Unsuspecting fish, mammals and birds, have no idea they are trapped until the net is puled tight; and then, every single living animal inside is killed!! We are the unsuspecting fish. Someday soon, the trap will be pulled shut. All Muslims need is someone to pull the trigger. And their *Stealth Jihad* against us will be accomplished.

If their wildest dreams came true, what would Muslims want for America? 9/11 was not a random plot hatched by some crazy fringe element. This was carefully planned and financed by Osama bin Laden, a Saudi. 15 of the terrorists were Saudis. Plus there were many Americans providing support; bound to Muslims by common religious and/or financial interests. Muslims want to defeat America and annex it into their Caliphate. They are using *Stealth Jihad,* moving slowly and methodically, working under the radar, and setting up their drift nets to trap us. If their wildest dreams came true, what would they be like?

Islamists would install a Muslim President who would spend every waking moment pursuing Muslim interests: He would help Muslim countries get rid of their dissidents by allowing them to come to America. He would prevent the States from closing our borders so that foreigners, including Muslim terrorists, could sneak into America. He would liberalize immigration policies to allow disproportionate access to Muslim "refugees" allowing more Muslims into America—the more radical, the better; so they could form the front lines of a *stealth* or actual *Jihad*. He would tax us to provide welfare and benefits for all these newcomers.

He would vigorously support building more mosques, knowing that once they are built, mosques cannot ever be taken down. He would undermine the religious freedom of Christians who founded this country and foster the spread of Islam and *Shari'ah* law. And he would do all he could to prevent Christians from exercising and strengthening their own beliefs, and upholding American values, knowing that a dispirited group of Christian Americans are easily defeated. And how better to do this than force Catholics to violate their religious beliefs by forcing them to provide abortions for all women in their hospitals, churches and schools?

He would minimize the threat of Islamic Terrorism (or even deny its existence with "New-Speak" and do all he could to protect the terrorists. He would release terrorists from Gitmo and return them to Iraq, Afghanistan, Yemen and Somalia. He would hand over our most vital defensive weapons to the enemy. He would disclose our vital national secrets. He would dismantle, demoralize and defeat the US Army by cutting their funding; firing active duty soldiers; denying them combat pay; insisting they allow gays into their ranks; preventing them from saying any Christian prayer, even before battle; and demanding that Muslims be allowed into the army without proper screening. To further demoralize them, he would ensure that our achievements in Iraq are turned into defeats and that we are vanquished in Afghanistan.

He would advance the Caliphate globally. He would prop up Dictators in the Middle East who hate us; and work to overthrow those who are friendly or at least neutral. He would ignore and abandon freedom fighters inside countries that are our sworn enemies; even as they seek freedom and democracy. And he would seek to curry favor with the Despots who rule those countries. He would dither and postpone taking effective action to prevent our enemies from acquiring nuclear weapons that they could use to strike at our allies and us. He would ensure that its enemies encircled Israel. And no matter how Iran threatens Israel; and no matter how many of our citizens Egypt jails; the Muslims' selected American ruler would support Iran and Egypt over Israel.

He would ensure America couldn't become energy independent and that it remained forever dependent on Middle East oil. He would demand *Jizya* from every remaining "Infidel" American Business by taxing them at every turn. Thus, he would ensure private businesses collapsed and private jobs were lost. He would demoralize and demonize any entrepreneur with chants of *"Millionaires and Billionaires who won't pay their fair share!"* He would take over all private enterprise; so every American would be dependent on his government for jobs and benefits; and also be compelled to vote for him.

He would give taxpayer funds to his cronies, so they would continue to support him. He would create massive new government bureaucracies and staff them with make-work jobs for his supporters. He would destroy our American economy with manic and unsupportable spending.

He would take away our First Amendment Rights, so we couldn't oppose him. He would do everything in his power to take away our Second Amendment Right to bear arms so we couldn't defend outselves. Gradually, he would denigrate and dismantle our US Constitution and replace it with some version of *Shari'ah* law, which he, as our Founding Father, would tell us was good for us.

He would make America a Caliphate; with us in a state of *Dhimmitude*, slaving for the Muslims who rule over us and paying almost every penny we earn in *Jizya* or taxes. Finally, he would reign over us as our Ruler of the new Muslim-controlled Caliphate of America.

Chapter 7

Think about what you have just read
And answer the Question

See how you have been lied to: Look at the vast amount of information your current media and the Islamists have hidden from you. And see how they have tricked you. You thought the attacks on 9/11 were isolated incidents. But, this was just the beginning of a plan of *Stealth Jihad* against us; softening us for blows yet to come.

Terrorist attempts and actual attacks against us have not stopped at all. All that has happened is that the media has concealed the extent and the number of attacks against us. For instance, when Nidal Hassan stood on a table and assassinated unarmed soldiers shouting "Allahu Akbar;" Obama instructed us not to rush to judgment; that this was a newly discovered illness: pre-traumatic stress. And later, he has determined that this was just "workplace violence!" Can you think of a better example of someone enabling *Stealth Jihad* against us by lulling us into a senseless torpor?

The original purpose of the TSA has been completely subverted. Instead of looking for terrorists and indications of terrorist threats; Obama is now concerned about not hurting the feelings of Muslims; and making sure that the orthodox Muslims, the ones most likely to be terrorists; are exempted from the regular TSA procedures that would protect us from another terrorist attack. Meantime, our own people have been humiliated, beaten down and forced to submit to unconstitutional and degrading searches.

As you have now seen, Islamists exert enormous power and influence over us in America. In fact, Muslims exert more influence in America than the Christians. We have to struggle and litigate to have crosses or crèches in the public square. But Muslims have their call to prayer blaring over loudspeakers from early morning to late night in certain cities and are allowed to block public streets to pray! They have tricked us into accepting tributes to Islam at our Flight 93 memorial; when we intended to pay tribute to those murdered on 9/11. They nearly got away with having their prayer to Allah waft over our dead at the World Trade Centers; which were brought down by terrorists acting in the name of Allah! Look at the sophistry of those who support Islamists. See how they call themselves a "Religion of Peace" and yet, are building Wahhabi Mosques all over the country; deliberately setting them up near Christian churches; and teaching their adherents to hate us and wage *Jihad* against us. The simple fact is that those non-Muslims who proclaim that Islam is a religion of peace do not have a clue about what Islam really is. They are just working with Islamists to soothe us so we won't worry about what is going on under the radar.

Look at the vast power Muslims are exerting on our universities, our justice system, our court system, our financial system and so many of our vital businesses. You wonder why the media lies to us all the time. And then, you realize that vast tracts of the media are owned by Islamists who are waging a *Stealth Jihad* against us. Keeping us ignorant facilitates their conquest of us.

The Washington politicians and big business, who do know what the Islamists are doing, either through greed to earn Arab money for themselves; or through sheer terror of what the Media, the Muslims and Obama will do to them; continue to support Obama with large donations and much praise. Working together, this unholy trio, the Media, the Muslims and Obama, has seen to it that you, the ordinary American, remain in ignorance.

When the JournoList starts up with its usual chant to cover up for Obama: *"This book is full of Hate."* *"The writer hates Obama because he is black;"* remember that when the Park Service tells you to watch out for Grizzly Bears; it doesn't "hate" the bears. It is simply warning you. So it is with this book. There is no "hate" for Obama; this book is just warning you.

There is a conflagration that is burning up our Constitution, our Freedom and our way of life. It is coming closer and closer to you and someone is shouting, *"Fire!"* But the JournoList, the Islamists and Obama will use their usual technique of finding some little thing wrong and inflating it to cast doubt on everything that has been said: *"It's all a bunch of lies and exaggerations!"* And they will castigate and threaten the messenger: *"This book is full of Hate." "She's just a liar! A bigot! And a racist!!" "The writer hates Obama because he is black!" "The writer hates Muslims!" "She is an Islamophobe!" "She has insulted Islam!!"* And then they will soothe you with: *"You are too sophisticated to believe that quack."* And contradict themselves with: *"Besides, the fire is just burning your neighbors. It is nowhere near you!"*

And I ask you again:

Will you believe Obama, the Islamists and the JournoList and wait in a trance until you and your country are burned to a crisp?
Or
Will you wake up and shout "Good God!! There really is a fire!" . . . ?

So, have the Islamists succeeded in their wildest dreams?
Read Part IV to find out.

Part IV of IV

Obama is waging *Stealth Jihad* against America

Table of Contents

Introduction

Introduction

Listen to Obama explain his Muslim Faith and read the details:
http://www.youtube.com/watch?v=Dc3PzHKCVGM&feature=player_embedded#!
http://conservapedia.com/Barack_Obama%27s_Muslim_Heritage
http://conservapedia.com/Muslim_agenda_of_the_Obama_administration

Admit it. You already had great doubts about Obama. But the two most powerful groups in America—the Media and the Islamists—tricked you into voting for him. In Part I, you understood how the Media helped hide Obama's secrets and tricked you into voting for him. In Part II, you understood Islam and how Islamists have tricked Europeans and pursued a Stealth Jihad to convert Europe into Eurabia. In Part III, you understood how Muslims are tricking you and pursuing a Stealth Jihad right here in America. And in this Part IV, I will tie these threads together and show you what Obama is doing to our country. I trust you will have the courage to face what your instincts tell you is true.

This is serious stuff; so don't waste my time and yours screaming about "racism." Obama is not an American Black. His American half, through his mother, is White and the other half, through his father, is African and Muslim. And don't talk to me about "Hate" and call me an "Islamaphobe" either. First, make up your mind: either it is OK to be a Muslim or it is not. If a Muslim is the same as a Hindu, a Buddhist, a Jew or a Christian; then it is not "hate" to say Obama is a Muslim. If, on the other hand, (a) Islam is not a religion but rather a very dangerous religious/political/military ideology, and its Qur'an commands all true Muslims to do Jihad against us and destroy us; and (b) in Muslim countries, non-Muslims are persecuted for practicing their religion and forced to live like Dhimmis, aka slaves or serfs; then it means extreme danger to you and our country. But it is still not "hate." Just as the Park Service doesn't "hate" grizzlies but simply warns you about the dangers; so it is with me. I don't "hate" Obama or Muslims. But I am warning you, because it is imperative that you figure out for yourself whether or not Obama is a Muslim, as I say he is; so you will watch what he is doing, and realize he is destroying America.

Also, don't tell me that 1.2 Billion Muslims are going to rise up to attack me. Of those 1.2 Billion, half are women. And they couldn't possibly want to remain as they do now, being totally subservient to men, and being subject to genital mutilation, rape and "honor" killings. Then, there are the vast numbers of decent and moderate Muslims who have escaped from the strictures of Orthodox Islam and are living in non-Muslim controlled countries. They want to get along with everyone; have no desire to "kill the infidel," like orthodox Muslims do; or be subjugated by Orthodox Muslims. Then, there are those Muslims who are neither radical Orthodox nor even more radical Salafist, living in Muslim countries, who have participated in the Arab Spring, and who are crying out, and even dying, to get our American freedoms for themselves. None of the above groups, which constitute the vast majority of those 1.2 Billion, would want to silence people like this writer. In fact, it is in their interest that the extremists be exposed. It is only the extremist and radical Orthodox Muslims that seek to destroy those with an opposing point of view. Today, these extremists profess to speak for the moderates; but they will destroy the moderates as soon as they get the opportunity; just as the rulers in Syria and Iran are killing the moderates within their borders.

Chapter 1

Obama confuses us because he says one thing and does another

What do you know about Obama? . . . Nothing at all! You knew absolutely nothing about his personal and professional life; and nothing about his eligibility, his brilliance, his socialism or his religion in 2008. So, when you last voted for him, you knew nothing. **And you know nothing even today**.

The last election was a triumph of Media marketing over substance; promoting Obama as the "American Idol." He bounded onto the stage with his great, practiced smile and used the reverb to bring power to his voice as he read from his teleprompter, what someone else had written for him. And the Media assured us *"He was the most brilliant man living!" "The world would love us now!" "The only way America could redeem itself of its sin of slavery was by electing a black man!"* Women fainted. Others lined up for hours "to collect some of Obama's stash," and believed he would make them rich. The excitement reached fever pitch. Like a giddy teenager, you fell for the good-looking dude who promised "Hope!" and "Change!!" And you handed over to him, our country, its great traditions and its enormous wealth.

Obama confuses us because he says one thing and does another: As you have seen in Parts II and III, Islam is not a religion but a religious/political/military ideology that seeks to destroy opposing ideologies like ours. Obama has permitted the installation of Mega Mosques throughout the country, especially in the Bible belt, right next to Churches. These Mosques are preaching a virulent strain of Wahhabi Islam, which views us as the enemy to be defeated. Obama says he is controlling the border and preventing illegals from entering. But he gets together with 19 foreign countries to sue Arizona, which is actually trying to prevent illegals from entering. He is importing the most primitive and violent Muslims, the Somali Muslims, whom he is setting up as our overlords and who are creating havoc in many quiet little towns in the hinterland.

He says Dictators should not be allowed to kill innocent civilians and sends our military to bring down the Dictator, Muammar Gaddafi of Libya. But he fails to take action against another Dictator, Bashar Assad of Syria, who is killing thousands more. And he just talks endlessly about Iran; but fails to prevent them from advancing their Nuclear Bomb program; or to give any support to the poor Iranians who are crying out for democracy and some rights for themselves.

He says he is "focusing like a laser" on getting jobs for Americans. But he cancels deep sea drilling, drilling for oil in Alaska, closes down virtually all coal plants and the Keystone Pipeline; all of which cost us huge job losses. And he provides US funding for deep sea drilling in Brazil and promises to buy their oil. He spends trillions on TARP, Stimulus and other programs supposedly to get us jobs and improve our economy. But 80% of this money has been wasted on Green Energy projects owned by his cronies, which do not produce many jobs here; which purchase their solar panels from China; and most of which are now going bankrupt. And though the number of people working has actually dropped and our economy has not improved; he keeps spending Billions more and putting us further into debt. He has set up a cadre of unconstitutional appointments, his Czars, his EPA, his DOE, his DOJ and other organizations, to stymie Corporations and prevent them from growing and providing jobs.

He took an oath to defend our Constitution, but he is shredding it with his edicts against **Religious Freedom**, demanding that Catholics pay for abortion pills, i.e. abortifacients; his war against **Freedom of Speech**, using the Executive Branch to bring constant pressure on Fox News or mustering his legions to try to silence Rush Limbaugh and by asserting the right to shut down the Internet; with his violation of the **Takings Clause**, taking away the property rights of bond holders in the Chrysler and GM bankruptcies to favor labor unions with other people's money; with his violation of the **Second Amendment Right to Bear Arms**, with his Fast and Furious ploy and his strong support of the U. N. Resolution which prevents us from owning guns; and with his violation of the **Advice and Consent Clause** by brazenly bypassing the Senate and instead using "recess" appointments, even when Congress is not in recess, to fill Administrative posts with left-wing appointees who could never obtain Senate approval.

Obama's administration is replete with examples of his total disregard and disrespect for the other branches of our government: He tells the EPA to implement the financial equivalent of cap and trade (not passed by Congress) through punitive regulations that will make it prohibitive to use carbon-based energy and other products manufactired with petrochemical feed-stocks. He tells the EPA to reject Texas' air pollution control plans properly adopted by the state of Texas using legal arguments that have already been rejected by the Supreme Court. He tells his Department of Labor to bring a lawsuit against Boeing, to intimidate and prevent them from opening a newly built plant in a right-to-work state, South Carolina, which would have created 2000 jobs. He tells his Homeland Security officials to cease enforcing our immigration laws generally and then brings legal action against the State of Arizona to prohibit them from enforcing their State law modeled almost exactly on federal law; a position so outrageous his own Supreme Court appointees refused to give it credence. Then, he tries to intimidate the Supreme Court as it deliberates ObamaCare by declaring that it would be an unprecedented, extraordinary step for "unelected judges" to "overturn a law that was passed by a strong majority of a democratically elected Congress." (Giving new meaning to the term "strong": a bare 219 to 212 in the House and the minimum of 60 aye votes in the Senate.) He has violated the separation of powers by stating his agencies do not need to honor FOIA requests made by the public, a direct violation of a law passed by Congress; thereby ensuring that we, the public, cannot find out what he is doing. Little wonder you are confused.

But do you remember, back at the end of Part III, when I asked you to imagine what Islamists would dream of, if their wildest dreams for America could come true? Isn't Obama fulfilling their wildest dreams?

The only way to explain what Obama is doing is to recognize that he is acting as a Muslim, pursuing Muslim interests: You ask: "What is he doing to further Muslim Interests?" In this Part IV, I will show you what Obama is doing to our country. And I will demonstrate to you how it parallels what Socialists do in Third World Countries and also parallels, **exactly,** what Militant Islamists are doing in Britain and the rest of Europe. As you go through each chapter, ask yourself: ***"Does this benefit America? Or does it benefit Obama and Islam?"***

Chapter 2

Keeping the border open at all costs, knowing Terrorists are Infiltrating

The Federal government owns 650 million acres in the Western States:[1] Much of this is in the Border States where more than 40% of California, New Mexico, and Arizona are government lands.[2] While that is not the whole story, this situation exacerbates the failure of our government to control the border, because when illegal immigrants cross the border they find ready hiding places on and unseen traffic corridors through federal lands with minimal to no oversight. When Obama refuses to control the borders; it means that anyone can come in illegally and penetrate deep into or country.

The FBI and Homeland Security have confirmed that terrorists are entering the United States from our Southern border.[3] They come from many breeding grounds of terrorism, notably in large numbers from the Taliban in Afghanistan and the Al Shabaab from Somalia. They migrate to cities like Detroit and New York where they can hide. Sleeper cell attacks have already taken place in the U.S. The first attack on the World Trade Center Towers in 1993 was the handiwork of a sleeper cell. The terrorists are patient and are waiting for the time to be right. A radical jihadist group responsible for nearly 50 attacks on American soil is operating 35 terrorist training camps across the nation, but the U.S. government refuses to include the organization on the State Department's list of foreign terrorist organizations Jamaat ul-Fuqra, known in the U.S. as "Muslims of America," has purchased or leased hundreds of acres of property—from New York to California—in which the leader, Sheikh Mubarak Gilani, boasts of conducting "the most advanced training courses in Islamic military warfare."[4]

Texas officials state that large numbers of illegals are entering this country who are not Hispanic. These illegals, who are working round the clock to infiltrate the U.S., are unable to speak Spanish and speak with an accent that is not native or Spanish. Homeland Security shows more than 40,000 illegals from countries "Other Than Mexico" or "OTM"s were apprehended in 2003-4. The number rose to 120,000 illegals in the 1st 6 months of 2005.[5] A congressional report states 1.2 million illegals were apprehended in 2004 and of those 650 were from terror-sponsoring countries. These OTM's wear patches on their jackets indicating they come from countries where Al Qaeda is active.[6] True, these infiltrations arose during the Bush administration, but they continue today at ever-higher levels today.

Knowing Terrorists are infiltrating into America through our southern border, Obama has done nothing to help the border patrol do its work. In fact, his rules hinder them. Vast tracts of Wildlife Refuges and National Monuments are so dangerous that the Bureau of Land Management has actually posted signs[7] warning U.S. citizens not to enter them, essentially ceding millions of acres of American land to Mexican drug smugglers and illegals, including terrorists. This includes 478,000 acres of the Sonoran Desert Monument, 3,500 acres of Buenos Aires National Wildlife Refuge, the Organ Pipe Cactus National Monument, 129,000 acres of Ironwood Forest National Monument, the Cabeza Prieta National Wildlife Refuge and 1.8 Million acres of Coronado National Forest, located in south-eastern Arizona and south-western New Mexico. These areas are being trashed by illegals. Nevertheless, because of the "environmental concerns" of the Obama Administration, our border patrols are forced to patrol on foot or on horseback.[8] The BLM has actually put up signs warning Americans not to enter American lands.[9]

Obama does nothing to discourage illegal entries, and in fact, to the contrary, his policies clearly encourage more illegal entries. Obama has permitted "Sanctuary Cities," like Los Angeles and San Francisco, which protect illegals in violation of Federal Law. Sanctuary Cities are now going broke under the increased burden of providing schooling, health care and various welfare programs to the large number of illegals in these cities. The city of Maywood, California was not only a Sanctuary City, but also a safe haven for illegal aliens seeking protection from deportation. Now, it has disbanded its police force and fired all its public sector employees because it has nobody left who is paying taxes and it can no longer afford to pay any workers.[10] *San Bernadino is a major California city that filed for bankruptcy on July 11, 2012. it is also a sanctuary city.*[11]

Obama has vigorously opposed States like Arizona that seek to prevent entry of illegals. Arizon'a laws actually mirror Federal law and merely provide that state and local law enforcement can enforce the federal law while performing their state or local duties. What's wrong with that? Well, as Obama's solicitor general said, it interferes with Obama's policy, which is to refrain from enforcing immigration laws at all. Even Justice Sotomayor, Obama's appointee, had trouble understanding that argument. And, while apologizing in countless countries around the world for American "interference" in their affairs over the years, Obama got his Justice Department to solicit 19 foreign countries to join him as he tried to inflict a beat down on Arizona.[12]

Of course, merely having an intergovernmental dispute with the State of Arizona is not good enough for Obama. He has to take the next step of telling Maricopa County, AZ Sherriff Joe Arpaio how to run his Sheriff's Department -remember his nationally televised lecture to that policeman in Cambridge? Obama's Injustice Department is investigating Sheriff Arpaio's Sheriff's Department for allegedly systemic practices of discriminatory policing and racial profiling against Latinos.[13]

Obama's Justice Dept. has also brought suit against a rancher, Roger Barnett,[14] who owned property on the Mexican border, which was constantly overrun by illegals.[15] Barnett had turned over 12,000 illegals to the authorities in the past 10 years. But instead of awarding him a medal, Obama's Justice Department actually claimed $32 Million[16] in damages from Barnett for "civil rights violations" of the illegals and for Barnett's "infliction of emotional distress" on the illegals![17]

The Sonoran Dessert is overrun by illegals who destroy the beautiful desert and create an ecological disaster with their trash and feces.[18] These illegals sometimes rape women and signify their conquests by hanging the women's bras and panties on a tree.[19]

Instead of controling the border, Obama has opened it up to illegals. Even worse, he has actually appointed a new Czar, Andrew Lorenz-Strait, as the nation's first public advocate to handle illegal aliens' complaints against ICE and Homeland Security![20]

On March 6, 2012, the ICE unveiled a $32 million 608-bed Immigration Detention Facility in Texas.[21] Only 4 people are housed in each room. There are TV's tuned to English and Spanish channels, microwaves and board games in the common rooms and washers and dryers in the laundry rooms. The Karnes facility is compliant with Obama's decrees for all detention facilities. It has a gym with weight-lifting equipment, a soccer field, indoor and outdoor basketball courts and sand and nets for beach volleyball. There's a law library, a walk-up pharmacy and a computer lab offering free Internet access. There are 117 pay phones charging cheap rates for both international and local service. Illegals have unfettered access to interpreters and legal services. Other benefits[22] include special "ethnically appropriate" meals, female hormone treatment for transgender detainees, abortions, undisclosed medical treatment, mental health services and access to preferred-religious materials.[23] Does it make any sense to spend this kind of money on illegals at a time when ordinary Americans are hurting?

The 9th Circuit just put its 7 deportation orders on hold pending Obama's new standards for the conduct of our ICE and Border patrol agents. And this has also cast doubt on whether any of the 1.6 million deportation cases pending before the courts could proceed.[24]

Take a double dose of extra strength Excedrin before you read the rest of this. Based on data for calendar 2005, $11 to $22 Billion is spent each year on welfare for illegals. $2.2 Billion a year on food stamps, WIV and free school lunches for illegal aliens. $2.5 Billion for Medicaid. $12 Billion for primary and secondary school education for illegals. Another $17 Billion for education of American-born children of illegals. $3 milion per day to incarcerate illegals, who commit two-and-a-half times the crimes as American citizens do. Illegals, commit nearly one million sex crimes a year and constitute 30% of all federal prisoners. A total of $90 Billion per year is spent for Welfare and Social Services for illegals. In 2005, 4-10 million illegals crossed the southern border, as many as 19,500 from terrorist countries. Total cost: $338.1 Billion a year.[25] You just know that the ballooning growth of the federal budget includes vast increases in expenditures on various welfare and social services for illegal immigrants in the seven years since.

Knowing illegals, including terrorists, are entering from our southern border, Obama has forced our border patrols to go on foot or on horseback to apprehend them. He has permitted cities to offer "Sanctuary" to illegals. And he has worked with foreign governments to sue Arizona to prevent it from enforcing state laws which mirror Federal laws against illegals. Obama has sued a Sherriff and even an individual who was aprehending illegals. He has appointed a Czar to protect the interests of illegals. **Do you really believe this President is interested in preventing terrorists from entering into America?**

Chapter 3

Importing people from
terrorist-sponsoring countries into the U.S.

The US provides resettlement for more refugees than all the other countries of the world combined. The entire refugee aid program has a $1 Billion dollar budget. Refugees are chosen by the U.N. (a majority Muslim body) and then sent to America with no training, no verification of their education or skills and no verification of their willingness to assimilate into America.[1] The Office of Refugee Resettlement ("ORR") spent $206 Million for cash and medical assistance in 2008.[2] But it has failed to produce a breakdown of ethnic groups they are bringing in because it has failed to provide any statistics for the years after Obama took office, namely 2009, 2010 and 2011.[3] (*It should be noted that this failure to provide statistics and information is typical of the Obama administration's modus operandii. When the news is bad; such as ORR statistics, or labor department statistics, it doesn't get reported! At least, not until it can be massaged to sound good for Obama!*)

Of all that is bad about Islam, perhaps Somalia exemplifies the very worst; and it is from there that Barrack Obama is unleashing a new form of terrorism on America.[4] And that fact may at least partially explain why there are so many Somalis among us, despite how inappropriate they are for America.

Refugee Resettlement Watch has determined that America has accepted more than 150,000 Somalis. Somalis are a primitive, nomadic people who normally practice polygamy, wife-beating, and female genital mutilation (at a rate of 98 percent prevalence, according to the World Health Organization). They are Muslims and keep their females covered up in the Islamic style. Plus, they are known for jihadist hostility to Western values, except money (supplied by the unwilling taxpayer) of course. These terrorists, known as al-Shabaab, are affiliated with Al-Qaeda. It was the Somalis who dragged the body of an American Soldier through the streets of Somalia. Remember *Black Hawk Down*? And it is Somali pirates who are killing passengers and demanding ransom for the ships and crew that they capture. Somalis are completely unwilling to assimilate into the American culture. Instead, they demand that we accommodate to their various barbaric practices.

When you look at reports from the various states, it is obvious that Obama has converted the Refugee Resettlement program into one which allows terrorst-sponsoring countries to send "refugees" here. However, this Refugee Resettlement Program has many supporters who get money from it and who, therefore, support it. In 2008, Catholic Charities got $58 million and Lutheran Immigration Services got $39 million.[5]

In meatpacking plants in Nebraska, Colorado, Kansas, Minnesota and Tennessee, Somalis demand scheduling that accommodates their Islamic prayers 5 times a day and time off for the month of Ramadan. This has led to fights with Blacks and Mexicans who are expected to take up the slack as Muslims take time off to "pray."[6]

Violent Somali street gangs have grown into vast criminal enterprises, as shown by the arrests of dozens of Somalis in three states in Minneapolis-St. Paul, Minnesota;[7] Columbus, Ohio and Nashville, Tennessee in November 2010 for child prostitution, safe cracking, and car theft. Three Muslim gangs called the Somali Outlaws, the Somali Mafia and the Lady Outlaws were forcing teenage girls into prostitution. Three Muslim women were charged with attacking key prosecution witnesses.[8] In Minneapolis-St. Paul, 29 Somali Muslims were indicted for kidnapping, raping, and selling underage white girls. The indictment accuses the gangs of finding and recruiting young girls for the purpose of prostitution in exchange for money and drugs between 2008 and 2010.[9] Other evidence points to an international reach of crime that includes credit card fraud, burglary, and witness tampering.[10] *If you look back to Part II, you will find the identical pattern of rape of underage white girls by Muslims taking place in Britain and other European countries too.. In Britain, the authorities ignored the problem for decades. In America, our media are also down-playing this problem. See the pattern?*

According to Representative Peter King, who had the tremendous courage to conduct hearings on the matter, more than 40 U.S. nationals have gone to Somalia to join the *Jihad.*[11] But, of course, some insist that Representative King is a *"racist"* and demand that we ignore his findings! Once again the claim arises, *"If there is a single Muslim who is not a terrorist, then you cannot call any Muslim a terrorist."* Incidentally, the reverse holds true for Christians, *"If any white person, not even a Christian, and not even white, like George Zimmeran, is found to be a terrorist or murderer or racist, then every Christian is a terrorist, murderer and racist!."* I have no doubt that Obama will punish Representative King by importing plane-loads of Somali "refugees" and settling them in Representative King's district! But Representative King has the courage to face all of that. We should make careful note of who, exactly, is putting pressure on Representative King. Right there, we will locate the Islamic supporters who are pursuing *Stealth Jihad* against America. Please, Representative King, I beg you, name them and out them!

Muslims also hate gays. Muslims in Minnesota chase and beat up gays.[12] In Washington, D.C. two Muslim youths brutally beat up two Georgetown medical students after asking if they were gay.[13] The media fails to report these crimes. Even in San Francisco, an actively gay-friendly city, when three Muslims fired a BB gun in a gay man's face, the media remained totally silent. And though the police did acknowledge that the suspects had come to San Francisco to target gays; they did not report this incident for 5 days and then, euphemistically called them "urban youths" and did not report the religious affiliation or the motive of the men.[14]

So now, under Obama, we have established a new hierachy for "Hate Crimes" and "Discrimination." Christians and whites are at the bottom of the pecking order. No one can ever commit a *"Hate Crime"* against them. Not even, as in Shrriff Arpaio's case, when an Obama supporter threated to kill him and his family.[15] Not even, as in the New Black Panther case, when blacks stand outside polling booths with nightsticks and batons and threaten whites who try to enter to vote.[16] And not even when black youths chase down a 13-year-old kid coming back from school, catch him as he is trying to get into his house, say "you get what you deserve, white boy," pour gasoline on him and set him on fire![17] And not even when, in Mobile, Alabama, on April 23, 2012, five months after black Tayvon Martin was shot by a hispanic George Zimmerman in Florida, twenty adult and teenage black males storm the home of a white man, Matthew Owens, and beat him up with brass knuckles, bricks, chairs, bats and steel pipes until his whole body is drenched in blood; and call out, as they are leaving, "Now that's justice for Trayvon!"[18] And not even when over 100 black youths attack a white couple as they stopped at a red light in Norfolk, Virginia, that the blacks considered their own area. In fact, the local policemen wrote this up as a "simple assault." And the local newspaper, for whom the victims worked and from which the victims took a week off to recover from their injuries, concealed all traces of this attack until national media attention forced them to acknowledge the black attack on whites had taken place.[19]

Next come blacks. Virtually anything a white does to a black is a *"Hate Crime."* If whites elect a Black President, they are still *"racists,"* but sort-of temporarily absolved from their "crimes." And no matter how Obama has destroyed the economy and America's institutions, if whites fail to re-elect the Black President; why then, they are reconstituted as *"racists!"* By this reasoning, whites will always be *"racists"* until they cede all power to militant blacks. *Should I tell all my white friends, "just get used to it?" Or tell them to develop a spine and confront these ridiculous allegations?*

Gays used to have a higher priority than Blacks. If a black and a gay got into a fight, it would be the black that comitted the *"Hate Crime."* But now, under Obama, we have a new top category: Muslims. If Muslims beat up gays because they are gays, it is not a *"Hate Crime."* It is hardly a crime at all. Just some attack by some amorphous "urban youths"! See the parallel to Britain where attacks by Muslim gangs on gays are called attacks by amorphous "Asians" as though the attacks could be by Indians or Philippinos or Chinese? In each case, the Muslim barbarisms are covered up. Anyone who objects will be called a *"racist"* and an *"Islamophobe."*

Should I say to all my conservative American friends, "Just get used to it"? Or should I tell them to observe the parallels to what has happened in Europe and speak out and object? What do you have to lose? You will be called an "Islamophobe," and put under tremendous political pressure. But you will be called that anyway. And, at least, you will save your country!!

Remember how Europe was converted into Eurabia? Militant Muslim "refugees" came in without any background checks; without the authorities recognizing that they would never learn the native language, assimilate into European culture or embrace Euroean norms; and with the authorities forcing the local poplations to accept these strangers and support them by paying enough taxes so the "refugees," their four wives and multiple children could obtain welfare and other benefits. Once the Militant Islamists reached a critical mass, they created separate Arab "states" within Europe where they followed Islam; obeyed only *Shari'ah* law; prevented native Europeans from entering; insisted women be covered; instituted all kinds of barbaric practices like polygamy, female genital mutilation, rape of women who were not fully covered in burkas, child pedophilia euphemistically called child "marriages" and "honor" killings where the Muslim male usually escaped any punishment; banned gays, pets, music and concerts; beat up European policemen and burnt their cars; refused to co-operate with the authorities in any criminal investigation; and ignored the European authorities and their laws.

Well, Obama is doing the same thing here in America. Obama has ordered the state of Tenessee to accept 10,000 Somali "Refugees" without any background checks, says Representative Rick Womick[20] (who, of course, has been called a *"racist,"* and *"Islamophobe!")*[29] Because of the various social and cultural problems the Somalis bring; and the huge amounts of money for welfare, remedial education, housing and even car payments that has to be spent on them by the State; State Senator Jim Tracy (another *"racist"* and *"Islamophobe"*) seeks to have his Tennessee legislature opt out of the Refugee Resettlement program.[21]

Under the radar, Obama has introduced violent *Jihadists* into many small towns in America, mostly in the Bible belt, but also in Seattle, Washington; Columbus, Ohio; Boston, Massachusetts and in many towns in New York and California. The plight of **Lewiston, Maine** is typical. Somalis have established an ethnic stronghold in this town. Actually, a strangle hold, would be a more accurate term. In this relatively poor town, many people have found government work providing services for the Muslim refugees, as social workers, security workers, remedial education teachers and the like. And so, they have become supporters of the concept of having "refugees." The town is all roiled up between these and the townsfolk who want "to do the right thing" and help the "poor refugees;" and others, who are appalled at the barbaric practices of the Somalis who have been foisted upon their town. The former group and the Militant Islamists, call the latter group *"racists," "Islamophobes,"* "xenophobes" and "nativists;" label them "unchristian" and "intolerant;" and accuse them of "discrimination" if the latter group dares to speak out.

It appears that the liberal authorities believe that all cultures are equal. A group of primitive, nomadic people who have no formal education, cannot read, have never had running water, electricity, heating, air conditioning, cars, houses, phones or even used a flush toilet; are deemed to be exactly equal to ordinary Americans. Their "right" to live in Muslim enclaves and violate the freedoms of their women, gays and children are deemed equal to our laws and standards. Their "right" to have ordinary Americans tax themselves to provide welfare and other support for them is deemed sacrosanct. And anyone who complains is abused as a "racist," and an "Islamophobe" and whatever other pejoratives there are; and thus shamed into silence.

Think about this. We now know from the European experience that these Muslims won't assimilate and don't even want to. So, why are we bringing these people into America? And then, if both cultures are actually equal, why are we trying to get them to assimilate into ours? Why are we spending millions teaching them English, how to drive a car and use modern toilets? Why are we bringing them here in the first place if their culture is as good as ours? See how liberals make you contort yourself into a pretzel trying to follow their edicts? It would be fun to watch, except that it is real people's lives and towns that the liberals are destroying.

Before we go further, consider the concept of "Discrimination." In Hawaii, raptors like crows, hawks and eagles are banned. Why? Because they would upset the delicate ecological balance of the native species and destroy them. Hawaii is "discriminating" against Crows. And that is perfectly o.k.

Now apply this concept to ordinary Americans like those in the town of Lewiston, Maine. Does it make any sense to forcibly introduce nomadic Muslims with their barbaric practices and who will never assimilate into American culture, into a bucolic American town? Will it not upset the "delicate balance" of the township? In fact, what Obama is doing is exactly like he was spreading botulism toxin in the various towns.

No good can come of it. And it will infect every town with its violence and its destruction of the social mores and culture of native Americans. *Tough words, I agree. But don't just yell at me. Tell me where I am wrong!*

According to its Mayor, Larry Reynolds, Lewiston, a city of only 36,000, has absorbed over 1000 Somalis in 18 months and cannot absorb more. He pleaded, "Our city is maxed out financially, physically and emotionally. Only half of Somalis have found work. The rest are supported by the taxpayers. General Assistance has more than doubled during the past 12 months and over half of the $528,000 budget is going to Somalis." Nevertheless, the poor Mayor has been reviled by Muslims as a *"racist"* and an *"Islamophobe!"* [22]

The use of the epithets *"racist," "Islamophobe" "xenophobe," "nativist," "right wing extremist;"* the labels *"unchristian"* and *"intolerant;"* and the accusations of *"discrimination,"* renders all those at the receiving end completely powerless. The Islamists know this. And that is why they use these epithets. And so, through manipulation and by shaming the locals, essentially by practicing *Stealth Jihad,* the Somalis have become the overlords of the local population, living off their hard work, and ridiculing the locals for their efforts to provide for them.

Why are we trying to bring nomadic tribes, with their culture stuck in the middle ages, into 21st Century America? Of what possible benefit is it to America to import these kinds of people? Are we trying to save the world? It never occurs to anyone to ask the Islamists how many Christians or Jews are treated equally in their Muslim countries. The usual answer from ill-educated Americans is that it doesn't matter. That we have to *"show the world that we are a better country."* But no one asks, *"Are you, yourself, going to show the world?"* Because the answer is, *"of course not".* These do-gooders always make sure they do not have to put themselves out. They just want other people to put themselves out. Next question: *"show whom?"* And *"for what purpose?"* Are we supposed to impress the rest of the world with our tolerance? Or are they laughing at us for our idiocy, committing suicide by trying to civilize tribes of people who will never assimilate into our culture? Did we take a vote on this? Did Congress authorize this? Of course not. This is entirely Obama's idea.

And do you realize what comes next? One, or many, of those Somalis will bomb something. In fact, they have already tried. As Representative King has told us, over 40 of them have gone to Somalia for terrorist training and some have returned and tried to inflict terrorist acts on us. Next, we call upon the police and the FBI to do surveillance of the Somalis. Next, the Muslim organizations will complain of "discrimination." Next, Obama will force our police and FBI to cave to those demands and keep a watch on everyone. Next, it will become obvious we will not have the resources to do watch everyone in America, in order to appease the Muslims and not watch just those we think are likely to be terrorists. And then what? We will go the way of Britain. Britain has now proposed it will spy into every single communication made by the public. Every single phone call, email or website visit, text messages and visits to social networking sites such as Facebook and Twitter would be tracked, monitored and stored in a massive database.[23] The British Public will lose all semblances of freedom and privacy. Big Brother will be watching everything they do. And that, my friends is what is coming to America.

See what I mean about Obama waging *Stealth Jihad* against America? Obama has destroyed our economy and rendered Americans poor and desperate for any job, even one providing services for Somalis. Then, he has imported *Jihadist* Somalis into this country and converted the Americans into *Dhimmis,* or slaves, providing services to their Muslim overlords; while, at the same time, paying taxes, *Jizya,* to support their Muslim overlords.

A Christian President would have focused on providing refugee status for Coptic Christians, or Iraqi Christians or some other Christian group that at least has a reasonable chance to assimilate. One has to ask, why does Obama want to import Somali Muslims? Why is he settling these people in the midst of the Bible belt? One only has to look at the European experience, described in Part II of this book, to get the answer.

The answer, of course, is that these violent and barbaric Muslims are the shock troops, being brought in by Obama to be the beachhead for advancing the cause of the global Caliphate by waging *Stealth Jihad* on America.

Chapter 4

Furthering *Jihad* against Christians in Africa

Obama's foreign policy is a disaster for America. Upon analysis of foreign policy actions that Obama has taken, it is clear he supports Muslim interests at every turn. Consider his actions in Africa.

Kenya: Even as he ran for the office of President of the United States, Obama was helping his fellow Luo tribesman, Muslim Leader Raila Odinga, wage *Jihad* against the Christians in Kenya. Obama always sides with the Muslims. Kenya's problems and their solutions are typical of how Obama handles international matters. Kenya was an oasis of wealth and stability in Africa and an ally of the United States. Mr. Kibaki, a Kikuyu Christian, was the President. The Kibaki government had been a leading supporter of the U.S. Government's efforts to dismantle Al-Qaeda cells in Kenya, which had been responsible for the Kenyan Embassy bombings in 1998.[1] The Kikuyus dominated business and politics. But they had also shared the riches of the country and intermarried with the other tribes and so the country was relatively stable.

Kenya was particularly vulnerable to terrorism because of its proximity to Somalia and Sudan. In fact, it was Kenyan Al Qaeda operatives who blew up embassies in Tanzania and Kenya during the Clinton Administration. Since the early 1990's, militant Islamic Imams have preached violence against Westerners, attacked the Kenyan government as the lackey of the United States and Israel and called for the implementation of *Shari'ah*.

Obama's fellow Luo tribesman, Raila Odinga is a Muslim and a violent and ruthless thug. His father, Oginga Odinga, was a communist. Raila was educated in East Germany and named his first-born son after Fidel Castro.[2] Raila Odinga had attempted a coup in 1982 and had failed. In 2006, when he was running for election against Mr. Kibaki, Odinga had signed a secret agreement with the leader of a major Muslim group in which he agreed to institute *Shari'ah* law in the whole of Kenya, including the Christian regions, in exchange for support. In addition,

Odinga had agreed that Muslims suspected of terrorism would be safe from extradition to the United States.

In the run up to the 2007 election, Odinga's supporters joined local Muslim terrorists in a pattern of violence designed to steal the election. The Kenyan press warned that Luos were stocking up on *parang*s or machetes.[3] Odinga would attend rallies of his opponents, publicly humiliate them and ask them to step down and support his party. In his strongholds, people who voted against anyone his party chose were killed. According to the Kikuyus, the Luos were stuffing ballot boxes in their areas and using violence and threats to prevent any Kikuyu representative from going near those polling places. (*Sounds just like the New Black Panthers in America, doesn't it?*)

In August and September 2006, in violation of the Logan Act, Obama went to Kenya and worked for the election of Raila Odinga.[4] Obama, in true community organizer fashion, followed his cousin's clearly racial strategy of arousing anti-Kikuyu sentiments and inciting violence against the Kikuyus. Obama's partisan support was so transparent that the Kenyan Government complained to the U.S. Government.[5] According to Joe Klein of Time Magazine, Obama had nearly daily conversations with the U.S. Ambassador in Kenya or with opposition leader Raila Odinga in the month leading up to the Kenyan election in 2007.[6]

What this means is that the press knew that Obama was heavily involved in Kenyan politics. But chose not to tell the American public of this involvement. Nicholas Kristof of the New York Times writes that Obama's grandfather was the first person in the area to wear western clothes rather than just a loincloth and that both Obama's father and grandfather were Muslims and polygamists. Kristof demonstrates his elitist view that we ordinary Americans should be kept in ignorance: *"I worry that enemies of Senator Obama will seize upon details like his grandfather's Islamic faith or his father's polygamy to portray him as an alien or a threat to American values. But snobbishness and paranoia ill-become a nation of immigrants, where one of our truest values is to judge people by their own merits, not their pedigrees. If we call ourselves a land of opportunity, then Mr. Obama's heritage doesn't threaten American values but showcases them. The step-grandson of an illiterate, barefoot woman in this village of mud huts in Africa may be the next president of the United States. Such mobility—powered by education, immigration and hard work—is cause not for disparagement but for celebration.*"[7] All this frippery was justification for concealing a key point about Obama:

Obama was actively supporting a Muslim candidate of his own Luo tribe, who had promised to inflict Shari'ah law onto Christian Kenyans, who opposed Kenya's cooperation with the U.S. to locate Al Qaeda operatives and who was an extremely violent man whose Luo tribe committed mass murder of Christians in Kenya! And, in fact, Obama has been exactly the "alien" and "a threat to American Values" that Kristoff was so anxious to conceal from us!

© SAYYID AZIM/AP/Corbis

Obama with his fellow Luo Tribesman, Muslim Raila Odinga Campaigning in Kenya against Christian Mwai Kibaki

Who gave Kristof the right to decide that these facts were not of importance to the American people? *What unmitigated gall!!* On any other subject, Kristof would be extolling the virtues of transparency and the sanitizing benefits of an open flow of information.

Mr. Kibaki, a Christian, ran on a platform of prosperity and vowed to keep Kenya's economy, one of the strongest in Africa, growing. Mr. Odinga, Obama's Muslim cousin, ran as a Socialist and a champion of the poor. (*Note once again, the similarity to our own Presidential campaign.*

217

Romney is running on a platform of prosperity through private business. Obama is running as a Socialist, promising to take from the rich and give to the poor!) When Raila Odinga failed to win the Presidency, the Luos rioted. They raped hundreds of Kikuyu women. They burned down 600 churches. In at least one instance, Christians, including men, women and children, had taken refuge inside their church. The Luos barred the doors, trapped the Christians inside, doused the church with kerosene and set it on fire.[8]

Despite all his violence and his obvious cooperation with Muslim extremists, Obama continued to support Raila. After he became President, Obama pressured the Christian President Kibaki of Kenya to agree to a power sharing arrangement with Raila Odinga, the Muslim contender, in order to stop the violence. Odinga was then appointed Prime Minister.[9]

Note this pattern carefully. First, the Muslims riot, loot, stir up ethnic tensions, destabilize the country and destroy its economy. Then, a "moderate" Muslim asks the Christians to sign a power sharing agreement. Then, usually, a do-gooder organization like Amnesty International adds pressure to the authorities by complaining of "police brutality against civilians" and by calling for "talks to ensure peaceful conflict resolution." The Christian authorities are terrified of the Muslim mobs and their violence. So they turn with relief to the "moderate" Muslims who seem to be offering a solution and agree to share power with the Muslims. Then, the Muslims use their newly acquired power to get more power. Finally, they destabilize the country with their terrorist acts and kick the Christians out of power.

Now, in Kenya, Al-Shabaab, an arm of Al Qaeda, has infiltrated Kenya from Somalia. In January 2012, Al Qaeda appointed Nairobi based militant Amir Ahmed Imam Ali to lead terror operations in the country.[10] And as of April 26, 2012, Stratfor, a private intelligence and defense organization, tells us that the U.S. Embassy in Kenya has informed U.S. citizens that it has received credible information of possible attacks against Nairobi Hotels and prominent Kenyan government buildings, meaning Raila Odinga's Luos are bombing and looting once again.[11] Elections are due in late 2012. Of course, if Odinga is not elected president, there will be more violence. *Sound familiar? Isn't this the same thing we are being threatened with if we don't re-elect our black President?*

Nigeria is under attack from Militant Islamists. What happens to it as it tried to cope holds very important lessons for America. Nigeria's economy will be Africa's biggest by 2015, on par with the economies of India and Brazil. It is Africa's top producer of crude, its oil exports have grown 7% since 2009 to 2.5 million barrels a day and it is the fourth largest supplier of oil to the U.S. The IMF forecasted that its economy would grow 6.6% in 2011. At present, the US supplies itself 7.7 Million barrels of oil per day. Saudi Arabia supplies 1.6 million barrels per day or 8%. Nigeria supplies 885,000 barrels per day or 5% of the US supply.[12] As such, Nigeria is a prize coveted by OPEC. Gaining control of Nigeria's oil would further assure America's serious dependency on OPEC oil.

Nigeria's population of around 160 million is projected to be the world's fourth most populous nation by 2050. With the growth in oil production leading a boom in retail and construction and under 19-year-olds comprising 50% of the population, foreign investors viewed this as a prime developing market. Nigeria is split roughly equally between prospering majority Christians in the coastal south and tribes in the north over which Boko Haram seeks to assert its control. Until recently Boko Haram had been dismissed as forest-dwelling fanatics armed with bows and poisoned-tipped arrows.

Southern Nigerians enjoy a per capita gross domestic product twice that of northerners. Though the majority of Southerners are Christian, millions of Muslims live among them. A great many of the extremely rich Southern Nigerians are Muslim. Aliko Dangote, a Muslim, is the richest man in Africa. His wealth dwarfs diamond kings, telecom giants and oil magnates, and his estimated $11.2-billion net worth is four times that of Oprah Winfrey's.[13] Many Christians were living in the north. The two groups got along reasonably well and the country was at relative peace.

But the Muslims in the north are largely uneducated, poor, unsophisticated and easy prey for militant outside agitators. The Al Qaeda terror network has been training Boko Haram, which means "Western learning is unclean." Boko Haram, a movement styled on the Taliban, also acknowledges an alliance with Al Qaeda in the Islamic Maghreb as well as Al Shabaab in Somalia.[14] Boko Haram, fed with a combination of anti-government and anti-Christian ideology and a mix of economic and political grievances, has now grown to 10,000 members.[15]

Intelligence reports say Al Qaeda taught the group to make car bombs, grenades from condensed milk tins and other improvised explosive device. In April 2011 more than 800 people died in protests after the election of President Goodluck Jonathan, a Christian. In the past decade, more than 1,000 people have been killed in Jos, the central Nigerian city that marks the dividing line between the country's dominant religions, Islam and Christianity. But the most recent attacks have centered on Kano a northern city.[16]

In 2009, Boko Haram accused police of shooting of its founder, Mohammed Yusuf, while in custody, a grievance at the heart of its anti-police violence. Since then, Muslim violence has increased with almost weekly occurrences of murders and bombings. Last Christmas 2011, they bombed churches while Christians were at services. In response, President Goodluck Jonathan placed the northern areas under emergency rule. In response to that, in January 2012, a Nigerian newspaper published a warning from Boko Haram, that Christians had three days to get out of northern Nigeria.[17] Boko Haram then started a wave of suicide car bombings, burning churches (often with women and children inside), burning Nigerian schools, bombing stores and workplaces, bombing soccer games and any place where people, particularly Christians, gathered.

On Easter Sunday, 2012, the militants bombed churches in the city of Jos. Police stations bear the brunt of Boko Haram attacks, particularly in Kano. In one particular instance, because their police station had been bombed, the police officers gather in the shade of trees across the street, many wearing a white robe rather than a police uniform because it is easier to make a getaway if they are attacked. Many police officers are missing. One ex-legislator said he hadn't seen his cousin, a police superintendent, in six months, that his cousin is in hiding and won't disclose his location. As a result of the total breakdown in law and order, many in this city of nine million people remain on edge. As of March 2012, three million Igbo Christians from the north have appealed to the government for help to relocate to the south.[18]

A 12-hour curfew has been imposed which prevents travel in and out of town. During the day, rows of shops stay closed as thousands of shopkeepers, many of them Christians, who had moved north, cram themselves, their families and their belongings onto overloaded buses to flee south. "Most men are sending their wives and their wares home," said Leonard Nwosu, president of a Kano community association that claims to represent three million Igbo people, largely Christian storeowners in the city. "A mass exodus has started."

Boko Haram leader, Imam Abubakar Shekau, declared in his first ever televised appearance that Boko Haram was "at war with Christians" and that its fighters "will continue to kill and are ready and willing to be killed themselves as martyrs." Ayo Oritsejafor, head of the Christian Association of Nigeria, called the killing of Christians by Boko Harem "systematic ethnic and religious cleansing." As such, Oritsejafor urged his followers to "do whatever it takes" to defend themselves against "these senseless killings," adding, "We have the legitimate right to defend ourselves."[19]

Africa's top oil producer and most populous nation is buckling under the weight of religious and political tensions. Given a raging Islamist insurgency, Christian genocide, and possible economic collapse, Nigeria may have already reached the breaking point. Though the Boko Haram attacks have not seriously damaged the oil, banking and retail industries that constitute the heart of Nigeria's economy, Nigeria has been compelled to devote nearly 20% of its budget to security.

The government has declared a state of emergency and authorized the police to search houses and makes arrests without warrants in patrols of the northeastern city of Maiduguri. The police are not particularly well trained or well qualified and are seriously underpaid. They may have been adequate at a time of peace, when civilians did not question their authority. But they are ill equipped to deal with a violent insurgency of the type that Boko Haram has initiated. Many police run away and hide. Those who remain complain their guns are antiquated, and that they lack handcuffs and other equipment. The jails are inadequate and need to be modernized. The government has its hands full trying to get its police force in shape to fight.

The police force in Maiduguri boasted of killing hundreds of alleged Boko Haram gunmen. Immediately, Boko Haram alleged police brutality by government forces. Amnesty International, which always take the side of what it perceives is the underdog, has accused the police of rape, theft and "unlawful killings."[20] Amnesty International has forgotten to denounce the killings and bombings of Boko Haram that precipitated the police action. And it fails to mention that there is no other way to stop the insurgency than by police or military action against the insurgency. And then, to add to the pressure on the government, Amnesty International has begun its usual chant of "*you are killing civilians!*"[21]

Government leaders hope Boko Haram may be running low on money after the death last year of Gaddafi. They have evidence that Gaddafi—who bankrolled insurrections across West Africa, including Nigerian oil militants—funneled money to Boko Haram's most hostile leaders. Boko Haram is fragmented and de-centralized according to authorities, making it difficult to identify its top leaders.

Mr. Jonathan's cabinet is quietly holding talks with envoys of Boko Haram who appears to be willing to talk. They gave the government nine demands. They ranged from job-creation programs to prisoner releases to state support for *Quranic* schools. Meantime, in early February, 2012, about 20 gunmen stormed a prison in Abuja, Nigeria's capital, and freed 120 inmates.[22] Boko Haram also seeks greater implementation of *Shari'ah* law throughout Nigeria. To the Christians, it is obvious that the wave of attacks and bombings is an ethnic cleansing geared towards driving the Christians out of northern Nigeria.

But the militant Boko Haram has no intention of stopping until everyone abides by *Shari'ah* law. In an interview with the Guardian on January 27, 2012[23] Abu Qaqa, a spokesman using a pseudonym, said the rights of the country's 70 million Christians, who represent half of Nigeria's population, "would be protected" under the group's envisioned Islamic state. "Even the prophet Mohammed lived with non-Muslims and he gave them their dues." But he immediately contradicted himself by saying that everyone must abide by *Shari'ah*, law: "There are no exceptions. Even if you are a Muslim and you don't abide by *Shari'ah*, we will kill you. Even if you are my own father, we will kill you. People underrate us but **we have our sights set on bringing *Shari'ah* to the whole world, not just Nigeria."**

Qaqa said Abubakar Shekau, their current leader, and others had travelled to Saudi Arabia for training and funding. "Al-Qaida is our elder brother.

During the lesser Hajj (in August 2011), our leader travelled to Saudi Arabia and met al-Qaida there. We enjoy financial and technical support from them. Anything we want from them we ask them." He said recruits from neighboring Chad, Cameroon and Niger had joined the group. A recent UN report said weapons from Libya might have been smuggled to Boko Haram and al-Qaida in the Islamic Maghreb via Chad, Niger and Nigeria. In a You Tube message posted recently, Abubakar Shekau threatened to bomb schools and kidnap family members of government officials. "Poor people are tired of the injustice, people are crying for saviors and they know the messiahs are Boko Haram," he proclaimed.[24]

While Nigeria tries to bring the insurgency under control and bring peace and stability to its country, America is failing to offer any support. Days after the Easter Sunday attack on a church that killed 38 people, Obama's representative, Assistant Secretary of State for African Affairs Johnnie Carson, obviously closing his eyes to the facts, said : *"I want to . . . stress one key point and that is that religion is not driving extremist violence either in Jos or northern Nigeria. While some seek to inflame Muslim-Christian tensions, Nigeria's ethnic and religious diversity, like our own in this country, is a source of strength, not weakness and there are many examples across Nigeria of communities working across religious lines to protect one another."* [25] When a mob attacked Muslims in Burma, the State Department issued an immediate condemnation. But while Boko Haram attacks and kills thousands of Christians, the State Department has been silent. Congress has repeatedly requested that Obama's State Department list Boko Haram as a terrorist organization. But it has refused. And now, Republicans in Congress are attempting to pass a law forcing Obama to act and designate Boko Haram a terrorist organization.[26]

Given all that has happened in Nigeria, and the public pronouncements by Boko Haram's leaders, no one can deny that militant Islam has infiltrated Nigeria and is inciting Boko Haram to undertake ethnic cleansing of Christians in northern Nigeria. There can be no possible explanation for the Obama Administration's willful and deliberate refusal to acknowledge these facts other than the Obama Administration's desire to encourage *Stealth Jihad* against Nigeria.

As in the Middle East and North Africa, sub-Saharan African nations share the same volatile mix of booming youth populations, low employment, and decades of ineffectual governance. *Shari'ah* law is already in place across 12 states in the Muslim-majority north, including Somalia, Sudan, Mali and Mauritania, which are all Muslim controlled now.[27]

As Pamela Geller says in her *Atlas Shrugs journal:* "The devout Muslim group Boko Haram's mission matches that of the jihadists in Egypt, Europe, Africa, and America *to the letter.* **And while Islamic supremacists gain ground across the world and swallow whole countries in the Middle East and North Africa; Obama has removed** *jihad* **and Islam from counter-terror training materials, and Muslim Brotherhood groups in America lead DOJ officials around by the nose.**"[28] [emphasis added.]

Chapter 5

Furthering *Jihad* in the Middle East and isolating Israel

If you look carefully at how Obama has handled the Middle East, you will realize that he has shown no care at all about Israel; that he has supported Middle East tyrants who are the enemies of Israel and ours; and that he has helped bring down Middle East Dictators who were friendly to Israel and us or at least neutral towards us.

America's biggest enemy is **Iran**. The mullahs had ruled Iran with an iron fist since Jimmy Carter allowed them to take over in 1979, over 33 years ago. Iran is steadily advancing in its Nuclear Uranium Enrichment program. Yet Obama has not done anything to stop them. In fact, on April 28, 2012, he signaled he will permit them to enrich any quantity of uranium up to 5% purity.[1] He has labeled Christian-American citizens "terrorists" and issued a threat assessment against them. But he has not said anything similar about Iranians. In 2009, Mir Hossein Mussavi, supported by the students and the ordinary people of Iran, won election against the incumbent Mahmoud Ahmadinejad, who was supported by the Mullahs. But the official declaration was that Ahmadinejad won. Iranians rose up objecting to the election fraud and asking for freedom. The Mullah's civilian armed forces, the *Basij* cracked down on the uprisings; killing many of them and dragging others away to be tortured. Neda Agha Soltan, a beautiful 26 year old, was gunned down by the *Basij* and died on the street. The students called out to Obama for help, "Obama, Obama, you are either with us or with them." But Obama was silent.[2] The revolution was crushed. Many were tortured and killed. And a great opportunity to bring democracy to Iran and neutralize our enemy was lost.[3] Why was Obama silent?

Then there was the Iran drone incident. The RQ-170 Sentinel is the most sophisticated unmanned aircraft America has, with cutting-edge sensor technology, sophisticated cameras and listening devices.[4] It has three different sets of GPS programs that, if the operator loses communication with the drone, enable it to fly back to its base and land itself.[5]

On December 5, 2011, an RQ-170 landed just inside the Iran border with Afghanistan in a remote desert area. It is not clear why it landed, but it appears that it was guided down, because it sustained only minimal damage. It is inconceivable that anyone would fly the drone, which is such a treasure trove of super-secret information, near enemy territory, without having planned what to do if the drone was captured. But the Obama Administration, the one we were told was the smartest in living memory, appears to have done so.

Obama had three choices: He could send a force to recover the drone, which we could have done. He could destroy the drone, which was really simple to do. Or he could ask Iran nicely, pretty please, would it return the drone? Anyone with a modicum of brains would have had the drone bombed before Iranians could find it. But the Obama Administration chose to allow the Iranians to capture it.

On April 24, 2012, the Christian Science Monitor showed a photo of our drone in front of their Azadi (Freedom) tower, and the Iranians bragged that they have reverse engineered it. They claim to have uncovered all the secret technology that we had used.[6] Once again, it appears that Obama bungled. But if you look at the actual outcome, the result it that he allowed our Muslim enemies in Iran to capture our most secret technology!

Just passing on to you a secret I learned in my native country. If someone appears to be bungling something, don't just assume he is stupid. Oftentimes, it is a cover for doing something really sinister. The bungling is just to put you off guard. Always check out the consequences of the bungling. Then, you can determine if it was stupidity or guile. So, why do you think Obama, the most brilliant man on earth, allowed the Iranians to get our top-secret technology?

Egypt is the largest and most powerful of the Middle-Eastern countries. If the world is to become a Muslim Caliphate, then Egypt must cease to be secular. This time, the dictator was Hosni Mubarak, who had ruled for 30 years.[7] Mubarak had stopped attacks on Israel and prevented terrorists from gaining access to Israel from his border. He treated the Coptic Christians decently. His was a secular regime and he prevented Islamists from taking power. Many Muslim Brotherhood members were jailed for being terrorists. Mubarak's army had trained in America and worked closely with us. And if not a friend, at least, Mubarak was not an enemy of America.

In the Arab Spring of 2011 in Egypt, there was a similar uprising to Iran's, with students protesting in Tahrir Square, begging for some freedom and democracy. This time, the Obama administration worked to help overthrow Mubarak. In so doing, Obama worked with the Muslim Brotherhood, from which the founder of Al Qaeda, Dr. Ayman al Zawahiri came. The stated goal of the Muslim Brotherhood is *"eliminating and destroying Western civilization from within."* [8] Dr. Essam Abdallah, an Egyptian liberal intellectual, writing in the Journal *Elaph,*[9] refers to reports coming out of Washington. These reports reveal the depth of the below-the-surface coordination between the Council on American Islamic Relations (CAIR), Hamas, Hezbollah, the Iranian regime and the Muslim Brotherhood in Egypt, Syria, Tunisia, Libya and Jordan.

The Obama Administration actually sent their operatives to help the Muslim Brotherhood gain seats in the Parliamentary elections that followed the Arab Spring.[10] They had their media put out stories of how the Muslim Brotherhood is not really a terrorist organization. According to the New York Times, the Muslim Brotherhood is comprised of "moderates" and "largely secular." They "want to build a modern democracy that will respect individual freedoms, free markets and international commitments, including Egypt's treaty with Israel."[11] Incidentally, the New York Times also thought that Ayatollah Khomeini was a great guy, far better than the Shah of Iran. But being wrong time and time again has never stopped the New York Times. The grey lady just gets older and stupider!

Egypt's current rulers actually copied Iran's 1979 behavior and detained ten Americans, including the Sam LaHood, the son of Roy LaHood, the U.S. Transportation Secretary. They were prevented from leaving the country. And the Egyptian authorities actually commenced trials against them for having "received illegal foreign funding and operating without government licenses." America has been supporting Egypt to the tune of billions of dollars a year since Carter negotiated a peace accord between Israel and Egypt in 1979. For the year 2012, Egypt had requested $1.55 Billion dollars.

When the Americans were imprisoned, Obama threatened to withhold funds from Egypt and cancel diplomatic relations until our Americans were released. *Oops! Sorry! That would have been an American President talking.* Instead, Obama promptly reassured the Egyptians he would not stop the multi-billion dollar assistance we give to Egypt.[12] And, as of April 2012, he has released $1.5 Billion of the funds to Egypt.[13] Apparently, the U.S. also paid a ransom of $5 million dollars, euphemistically called "bail," for the return of our Americans.

After the Muslim Brotherhood won substantial support in the parliamentary election, Obama stated that America has to work with, and officially recognize, the Muslim Brotherhood because "it had obtained popular support"![14] Yes, the same "support" that the Obama Administration itself had organized. As you can see, Obama uses the media to make us accept what was not acceptable to the American people. And he is incredibly devious in how he accomplishes his goals.

And now, Muslim Brotherhood operatives from Egypt are welcome guests at the White House.[15] According to George Selim, the White House's new director of community partnerships, CAIR, widely reputed to be an affiliate of the Muslim Brotherhood, has had hundreds of closed door meetings with President Obama's deputies.[16] Unlike Bibi Netanyahu of Israel, who is barely tolerated and has to beg for an audience! And Egypt's secular revolution seems to be coming apart at the seams. Two of the three choices the people have are either the Muslim Brotherhood supported candidate, or a Salafist, who practices an even more virulent form of Islam than Wahhabism. As of early May 2012, Salafists, the Gamaa Al-Islamiya, a terrorist group and the Muslim Brotherhood are on the march, proclaiming, "Save the Revolution!" "Victory or Death!" and "Jihad, Jihad!" Whom are they fighting? The Egyptian Army, the one group that had earned the respect of all of Egypt! And who is leading them? **Among their leaders was Muhammad al-Zawahiri, who had been recently released from prison for terrorist activities and who is the brother of al-Qaeda leader Ayman al-Zawahiri.**[17] (If you recall, once Obama killed Osama, Al-Zawahiri became the new al Qaeda leader. Or should I say, "Because Obama killed Osama, Al-Zawahiri was able to become the new al Qaeda leader"?) Either way, *Shari'ah* law will be imposed on the people of Egypt and their uprising will have been in vain.

Libya's Muammar Gaddafi, who had ruled for 42 years, was one of our allies in the Middle East. Since Reagan bombed Libya in 1988, Gaddafi had cooperated with the West, renounced war and even allowed western authorities to inspect his arsenal. I am no friend of Gaddafi, but he did not pose any threat to American interests and had not done so for long time.[18]

In the Arab Spring of 2011, Libyans rose up against Muammar Gaddafi. Obama sent our troops and jets to support the rebels. He claimed we were "leading from behind," but, in fact, it was our advisors on the ground and our military jets that provided the support to overthrow Gaddafi. In fact, the Obama Administration, which, abiding by liberal principles, should have consulted Congress before going to war, justified its action by claiming it was not a war, but rather a "Kinetic Military Action Promoting Humanitarianism"[19] It has been documented that Al Qaeda and the Libyan Islamic Fighting Group (LIGF) fought along with the Libyan rebels[20] and has infiltrated the anti-Gaddafi groups. Yet, the Obama administration provided training and support for them.[21] Very soon, now, we will be told that Al Qaeda is not all bad. That there are some good Al Qaedas and that Obama is helping only the good ones!

Syria's Bashar Assad is also a Middle East dictator who, together with his father, has ruled for 31 years. Bashar Assad provided heavy support to Saddam Hussein when we attacked Iraq to overthrow that dictator. Bashar provided a safe haven for Al Qaeda fighters to attack our forces in Iraq. Bashar Assad is a proxy for Iran and helps fund Hezbollah and Hamas, two terrorist organizations that encircle Israel. During the Iraq war, Assad kept Suria's border with Iraq wide open to allow Al Qaeda to infiltrate Iraq and kill or main American soldiers. Bashar Assad is no friend to America or Israel.[22]

There was an uprising in Syria too.[23] But though Bashar Assad has killed thousands of his people and is leveling whole cities with aircraft, helicopter gunships, tanks, artillery and military weapons; the Obama administration has been unable/unwilling to do anything but talk. When Hillary Clinton recently spoke out against the continuing Russian supply of helicopter gunships to the Syrian military, she was shut down by Obama's enforcers.

To summarize: The Middle East is ruled by Dictators who have ruled for decades; giving no freedoms to their Muslim populations; and sharing none of their country's wealth with them. This is what is in store for us if/when we are controlled by a Muslim ruler. And, as for Obama, when the Dictator is an avowed enemy of America and Israel, like Iran's Ahmadinejad or Syria's Bashar Assad; Obama does nothing. When the Dictator is neutral or an ally, like Egypt's Mubarak or Libya's Gaddafi, Obama works to dethrone them. **One has to ask, whose side is Obama on?**

Chapter 6

A Foreign Policy in Iraq
that also furthers the cause of *Jihad*

Obama has ensured that our hard won victory in Iraq would become a failure. For those who have forgotten, it was President Clinton who signed the Iraq Liberation Act of 1998 calling for regime change, the overthrow of Saddam Hussein and support of democratic movements in Iraq. It stated that Iraq had used, and continued to stockpile, various biological weapons like botulism and anthrax, was stockpiling SCUD missiles, which it had aimed at Israel and U.S. troops in Saudi Arabia and was developing other weapons of mass destruction. This Act was passed unanimously.[1]

For 12 years, Hussein thwarted UN Nuclear inspectors and to use the UN Oil for Food program to enrich himself. All politicians, including Clinton and other Democrats, called for regime change.[2] In 2001, both the House and the Senate passed resolutions authorizing George Bush to invade Iraq.[3]

However, when George W. Bush started Operation Iraq Freedom and toppled the Dictator Saddam Hussein; the Democrats, pretending that they had never supported the war at all, began the chant *"Bush Lied and People died!"*

It was George Bush's vision that if a large and powerful country like Iraq could be democratic, other countries in the Middle East would follow suit; and people in the Middle East would obtain their freedom from Middle Eastern Dictatorships. In fact, Bush was correct, witness the uprising of Iran in 2009 and the uprisings of Yemen, Algeria, Bahrain, Libya, Egypt and Syria in the Arab Spring of 2010-11. But Bush is, after all, anathema to the political left and the scapegoat for all of Obama's failings. How could we possibly give any credit to Bush?

Remember when Al Qaeda terrorists in Iraq captured four Blackwater contractors in Iraq? They mutilated and decapitated them, burnt their bodies and hung them from a bridge.[4] Of course, liberals, who sit behind their desks in comfort while others fight for them, will say that anyone who works for Blackwater deserves to die. But these were Americans providing security for our diplomats and others in a very dangerous place, Iraq. They were fathers, husbands and sons of grieving families. No one deserves this kind of death.

In 2004, four Navy SEALs were dropped by helicopter right into the battlefield to capture the terrorist who masterminded this atrocity, Ahmed Hashim Abed. An al Qaeda training manual captured by British authorities advises: "brothers must insist on having the opportunity to show that torture was inflicted on them by state security before the judge. Complain of mistreatment while in prison." Sure enough, Abed claimed he had been beaten and given a fat lip.

This fat lip, according to the Maj. Gen. Charles Cleveland, commander of Special Operations Command Central, required that all three SEALs: who risked their lives to capture this terrorist, must be court martialed for "abuse". One for supposedly "abusing" and the other two for "failing to protect the terrorist from "abuse" and for "covering up" the "abuse"!! The General insisted: *"The abuse of a detainee, no matter how minor, creates strategic repercussions that harm our nation's security and ultimately costs the lives of U.S. citizens."* [5]

The fact that terrorist training manuals advised terrorists to claim abuse when there was none; that Abed was lying; that court martialing our soldiers when they risk their lives to do their job demoralizes them and the rest of our Armed Forces; that his actions causes the terrorists to lose all respect for us; that this caused the Arab world (most notably war zone Iraqis and Afghanis) to laugh at us for our weakness and also lose respect for us; and that all of this "ultimately costs the lives of U.S. Citizens;" does not seem to have entered the spineless General Cleveland's mind. Our SEALs were under threat of jail for another 6 years until finally, one of them was cleared in April 2010 and the last found not guilty in May 2010.

On December 16, 2011, Obama handed over the terrorist Al Musa Daqduq to Iraq, without trying him for the murder of at least 4 of our soldiers. Senators John McCain, Mitch McConnell, Joe Lieberman, and

Lindsey Graham called the transfer of Daqduq "disgraceful," and argued that he should have been tried by a U.S. military tribunal. The White House said they decided to transfer Daqduq to the Iraqis because "it was the fastest possible way to bring him to justice."[6] My head spins. Obama and his best bud Eric Holder say they refused to lift a finger to bring Daqdaq to justice, because they do not want to use military tribunals established by the US Congress and blessed by our Supreme Court because they do not reflect fairness and justice, but sending him to Iraq is "the fastest possible way to bring Daqduq to justice."

Has he "been brought to justice?" Who knows? Our media will not ask. But I will bet you; Daqduq is back on the battlefield. Our 3 Navy SEALS were under threat of jail for an imagined "fat lip" claimed by a terrorist. But the murder of 4 Americans has been forgiven by our President.

Notice how Obama is corrupting the U.S. Army with his politically correct thinking. No doubt, General Cleveland will get many, many promotions; while any General who opposed this travesty will not. Notice also, how Obama shows more concern for Islamic terrorists than for American citizens who were killed by terrorists or for our own Navy SEALs who risk their lives for us.

Remember General Petraeus, whom the liberals called General Betray Us in a paid advertisement in the New York Times? Well, his surge in Iraq was successful and brought a measure of peace to Iraq. The three different sects, who had warred against each other for centuries, finally agreed to share power. Nuri al-Maliki, a Shi'ite supported by Iran became the Prime Minister; Kurdish Masoud Barzani became the President; and Ayad Allawi of the Sunni Iraqiya group supported by Saudi Arabia, got the speaker's post.[7] Shouldn't our Commander in Chief be focused on trying to maintain the benefits won with blood and treasure?

Are you kidding me? No way is he concerned about us. When the Army Generals recommended that the U.S. Army stay in Iraq to stabilize the country, they recommended that nearly 20,000 personnel remain to carry out counterterrorist operations, support American diplomats, and provide training and support to the Iraqi security forces. Under Administration pressure, that figure was whittled down to 10,000, which was judged to be the absolute minimum needed, by Defense Secretary

Leon Panetta and Admiral Mike Mullen, chairman of the Joint Chiefs of Staff. Obama, however, decided that only 3,000 to 5,000 troops were needed in Iraq post-2011. The only person known to agree with him was Joe Biden and the Iraqis were not willing to stick their necks out for such a puny force. Obama claimed victory, declared "promise kept" (his promise that US troops would be out by December 31, 2011) and proclaimed that we leave Iraq with our "heads held high."

A week after the withdrawal, al-Maliki put his Sunni opponent in jail. Al-Qaeda has returned. There have been a string of deadly explosions killing scores of civilians. And the country is hopelessly destabilized.[8] **Over 3500 of our troops gave their lives in this combat. And Obama has spat upon their sacrifice.**

Chapter 7

A Foreign Policy in Afghanistan that also furthers the cause of *Jihad*

Obama has also ensured that we will also lose in Afghanistan: Liberals always want our soldiers to kill the enemy but not kill any "innocent" civilians. This would be workable if this were the 18th century, when the two warring factions would line up opposite each other and fight until someone won. But, even as early as the Civil War, it started to become impossible to avoid unfortunate deaths of civilians. I can understand that our army should not deliberately target civilians. But when we are involved in a guerilla war, and the enemy hides amongst the civilians, what are we supposed to do? Think. Do you have a clue how anyone could catch a terrorist without hurting a civilian?

Nobody has any clue, except the Obama Administration. It has worked with Karzai to issue Rules of Engagement, the "Karzai 12," that will make your head spin. Or, if you are a parent with a kid in the armed forces, make you want to bring your child home right away. These rules are designated "top secret"—top secret from us, so we won't rise up and scream!! The Taliban, of course, already know them because they are benefitting from them and probably drafted them in the first place.

Here are seven of them: No night or surprise searches. Villagers are to be warned prior to searches. Afghan National Army, or ANA, or Afghan National Police, or ANP, must accompany U.S. units on searches. U.S. soldiers may not fire at insurgents unless they are preparing to fire first. U.S. forces cannot engage insurgents if civilians are present. Only women can search women. Troops can fire on insurgents if they catch them placing an IED but not if insurgents are walking away from where the explosives are.[1]

O.K. Let's get our instructions straight, put on our boots and go out on a raid. First, we have to let the villagers, and the terrorists hiding there; know that we are going to conduct a "surprise" search. Then, we have to go with Afghani units. By the time we round up our Afghani "partners," someone will have told the terrorists we are coming. And how can a US soldier give his full attention to the mission at hand, when he also needs to think about whether his Afghani "partner" is going to kill him? Can you catch a terrorist this way? Then, we cannot fire until they "prepare to fire." We are to watch them, like at the OK Corral, and wait until they draw first. Except they are hiding in the hillside or in somebody's house and we won't see them until they actually shoot us. What do we do then? Next, we can't fire if there are civilians present. But they hide among civilians, so we cannot ever fight. Lastly, we cannot fire even if we catch them placing an IED that will kill us; if they spot us first and turn and walk away. We have to let them get away so they can return and place more IED's to kill more of us. Now tell me, how many terrorists did you catch? Do you even want to go out on a raid? If not, why are we asking our soldiers to risk their lives this way?

The soldiers know these rules are idiotic. As one of them said, "We have to follow the Karzai 12 rules. Our soldiers have to juggle all these rules and regulations. But the Taliban has no rules." Many times, the insurgents escaped because of these rules. And the toll of U.S dead and injured is mounting. The U.S. Army now has to follow the Karzai 12 rules and break its own rules so it can bring women into combat zones to conduct searches on Afghani women.

One former soldier reminded me that even civilian Police Officers are allowed to use deadly force if they feel their lives are in danger. But that these Rules of Engagement required that one of our soldiers has to have 100% certainty he is facing a Taliban fighter before he can shoot to kill, making his job impossible and making it far more likely the soldier himself will be killed or captured. And so, he saves a bullet for himself so he would not be taken prisoner by the Taliban! Where is the American outrage at the monstrosity of the rules Obama has inflicted on our soldiers?

But the Taliban has no such restrictions. Our soldiers frequently have to face armed men hiding under burkas. The soldiers have now commenced a practice of asking the burka clad "woman" to say her name before they put forward our women soldiers to do the search. That way, they can determine if this is really a woman, or a terrorist planning to kill our soldiers. In fact, in May 2012, just hours after Obama flew to Afghanistan and declared that America was negotiating peace with the Taliban; burka clad Taliban detonated a suitcase bomb that killed seven civilians, most of them children, in a fortified guesthouse used by Westerners.[2]

Because of the lack of security, non-governmental organizations (NGO's) do not work there. The soldiers have to clear and hold an area before the NGO do-gooders will arrive. Once our soldiers do the dirty work, the NGO's arrive to "do good." Almost the first thing the NGO's do is to find fault with the way the war was conducted. How our soldiers didn't protect the civilians. How our soldiers used too much weaponry, etc. If they can discover enough "evidence" against our soldiers, they will delight in bringing it to Amnesty International or some such group so they can bring suit against our soldiers. These nincompoops never find fault with the Taliban and how they behave. They only prosecute our own people. If anything, the NGOs behave treasonously, buddying up to the Taliban, excusing all their bad behavior and blaming our soldiers. They do not even consider how difficult it is for our soldiers to have to follow all those Rules of Engagement and face an enemy that fights with no rules whatsoever and which will behead our soldiers if they capture them.

Why are U.S. based NGOs even allowed to go to the battlefield? Why do our soldiers provide security for non-U.S. based NGO's? They use our money, have no loyalty to the United States and do their best to put themselves up and tear down our soldiers. And once again, we have to defend ourselves as these liberal do-gooders tell us, *It doesn't matter what the Taliban do. We have to set a higher standard.* For what purpose? Whom are we trying to impress? The barbaric Taliban? They would only laugh at our weakness. Dear God, if the do-gooders really believe this, why don't they come out on the battlefield before it is pacified and show the world how America has that wonderful higher standard? Better still, why don't we withdraw our troops and send the State Department into Afghanistan? I am sure they could chit chat, sip some tea, negotiate peace and make friends with the Taliban; exactly like they are asking our soldiers to do. I simply marvel that our soldiers have the discipline they do. If it were me, I would shoot one of those whiny do-gooders and tell them to go get "compassion and care" from the Taliban.

While on patrol, one group of soldiers went to a Mosque and discovered handguns, which only terrorists carry. The Imam made no apologies and offered no information about how the guns came to be there, but he asked the army to provide his village with clean drinking water. But it was too unsafe for the NGOs to do what is clearly their job. So it fell on the soldiers, who are supposed to be prosecuting a war, to build the infrastructure to provide the water for the Mosque so we can "make friends" with the locals. Also, to "make friends," the US Army has opened a clinic in which they are treating the locals. Despite all this, Imam Sahed said, the U.S. Army "needs to go . . . . Between Islam and the infidel, there can never be a relationship!"[3]

Note carefully what the Imam said. "There can never be a relationship between Islam and the infidel." He didn't apologize for allowing armed terrorists who plan to kill us to hide inside his Mosque. He asked the US taxpayer to pay for, and our soldiers to do, manual labor, to provide him with the services he wanted. Then, he told us we were unclean and to get out.

Is it not obvious that the Afghanis totally disrespect us? If that is the attitude of Afghanis, why, in heaven's name, is Obama calling upon our Army to befriend the Afghanis? Why are we building schools, running clinics and doing all the rest of that stuff before we first get their respect? Why are we putting our soldiers in harm's way if we do not intend to prosecute a war?

Obama has also converted the war into a sort-of police operation. He is being advised by high powered attorneys, no doubt from Ivy League schools and hot-shot law firms, who are lawyering up the terrorists even before they are captured. Obama is requiring that the Army produce evidence from the battlefield sufficient to bring civilian trials against captured terrorists. If this standard cannot be met, the captured terrorist must be released.

Let me tell you how Obama wants it to work. After going through all the Rules of Engagement, our soldier finally captures a terrorist. He has to then call upon two other soldiers to stop fighting and witness as the first one reads the terrorist his Miranda Rights. Then, all three have to stop fighting and collect evidence, in sterile bags so it won't get contaminated, so they can prosecute the terrorist in a civilian court.

I am not joking. In several instances, Taliban detainees, who had been captured after being observed placing bombs in the culverts of roads used by the military in Kandahar were fed, given medical treatment and then released. The American soldiers had a mountain of evidence, including a video of the men planting the bomb, and chemical traces of bomb residue on their hands, but this was deemed insufficient. In another instance, the 2nd Stryker Cavalry Regiment survived an attack by a suicide bomber because his device failed to detonate. The soldiers managed to capture the suicide bomber. But he too had to be released. Internal Security Assistance Forces (ISAF) admits that releases like this are common. Though General Stanley McChrystal and General Petraeus had assured that their strategy would result in the control of at least 40 Afghan districts by 2010; this has not happened. The troops say it is impossible to hold terrain when the insurgents know that if captured, they cannot be held.[4] All that this "catch and release" policy is doing is maiming and killing our soldiers and destroying their morale.

Nighttime raids were the most successful tactic for killing the Taliban fighters and making progress pacifying the Taliban held provinces. And now, the Obama Administration has added another rule that our soldiers will only act as "support" for Afghani soldiers during nighttime raids. (I think the idea is that our soldiers must take orders from the Afghanis, and walk humbly behind them. But if there is trouble, then our soldiers must be the ones who risk their lives. Someone correct me if I am wrong!) If this were not enough, if there is credible intelligence that there is a Taliban target in the region, Obama now wants the Army to go to an Afghan Judge and obtain a warrant. Look at the implications of this order. Obama insinuates that our Armed Forces cannot be trusted to do their job. That someone superior to them, an Afghan Judge, has to grant approval for our soldiers to mount patrols that risk their lives!! Steve, who writes at America's Watchtower, puts it best: "*Never before in the history of warfare has a country willingly or knowingly provided advance notice of an operation designed at rounding up the enemy and Barack Obama is on the verge of doing just that.*"[5] In fact, Obama has since done exactly that which Steve feared. I don't know if there are Afghani Judges where the fighting is taking place. Even if there are, why do our Armed Forces have to take orders from an Afghan Judge?

Do you really think Obama is serious about catching the enemy? Or that he is concerned about the safety of our troops? Just for a second, let's contrast Obama's attitude with Churchill's: "*We shall go on to the end. We shall fight in France, we shall fight on the seas and oceans, we shall fight with growing confidence and growing strength in the air, we shall defend our island, whatever the cost may be. We shall fight on the beaches, we shall fight on the landing grounds, we shall fight in the fields and in the streets, we shall fight in the hills; we shall never surrender.*" "*We have before us an ordeal of the most grievous kind. We have before us many, many long months of struggle and of suffering. You ask, what is our policy? I will say: It is to wage war, by sea, land, and air, with all our might and with all the strength that God can give us; to wage war against a monstrous tyranny never surpassed in the dark, lamentable catalogue of human crime. That is our policy. You ask, what is our aim? I can answer in one word: It is victory, victory at all costs, victory in spite of all terror, victory, however long and hard the road may be.*"[6] So, what is Obama's concept of victory?

As you can see, the focus is now on making friends with the civilians, instead of fighting the enemy. God knows who thought up this stupid strategy. My guess is that it was those effete liberals at the State Department. The first thing they should have done is to study Islam. Second, they needed to analyze the Afghani culture. They have done neither.

Think. This is an alien culture. They do not have a history of civilization like the Iraqis do. They never have. Except in the few cities, they are extremely poor and live in tribes where tribal elders organize every aspect of their life. Their culture is an extremely primitive and hierarchical one and they have a sharply stratified society. At the top of the heap is the tribal elder, then the men and way beneath that, the women and children, somewhere near the cattle and livestock, or perhaps beneath the cattle and other livestock. Afghanis, especially their nomadic tribes, function solely on the basis of respect, enforced by fear of certain death for failure to show proper respect. Whom do they respect? People who are trying to be their buddies? Or people they are terrified of? What would King Abdullah have done if he went to Afghanistan? Would he prostrate himself and apologize left and right? Of course not! All Muslims, including Obama, prostrate themselves to King Abdullah. In short, if you are going to conquer, then you must behave like a conqueror.

Our style of ordering our soldiers to "show compassion" to the Militant Muslims who are trying to kill us, does no good whatsoever. It only earns us their contempt. It does not work in Britain or in Europe. It does not work in Lewiston, Maine. And it won't work on the battlefield either.

Their national sport, *Buzkashi*, is similar to polo, but played with the fresh bleeding carcass of a goat tossed or tugged away from one horseback rider to another. All civilized, just like our sports, right? Their literacy rate is only 34%.[7] And our soldiers are supposed to teach these people how to fight with our weapons when they can't even read the manuals. Like all Muslims, they also practice genital mutilations, polygamy and "honor" killings. 57% of Afghan girls under the age of sixteen, and many as young as nine, are in arranged marriages.[8] It is a common practice, known as *baad* or *baadi*, to sell a young girl, as young as 7 or 8, into slavery to pay off an elder's debts. The girl had less value to them than the livestock. The parents of the girls would choose giving the girl over giving livestock, which would bring in money. The child would be kept locked and tied up in a dark room, beaten, starved, made to work and raped. When she finally got pregnant, if she produced a girl, then her tribulations would continue. If she produced a boy, then perhaps, her life might improve.[9]

As of October 2011, the Taliban still enforced stoning deaths as punishment for adultery.[10] A young 19-year-old girl and a 25-year-old man ran away together to avoid arranged marriages. The two families had negotiated a payment from the boy's family to the girl's intended husband's family to avoid further punishment. But the Taliban insisted on the punishment of death and also insisted that the families attend the *"sangsar," the* "ceremony" of stoning to death. Note: they even have a name for the procedure by which they stone people to death!

They buried the girl in a four-foot hole. And then, the villagers took turns to throw rocks at her head until she was nearly dead. Then, they finished her off with a couple of bullets. They did the same thing to the man.[11] This is the barbarism they practice. They treat their women as chattel and barely better than livestock. And this is what our liberals consider equal to our culture!! And we are stupid enough to acquiesce in their demand that we treat their women with the utmost respect!! Don't our liberals even understand that the moment we order our soldiers to start showing their women such profound respect, while the villagers themselves have absolutely no respect for those same women; our soldiers have abased ourselves and relegated themselves to a position far lower than even their women and their livestock?

If we want to resolve this problem, the first thing we need to do is forget about all that stuff the liberals are saying and stop contorting ourselves into pretzels trying to please them. Liberals know nothing about Islam, the culture of the Afghanis, or how to win a war. All they do is hamper our soldiers. Actually, what they do is like that Monty Python skit—they cut off our soldiers' arms and legs and ask them to fight. And when we can't win that way, the liberals sneer at our soldiers and say things like *"The proud Afghanis have never been defeated by any force on earth!" "It was hubris on our part to think we could defeat them!" "We are mired in defeat in a disastrous foreign war!"*

What we need to do is command the respect of the Afghanis. *Incidentally, talking of respect, does the Obama administration show Christians any respect at all? Even the respect they demand that our soldiers show to Afghani women? This gives you a clue about what Obama thinks of us.*

Anyway, our soldiers need to command respect through fear. Afghani tribesmen need to be more afraid of us than of the Taliban; otherwise, they will always cooperate with the Taliban and double—cross us. Once we fight and defeat a tribe or village, we should wait until they come and ask us for mercy and help. And the terms under which we give any help at all is that they surrender the Taliban hiding amongst them. This way, they will respect us and not mess with us. This way, we establish we are the conquerors and won't have to waste blood and treasure fighting over and over again to hold the same ground.

But all we do is show weakness. In so doing, we ensure that more of our soldiers will be killed and none of our achievements will last for an instant after we turn our backs. There have been more than 30 insider attacks by our so-called Afghani partners in the past 2 years.[12] Many of these were fatal.[13] Last June 2011, following Obama's idiotic strategy and Rules of Engagement, we lost 66 of our soldiers, more than in any month previously.[14] On April 27, 2012, there was yet another murder of an American soldier and his Afghani interpreter by an Afghani partner. In the past four months, at least 16 of our coalition troops have been attacked by our Afghani "partners." This brings to at least 36, the number of international service members killed in Afghanistan in April 2012. Since 2007, more than 80 NATO members have been killed by Afghan security forces. More than 55% of those attacks have occurred in the past two years.[15] And now, even AP reports that while reporting overall numbers of soldiers killed by an Afghan in uniform, the DOD does not report insider attacks in which the Afghan wounds—or misses—his U.S. or allied target. It also doesn't report the wounding of troops who were attacked alongside those who were killed.[16] In June 2012, three more of our soldiers were killed by our Afghani "partners."[17] And yet, the DOD has acquiesced in Obama's policy that our soldiers must live inside compounds with Afghani "partners" and go out on missions with them.

When Obama was elected, he ensured that we would lose in Afghanistan by dithering around for months, and then refusing to provide the number of troops that the Army recommended as necessary to make the surge there work. In January 2011, he informed the world that the Afghanistan surge would not last more than 15 months and that all of the surge troops would get out of Afghanistan by September 2012, just in time for his re-election.[18]

Of course, this meant that Karzai would feel abandoned and look to someone else to support him once we left. No wonder he's sending money to his bank accounts abroad as fast as he can, chosen to side with the Taliban, ceased cooperating with us and regularly undercuts our authority in fighting the Taliban.

This was made abundantly clear during the *Qur'an* burning crisis of February 2012. Some soldiers were ordered to burn papers, which prisoners were using to communicate with each other. In this collection, there were some *Qur'ans*. If Karzai wanted to support us, he would have downplayed this and told his people it was an accident. But he didn't. People in the Karzai Administration informed the local populace, which is illiterate and could not have read the news on the Internet, which then started rioting and looting and murdered (yes, I use that word advisedly) 8 of our soldiers and coalition troops.

Obama and various military officials made the most abject apologies to the Afghani people. Incidentally, you now know why Obama apologizes and prostrates himself on behalf of America to other Islamic nations. It is his way of denigrating and abasing America! One of Obama's military staff even apologized to the Muslim populace in America! *(Did you hear someone in the Obama or the Karzai Administration apologizing to the American people for the murder of our soldiers? I missed it. You must have missed it too!)* Obama himself wrote a personal letter of apology to Karzai!! But this didn't stop Afghan soldiers inside the security compound from killing six of our troops.[19]

Obama actually said the soldiers who burned the *Qur'an* would "be brought to justice", implying that they did it on purpose; and that what they did was a capital offense. Essentially, Obama was enforcing *Shari'ah* law.[20]

He has even gone one step further and countenanced the possibility that he may hand over our soldiers to the Afghans. They, of course, would try our soldiers under *Shari'ah* law, without any attorneys, any rights, or any discussion of mitigating factors, such as following orders, or not realizing there were *Qur'an*s among the documents burned, or even that these were not intentional acts. In fact, none of the Constitutional protections that we provide to Islamic Terrorists will be available to our soldiers. They will be tried for burning a *Qur'an*. And for that "crime," they will be executed. Well, we have not done that (Thank God!), but do you think even for a minute that it was Obama's backbone that saved our soldiers?

Contrast this to what the Obama Administration itself did in 2009. It ordered the burning of Christian Bibles, which had been translated into Pashtun and Dhari and sent to Afghanistan. They forbade a soldier from handing them out during his off time, confiscated all the Bibles and burned them, so Afghanis would not be "offended" by our Bible.[21]

Did Obama demand (or even humbly request) that Karzai discover who killed our soldiers? He did not even ask for any apology for the killing. See the pattern here? Obama is more concerned about Islamic sensibilities than about the lives of our soldiers.

The Obama Administration has also agreed to hand over to Karzai the entire Bagram AFB and the 3000 prisoners captured by U.S. forces.[22] We would have spent billions on that base. And now, it appears we are gifting the Bagram AFB to the Taliban! Because Obama is now pursuing peace talks with the Taliban. Before obtaining anything from them, it has agreed to release 5 of Mullah Omar's chief lieutenants to Qatar, which will then release them to the Taliban.[23] The Taliban itself is now declaring a victory.[24] No doubt, very soon, we will be told that the Taliban, like Al Qaeda in Libya and the Muslim Brotherhood in Egypt, are not all bad. That there are some good Taliban and that Obama is negotiating only with the good ones! Sure enough, NPR, a proud member of the Journolist which disperses propoganda for Obama, started running a story about the "good Taliban" the week after July 4, 2012!

Worst of all, Obama's precipitous retreat from Afghanistan has reversed all the gains made by Afghani girls. Before 2001, the Taliban had subjected Afghan women to a terrifying *Shari'ah* nightmare that forbade them from working outside the home or even leaving their homes unless accompanied by a close male relative. Failure to abide by these restrictions[25] resulted in public whippings, beatings or stoning.

School enrollment had grown from several thousand girls in 2002 to more than 2.7 million girls in 2011. But in 2010, the Taliban recommenced their barbaric attacks on schoolgirls. Ten Taliban fighters were arrested[26] for squirting acid[27] onto 15 girls who were walking to school in Kandahar. Taliban gunmen beheaded the headmaster of a girls' school in Kabul; and insurgents destroying over 240 girls' schools throughout the country. Those attacks included[28] poison spray being used on four girls' schools in Kanduz, which hospitalized over fifty teenage girls; a gas poisoning[29] of a girls' high school in Kabul, which hospitalized 46 students and nine teachers; and a poison spray attack[30] on a girls' school in the northern province of Sar-e-Pul that hospitalized 20 students.[31] In April 2012, in order to prevent their attendance at school, the Taliban poisoned[32] the drinking water and injured nearly 150 Afghan schoolgirls.

On May 1, 2011, Navy Seal Team 6 members took out Osama bin Laden. He had been living for 7 years in Abbottabad, a wealthy enclave of military officers 35 miles north of Islamabad, the capital of

Pakistan. His house was reputed be worth $1 million. It is simply not credible that the Pakistani Army did not know that Osama lived there. In a small exclusive community, every newcomer would be subject to natural curiosity, especially one who is an unusual 6'4" tall and who live concealed by 18-foot high perimeter walls.

The stealth helicopters used were top secret, totally silent and able to avoid radar. One stealth helicopter went down during the raid. Though the Seals tried to destroy it, the tail section remained intact. The Pakistanis promptly sold the part to China.[33] The Obama administration has taken no action whatsoever against Pakistan for having concealed and given shelter to Osama bin Laden all these years, or for having sold top-secret technology to the Chinese. Instead, it has continued to give Pakistan the billions of dollars that have been given in the past.

Evidence that helped located Osama had been discovered through the use of enhanced interrogation techniques on Abu Zubaida and on Khalid Sheik Mohammed, who had organized the 9/11 terrorist attacks. But Obama had accused the previous administration of torture and said in 2008, "Guantanamo is entirely unnecessary and the detainees should not be interrogated." It was Obama, who said in 2008, "Bin Laden was innocent until proven guilty and must be captured alive and given a fair trial." Just before the raid, Obama had been playing golf and had to be asked to cut short his game to come into the situation room to watch the raid. Of course, that did not get much coverage in the Situation Room pictures or in the claims that Obama "made the tough call" about killing one of America's most hated enemies. I mean, seriously, was Obama ever going to say "No, don't kill him. Let us make friends with him?" It was Obama who decided that Osama's compound could not be bombed, but rather, that the Seals had to risk their lives to go in to get Osama.[34] It was Obama who sneered in 2008, "Navy Seal Team 6 is Cheney's private assassination team."[35] According to some reports, Obama and Valerie Jarrett opposed giving the go ahead and Leon Panetta had to take charge and give the command.[36] Finally, it was Admiral William McRaven, a former SEAL, who made the decision to take bin Laden out.[37]

But having sneered at all the work done by the Bush Administration that helped locate Osama and sneered at the Navy Seal Team 6 that risked their lives to undertake the mission, Obama went on national and worldwide TV immediately after the successful raid, and took virtually all credit for himself: *"I can report . . . I was briefed . . . I called Leon Panetta . . . I met repeatedly with my national security team . . . I put together a team . . . I determined that we have enough intelligence (to proceed) . . . At my direction, the US launched (the) operation . . . I, as commander in chief. . . ."*[38] Obama also disclosed that it was the Navy Seal Team 6 that undertook the operation. This caused tremendous concern among those who understood that it was vitally important to keep operational details secret and particularly, to keep the identity of the team that did the operation secret because it was certain that Osama's supporters would try to take revenge on them.[39]

Obama has given unprecedented access to confidential security information to two academy award winning film makers, Kathryn Bigelow and Mark Boal to make a movie about the Osama bin Laden raid. Representative Peter King has asked for information about possible releases of security information. Obama has laughed that off. The movie was made in June 2011. But, curiously, it will not be released until October 2012, a month before Obama's bid for re-election. Clearly, all this was done to get Obama maximum credit and make the most extensive political use possible of the raid. I wonder, is it possible we'll get a shot of Obama on the golf links just before the raid? On the one-year anniversary of the raid, Obama released a video giving himself full credit for the take down. He spent a week celebrating his "accomplishment," and mocking Romney saying Romney would not have made that "brave decision" that Obama made. Obama flew to Afghanistan on the 1-year anniversary and grabbed more headlines and kudos.

Meantime, two months after Obama disclosed that it was Navy Seal Team 6 that undertook the mission, a military helicopter was shot down in eastern Afghanistan, killing 31 U.S. Special forces, most of them from Navy Seal Team 6.[40] There is no doubt that Osama's supporters took down this particular helicopter because Navy Seal Team 6 members were in it. And there is no doubt that Obama's reckless disclosure of their involvement got them killed. Shortly after the raid, Obama's people disclosed that they tracked Osama down using a phony vaccinating program to obtain a sample of Osama's DNA. This clued the Pakistanis onto Dr. Shakil Afridi, who had helped the CIA identify Osama by setting up the fake vaccination program. Afridi was then tried for treason by Pakistan and jailed for 33 years.[41] In June 2012, the New York Times disclosed that Obama himself ran the "Kill List" of people who were to be executed by the unmanned drones. It also disclosed that Obama was in charge of the secret computer program where the U.S. had collaborated with Israel to develop and insert the computer worm Stuxnet into Iran's nuclear control room computers and slow them in their uranium enrichment program.[42] David Sanger also disclosed that the former Secretary of Defense, Robert Gates has confronted Tom Donilon, a former political operative for Obama and now the National Security Advisor and told him to shut the F*   *   * up; essentially charging Donilon of being the person responsible for the leaks.[43] As Representative Peter King said, all these leaks were clearly designed to create a "tough on national security" image for Obama.[44] In so doing, 31 of our Seal Team 6 members were killed, the Pakistani doctor who helped us was jailed for 33 years, we betrayed our ally Israel, and we made public a very dangerous assertion, that our President personally ordered the execution of select enemies who were on his "kill list." In short, Obama put his personal political image before our National Security.

It is clear that Obama does not want to win either of the two wars. Obama's approach is to tie down our Armed Forces with demands it cannot possibly meet. Like those Rules of Engagement that expose our soldiers to greater harm but ensure no terrorist can be caught; performance demands for doing more with far, far less troops than the Army needs; and demands that the Army "make friends and win the hearts and minds" of the Afghanis and the Militant Taliban, which no one earth has done. Then, he gets to withdraw from Afghanistan and blame the Army for his failures!

His approach of abject apologies for an inadvertent burning of *Qur'ans* coupled with deliberate burning of Bibles; failure to demand that terrorists who kill our soldiers be brought to justice, negotiating with the Taliban and returning captured Taliban to the battlefield; all ensure that the war in Afghanistan will also be lost. And his reckless disclosure of Navy Seal Team 6's involvement in the Osama bin Laden raid is inexcusable. **We have already lost 3004 soldiers in this Afghanistan war. And tens of thousands have been injured. And Obama spits on their sacrifices.**

Chapter 8

Demoralizing and Defeating the U.S. Army

The U.S. Army is the finest fighting force in the world. It is an all volunteer force of young men and women who love their country and are willing to give up their lives for us. For all of those who sneer at them and call them rednecks and hicks; I have a challenge. Volunteer to go to Afghanistan, read Obama's Rules of Engagement closely; and see if you have the courage to go out on patrol with our soldiers for just one day.

The men and women of the Army mostly vote for conservative candidates. For that reason, Obama and his Democrats do all they can to dienfranchise them. In the 2004 Bush—Gore election, they didn't allow the votes of the soldiers to be counted in Florida. Various states under Democrat control regularly "forget" to send out the soldiers' ballots on time so they can be returned in time to be counted. This, from the party that is so passionate about not disenfranchising anyone!!

The Armed Forces fight and give up their lives so we can have freedoms and our Constitutional Rights. They have to tolerate abuse by liberals who spit on them and call them names, because that is deemed to be an exercise of Constitutionally protected Free Speech. But they themselves have neither Freedom of Speech nor Free Exercise of Religion. They cannot say anything against the governent in power, not even in their off time. Seargant Garry Stein, a 26 year veteran, was punished and fired for posting, during his free time, "political statements about the President of the United States,"[1] on his Facebook Page entitled the "Tea Party Armed Forces."[2]

Our Oath of Allegiance has been rendered meaningless. Soldiers are required to obey and submit to orders from above. When the whole chain of command is operating to protect and defend our country, their rules and their oath make absolute sense. Our soldiers know and trust that those higher up are looking after their best interest, and they obey all commands given to them, even ones which will result in the loss of their own lives. But when those higher up start kow-towing to political correctness and fail to defend their own soldiers, the whole chain of command breaks down.

Their oath states: "*I do solemnly swear that I will support and defend the Constitution of the United States against all enemies, foreign and domestic; that I will bear true faith and allegiance to the same and that I will obey the orders of the President of the United States and the orders of the officers appointed over me, according to the regulations and the Uniform Code of Military Justice. So help me God.*"

But this system does not work today. There are five major problems with the way our Army is dealing with this oath. First, God is being removed from the Armed Services. Secretary Michael Donley is working overtime with the Military Association of Atheists and Freethinkers (MAAF) to remove all vestiges of Christianity from the Armed Forces.[3] If we are going to allow a small minority to be "offended" by the word God, and remove God from every place in the army, how can anyone take the oath, *so help me God?*

The second problem is that an Orthodox Muslim cannot take this oath. As has been documented above, a Muslim swears fealty to the *Qur'an* and *Shari'ah* law, both of which are an intrinsic part of Islam. They forbid a Muslim from obeying any law other than the laws of Islam. How can a Muslim possibly swear to uphold our Constitution, which differs from *Shari'ah* in virtually every aspect? So why are we allowing Muslims into the Armed Forces?

Third, there is a problem with the words *"orders of the officers appointed over me."* It is not in the Constitution that the Armed Forces must submit to civilian authority. Article I, Section 8 states, Congress has the power to "raise and support armies" and "to provide and maintain a navy." Article II, Section 2 states, "The President shall be the Commander in Chief of the Army and Navy of the United States, and of the Militia of the several States when called into the actual Service of the United States." Congress has the power to declare war and <u>to make the rules for governing the military</u>. But nowhere does it say that various attorneys and other civilians appointed by the President have the right to give orders to the Military. And nowhere does it say that our generals have to obey the civilians even when they give clearly unlawful orders. In many other counties, self-respecting generals would have staged a coup, rather than let Obama order their soldiers to go off to die for no reason. But our generals now seem to be more interested in mindlessly obeying civilians and doing what is politically correct, than in protecting our soldiers.

Why have our senior generals agreed with Obama and liberal civilians that Nidal Hassan's murder of our soldiers was "workplace violence?" In so doing, they have dishonored our dead. And they have engendered distrust among the grunts. If our generals side with those that kill them, how are our soldiers supposed to trust our generals? Why did our generals agree to keep Nidal Hassan in the military in the first place when they had ample evidence he was sympathetic to the terrorists? Obama has insisted that there are no Muslim terrorists. Why have our generals agreed to fight an undefined and nameless enemy? Why have our generals agreed to permit gays to openly practice their sexual behavior in the army without registering a single peep of protest? They are demonstrating they do not care for the health and wellbeing of our soldiers who may be exposed to AIDs on the battlefield. How can our soldiers trust them?

It was a civilian attorney, just as we started the war in Afghanistan, who instructed the Air Force not to release the missiles that had targeted Osama as he escaped from Afghanistan because he had his wife and daughter with him. And this gave rise to at least eight more years of war in Afghanistan. I wonder, is the rest of the world admiring us for our concern for civilians, or are our own dead cursing this attorney for having caused so many of our soldiers to lose their lives? It is various civilian attorneys who are making up those "Rules of Engagement" which are killing our soldiers. And our generals are going along with these rules, knowing they make no sense at all. When the media gets all huffed up about our soldiers posing next to Taliban they have killed, our senior Army officers immediately issue apologies and promise to discipline our soldiers. Why do they never defend our soldiers and point out how the Taliban treat our dead soldiers? When Karzai and the Afghanis have a hissy fit over the burning of *Qur'ans*, why do our senior officers promise to discover the "miscreants" who burned the *Qurans*? Why are they unable to say that this was not intentional at all? Why do they hide "insider" murders of our Soldiers by our so-called Afghani partners, instead of demanding that our soldiers not be forced to "partner" with those that are likely to kill them?

It is civilian attorneys who first refused to use military tribunals to try terrorists at Gitmo and then dilly-dallied and dragged their feet before starting to use military tribunals after it became apparent that the Congress would not allow the trials in civilian courts. These rules are passed along by various military officers who are putting their personal agendas and political interests before those of the soldiers under their command. Obama is releasing various terrorists from Gitmo. It took countless lives and lots of suffering for our soldiers to catch those terrorists. Why aren't our generals protesting?

Various politicians blatantly lie about what the soldiers are doing. For at least 5 years, Democrats, particularly Obama and Nancy Pelosi, have alleged that terrorists are being tortured in Gitmo and that they knew nothing about it. This has caused our army to lose public support for the war and caused morale to suffer. Finally, in April 2012, Jose Rodriguez, an ex-CIA officer, informed the American public that Pelosi had lied. Why has no one else high in the chain of command ever spoken up? Is Jose Rodriguez the only person with cojones in the American Army? Do they not realize that by being silent, they encourage Democrats to lie about the military and its accomplishments and denigrate and demoralize our soldiers? And that this failure to speak harms the reputation of the armed forces and the nation?

Right now, the Military Tribunal trying KSM and other terrorists in Gitmo has been turned into a circus. These are the terrorists who murdered 3000 of our people on 9/11 and have admitted to doing so. Khalid Sheik Mohamed is the one who claims to be the mastermind of the 9/11 attacks and who actually made and publicized a video of himself slitting Daniel Pearl's throat.[4] Now, they come into court, and promptly whip off their headsets so they cannot hear the Arabic translation of the court proceedings, which we are providing to them to ensure procedural fairness. Right in the middle of the trial, they suddenly kneel down and start praying. They yawn and turn their faces away. One of them removes his shirt to show the marks of his "torture," though none are to be seen. One of them turns round to the victim's next of kin and flips them the finger. Another **flies paper airplanes** toward the victims' relatives.[5] Some idiot woman lawyer comes to court dressed in a Burka and demands that all women in court be ordered to dress the same to "show respect" for the terrorists!

First question: What does the Arab Street think of this spectacle? Do they respect us for our superior civilization, tolerance, fairness and kindness to the terrorists? Of course not! They know, first hand, what "torture" really is. They witness it daily. They have seen the women with acid thrown on their faces. They have personally beheaded those who didn't obey their leaders. They have watched that wonderful "*Sangsar* ceremony" where women are dumped in a four-foot hole, covered with dirt up to their necks and stoned to death. They know that if we had actually tortured the terrorists, they would have been cowering in fear. Instead, the terrorists are showing the most profound disrespect for us. In a culture where respect is the first thing, and almost everything, what do you think the Arab Street is thinking of us? They are laughing at us! At our impotence and our inability to control the terrorists. Just by mocking us, and flying airplanes at the relatives of the dead, the terrorists have set themselves up as heroes to the Arab Street!

Second question: So, to whom do we show respect? Does our prosecution wear black armbands to show respect for our dead? Do we penalize the terrorist who deliberately mocked and insulted the relatives of those he had already murdered by flying paper airplanes in their faces? Do we penalize any of the terrorists for disrupting the court proceedings? Do we tell that woman lawyer that if she wants to show respect, she should first show it herself by following all Muslim traditions and getting her clitoris cut off? And not selectively picking and choosing what traditions she will follow, and then trying to make all women in court follow what she dictates? And that she must show respect for the court by stopping the antics of her clients? Do we demand that all terrorists show respect for our Tribunal? And tell them if they cannot behave themselves, they will be brought to court strapped in a wheelchair, so they cannot kneel to "pray" in order to disrupt the proceedings and with their hands strapped down so they cannot insult and humiliate the next of kin and cause them further pain of mind by mocking them and flying paper airplanes in their faces? Of course not.

Our Army is worried that Obama will start carping about us not showing enough "respect" for the terrorists and for Islam!! Our Generals are so terrorized they cannot even understand that by conflating the terrorists and Islam, Obama has admitted that Islam does support terrorism! *And, once again, Obama's Stealth Jihad works to demoralize and defeat our army and make a laughing stock of America throughout the world.*

At some point, those higher up in the chain of command have to realize that when they do not defend their soldiers' interests, the whole system collapses. At some point, our generals have to say to the Democrats, *"Enough! You have gone too far."*

Fourth, there is a major problem with the words "*I do solemnly swear that I will support and defend the Constitution of the United **States against all enemies, foreign and domestic** . . .*" Do we have foreign enemies? We seem to be trying to make our Armed Forces make friends with them, even when we know they can't ever succeed. If nothing else, this creates a cognitive dissonance in our soldiers' minds. Are they fighting or making friends? And with whom? Obama refuses to allow anyone to call the enemy "Islamic Militants." What about those who pretend to be our civilian friends during the day and then take up arms against us at night? Ask any Psychologist whether putting our soldiers in deadly peril, while at the same time asking them to make friends with our enemies, can cause profound psychological harm to our soldiers. Any fool could see it does. And what do Obama and our liberals do? Having caused all this immense psychological harm in the first place, they now profess to care deeply for our soldiers and constantly appear in photo ops with our soldiers, lovingly discussing how to take care of the psychological and economic problems of our soldiers. *It makes me want to puke!!!*

Lastly, we have the major problem that no one dares to broach. *(And I thought our generals had courage!!)* What if we have a domestic enemy who is issuing commands that actually prevent us from defending ourselves and result in failure for our Armed Forces and our Country? Then what? Do we just shut up and obey? And March into the Valley of Death?[6] Is this how it is supposed to be?

Terrorists to the left of us, Terrorists to the right of us,
Terrorists behind us, Terrorists in front of us,
And Terrorists amongst us,
Into the valley of death, marched the U.S. Army?

There is an unremitting attack on the Christian religion in the Armed Forces. Think about it, it is faith and prayer that gives our soldiers the courage to face the dangers they face. It is their sense of duty and loyalty to their country, encouraged by their religion and the comradeship it brings, that enables them to conquer their fears and overcome their sorrow at the deaths of their conmrades. Why are we denying this comfort to them? It appears that the rule for the Obama Administration is that all religions, including the smallest ones and even no religion, are all equal; except that the majority religion of Christianity must be hampered and restricted. Once again, Obama plays the trick of taking a concept and expanding it to include so many things that the concept ends up having no meaning.

Remember what I told you about water. When you start chattering about the particulates in the water, the bits of grass in it, the bird droppings and everything else, it ceases to be water. So it is with religion. When you include atheists, who have no religion, and orthodox Muslims, who do not have a religion, but rather a religious/political/military ideology that does not honor our constitution or our traditions, but rather is at war with it; then you cease to have any religion at all. To give you another example. What if I demanded the right to be a professional basketball player and said I am "offended" that you won't allow me to play? Would you be "discriminating" against me and showing a "lack of respect" if you laughed in my face? Or do we have to truncate the court, shorten the net, tie the legs of the professional players together and get them to stand aside so I can walk over to the net and dunk the ball? After we do all this, would it still be basketball?

Some atheist have called upon Camp Pendleton to remove crosses put up on its grounds to memorialize Marines who died in battle. This, even after the soldiers who put up the crosses themselves died in a later battle.[7] Atheists and Muslims are constantly battling to prevent our soldiers from praying, asserting that these Christian or Jewish prayers are "offensive." They have demanded that the Gideon Bible be removed from on-base lodging.[8] MAAF has actually ordered the Air Force to remove the word God from the log of its Rapid Capabilities Office.[9] Franklin Graham (Billy Graham's son) was prevented from giving a prayer at the National Prayer Breakfast at the Pentagon because he had said Islam is not a religion of peace. *(A fact I have demonstrated is true!)* But the Pentagon does observe the Holy Month of Ramadan.[10] Obama has banned prayers in in all Federal Buildings and property.[11] I wonder, since even grounds of the base are Federal property, does a soldier have to go outside the base if he wishes to pray? But, as has been noted, Obama does hold lavish *Iftar* dinners at the White House.

Meantime, as has been discussed, Obama has introduced Muslims into the army without vertting them. And there have been numerous attacks on our armed forces by our "partners" in Afghannistan, and also here in the United States. Among the latter was the June 1, 2009 Little Rock murder of Army Private William Long by Islamic jihadist Abdulhakim Mujahid Muhammad. Though Muhammed has acknowledged he was acting in the name of Allah, this shooting has not been listed as a terrorist act.

Nidal Hassan is another case in point. He was promoted by the army even though he was a medicre candidate. He was provided with a full scholarship to do his medical studies and post graduate studies as a Psychiatrist. All this, though he was an inferior student and also clearly displayed a hostility to American values. Making a medical presentation to his colleagues, he presented a power point on suicide bombers and *jihad*.[12] The business card he handed out listed him as an MD and also as an SOA, a Soldier of Allah. But the Democrats' political correctness knew no bounds. They pushed the their affirmative action agenda to make it impossible not to promote him and used the club of political correctness to encourage Hassan's superiors to ignore or minimize obvious warning signs.

When unarmed soldiers were attending a graduation ceremony, Hassan got up on a table, pulled out his guns, and massacred 13 of our soldiers and wounded 30, shouting out all the while *"Allahu Akbar!"*—Allah is great!

Obama "rushed to judgment" instantly and cautioned us not to "rush to judgment." Later on, his minions informed us, this was "pre-traumatic stress syndrome"—a mental illness unknown to the DSM. *(But Obama is so brilliant, who are we to tell him he can't invent a disease no one else has discovered before?)* We were to believe that that Hassan, who joined the U.S. army at a time we were at war with two Muslim countries Iraq and Afghanistan; was so stressed out at the notion of fighting fellow Muslims that he killed 13 unarmed Christians and Jews!! Obama, of course, was just covering up for yet another militant Islamist. It was later discovered that Hassan had been attending the Mosque of radical Imam Al-Awlaki; had been in email contact with him and was, in fact, a Muslim Terrorist.

Contrast this with how Obama handled the shooting of Gabrielle Giffords by a mentally unstable white man. Obama instantly "rushed to judgment" and pronounced that this happened because of Tea Party extremists and Christian Right Wing extremists. This, even though that shooter had nothing to do with Christians, Tea Party goers or the Right Wing of the Republican party. Also contrast this tender care for Muslim Terrorists with Obama's DHS, which issued a broad based "Threat Assessment" against all Tea Party Supporters, Christians, Right Wing "extremists" and "Disgruntled Military Veterans." Apparently, actual terrorists are not terrorists, but any person who oppposes Obama's policies could be a terrorist![13]

In order to show his "sympathy and concern" for the soldiers who were murdered, Obama's DOD officials have now determined that Hassan's terrorist acts were mere "workplace violence." This ensures that those who promoted Hassan and failed to take action against his obvious *jihadist* leanings go unpunished, and the government is excused from looking into the deleterious effects of political correctness and the threat it poses to safety. This also ensures that the victims' families do not get any combat death benefits due when they are murdered by an Islamic Terrorist or the Purple Heart, which their families would treasure.[14]

Repealing Don't Ask, Don't Tell: To make matters worse for the Military, the Military top brass fudged polls showing the military personnel approved of including gays in the military.[15] And the President was able to issue an order. And the Military has commenced indoctrinating its 2.2 million active and reserve personnel to accept gays. They are being "taught" how to accept gays kissing; that gays in civilian clothes can march in gay pride parades. I suppose we have to be grateful that the Military still does not accept transgender and transsexuals.[16] (Notice it is A-OK for sodiers to assert their Freedom of Speech rights and make political statements and march in GayPride parades during their off duty time if they are gay, but not OK if they are making other kinds of political statements such as their belief in orthodox Christianity!) Since the repeal of "Don't ask, don't tell," the Obama administration has issued rules that violate the free exercise of religion of all traditional religions. At their worship services, Chaplains are permitted to express their sincerely held religious and moral beliefs that homosexuality is a sin. **But neither they or any soldier, is allowed to express these views openly outside the chapel or for that matter have thoughts anywhere, including outside the church, that are reflective of those religious beliefs**. And they could be "punished" for their resistance to the indoctrination of homosexual behaviour in the ranks.[17] Of course, this is a blatant violation of the Free Exercise of Religion. (Don't you wonder what would happen if an Orthodox Muslim in the military refused to set aside the religious teachings of his faith with respect to homosexuality? Remember the Gitmo trials? Our Army was showing understanding and excusing the terrorists and admitted murderers for disrupting proceedings by kneeling to pray. Why the double standard?) But this is the army. The can, and do, treat our kids like dirt.

If you were a young woman, would you want to share a shower or a bunker with a hormonally charged unknown young man? Why not? Because you wouldn't want him making passes at you. And you certainly wouldn't want him alleging you made passes at him! Now, how is this different when you introduce a hormonally charged gay youg man among other straight men? Can't you just see the Army stopping in its tracks on the way to war and conducting hearings on "sexual harrassmenet" and "hate crimes;" to ascertain who made passes at whom; who said what "offensive" thing to whom; who "discriminated" against whom; etc? Clearly, a field day (and lots of attorney fees) for the ACLU and other plaintiff's lawyers.

Add to this one other consideration. When medical personnel handle patients, they take "universal precautions" by wearing double gloves etc. Even the TSA wears thick blue gloves as it searches people. We all know that coming into contact with infected blood exposes us to AIDS.

And we want to make sure the personnel do not catch any disease, particularly AIDS, from the people they inspect. The Navy has seen its HIV rate increase fourfold since 1999.[18] All through unprotected sex and not through IV drug use. Our soldiers have a proud rule that they will not leave any fellow soldier behind on the battlefield. When two soldiers are injured and bleeding on the battlefield, and one has HIV, what "universal precautions" is the other supposed to take? How will he even know? Has the Military taken this into consideration? Or, like pretending we do not have Muslim Terrorists inside the army, is it pretending there is no problem here either?

Not content with all this tender care, Obama has imposed draconian cuts on the army budget—the only place he wants to cut any spending. He has fired 80,000 soldiers; and plans to shrik the military drastically. So much so that it would no longer be able to handle more than one war at a time.[19] He has increased the amount soldiers have to pay for their health care coverage; while leaving the requirements for unionized civilians untouched.[20]

He has also cut combat pay. Simply being in Afghanistan while the Taliban takes pot shots at you and where our Afghan "partners" inside the army camps kill you, is not enough to be classified as "combat." You have to actually go outside on a mission to earn combat pay.[21]

If our soldiers had only consulted me, I would have solved all their problems. I would have had them unionize. And voila!! They would not be laid off without civil service hearings; meaning they would never be laid off. They would get not only their combat pay; but they would double or triple their base pay; work only 8 hour shifts; get overtime and time and a half on holidays; get all the benefits our government workers get; and get to be like the GSA and go on $850,000 junkets to Las Vegas! Obama would be delighted and bend over backwards to reward them because he would get a "cut" (percentage) of what the unionized armed forces would pay to the unions. . . . And I too would get a cut of the benefits I obtained for the Armed Forces and be rich for life!!

But let's stop laughing for a while and take a serious look at what Obama is doing to our Armed Forces. He has demoralized them with the way he has conducted (or failed to conduct) the wars in Iraq and Afghanistan.

They are dying out there, but there is no mission and no notion of what a "victory" would be. In fact, their present mission, to "make friends amd win the hearts and minds" of the Taliban, is impossible. As you have seen over and over again in this book, Militant Islamists do not wish to "make friends" with us. They only seek to kill us. To them, we are alien beings, infidels. We will not become properly human until we accept Allah! How, in heaven's name, are we supposed to "make friends" with them?

Obama has denied our soldeirs the very rights they fight for. They are prevented from speaking out and from saying prayers. He has introduced Muslims and Gays into the arnmed forced without considering the deleterious effects this will have on army discipline and unit cohesiveness. And then, he is reducing our soldiers to penury with his penny pinching.

Why is he is doing all this? You have already seen why. You just haven't recognized it. Or maybe you just don't want to believe what your common sense is telling you. Have you seen any stories about how amazing the Armed Forces are, taking ordinary kids, some with little education, some quite troubled, and transforming them into a wonderful fighting force? Have you seen any media coverage of brave soldiers who performed excellently in war? Any stories of their valor on the battlefield, giving their lives to save their fellow soldiers? Or how smart and well spoken they are? Or how disciplined they are? Or how mere 22 and 24-year-olds know to lead their troops into battle? Or how they are able to make split second decisions on matters of life and death? Or what a marvel all this is, when you consider how young our soldiers are? Or any contrast with the average 20-year-old back home, lounging around their parent's house; playing video games and smoking bongs? Why do you think that Obama, the Commander in Chief of the Army and a Democrat who has so much control over the media, does not insist on some positive stories about our soldiers?

There were positive stories at the start of the Iraq war when the media embedded reporters with the troops. The embeds got to see, first hand, what a wonderful fighting force our Army was. But as their reports came back, they were pulled from the battlefield because the Democrat controlled media cannot allow the American public to show respect, sympathy and admiration for our Armed Forces. They must be induced to "*hate the war.*" In fact, there is a constant drumbeat about "*Americans weary of the war.*" I must ask, which Americans are "*weary?*" Are these the same ones who have done nothing whatsoever for the war or for our warriors?

No, Obama's whole goal for the U.S. Army is to discredit and demoralize them. His "threat assessment" against "right wing extremists" included "army veterans returning from war." He and his media minions are constantly producing sob stotires about how our arrmed forces are returning home psychologically damaged and/or crippled; suggesting to us that all our Armed forces are damaged goods, on the verge of a nervous breakdown and in need of the ministering hands of government workers; aka the Democrat Party! Obama pretends to care for them by asserting that they shouldn't have to pay so much interest on their student loans. This after he took over all student loans and after he and his fellow Democrats arrange to raise the interest rates!![22] So, Obama has arranged for our soldiers to be poor. Similary, Obama also pretends to care for them by constantly admonishing private corporations to hire them. This, after he has just finished firing them![23] Similarly, Obama also pretends to care for them by constantly admonishing private corporations to hire them. This, after he has just finished firing them![24] And finally, Obama has arranged for our soldiers to be out of work. According to Obama, our soldiers are potential terorists, crippled in mind and body; and he has arranged that they will be penniless and out of work. In short, Obama is turning our soldiers from warriors into victims!

Remember, when talking about his plans to double the size of the Peace Corps and nearly quadruple the size of AmeriCorps and the size of the nation's military services, Obama made this rather shocking (and chilling) pledge just before his election in 2008: "*We cannot continue to rely on our military in order to achieve the national security objectives we've set. We've got to have a civilian national security force that's just as powerful, just as strong, just as well-funded.*" [25]

What Obama aims to do it to demoralize our military men and women and convert the finest Army in the world into his personal army, just like the Iranian *basij;* who, because they are poor and desperate, will do whatever their Dictator commands them.

Chapter 9

Pampering State Public Unions & Bankrupting the Taxpayer

The problem with public unions is that they negotiate with themselves. A private union makes sense because union leaders negotiate with a boss who is doing whatever he can to maximize profits for himself and his shareholders and perhaps, might neglect workers' interests. A government union makes no sense at all. It has no boss interested in saving money for its shareolders, the taxpayer. Instead, Democrat bosses are more interested in hiring more workers, who will pay more union dues, which will give over 99% of its campaign contributions to the Democrats, who "negotiate" with the government unions. The taxpayer is never respresented in Government Union negotiations. Instead, after giving the unions more, Obama flies around the country on Air Force I, at our expense, and demands that thos who pay the most in taxes must *"pay their fair share"* and pay more taxes!! *How much more would be fair? Obama, he knows; but Obama, he not say!!*

Democrats regularly give government workers more pay and more benefits. Over 20 million people work for federal, state and local government. That's one in seven workers in America. Their salaries and benefits total roughly $1.5 trillion of taxpayer funds each year (about 10% of GDP). They spend another $2 trillion. If government could be run more efficiently by 30%, that would result in annual savings worth $1 trillion.[1]

In exchange for hiring all these workers, Democrats get votes from their 20 million workers, millions of dollars in donations, boots on the ground for political campaigning and campaign ads paid for by unions which are totally partisan, but still tax exempt! The AFSCME contributed $90 Million in the 2010 off-year elections alone.[2] Together with the NEA and the SEIU, these three unions spent $170 Million dollars cash (not counting the door to door work, the phone banks,and all the other support) on the elction in 2010, over 95% of it on Democrats.[3] Remember this the next time you hear the chant, *"Let's take the money out of politics.*" Or when Obama abuses and disrespects the Supreme Court for its *Citizen's United* decision, which enabled corporations and unions to spend money on politics. Neither Obama nor his henchmen have any intention of stopping the unions, which spend the most "money in politics," from spending money on the Democrats.

© First-Amendment-Rights.com
Where the Union Money Goes

The result of Democrat perfidy is that Democrat controlled states are broke. California's Governor Brown was elected by the SEIU. The SEIU provided cash, campaign "volunteers," ads and also had its nurses' union bankroll Meg Whitman's housekeeper's lawsuit. The woman, who had produced forged papers when she was hired, wept crocodile tears at her "ill treatment" by Meg who paid her a high-40 thousand dollar salary plus her benefits; but who terminated her when she was discovered to be an illegal. Brown won hands down. In exchange, Brown has to support whatever the unions want. One of its members openly threatened state legislators, *"we helped getchu into office . . . if you don't back our program, we will getchu out."* [4]

Democrats have provided government workers pay and perks vastly greater than private sector workers get. They have hired far more workers. In 2010, there were only 7.1 million unionuzed private workers. But there were 7.9 million unionized government workers, though there were five times as many private workers as public workers.[5] As public union pay, perks and benefits get increased, their states go broke and become unable to pay for government workers' large pay packets. Then, these Democrats increase taxes on poor citizens who are earning much less than their counterparts in the government and cut services to the public in order to maintain the government payroll.

According to a study by Andrew Biggs and Jason Richwine confirmed by the CBO, government job security is equivalent to about a 15% increase in compensation, and government workers in California, including pay and benefits, are compensated up to 30% more generously than are similar employees in large private firms.[6]

Most of our biggest States & Municipalities have done nothing to control pay and perks. Most of the lifeguards in Newport Beach earn more than $100,000 in total compensation per year! In at least two instances, pay had topped $200,000 as the city struggled to rein in pension costs. When outraged citizens demanded an explanation, they were told that lifeguards *"hold management roles, have decades of service and are considered public safety employees under the fire department, the same as fire captains and battalion chiefs!"* [7]

California is no longer the Golden State. It is blue and it is broke. California's extreme dereliction of duty came to light when the LA Times investigative reporters headed by Jeff Gottlieb discovered that the City Manager of Bell, Robert Rizzo (a Democrat, of course), had received an annual salary of $787,637, and once benefits were added, total compensation rose to more than $1.5 million per year![8] He was also entitled to 26 weeks' vacation per year. Rizzo had also made many $400-$500,000 illegal "loans" to cronies that were not properly authorized and were never paid back.[9]

Of course, this is peanuts compared to the $2.4 Billion wasted by Obama on "green energy" schemes supported by the owners of Google and Robert Kennedy Jr., the $565 Million wasted by Obama on Solyndra, now bankrupt; the $400 Million wasted on Abound Solar, also bankrupt; and other waste we saw documented in Part I of this book. But the basic point remains.

When you allow a government to take more and more of your taxpayer money; it will get more and more corrupt. Your money is safest in your own pocket, where you can look after it yourself!

The Bell scandals lead to further investigations by the State Treasurer, John Chiang. In 2009, at least 15 local government agencies across California paid top executives more than $300,000 per year. Many were heads of water or utility districts. In 2009, East Bay Municipal Utility District, which provides water for several Bay Area cities including Governor Brown's Oakland area, paid its top executive, Dennis Diemer, $420,220. In 2009, Expo Line Construction Authority Chief Executive Richard Thorpe and former Metrolink Chief Executive David Solow, made $371,917 and $340,381, respectively.[10] Bruce Malkenhorst, who worked for the City of Vernon, received the biggest public pension in California, $545,000 a year. Malkenhorst held as many as 10 positions during his 29-year tenure in the city government, including city administrator, clerk, finance director and executive director of the Vernon Historic Preservation Society. Through those positions, he was able to earn as much as $911,000 per year in total salary. Because of innumerable irregularities discovered upon audit, his pension is going to be reduced to a measly $115,000 a year. Both he and his successor were also awarded "public safety" pensions even though they were staff attorneys. His successor, Eric T. Fresch, made $1.6 million a year and it was expected that when he retired, he would get a $300,000 a year pension. Fresch worked as city administrator, city attorney or assistant city attorney. But his pension is going to be stripped from him because he never took an oath of office for these positions. How quaint! If he had only taken that oath of office, even with all those irregularities, he could have held onto his pension.[11] The City of Cudahy is one of Los Angeles County's poorest. Their city hall failed to keep records, did not produce minutes for its meetings failed to account for a $250,000 state parks grant and lost the opportunity for a $2.5 million grant. But the city manager, George Perez, who started as a janitor, earned a final paycheck of $186,000 a year. He also earned $23,500 as director of a private company that provided water to the city, which he, Perez, wearing his other hat as City Manager, purchased. His contract required an 8% annual raise and an additional cost-of-living allowance of 2%-4.5%. *Nice work, if you can get it!*[12]

Governor Brown totally caved to the 30,000 member Prison Guards union, which had spent $2 million on his election. Because prisons operate around the clock, prison guards have an average of 133 days of leave accrued. Brown increased their accrued vacation from 80 days, and permitted unlimited vacation accrual. Leave accrued years earlier, when the guard was earning far less; are paid for at current rates when the guard retires. It's as good as money in the bank earning interest. And, if you happen to be in a job that bases your retirement pay on your last year or two of compensation and your accrued vacation can be cashed in and used to increase your compensation in the last year before retirement; it is much better than money in the bank!

The total value of the accrued vacation for prison guards was $600 million. In 2009 alone, prison guards collected a total of $111 million. for accrued vacation that was being cashed out. 80 officers got payments exceeding $100,000 when they left service in 2010; payments which were much larger than their annual salary.

The staff also got 18 more days off over the life of the contract and the typical prison guard now gets more than 8 weeks' vacation in their first year. Before, they got $130 per month extra for meeting certain fitness standards. Brown watered this down in the new contract. They get the money for simply going to a doctor for an annual physical.[13]

California has also been grossly derelict with loans made to employees. An audit of 11 state employees retirement funds found that more than $13 million had gone uncollected. The Department of Transportation, the Department of Forestry and Fire Protection, and the California Highway Patrol were among the agencies scrutinized by the controller's office.[14]

Waste is not limited to California. In **New York**, once he came into office, Mayor Bloomberg increased the sanitation budget by 350%. Residents of the Big Apple have to pay enough taxes to pay $144,000 a year in salary, health and pension benefits for garbage workers, who are unionized, but basically unskilled laborers.[15]

L.I.R.R. workers live in hog heaven. They have work rules that enable them to earn 4 day's pay for one day's work. They can retire at 50. They are paid astronomical sums. The 12 highest paid L.I.R.R. engineers in 2006 were earning over $200,000 per year when they retired and then went on disability. Some workers' retirement income is over $170,000 per year. Disability adds about $36,000 per year to a New York Long Island Rail Road worker's pension. One couple, both in management, are now retired and take in about $280,000 a year in retirement and disability benefits. Over 90% of LIRR workers, even those with desk jobs, retire with "disabilities." One year, the number receiving disability payments rose to 97% of the retirees![16] The cost to New York City taxpayers was $300 million. Disability fraud is not limited to the LIRR. 82% of California State Troopers are also "disabled" before they retire.[17]

In **Wisconsin**, one Madison bus driver, John E. Nelson, was able to make $159,000 in 2009, about $100,000 in overtime pay. Seven bus drivers took home more than $100,000 that year. As Ann Coulter says so brilliantly: *"Fine, we understand that Wisconsin public sector employees like the system that pays them an average of $76,500 per year, with splendiferous benefits, and are fighting like wildcats against any proposed reforms to that system. But it's madness to keep treating people who are promoting their own self-interest as if they are James Meredith walking into the University of Mississippi."* [18]

State and Municipalities' Public Pension Funds and their associated Employee Retiree Health Plans are Broke: Because of all the shenanigans listed above and because the politicians and government employees who manage the pension funds have consistently overestimated their returns, enabling the States and Municipalities to suspend making required contributions and/or increase benefits; many States, Cities and Counties are in a financial mess. In early 2011, estimates of the underfunded pensions for state pension plans ranged from $700 billion to $3 trillion, with the large range attributable to differing forecasts of the return on investment for the trust funds of these state plans.[19] Illinois alone has unfunded pension obligations of $80 billion and unfunded retiree health obligations of about $40 billion more. According to a Pew Foundation estimate in 2010, the unfunded state pension liability was closer to $3 trillion. Adding liabilities of municipalities would make this sum much larger and if you add in liabilities for unfunded retiree health obligations, which are not included in the above figures, the aggregate liability would be much more than $3 Trillion dollars![20] This has been confirmed by a confidential report made by JP Morgan Chase, one of the biggest underwriters of municipal bonds which was disclosed in June 2012. According to the study, the State of Massachusetts must cut its spending by 20.1% or raise taxes dramatically or do both to fully fund its pensions. Even after Governor Christie's reforms, New Jersey, has to increase taxes, increase the retirement age by 9 years, increase employee contributions to their pensions by 23%, cut the state budget by 7% and cut cost of living adjustments by 2%![21]

CalPERs & CalSTRs are broke: In California, school districts have helped boost annuity payouts to teachers and administrators through the practice of spiking, or offering double-digit pay raises. This is one reason why California's Teachers Retirement System faces a $56 billion deficit.[22] The California Public Employees' Retirement Systems (CalPERs) has $235 Billion in assets. And CalPERs officers have been involved in fraud and waste of these funds. CalPERs used friends and cronies of senior management as "placement agents" to introduce money managers to its pension funds. For this "introduction," the placement agent, meaning the friends and cronies, received fat fees from the money manager. This also suggests that CalPERs did not get the best money manager it could have. And this resulted in relatively poorer performance and this, in turn, contributed to the underfunding. There is now a spate of state and federal investigations of the "pay to play" system used by CalPERs. The former CEO of CalPERs s, Frederico R. Buenrostro and his friend Alfred J.R. Villalobos received $60 million dollars in fees for acting as placement agents while Buenrostro was CEO of CalPERs. The SEC is suing them to recover any ill-gotten gains and other penalties.[23]

VEBA's are also broke: Retirement Trust funds or Voluntary Employee Benefit Funds, known as VEBA's, created to cover billions in medical costs promised to union workers and their families, are also running short. The biggest fund, a trio of United Auto Worker trusts covering benefits for more than 820,000 people, including Detroit automaker retirees and their dependents, is underfunded by nearly $20 billion dollars.[24]

Pension Liabilities & Fraud are Bankrupting States: State governments in the U.S. have an aggregate of pension liabilities exceeding $3 trillion for state civil servant and teachers' pensions. This has caused heated battles in states such as Wisconsin, Ohio and New Jersey between school reform activists and public-sector unions.[25] Municipal pensions are likely underfunded to the tune of $574 billion, according to Novy-Marx and Rauh. This includes a whopping $53 billion pension deficit for both the city and the county of Los Angeles, and an even bigger $122 billion deficit for New York City.[26]

The unfunded pension liabilities of California's state and local governments exceed $700 billion. California state government payments for retirement benefits have grown at an alarming and unsustainable rate, exceeding $5 billion a year, more than state support for the entire UC system. In 2002, Los Angeles taxpayers contributed just under $100 million to the Los Angeles City Employees' Retirement System, and it was fully funded. Today, that taxpayer contribution is more than $400 million, and the Los Angeles system is underfunded by more than $2.3 billion.

As a consequence, various cities throughout the country are declaring bankruptcy or considering it. Many experts fear that a surge of municipal bankruptcy filings is unavoidable.[27]

Among the cities filing are **Harrisburg, Pennsylvania, which** was compelled to file for bankruptcy even though its Mayor, elected with the help of unions, opposed it.[29] **Central Falls, Rhode Island** has also filed for bankruptcy.[30] **Detroit, Michigan**, now has junk bond status. It had closed dozens of schools and parks and cut other city services. But employee pay packages are still top big. **Jefferson County, Alabama**, is considering bankruptcy.

California, with its sanctuary city policies which have attracted huge populations of illegals; its expansive public welfare systems; and its massive public union pay and benefit packages; has a huge number of cities in trouble. Three major cities filed for bankruptcy within the months of June-July 2012.[28]

California filings include the city of **Maywood, California**, a sanctuary city, that has so many illegals not paying taxes that it can no longer afford any public services. It fired all its public employees in June, 2012.[31] The city of **Vallejo** has filed bankruptcy. There is pressure on **San Diego** to consider filing bankruptcy as a way to get around the benefits package for public workers, though its mayor opposes it. As recently as February 2010, the city of **Stockton** filed for bankruptcy.[32] **Mammoth Lakes** also filed for bankruptcy protection.[33] **San Bernardino** officials knew for years that it was in financial trouble. It knew in 2010 that its budget shortfall of $22 million would balloon to $38 million in 2012. Officials knew they needed to cut spending. But because of intense political pressure, they tried to make do by increasing taxes and making relatively minor spending cuts. In July 2012, it finally announced it would be filing for bankruptcy protection.[34]

These huge and growing slices of the budget pie are needed to pay for average state retirement packages now valued at more than $1.2 million each. The taxpayers who pay for those retirement benefits have only 5% of that amount, an average of $60,000, saved for their own retirement.[35]

Democrats are planning to cover the liabilities of Union Pension Funds: In 2008, 230 multi-employer union pension plans were either endangered (<80% funded) or critical (<65% funded). By 2009, the number had soared to 640. In 2010, Senator Casey, (D) of Pennsylvania proposed that these pensions be transferred to a separate fund at the Pension Guarantee Benefit Corporation and that $165 Billion of taxpayer funds be provided to pay the retirees.[36] In other words, multi-employer union pension plans, which have long been notorious for poor or corrupt management, will be bailed out to the tune of $165 billion. It's not the $400 billion bailout that TARP was, but then again, the TARP money has for the most part been paid back with interest. This money will never be paid back, and if we bail out union pension plans this time, how can we justify not doing it again?

You really don't need all of these mind-numbing statistics to understand what is going on. Obama and his Democrats want union votes, so they permit the unions to do whatever they like in terms of work rules, preventing discipline of slackers, preventing firing of incompetent workers, giving unnecessary overtime, double counting pay, allowing workers to pad their last year's salary with "unused" leave and "sick pay" when calculating their pensions, giving early retirement, and allowing extremely lax rules to determine whether the worker is entitled to disability.

Then, exactly like in my native country, Obama goes around the country, denigrating the working people and calling them "*the rich*," chanting, "*The rich must pay their fair share!*" and pretending to love the poor people. He pretends that raising taxes on people will have no effect on the economy; even while there is empirical evidence that doing that in the past three years, and constantly threatening to do more of that, has caused our economy to stall. Taxes are raised on the rich, as well as the middle class, to support all these pay and retirement schemes for State Public Union workers. Exactly like in my native country, the poor remain poor. Obama gets his votes. And the economy of the country slowly dies!

Chapter 10

Pampering Federal Public Unions & they'l have fun, fun, fun 'till the Tea Party takes their T-Bills away

Obama has doubled the federal workforce and their pay. The federal government now employs about 2.3 million civilian voters, sorry, I meant workers, which is about 1.7 percent of the total U.S. workforce. Another 2.3 million uniformed personnel are employed, including 1 million reservists, and 800,00 people work for government enterprises such as the Postal Service. In 2010, the federal workforce topped 2.15 Million, higher than the previous high of 2 million emloyed before President Clinton started paring down the federal workforce in 1994 and double the workforce of 1.2 million when President Bush left office at the end of 2007.[1]

The average federal pay, including perks, is $126,000 per year[2] Washington D.C. has one lawyer for every 12 residents, all the better to lobby the government. In contrast, even New York has only one for every 123 residents. The median income of Washington D.C. is now greater than that of Silicon Valley. The three richest counties, Loudon, Falls Church and Fairfax counties all in Virginia, all have a median annual income of over $105,000 and all get the majority of their income from the federal government.[3] Remember those "Millionaires and Billionaires" that Obama so hates? Well, over 50% of the U.S. House are millionaires and the median wealth of the U.S. Senators is $2.38 Million.[4] And Obama himself is a millionaire!

In 2010, more than 77,000 government employees earned more than the governors of the states they worked in. In Maryland, 7,283 or 7% of federal employees, earned more than Gov. Martin O'Malley's $150,000 salary. In 2009 in Colorado, 10,875 employees made more than the $90,000 salary of the governor, Bill Ritter.[5]

In 2005, only 7,420 federal workers were making $150,000 or more per year. A mere 5 years later, under Obama in 2010, an astounding 82,034 federal workers were making $150,000 or more per year! In 2008,

272

when Barack Obama took office, the U.S. Department of Defense had 214 civilians earning $170,000 or more. In June 2010, this number had increased nearly fourfold, to 994 civilians.[6] During this same period, from 2008 to 2010, Overall, federal workers earn 16% more in total compensation, including wages and benefits, than comparable private-sector employees, according to the Congressional Budget Office. But the key difference is in benefits, where federal workers average more than $20 per hour in compensation, 48% higher than the $13.60 in prorated hourly benefits in the private sector. Added together, the CBO said, that means significantly higher pay for government employees.[7]

In 2008, according to the Commerce Department's Bureau of Economic Analysis, the 1.2 million civilians employed by Uncle Sam were paid an average annual salary of $79,197. The average private employee earned just $49,935. The difference between them came to more than $29,000, 4 times more than in 2000. Once benefits are included, the federal advantage is enormous. Total federal civilian compensation in 2008 averaged $119,982, more than double the $59,908 in wages and benefits earned by the average private-sector employee.[8] To be exact, federal employees now average $123,049 in pay and benefits, while private-sector employees make $61,051 in total compensation, according to the government's own Bureau of Economic Analysis. That's a pay gap of $61,998—up from $30,415 in 2000. And that's not even counting the absurdly generous retirement benefits that allow many federal employees to retire with lifetime pensions and health insurance after little more than two decades on the job.

So what have all these expenditures got us? **The Postal Service is broke**. It lost $5.1 Billion for the year ending September 30, 2011. It lost $3.2 Billion in the quarter ending March 31, 2012. It even lost $3.3 billion during the Christmas quarter, normally its most profitable.[9] It is Christmas, celebrated by Christians sending thousands of Christmas cards, which make the Christmas quarter the most profitable for the Post Office. But they have steadfastly refused to stock Christmas stamps that would appeal to their Christian clientele. I, for one, have taken to sending e-cards rather than be forced to buy E'id stamps or Mickey Mouse stamps for Christmas. Is it just possible that the total lack of a focus on marketing and service to their customers might have something to do with the losses during what was their most profitable quarter?

The Postal Service proudly tells us they do not take a dime of taxpayer money. It just "borrows" it. Kinda-Sorta like your kids "borrow" money from you! They owed the Treasury $12.1 Billion as of January 31, 2012. Notwithstanding this dismal performance, the Democrat-controlled Senate has recently passed still more deficit funding for the USPS refusing to allow the closure or curtailment of operations at thousands of rural post offices. One of the key justifications for maintaining a bloated USPS is that allegedly things are not as bad as we thought they were because the USPS overpaid its contribution to the Federal Employees Retirement System and will get a refund. Sound familiar? Isn't that the ploy our state governments have been using to avoid funding state pension trust funds? And Senator Carper of Delaware is planning to use $10.1 Billion which is claimed to be an overfunding of the postal office retirement system; use $1-$2 Billion for incentives to get some long-time employees to retire; and is also trying to get the House to "do its part" by passing more funding for the Postal Service.[10]

Amtrak is also broke. It gets funds from three, sorry, four, no actually, five sources. States and local governments provide operating revenues and fund. The DOT applies for funds for Amtrak, and also applies directly to Congress for other funds. As of 2010, Amtrak was receiving $1.56 Billion a year from Congress. In addition, it received $1.3 Billion from the American Recovery and Reinvestment Act of 2009.[11] And the fifth source? Why, the sums you pay for your tickets, of course. Airlines manage with just the income from ticket sales. But it is just too much to expect that from Amtrak.

Even the Secrete Service is corrupted: It was disclosed in May 2012 that secret service agents on an advance trip to Cartagena, Colombia, hired prostitutes at $800 a night. Hopefully, they paid with their own money. But given the large amount, it sounds like this was being expensed to the taxpayer. And also, how else could the agent explain these sums to the wife back home? Even worse, women hired by hostile foreign countries could have compromised them and discovered state secrets. The matter is still being investigated. But the fact remains that these government agents considered it perfectly in order to be frequenting prostitutes while they were on official business.

The GSA takes the Cake: According to its own website, the mission of the GSA is to foster an effective, sustainable and transparent government for the American people. Its vision is to position the government to better serve the public. To do so, it believes in transparency, to manage resources with utmost care and an obsession with "no waste."[12] The GSA is an independent agency of the United States government, established in 1949 to help manage and support the basic functioning of federal agencies. The GSA supplies products and communications for U.S. government offices, provides transportation and office space to federal employees, and develops government-wide cost-minimizing policies, and other management tasks.[13] In short, the GSA is the procurement and operational services arm for the government, which spends approximately $3.7 Trillion a year.

Having all this money sloshing around in Washington has clearly gone to its collective head. The GSA recently spent $300,000 to relocate a single employee to Hawaii. It authorized many staff members to spend 7 days in Hawaii in order to attend a one-hour ceremony. No doubt, other details will come out as the investigations proceed.[14]

But the one that caused the explosions in the House in early May 2012 was an October 2010 trip GSA staffers took to the luxury M Hotel in Las Vegas. Jeffrey Neely, regional commissioner, organized it. According to him, it was all right not to get competitive bids because he was paying for quality.[15] To prepare for that meeting, he flew 50 "managers" on 8 separate "scouting trips" to the same luxury Las Vegas hotel. They stayed at Loft suites, with 2,300 sq. ft. in two stories with spa tubs and all the trimmings and a rack rate of $1,179 per night. Other "scouting" members stayed at Flat suites which ran $449-$599 per night. The total cost of these pre-conference "scouting" trips was $130,000. Travel cost another $100,405 and catering costs totaled over $30,000. Then, in October 2010, over 300 "leaders" were flown out to Las Vegas for a "team building meeting." The staff was provided with tuxedo rentals, commemorative coins, mind readers, motivational speakers and everything a guy could dream of. One of them was foolish enough to post a video on You Tube.[16] The staff had fun, fun, fun!

This party alone cost us taxpayers $823,000! We'd better take those T-bills away from Obama, the federal government and its workers come election time.

Chapter 11

The Magic Mystery Money Machine &
The Almost-October Surprise

Good Morning, boys and girls. Take a seat. Let me put on my cap and gown and start my lecture. Today, we will discuss, *"High Finance—Everything You Plebeians Always Wanted to Know about High Finance but Were Afraid to Ask."* High Finance can be explained by asking two simple questions:

Question #1: "If you had a trillion dollars, and you lent it out at 1% per annum, how much money would you make per year and how much per day?"
Answer: A Trillion is a 1, followed by 12 zeros or $1,000,000,000,000. So, an annual return of just 1% of a Trillion is a 1, followed by 10 zeros, $10,000,000,000 or $10 Billion dollars per year.[1] That is $27,397,260 per day or $27 million and change per day. *(Of course, the "change" is more than quadruple your annual salary, but let's not quibble.)*

Question #2: "Now, if you were making that kind of money, would you be rich enough to buy everything and everyone in America?"
Answer: Think hard. . . . There!

Now, you know everything you need to know to understand high finance. That is the end of the lecture. Thank you.

You have been shouting; *"Tell us about the Magic Mystery Money Machine."* First things first. Do you even know what the Fed is? The Federal Reserve Board is a privately owned Bank, with 7 Board members. The 12 Federal Reserve Banks own the Fed. These Banks are, in turn, owned by major commercial banks. Some say these commercial banks, in turn, are owned by interlocking directorates[2] controlled by a cartel of rich families, some in Germany, Italy, France and England and some in America.[3] But no one knows the details of its ownership. Only one thing is clear, the federal government does not own the Fed.

It is totally independent of both Congress and the President; and, as Congressman Ron Paul has been telling us for decades, is totally unconstitutional because it is not answerable to any of the three Constitutional branches of government. It is a privately owned central bank. The word "Federal" in its name does not mean the U.S. Government owns it any more than it owns Federal Express because of the word "Federal" in its name. The word "Reserve" is also misleading because it does not have any "reserves."

The President appoints the chairman and 6 other Board members of the Fed and the Senate approves it. But this is not the normal "advice and consent" of the Senate because the appointee is not going to be a Federal employee, and is not going to be accountable to the President and Congress. Also, no Senator or Congressman can be a member of the Federal Reserve Board or an officer or director of a Federal Reserve Bank.[4]

The Fed is a private monopoly that creates our money, sets our interest rates, regulates our banking system and makes secret loans to whoever it wants. And the Fed makes its decisions independent of Congress and the President. And nobody, not Congress, not the President and not the Courts, can overrule decisions made by the Fed.[5] The Fed is supposed to be setting monetary policy and making sure that our fiscal house stays in order. To do so, since 1913, it has been given the right to print money. (*For those who like little tidbits of history, Congress passed the Federal Reserve Act on the day before Christmas Eve, when most of the lawmakers had already gone home, and President Woodrow Wilson signed it into law.6 Co-incidentally, the 13th Amendment permitting the federal government to assess income taxes against us, was also passed within 6 months of that.*)

The Fed has enormous power over us. Since the Fed sets the interest rate; it can lower it, causing retirees living on their savings to lose money; and it can raise it, causing homeowner's mortgage payments to rise. When vast numbers of borrowers have floating rate mortgages; if the Fed raises the rates, then the monthly home loan payment rises so sharply that the homeowner goes into default and the homeowner gets evicted. And this, in part, is what caused the recent economic crisis. To complete the circle, the Fed and its associated banks then purchase mortgage backed securities at a discount and make a lot of money.

Here is where the Magic Mystery Money Machine part comes in.
Actually, the Fed does not "have" money in the sense of owning an
equivalent amount of assets for the money it says it has. For example,
we say we are worth $200,000 when we have a house, or own other
real estate, stocks or financial instruments worth $200,000 to back up
that assertion. The Fed definitely does not have real assets worth the
Trillions it lends out. Furthermore, it does not "print" the money on
paper. Instead, it has a little old clerk sitting in a fortified dungeon in
front of a gold plated computer. He adds a bunch of zeros to a 1 on the
Fed's computers, and presto, it creates money. Yes, exactly like your kids
playing computer games, the Fed creates money! But it is not funny
money. It is not funny at all. Because we, the taxpayer, are liable to pay
for the debts the Fed creates as it induces the government to borrow and
spend more and more; and we also incur the costs of the inflation this
printing of money generates.

To earn its income, the Fed first creates money through the Magic
Mystery Money Machine, actually out of thin air. The Fed then invests
this money on securities, mostly government securities, or Treasury
Bonds. The federal government, meaning us the taxpayers, pay interest
on the bonds that the Fed purchases with the money it creates with its
computer. Then the Fed loans its income, meaning the interest we paid
it, to select dealer banks who then earn their income from the spread
between the interest rate the Fed paid us and the interest rate they
charge their customers.[7] In 2009, loans of $113.1 Billion were made at
below market rates of 1.2% to its member banks through the Fed's Term
Auction facility for 28 days. And these banks then were able to charge
3.8% on loans they made, tripling their profit on the loans.[8] *Quick, do
the math. What is a 2.6% profit on $131 Billion? You get an A. The answer
is $3.406 Billion per year!!*

Ron Paul Tries to Stop Feds from making Secret Loans

In fact, the Fed and its secret financing helped America's biggest financial firms get bigger and go on to pay their employees huge bonuses at the height of the housing bubble. According to a recent Bloomberg article, the big banks profited an estimated $13 billion by taking advantage of the Fed's below-market rates. Total assets held by the six biggest U.S. banks increased 39 percent to $9.5 trillion on September 30, 2011, from $6.8 trillion in 2006. They paid $146.3 Billion in compensation in 2010, or an average of $126,342 per worker.[9]

In 2009 the Fed purchased 80% of the $2.109 Trillion of Treasuries that Obama's government borrowed. That is $1.69 Trillion. *Now that you have taken your course in High Finance, you know that this means the Fed made a profit of at least $16.9 Billion, even if it made only 1% profit on the purchase.* In 2011, the Fed purchased 61% of the Treasury Bills issued by the government.

Thanks to Obama, we now owe $15.7 Trillion, mostly in short-term debt, which has to be refinanced. And, as you already know, when we refinance, we incur further costs for commissions. We are often told that our finances are sound because the Chinese are buying our T Bills and lending us money. But this is no longer true. Between May 2009 and March 2011, the Chinese government, being smart, divested itself of 97% of the Treasuries it once owned.[10] China has also started divesting itself of long term Treasury Securities.[11]. When people stop buying our debt and our debt becomes unmarketable, we have to pay a higher interest rate to sell our Treasuries. *Quick question: If we pay an extra 2% on this $15.7 Trillion debt how much extra will we pay? See how smart you are, you already know the answer. Yes, we will pay another $31.4 billion each year!! Yes, we will have to pay an extra $86.03 million a day to our bankers if our debt becomes unmarketable. That, my friend, is why we have to worry about running up the debt. And that, my friends, is probably why Obama does not care about running up the debt!!*

We also pay the Fed for services the Fed provides as "fiscal agents." I think this means we pay commissions to the Fed for brokering its purchases of our Treasury Bonds. So, the more debt we issue, the more money the Fed makes. What this sets up is a never-ending spiral where the amount of money and the amount of debt are continually increasing. *Notice that*

Obama keeps borrowing and spending and does not care at all about our debt. Ever wonder why?

I have not been able to discover exactly what the gross income of the Fed is. But there are audited financials showing their net income after "expenses." These expenses include salaries, the 6% dividend it makes to its member banks and other expenses. There is a fixed amount the Fed has to pay the Treasury. I do not know who negotiates this amount or how this amount is calculated. In 2010, according to the Fed's own website, this amount was $78.4 Billion.[12] But you must remember that it is the taxpayer who paid most of the Fed's income to it in the form of interest payments on Treasury debt and fees for acting as fiscal agents. *So money went from us to them. They deducted salaries, expenses and commissions; and then returned some of the money to us. Got it?*

The other important fact to know is that the Fed, though a privately owned corporation, is exempt from taxes by the federal government and the states.[13][14] Think about Question #2 and its answer. Now, ask yourself, why is Obama not chanting, as he usually does, *"The Fed pays nothing in taxes. These Millionaires and Billionaires are not paying their fair share!! The Fed should start paying taxes"*?

Even in the middle of the financial crisis of 2007-2008, the Fed never disclosed it had lent money to various banks. The excuse Bernanke made was that if creditors and investors discovered the particular bank had borrowed from the Fed, they would shun that bank.[15] And the banks themselves never disclosed this and instead touted their particular bank as being very sound. Jamie Dimon of JP Morgan Chase, a great Obama supporter, told his shareholders that he only used the Fed's Auction Term Facility "at the Fed's request" to help motivate others to use the system! In fact, his bank had borrowed $391 Billion!

The amount loaned by the Fed dwarfed the $700 Billion dollar federal TARP program, which was supposed to bail out failing banks. According to Bernanke, the fact that the Fed lent to the same banks that the Federal Government lent under TARP ensured that the banks would not collapse and thus protected the Treasury's TARP investments. According to Bernanke, the Fed did it to help the government, you see. Bank of America and Citigroup each received $45 Billion from TARP.

The six largest banks, JP Morgan, Bank of America, Citigroup, Wells Fargo, Goldman Sachs and Morgan Stanley, accounted for 63% of the average daily borrowings from the Fed. According to Senator Bernie Sanders, the GAO report disclosed that he total loaned to 18 current and former Federal Bank reserve bank directors' banks amounted to $4 trillion dollars![16]

The amount that the Fed had loaned, and the number and variety of the institutions it had lent to, stunned everyone. Unbeknownst to all of us plebeians, around 2007, the Fed started up a series of loan programs amounting to—*O.K., sit down now and take a deep breath*—amounting to **$16.1 Trillion dollars!**

That is even bigger than the total U.S. National Debt of $15.7 Trillion that Obama has run up. It is more than the U.S. Government has spent in the last four years! It is more than the $14.58 Trillion dollars that was the GDP of the United States for the entire year of 2010![17] And, at even 1% annual return, that money has made the private owners of the Fed $161 Billion dollars a year. In fact, the more it lent, the more money it made. Little wonder that the Magic Mystery Money Machine kept cranking on and on.

As you have seen, the Fed spent a great deal of its money purchasing Treasury Securities. The rest of the money that the Fed created went, essentially, to well-connected people. And, as you already know, you and I are not among them. Once again, the pattern repeated itself. If you were an Obama supporter and a Democrat, you got loans. Once you did, you showed your gratitude by making campaign donations to Obama. And it ended up that Obama owns you. That is why we have all those millionaires in Wall Street and in California supporting Obama even as he denigrates them and mocks them.

Representative Paul believes that the Fed is the chief culprit behind the economic crisis. Its unchecked power to create endless amounts of money out of thin air has brought us the boom and bust cycle and causes one financial bubble after another. Since the Fed's creation, the dollar has lost more than 96% of its value.[18] This is because as the Fed prints more and more money, it causes the value of the dollar to fall and price of goods to spike. Rep. Paul had been trying for at least 30 years to get an audit of the Fed but each time, Democrats, some Republicans and the Fed itself, stymied him. Finally, after two more years of litigation going all the way up to the Supreme Court, in December 2010, after a limited GAO Audit, the Fed released some information.[19]

Senator Bernie Sanders was another member of Congress who insisted on an audit. He said, "As a result of this audit, we now know that the Federal Reserve provided more than $16 trillion in total financial assistance to some of the largest financial institutions and corporations in the United States and throughout the world."

The Fed kept the Discount window open to banks to borrow. It helped them make bets on credit default swaps and covered them if they lost. It has loaned to 700 American and foreign banks. But because they are deemed to be financially incapable of handling such large sums, or perhaps because they are too small for lofty enterprises like the high finance of the Fed, **the Fed has not loaned to any small American banks.**

The Fed created or expanded 11 separate lending facilities. The Primary Dealer Credit Facility (PDCF) provided collateralized loans to brokers. In some instances, the collateral was worthless. Over $1.5 Trillion of loans were made to borrowers pledging collateral with "ratings unavailable," a euphemism for junk bonds. Don't ask me which instances. The Fed won't elaborate further.[20]

The Fed was able to pick winners and losers in America. Lehman Brothers, for reasons yet unknown, was allowed to fail, even though Barclays Bank wanted to purchase it. Bear Sterns was also failing, but arrangements were made for it to be taken over by JP Morgan Chase. Others like Citigroup, JP Morgan Chase and Morgan Stanley, were not only helped, but also paid to manage the program. Libya's assets were frozen, but the Arab Bank, substantially owned by Gadhafi, was allowed to operate, though not with Libya.[21]

We were told the banks were bailed out so they, in turn, could make loans to our small businesses and help those whose mortgages had become unaffordable. Instead, the banks kept the money and invested in various financial instruments like credit cards loans and bundled mortgages, which were selling at a severe discount, which brought them great profits. *Think about it. Would you make mortgage loans, which bring less than 6% a year; or credit card loans, which bring in around 22% a year? Yup. You got the answer right. See, I told you; you are now an expert on High Finance.* **And now you know why no matter how much was loaned to the Banks and despite all of Obama's posturing about this or that plan to help homeowners stay in their homes; the banks have not passed on that money to help poor homeowners who were trying to refinance.**

Banks and other lenders often bundle their loans into securities and sell them to investors, providing the banks with cash to make new loans. But that market all but dried up in 2009. That's when the Fed started the TALF, or Term Asset-Backed Securities Loan Facility, which made low-interest loans to pension funds, hedge funds and other institutions willing to invest in these securities. They and other big investors took advantage of the $70 billion Federal Reserve loan program designed to pump money into the consumer and business lending markets.

There were at least two Pension Funds that benefitted hugely from Fed money. With $5.14 billion borrowed from the Fed, the California Public Employees' Retirement System, CalPERs, invested in a portfolio of high-performing credit card loans. CalPERs put in $350 million of its own money and earned a $175 million profit, a return of around 50 percent. CalPERs has repaid the Fed loan. The state's other big pension fund, the California State Teachers' Retirement System, CalSTRs, borrowed $225 million from the Fed and invested in commercial mortgages and student loans and made very good returns.[22]

To manage the borrowing, the Fed even paid over $649 Million to private contractors like JP Morgan Chase, Morgan Stanley, and Wells Fargo, the very banks that had caused the financial crisis in the first place. The same firms also received trillions of dollars in Fed loans at near-zero interest rates.[23] *Ask yourself, if the big banks were failing so badly, why were they given money and not the small American banks?*

As Rush Limbaugh has said, "The thing about TARP that was so unprecedented and so dangerous is that TARP gave government regulators the power and the money to buy up equity, that is, they were buying up ownership of companies. It means that the government is in a position to help friends and punish enemies on a scale not seen since the 1930s . . . . Obama can't let these people go under. They fund his existence. It would hurt the Democrat Party if these people went south. This is about a certain class of people protecting themselves, and the best way to protect themselves is to be in bed with Obama, in bed with the regime. This is about a certain segment of the rich protecting its political investment in Obama and Obama protecting their political investment in him. Let me tell you, these are the people who fund the Democrat Party. That's who's being bailed out."[24]

You may recall what I wrote in my Preface. I told you I wrote this book because America was becoming like a Socialist Third World country, corrupt to the core. I told you that in my native country the government picked winners and losers. Those who were on the side of the government got preferential loans. Those who were not were out of luck. So even they soon learned to pay ball. They put the government authorities' cousins, uncles or sons on their boards. And all the private institutions soon became wholly owned subsidiaries of the government; doing the government's bidding, appearing at events with government officials, voting for them and making sure the opposition party got none of their contributions. Well, now that you have learned how Obama and the Fed operate, is it any different?

The GAO investigation revealed some absolutely stunning conflicts of interest. The main problem with the Fed's lending is the complete lack of Congressional oversight, and the way the Fed seemed to pick winners who would be protected at any cost."[25] Solid evidence of the looting of America has been put right in front of us, and yet the mainstream media does not even seem interested. Instead, it appears the mainstream media is doing its best to cover up of the whole matter. *Yet another reason why you need to read and listen to conservative media!*

Many Fed officials giving out the loans also had very large investments in the financial institutions that were receiving these secret loans. So how were these conflicts handled? According to Senator Sanders, "the Fed provided "conflict of interest waivers" to employees and private contractors so they could keep investments in the same financial institutions and corporations that were given emergency loans." *See how it works. If you are well connected, you get to sit on the Board of the Federal*

Reserve or one of its 12 Federal Reserve Banks. As such, you get to vote on some loan program or another. The Fed implements that lending program by asking the guy at the computer to print a 1 with a bunch of zeros after it. And voila! The money is created. You then vote on who should receive this loan. And you, wearing your other hat as a well-connected bank or individual, get to borrow the money and make more money!

Senator Sanders noted one example of an egregious conflict of interest. The CEO of JP Morgan Chase, Jamie Dimon, one of Obama's good buddies, served on the New York Fed's board of directors at the same time that his bank received more than $390 Billion in financial assistance from the Fed.[26] Moreover, the Board also made the decision to loan the funds for Jamie Dimon's company, JP Morgan Chase to purchase of Bear Sterns for pennies on the dollar.[27] JP Morgan Chase also earned income as one of the clearing banks for the Fed's emergency lending programs. On May 11, 2012, Jamie Dimon disclosed that JP Morgan had lost $2 Billion in derivatives trades. Apparently, Dimon had transformed its Chief Investment Office (CIO), which manages risk for the company, to make bigger and riskier speculative trades with the bank's money.[28] Those in this group were aware that Bruno Michel Iskil, a JP Morgan trader at its London office, had made bets on credit default swaps with a face value of over $100 Billion.[29] As you can probably guess, another bailout is going to be needed. And you, the taxpayer, is going to have to pay yet again. And this demonstrates that banking establishments are more dangerous than standing armies.[30]

From December 2007 to October 2008, the Fed also opened swap lines with foreign central banks, allowing them to temporarily trade their currencies, steadily becoming worthless, for U.S. dollars, to relieve pressures in their financial markets.[31] You are shouting again: "***Where did all the money go?***" *Don't shout at me! And sit down before you get a heart attack!* Well, here is a partial list of who got the loans:[32]

$7.7 Trillion for U.S. Banks & Financial Institutions:
- **2.5 Trillion** for Citigroup
- **$2.03 Trillion** for Morgan Stanley
- **1.0 Trillion** for Merrill Lynch, acquired by Bank of America
- **$1.3 Trillion** for Bank of America
- **$853 billion** Bear Sterns, acquired by JP Morgan Chase

- **$814 billion**—Goldman Sachs
- **$391 billion**—JP Morgan Chase
- **$159 billion**—Wells Fargo
- **$142 billion**—Wachovia **zero** for small American banks

$3.08 Trillion to Foreign Banks & Financial Institutions:[33]
- **$868 billion**—Barclays PLC (UK)
- **$541 billion**—Royal Bank of Scotland (UK)
- **$354 billion**—Deutsche Bank (Germany)
- **$287 billion**—UBS (Switzerland)
- **$262 billion**—Credit Suisse (Switzerland)
- **$181 billion**—Bank of Scotland (UK)
- **$175 billion**—BNP Paribas (France)
- **$159 billion**—Dexia (Belgium)
- **$135 billion**—Dresdner Bank (Germany)
- **$124 billion**—Societe Generale (France)
- **$183 billion**—Lehman Brothers
- **$35 Billion** to Arab Banking Corp, part owned by Libya's Muammar Gadhafi, Abu Dhabi Investment Authority and Kuwait Investment Authority
- **Bank of China**[34]
- Norinchukin Bank
- European Central Bank[35]
- Central Banks of Australia, Denmark, England, Japan, Mexico, Japan, Norway, South Korea, Sweden and Switzerland
- Mizuho Securities
- BNP Paribas of France
- Sumitomo

$2.639 trillion for "All Other Borrowers." Among them:

Pension Funds:
- CalPERS
- CalSTRS
- Philadelphia Teamsters
- Omaha's Teachers
- City of Bristol, Connecticut general Retirement System
- Insurers and pension funds in Sweden and South Korea[36]

Corporations:
- $116 Billion General Electric
- Detroit Automakers
- $2.3 Billion Harley Davidson
- $1.5 Billion Verizon
- Caterpillar
- Toyota
- McDonalds

Individuals TALF:[37]
- John A. Paulson
- Michael S. Dell
- H. Wayne Huizenga
- Julian Robertson
- Kendrick R. Wilson III, a former Goldman executive who had been a top aide to Henry M. Paulson Jr., the Treasury secretary during the crisis
- Christy K. Mack, the wife of John J. Mack, the former chief executive of Morgan Stanley. [38]
- The mutual fund industry sold assets to Fed-financed buyers during the credit crisis, including funds sponsored by Fidelity, Black Rock, Merrill, T. Rowe Price and Oppenheimer

There is one commentator that says these numbers are being used to "rouse the rabble" *(meaning you and me.)* He claims there was never any loss for us to worry about. That all the money owing was repaid before new loans were made.[39] This is not true with respect to Bear Sterns, Lehman, Countrywide and Merrill Lynch, all of which went under. This is also not true with respect to loans made against insufficient or worthless collateral like the mortgage-based securities.[40] Furthermore, as you now know, as each Trillion was lent out, the Fed Reserve's private owners made $27 Million a day even if it lent at 1%. And, as our federal government got further into debt, we have to pay interest on that money. And as the Fed prints more and more money, our dollar becomes more worthless and the price of our goods like milk, bread and gasoline goes up. And Obama, that brilliant solver of all problems big and small, will chant, *"It is all the fault of the oil companies!"*

You ask, *"How can you get a computer that you can use to print ones and zeroes and make millions a day?"* Well, you can't use that computer. It is reserved for those smart and wise people who are looking after the finances of the country and preventing a meltdown of the financial system. Look how hard they worked in 2008-2009 to stabilize the markets. You ask, *"How did the markets get so destabilized in the first place if they were looking after them?"* Good Question. Next Question. You ask, *"Where is the discount window you can go to get those loans?"* Well, did you make donations to Obama's campaign? If you didn't you are SOL!

The Almost-October Surprise: I have gone to great lengths to let you know how the Magic Mystery Money Machine works so you will understand what comes next. When the Fed can simply type in ones and zeros into their computer and create money and bail out anyone it pleases; does it make any sense that there could be a financial crisis where big financial institutions couldn't get money?

Well, there was. And this is where the Nearly-October Surprise comes in. It all started with Indy Mac, a thrift, which was stuck with $10 Billion of underperforming mortgage loans it was unable to sell. In May 2008, Oaktree Management LP looked over its books as a condition of providing a $1 Billion loan to Indy Mac. According to Howard Marks, Chairman of Oaktree, it decided not to invest, but rather checked out what assets of Indy Mac it would buy if the bank failed. "We're bargain hunters. And we have a long history in distress," he said.[41]

Within days after Oaktree's decision; Senator Schumer chairman of the Senate Banking Committee, issued a press release disclosing confidential and very sensitive information about the precariousness of Indy Mac's situation.[42] Bank regulators were outraged. As the director of the Office of Thrift Supervision, John Reich pointed out the FDIC insured all the depositors and there was no risk to them. "As a regulator of insured depository institutions, we do not publicly comment on the financial condition or supervisory activities related to open and operating institutions," Reich wrote. "We believe it is critically important to maintain the confidentiality of examination and supervision information." John Hawke, US Comptroller of the Currency wrote: "If Schumer continues to go public with letters raising questions about the condition of individual institutions, he will cause havoc in the banking system. Leaking his IndyMac letter to the press was reckless and grossly irresponsible. I don't see how he can be trusted with confidential information in the future. What this incredibly stupid conduct does is put at risk the willingness of regulators to share any information with the [congressional] oversight committees. After this, you'd be crazy to share information with Schumer."[43] As you have probably realized by now, if you, as a private individual disclosed confidential information about a bank, all kinds of Federal Agencies would be on your case. But a Senator does not face any liability for doing the same thing.

Schumer's unwarranted disclosures had exactly the result the bank regulators had feared. Long lines of worried depositors snaked around the bank as they waited to withdraw their savings. Panic ensued. The Bank failed. In July 2008, the FDIC took over IndyMac and its assets, which then would be sold at fire sale prices.[44]

Incidentally, and perhaps not so incidentally, Oaktree owners are big political contributors, predominantly to Democrats. They have donated more than $700,000 to Senate Democrats and the Democratic Senatorial Campaign Committee during the four years that Sen. Schumer has chaired the campaign committee. Oaktree's Mr. Marks gave the Democrats' Senate Campaign Committee $20,000 in late March 2008. Mr. Marks said he is a longtime Democratic donor and has gotten fund-raising calls from Sen. Schumer. But, he said, "I know him socially. I've never talked business with him."[45]

So we have a bank that is in trouble. A strong supporter of Democrats and big donor to Senator Schumer investigates the books of the bank and decides not to lend but to buy assets if the bank failed. Senator Schumer discloses confidential deleterious information about the bank, which causes a run on the bank. Bank fails. It is taken over by the FDIC and its remaining assets have to be sold in a fire sale.

Back in my native country, everyone would understand that this is how business is done. And that is why all businessmen make sure they donate to the party in power. At best, they would say, "They are shocked! Shocked!" Just like Inspector Renault. Over here, everyone will be horrified. "These things shouldn't happen in America," they will fulminate. And that will be the end of the story. And politics, both in my native country and here, will go on as usual.

After this, there were a string of failures of financial institutions. Fannie Mae and Freddie Mac used to be privately owned. The Fed authorized new loans and the Treasure increased their credit lines on the same day in mid-July. President Bush signed a law creating the New Federal Housing Finance Agency (FHFA) in late July. On September 7, the FHFA took over Fannie Mae and Freddie Mac. On September 14, the Fed arranged for Bank of America to take over Merrill Lynch. On that same day, the Fed denied support to Barclays Bank as it sought to take over Lehman Brothers and they had to file for Chapter 11 Bankruptcy protection. The very next day, the Fed authorized a loan of $85 Billion to AIG.[46] *One can only conclude that Lehman must have been giving its campaign donations to the wrong party!!*

In 2007, AIG was the world's biggest insurer. Goldman Sachs was one of the world's biggest banks. Its former executives held high positions in government. Hank Paulson, a Goldman CEO was Treasury Secretary under George Bush and later, under Obama. Paulson insisted that AIG had to be bailed out because it was "too big to fail" and that repercussions of an AIG failure would ripple throughout and bring down the world's economy.

Within weeks of receiving funds, AIG funneled over $90 billion of the taxpayer funds to various U.S. and European banks. Societe Generale received $11.9 billion, Deutsche Bank $11.8 billion and Barclays PLC $8.5 billion. But the biggest beneficiary was politically connected Goldman Sachs Group Inc., which received $12.8 Billion. If AIG had defaulted, then Goldman would have received only pennies on the dollar. Under the agreement made with Obama, Goldman received full payment. And that triggered suspicions of conflicts of interest and favoritism to Goldman Sachs. *Once again, Inspector Renault is "Shocked! Shocked!!"*

After Schumer set in motion the financial crisis for Indy Mac, it was Paulson who set up the chain of events that led to the financial crisis of August 2008, just months before the November 2008 Presidential election. At the time, Senator McCain was leading in the polls. After that, Senator Obama took the lead and went on to win the election.[47]

In September, Paulson informed President Bush that the sky was falling and would crash the financial markets unless Congress approved the

$700 Billion Troubled Asset Relief Program, TARP, to bailout financial companies. After approval was obtained, this was extended to include bailouts of automakers.

Republicans and some Democrats in Congress balked at providing this money. They wanted time to consider the implications on the taxpayer. Paulson insisted that there was no time, that the stock market was crashing and that TARP had to be approved instantly, immediately, right away, this very minute! [48] It appears that most members of Congress were unaware of the existence of the Magic Mystery Money Machine that could have printed more than enough money to stop all stock markets from crashing. Paulson knew, but didn't tell!

Finally, Paulson got Bush to call a meeting with Bernanke, White House officials and senior members of Congress. Senator McCain suspended his campaign, flew back to Washington and insisted on participating in the meeting. According to Paulson himself, first, he tried to get the White House to prevent Senator McCain from coming. Then Paulson says he spoke with McCain who made it clear that they needed to protect the taxpayers. Paulson says he then resorted to a veiled threat that if McCain stopped the passage of TARP, Paulson would inform the public that it was McCain who caused the markets to fail. When that failed, Paulson himself called Obama and told him to come back too.

At the meeting, Bush said he trusted Bernanke and Paulson to be doing the right thing. Paulson then described the dire situation. He then asked Nancy Pelosi to speak, but she deferred to Obama. According to Paulson, it was clear that the Democrats had planned how to humiliate McCain. Obama then went through in detail (even without a teleprompter, as an admiring Paulson reports) what Paulson was asking for and said that the Democrats would deliver the votes. Then, he "sprang the trap" on McCain. The Democrats set up the story line that McCain's intervention had polarized the two sides and that the Republicans were walking away from an agreement because of McCain's interference and that McCain nearly caused the country's economy to sink. [49] This was not true. There had been no agreement. But McCain was boxed in and totally humiliated. The Democrats would not allow McCain to get any credit for anything.

And the Media-Mafia lackeys of the Democrats came in on cue. Once they had praised McCain and coaxed the Republicans to choose him over all other Republican contenders. McCain had believed that this mean the Press loved him. But it was not to be. The press pilloried McCain. He was incompetent. He was impulsive. He did not know how to manage finances. He did not know how to work with the other side. He was a bumbling old fool who suspended his campaign to come back just for show. It went on for weeks in every newspaper and every TV channel. When all this was over, McCain had slumped in the polls and never recovered. The nearly-October surprise had captured yet another Republican victim. And Obama coasted to victory in November.

So now, you know all about the Magic Mystery Money Machine. So let's recap:

1.   You know High Finance and will never again allow anyone to put you down and say you don't understand it. And you know that if they tell you it is too complicated for you to understand; then they are hiding something from you that you should know.
2.   You know that the Media hid all this information from you and you realize you have to go to the conservative media if you want to find out what is going on in this country.
3.   You have seen how Senator Schumer "unwittingly" assisted a big Democrat donor whose business was purchasing assets at a fire sale, and who never talked to Schumer about business, but magically Schumer divulged confidential information about a Bank that caused it to go under and be forced to sell its assets in a fire sale. So you know that sometimes, at least, it is not merely conspiracy theories at work.
4.   The whole rationale for allowing the Fed to print money is for it to protect our markets. But it has failed miserably at this task. Why should we continue to give it the right to create money? Isn't it time to fire that little clerk in that dungeon and smash that gold-plated money machine? Ask your Congressman what he plans to do about the Fed.
5.   Was there any reason why the Magic Mystery Money Machine couldn't have created enough money to prevent the markets from tanking?
6.   Since the Fed could have created the money needed, what was the purpose of that super-rush in which TARP was created and McCain

was humiliated; if not to give Obama a chance to look good and get elected?

7.   If Obama and the Fed are not in bed together, why does Obama not call upon the Millionaires and Billionaires in the Fed to pay their fair share and pay more taxes? Or at least, some taxes?

8.   Why has Obama not even told the American people about the federal government's arrangement with the private bank that is the Fed?

Chapter 12

Crucifying Private Industry

I have told you before about the Drift Nets surrounding Americans: Obama and his Czars and Regulators are operating exactly like those who use drift nets for deep-sea fishing. These "Walls of Death," made of virtually invisible plastic filaments, extend 50 feet down and extend 30-40 miles across the ocean. Unsuspecting fish, mammals and birds, have no idea they are trapped until the net is puled tight; and then, every single living creature inside is killed!! We are exactly like the unsuspecting fish, tangled in the drift nets. We are all uneasy. Something is wrong in America. The Constitution is being ignored whenever it suits Obama. Laws and Regulations are being changed with great speed. And wherever we turn, some Regulator is harassing us. Our people are all getting poorer and there seems to be no hope. Our Middle Class is sliding down into poverty. We are constantly being called racists and made to feel like evil people. But we can't quite put our fingers on it. Someday soon, the trap will be pulled shut. All that is necessary is for Obama to hit the switch. And his *Stealth Jihad* against us will be accomplished.

Have you thought about how much power the federal government has over you? Of course not, because you have assumed that you are just a small fry and, in any event, the government would not be malevolent towards someone so unimportant. But you must understand that the Government is the most powerful entity on earth. The "government" consists of the IRS, the DOJ, the EPA, the DOL and all those twenty million federal, state and municipal bureaucrats and regulators who have all that power over you and nothing to do but to torment you.

Obama and his Regulators, Steven Chu, Lisa Jackson, Ken Salazar, Janet Napolitano, Kathleen Sibelius and Eric Holder Will Trap You and Destroy You!

Think about it. Does the government do anything productive? Manufacture widgets? Produce anything that makes money? No. Every public corporation is required to produce balance sheets accounting for all its income and all its expenditures. You have seen Henry Waxman at work, demanding that those who received government money explain what they did with it. Now ask yourself a question. Have you ever seen an accounting of what government does with your money? How many pot holes does it fill? How much overtime does it pay? What are the wage scales? What are the perks? How does the government balance its books? You have seen nothing. All you know is that whatever you have paid in taxes, sales taxes, gas taxes, property taxes, whatever; it is not enough. Obama will continue to fly around the country at our expense, chanting *"Jizya! Taxes!! I need more taxes!!"*

Except for our Military and our FBI, all the government does is regulate you and tax you. And that does mean you! Just a simple example will suffice. A friend of mine got a $150 ticket for parking outside a mailbox. No, it wasn't the Postal Service's mailbox. It was her mailbox outside her own home, in a quiet residential cul de sac with no restrictions on parking! And she parked after 6.00 p.m. when the mailman was long gone. Can she get this silly law changed? Of course not. Can she call to complain? She will get a machine asking her to "press 1 for English, 2 for Spanish" and an array of extensions she could pick. But, this being a government department, there will not be any customer service extension she can call to complain. Frequently, she will be recycled back to the main menu and have to go through the whole process again. If she finally finds an extension with the right person, she will have to wait on hold for ages. And then, when she finally gets a live person, she will be told there is nothing that can be done, this is the law. Can she contest this? She must first pay the ticket. Then lose income and take time off from work to hang around in court. Then, even if she wins, she has to wait months for her refund to be issued. Most of the time, when trying to reverse an unjust fine or fee, it is so onerous and time consuming, we just pay up and shut up! See how it works: Silly regulations. Punitive fines. And she is trapped in the drift net, spending money she can ill afford to fund a bunch of regulators who will continue to promulgate ridiculous laws with which to torment and fine her and the rest of the public for the rest of their lives!

Onerous regulations are being issued first by one, and then another, of Obama's regulators, making it more and more difficult for small businesses to make a profit. And so they are laying off workers. Taxes are going up. Prices are going up. People are losing their jobs. It is these Regulators who have the power to destroy any business, any industry and our economy and make the prices of your everyday essentials rise. It is your electricity, your water, your heating oil, your gas, your food bill, your clothing bills and your healthcare costs that rise as the government promulgates new regulations and forces businesses to incur unnecessary costs and increase the prices of goods you need, or shut them down altogether, also causing your prices to rise. And as a consequence, Americans are being squeezed into poverty, a little bit here, a little bit there. This is making us more dependent on our ruler Obama, and his government, to provide us with money to live; and is making our country more and more like a Muslim controlled Caliphate.

Unfortunately, Government thinks it should be a growth industry; if they aren't growing, they think they're not doing a good job. Even worse, the Socialists/Communists know that by growing Government they are growing their core supporters. And the regulators know that if they stopped regulating you, it would be an admission that they are unnecessary and they could be fired. So, the regulators will always find things you do that they must regulate. And as government gets bigger, they will regulate you even more and become more entrenched. And how do they regulate? Al Armendariz, an EPA Regulator, told us how:

"You make examples out of people . . . . And you hit them as hard as you can and there is a deterrent effect there. These companies respond to both the public image but also financial pressure . . . . It was kind of like how the Romans used to, you know, conquer villages in the Mediterranean," Al Armendariz, an Environmental Protection Agency official, told a town hall meeting in 2010. *"They'd go into a little Turkish town somewhere, **they'd find the first five guys they saw, and they'd crucify them**. And then, you know, that town was really easy to manage for the next few years."* [1]

When this little glimpse behind the curtain was leaked in May 2012, Mr. Armendariz was given his marching orders. He had gloated over that dirty little secret the American public was not supposed to find out. That the Obama Administration was using all available tools to terrorize and subjugate American Industry and the American people. Notice their philosophy. It did not matter whether the person or corporation was big or small, guilty or not. ***Find the first five guys you see and crucify them. And then, the Country will be really easy to manage!***

It is Obama himself who has led the pack in terrorizing our people. In 2008, AIG was the world's biggest insurer. AIG's bankruptcy was averted with an infusion of $82 Billion of taxpayer money, which, as you saw in the last chapter, went primarily to Goldman Sachs. If AIG had defaulted, then Goldman would have received pennies on the dollar. But under the agreement made with Obama and organized by Secretary of the Treasury Hank Paulson, a former Goldman Sachs Chairman, Goldman received full payment. But it was AIG that was vilified for being "the one who took the bailout."

A week later, **AIG** hosted a previously scheduled corporate event to St. Regis Resort at Monarch Beach. The hosts were not the traders/speculators who put AIG in the soup; these were the people who were selling good insurance products and making money for AIG. The event cost $440,000 and included $200,000 for rooms, $23,000 for spa and related services and $7,000 for greens fees.

Obama acted outraged. He went around the country criticizing companies that received federal money for taking corporate junkets and ginning up hatred against them. *"You can't go take that trip to Las Vegas or go down to the Super Bowl on the taxpayers' dime,"* he shouted. During a subsequent meeting in New Hampshire, Obama insisted we should curb spending during tough economic times. *"When times are tough, you tighten your belts,"* the president intoned. *"You don't go buying a boat when you can barely pay your mortgage. You don't blow a bunch of cash on Vegas when you're trying to save for college."*[2] Obama's press acolytes picked this up and magnified it. So, in no time flat, the whole country was terrorized.

Henry Waxman, that great investigator of all things big and little, demanded that AIG provide his Committee with a listing of all conferences, events, or retreats paid for by AIG, its subsidiaries, or affiliates, documenting the charges paid for each conference since January 1 to 6 months hence. Waxman also demanded all payroll information for every employee of AIG, its subsidiaries or affiliates; all participants in the Partners Plan; all participants in the Senior Partners Plan; and all employees in the Financial Products Division. Finally, Waxman demanded every single email, document or other communication sent or reviewed by Joseph Cassano, William Kolbert, Pierre Micottis, and Doug Poling during a two-year period.[3] There was nothing that Waxman didn't insist on investigating, no matter how remotely related to the corporate event in question.

AIG explained that no corporate executives attended this event. That this was a previously scheduled event held for its best customers.[4] But this was no excuse. If the AIG executives had done anything wrong, and even if they hadn't, Waxman was going to get them. And, worse than even Waxman's inquisitions, its executives were targeted with death threats. AIG workers were instructed not to travel alone at night and to park in well-lit areas. They hired security guards to protect their wives and kids at their homes. Busloads of union activists, exhorted by Obama's brown shirts, the SEIU and Acorn, armed with bullhorns and placards arrived at the homes of AIG executives in Connecticut. Fortunately, the presence of the security guards prevented any violence.[5]

Next, Fannie Mae and Freddie Mac finally slipped into default. These private entities (with Government backing) provided the fuel for the fire by fecklessly lending money to the subprime lenders. The Democrats' social engineers hounded Banks for discriminating against minorities and forced them to lend without regard for accepted underwriting standards, even if the minorities had bad credit. The result was no doc, no equity loans that never should have been made. When the economy turned, people were unable to refinance, and vast amounts of mortgages went into default. Countrywide went into default. The whole mortgage system ground to a halt.[6]

Franklin Raines, one of the chief executives of Fannie Mae who presided over this slide into the abyss, made $115 Million between 1997-2004, of which $52.6 million was bonuses for growing the Fannie Mae balance sheet with billions of subprime loans that went into default as soon as the merry-go-round stopped (conveniently after he was gone). **James Johnson** received $35 Million from 1993-1998 and total compensation of $100 million.[7] **Jamie Gorelick**, yes the same Jamie Gorelick that created the wall between the FBI and the CIA, which prevented them from discovering the 9/11 plot, also worked at Fannie Mae as its Vice President. She collected $26.5 Million dollars in salary, bonuses, performance pay and stock options in 1998-2003, working diligently overseeing the collapse of Fannie Mae.[8] **Barney Frank** (D-MA), got his boyfriend, Herb Moses, a six figure job with Fannie Mae. Then, using his foul mouth and bullying style, together with other Democrats, he made sure no one could investigate these two lenders or rein in their reckless practices.[9] Later on, an investigation by OFHEO revealed that during Raines' tenure, Fannie Mae "systematically manipulated accounting estimates, ignored accounting requirements it had lobbied unsuccessfully against and operated with weak internal controls that helped obscure the other problems," overstating profits by $10.6 Billion.[10]

But before that, Fannie & Freddie had helped their Democrat sponsors. But this was really just one big back-scratching marathon, as Fannie & Freddie made their biggest donations to Democrat protectors: **Chris Dodd got $165,000; Barack Obama got $126,000 and Billionaire John Kerry got $111,000.**[11] Countrywide, and its Chairman Angelo Mozilo, which owed its good fortune almost entirely to Fannie and Freddie, had its VIP program where they provided discounted home loans to **Democrat Senators Chris Dodd and Kent Conrad. Jim Johnson** himself got more than $7 Million in below-market loans from Countrywide.[12] Little surprise, years later Jimmy became an Obama bundler and was on Obama's select committee to vet his Vice President.

As we now know, both Fannie and Freddie went into conservatorship. The government took them over and gave them $116.1 billion and $72.3 billion respectively in bailout funds. As of May 2012, Fannie still owes $93.5 billion and Freddie approximately $54 Billion.[13] But we're still not finished. The SEC sued Fannie & Freddie and its top executives.[14] But not to worry, the taxpayer is paying for their defense. **As of February 2012, we have paid $99.4 million dollars to defend just 3 Fannie Mae executives.**[15]

But Obama and his cronies blamed the banks for the entire mortgage crisis. Laughably, Chris Dodd and Barney Frank have now collaborated on the eponymous Dodd-Frank bill "to rein in risk-taking by the Banks!" (less than ten years after they exhorted them to abandon all underwriting standards when it came to making mortgages); and "to restrain executive salaries in the future" (after their good buds and benefactors, Raines, Johnson and Mozilo skated with millions in bonuses for inflating the real estate bubble and bringing us the Great Recession).

And to make sure the Bank executives understood they were going to take the blame, Obama arranged the SEIU and ACORN to picket the homes of the bank executives, calling them "Greedy Rich Bankers." In one instance, over 500 thugs arrived in 14 school buses and cars at the home of Greg Baer, a relatively junior Bank of America executive and a Democrat who had worked for President Clinton. They poured out of the busses, carrying placards, shouting slogans over bullhorns, and climbed up the front steps to the front porch of the home on a weekend when no one other than a 14-year-old child was at home. In terror, he locked himself in the bathroom. After that, they went on to the home of a JP Morgan Chase official.[16] This protest certainly terrorized and intimidated the bank executives.

Of course, there's a backstory. The SEIU owed Bank of America $90 million of principal and another $4 million in interest and fees, and was in the midst of a campaign to organize bank tellers and call centers. Not a bad way to worsen employee morale and batter Bank of America's image through protests, making workers more susceptible to union calls to organize. Incidentally, the SEIU spent $70 million on Obama's election and the election of other Democrats in 2008.[17]

All this makes me sick. This is exactly what happened in my native country. The Socialists making themselves rich; working with union leaders using bull horns and placards to incite workers to hate "the rich;" instigating class envy and hatred; and creating havoc in the country. Remember what Obama did with his fellow Luo tribesman, the Muslim Raila Odinga, in Kenya? He instigated class envy and hatred among the Muslims for Christians in Kenya. In Kenya it ended with Muslims burning over 600 churches with Christians inside them. Tell me, why is Obama bringing Third World politics into this country? Is he planning to generate chaos in this country too?

You will recall that the automakers were so terrorized by all this that they left their company jets sitting back in Detroit, and took cars to get themselves down to Waxman's hearings!

As a consequence of Obama's extremely harsh criticism, militant picketing outside the homes of AIG and Bank executives by ACORN and SEIU thugs and Waxman's ruthless inquisitions, the whole country went into a funk. Business came to a standstill because no one wanted to take any risks. And no one wanted to stand out as someone who was spending too much. No more spending at all. No more giving your staff meals. No more entertaining your customers. Hunker down, and hope Obama's menacing eye won't bear down on you.

This was the actual beginning of the Great Recession! I don't want you to think that I am in favor of profligate spending. I'm not. But undoubtedly the vituperations heaped upon private industry by hypocritical Democrat leaders sure tamped down private sector spending at a time when that spending would have been a great stimulus for the economy.

Virtually all corporations cancelled their previously scheduled corporate events. And since hotels and resorts rely on corporate events to provide them with over 60% of their business, a great many of them went into bankruptcy. Among them, the Ritz Carlton of Half Moon Bay, the Ritz Carlton of Dana Point,[18] the Tamarack Resort of Idaho,[19] the Wigwam Golf and Spa Resort of Arizona,[20] the Amelia Island Plantation Resort of Florida, and the Illikai Resort of Hawaii.[21]

Law Vegas was devastated. Consolidated Time Share Resorts,[22] Consolidated Condo Resorts,[23] the Fontainebleau Resort[24] and others went into bankruptcy. A multi-billion dollar project, the City Center, with 5 different hotels, including the Aria and Crystals, nearly went into bankruptcy and only opened a scaled down version 2 years later.[25] Croupiers, waiters, cooks, dancers, costume designers, hair stylists, manicurist, cab drivers and countless other workers lost their jobs. House values fell, delinquencies rose and now Nevada leads the nation in foreclosures. Even today, 3 years later, Las Vegas is in dire financial trouble.

Meantime, the Obamas have spent our money liberally on themselves. They have gone on 16 vacations in 3 years. Obama has played 90 rounds of golf, which, at the rate of 4-5 hours per round, and 25 hours of work per 4-1/3 weeks per month, amounts to another 3 months' vacation.

Among the vacations is an August 2009 vacation at Martha's Vineyard where Michelle took an Air Force 2 jet just four hours ahead of Obama, who came on Air Force 1. Three Christmas vacations to Hawaii at $1.5 Million dollars a pop. In 2010, Michelle flew ahead of her husband to Hawaii, at an extra cost of over $100,000.[26] Michelle and Barack flew to New York on Air Force 1 to have a dinner date. Michelle's trainer is flown down from Chicago to D.C 2-3 times a week.[27]

Hawaii. Vail. Martha's Vineyard. Costa del Sol, Spain. African Safaris. India. All are included in the Obama vacation itinerary.

In 2010, Obama flew on Air Force 1 for his birthday bash to Chicago. Meantime, according to the London Daily Mail, Michelle took her younger daughter and 40 friends to a $650 a night Villa Padierna Palace Hotel where they had reserved 69 out of 129 rooms. They were accompanied by 86 agents and had an entourage of 14 cars.[28] Judicial Watch had to bring a FOIA lawsuit to get the details. But still, only scant details were provided. The Air Force Jet is said to have cost $189,323. The 15-member flight crew stayed at a separate hotel costing around $15,000. The secret service cost $254,481 of which some $50,000 were fees paid to a travel planning company half-owned by George Soros. The White house claimed that only 10 people went and that the 4 friends paid their own way. They have declined to give the cost of food, spa, transportation, etc.[29]

In June 2011, Mrs. Obama also took another trip to South Africa and Botswana. For this trip, Judicial Watch was only able to obtain the cost for the flight and crew—$424,142. Once again, the expense records and passenger manifests, off flight food, transportation, security costs, etc., were not supplied, on "security" grounds. On President's Day 2012, Michelle and her eldest daughter flew to Vail, Colorado. We don't have the numbers for that either.

Check out the details listed above, required by Waxman from private corporations when they held corporate events for their clients with their own money. But our tax money, when spent by the Obamas, is secret! If only Henry Waxman were in charge, he would have pinned down all the details for us. . . . Not!

Then, there was Obama's India trip, hastily arranged when it became obvious the Democrats were going to lose big in the 2010 elections.[30] Forty planes and helicopter gunships were used. Three Marine One choppers were disassembled, flown to India and reassembled for Obama's use. Forty cars were used, including 6 armored cars equipped with the nuclear codes. Thirty sniffer dogs were put in service. The President's chef was brought along. 547 rooms were booked. All the rooms and banquet rooms in the top of the line Taj Mahal Hotel were fully booked and the staff put on curfew, so they had to stay within the hotel premises, and obviously, be paid time and half overtime pay for the extra work. 125 additional rooms were booked at the Taj President and 80-90 rooms at the ITC Grand Hyatt.[31] An Indian newspaper estimated the cost at $200 Million dollars a day, taking into account the cost of the advance staff and the various local security services.[32] Obama's defenders have informed us that that is a gross exaggeration, but that the detailed costs cannot be provided for us because of "security concerns."

Don't laugh. There is a "security concern" about not letting the American public know of the extravagance of our President at a time when the rest of us are hurting. He wouldn't get re-elected if they found out what his trips cost!

Then, there was Obama's 13-year-old daughter's spring break in Mexico. She took 12 friends and was accompanied by 25 secret servicemen acting as bodyguards. Presumably they went in an Air Force plane. And, of course, we are being given no details about the cost to the taxpayer, except that it cost around $1 million dollars.[33] Even worse, various liberal newspapers and web sites, the London Telegraph, Huffington Post and Yahoo News, which first reported the story, have now taken it down, in craven submission to their Muslim ruler.[34]

Abusing the private industry while wasting public money on themselves is a common practice among Dictators and Rulers. And their flunkeys do the same. That is why the GSA is spends $823,000 on 3-day junkets to Las Vegas. And why the Secret Service is hiring prostitutes on our dime at $800 a night.

Armendariz is not an isolated case. Obama has created a two-tiered government, fronted by Cabinet Secretaries who were able to

withstand public scrutiny and then, behind the scenes, another tier of Czars, who work in secret and who could not withstand public scrutiny. Obama has appointed 35 czars, whom he has not presented for Advice and Consent to the Senate as required by the Constitution. This means that the FBI has not vetted them and they have not received any security clearance because they have secrets in their background that would preclude them from getting a clearance. A good example of this would be if you were a member of the Communist party or some radical group that advocates the overthrow of our government. Under this principal, Obama himself could not qualify for a National Security Clearance. He has not disclosed his various associations with communists—Frank Marshall Davis, his mentor in Hawaii, Bill Ayers and Bernadine Dohrn, admitted members of the anarchist, terrorist Weather Underground, Khalid Mansoor, the Black Nationalist and Black Muslim who sponsored Obama in college and Jeremiah Wright, who calls himself a Christian and yet preaches a virulent hatred of Jews and America itself. Many of the Czars have jobs that are duplicated by official Cabinet Secretaries. And they are among the highest paid staffers at the White House.[35] This means we are paying twice for the same job. *But you are not going to be so cheap as to deny Obama a few extra regulators, are you?*

Take a look at the results of Obama's "green" energy programs. Solar energy companies have gone bust or shipped their production to China. Wind produces energy only 20% of the time and kills thousands of birds. Green slime costs so much no one can afford it, and it will stink so much no one will want it anywhere near their homes. The only reason anyone can want "green" energy is that they are benefiting financially from government subsidies and tax breaks or else, they are working with Middle East oil potentates to see to it that we never become energy independent of them.

Liberals vehemently oppose finding our own sources of traditional energy in the U.S. Obama has done everything in his power, and some things outside his power, to prevent us from getting our own energy. It was his punitive actions on that most American of all energy industries—Coal—and his actions during and after the Deepwater Horizon oil spill that made me question his motives.

I knew he was a Socialist. I knew he would favor his rich cronies. But I couldn't understand why he would harm the country to such an extent. Think of what he did. First, exactly as he planned, he destroyed the coal industry with his EPA rules, shutting down dozens of coal-fired plants near term and making it economically impossible to build or renovate or expand any other plants. Next, he went after Oil.

Who benefits when we don't have coal and can't get our own oil? Why, Obama's Muslim brethren, of course. Explain to me why Bloomberg, who is in partnership with Prince bin Talal, is giving $50 million to the Sierra Club to destroy the coal industry? And don't tell me about the environment and how only Obama and liberals love the environment. Look at how even the Sierra Club has been bought off! They triumphantly "defeat" coal industries and put thousands of people out of work. But when thousands of birds are being slaughtered in "lethal takes" by Democrat-owned Wind Farms, the Sierra Club is silent. And can somebody explain to me why Obama is making America more dependent on OPEC if he is not pursuing *Stealth Jihad* against America?

Destroying Traditional Energy Sources, particularly Coal, is, and has always been, the goal of this Administration. A true President of the country would work with business leaders to ascertain what our energy needs are now, and how much increased capacity we would need in the future. And he would then do everything in is power to see to it that our needs are met. A true President would know of the danger to America of us relying on Mid-East oil. He knows that when we become too dependent, we have to obey what they say. He knows they would use their wealth to buy up more of our businesses and make us even more dependent on OPEC potentates. And our leader would do his best to help us find our own energy sources.

But instead, Obama is using EPA mandates to close down coal plants; preventing us from drilling on 97% of federal land and 98% of offshore federal properties; getting his EPA to shut down shale extraction; and personally shutting down the Keystone XL pipeline which would bring us oil from Canada. Does this sound like a leader who loves his country and cares about the economic plight of his people? Does it even sound like we are his people? Take a look at what he has done to coal, electricity, shale and the pipeline.

Before the 2008 election, Obama gave himself away to the San Francisco Chronicle when he said, *"Under my plan of a cap-and-trade system, electricity rates would necessarily skyrocket. Even regardless of what I say about whether coal is good or bad. Sure, if the industry wants to build coal-fired power plants, they can go ahead and try. But they can only do it in a way that will bankrupt the coal industry."*[36] When Sarah Palin pointed out that the Chronicle downplayed this; the Chronicle made a big deal about how they had not downplayed it and how Palin was lying about the downplaying, etc.

Note carefully how the media distracts you. The whole discussion after this event became one of whether or not the Chronicle had disclosed this properly or downplayed it. And they obfuscated what Obama had actually said. Today, three years later, you can see for yourself how important it was for us to have known that Obama planned to destroy the coal industry!

Remember always, the Media is not trying to inform you. They are doing what it takes, including lying, to get their man Obama re-elected!! So when the media tries to distract you by playing 3-card Monte with you; focus, focus, focus, on what they are trying to hide!!

It was Stephen Chu who "joked" that he wanted U.S. energy prices to reach European levels of $8 to $10 per gallon. Working with him is Secretary of the Interior, Ken Salazar, who claimed that even $10 a gallon gas would not help him change his mind about permitting offshore drilling; and Lisa Jackson, the EPA administrator, who has passed EPA rules that are causing coal fired plants, that produce the cheapest energy and produce 45-50% of the country's electricity, to either shut down or consider shutting down. Is it any wonder that oil prices are out of control, never falling much below $100 a barrel?

Their goal is to make solar, wind energy, green scum energy and other "green" energy competitive with regular oil, gas and hydro energy. Since they are unable to bring down the price of their green energy to come even close to the price of traditional energy; they have "solved" the problem by issuing regulations to ensure that the price of traditional energy goes up. But do we really need "green" energy?

We have more oil, gas and shale oil reserves that any OPEC nation.[37] We have enough crude to fuel the American economy for 2041 more years. Underneath the Rocky Mountains alone is a reserve of 2 Trillion barrels of oil. We have 8 times as much as Saudi Arabia, 18 times as much as Iraq, 21 times as much as Kuwait, 22 times as much as Iran and 500 times as much as Yemen.[38] We also have coal. A quarter of the world's recoverable coal reserves are in America. We have more energy in the form of coal than the entire Middle East has oil. Coal can meet current domestic demand for more than 200 years. Question: So why this mania for "green" energy? Answer: How else can we funnel billions of dollars to our cronies?

(a) Coal is the first industry Obama has crucified: Almost immediately after taking office, the Obama Administration began rewriting and dramatically altering a recently completed coal regulation, the 2008 Stream Buffer Zone Rule (Rule) that had been promulgated only after an Environmental Impact Statement (EIS) was issued after five years of environmental analysis and careful scientific consideration.

Obama hired another contractor to write an entirely new EIS to justify rewriting the Rule. But an AP report revealed that this draft EIS concluded that Obama's new regulation could cost over 7,000 mining jobs and cause economic harm in 22 states. Shortly thereafter, the Obama Administration criticized and dismissed the contractor it had selected to conduct this analysis.[39] *The millions wasted on the new EIS? Chump change. Besides, who cares? You do want Obama to fulfill his promises and destroy the coal industry, don't you?*

To prevent "Global Warming," enforce Cap & Trade on the Sly: So what is Cap & Trade? The most important thing you need to know about it is that Al Gore would have made billions off it. Cap & Trade rations energy, so we don't use "too much" of it, so we prevent "global warming." Incidentally, it also destroys economic development, which cannot take place without a stable and reliable source of energy. *(For all you Silicon Valley liberals, what would happen to your computers if I cut off electricity; or made the price of electricity "necessarily skyrocket;" to your server farms in the mid-west and other cheap electricity regions?)* Cap & Trade "Caps" the amount of emissions each and every company can emit. If they exceed their allotment, they have to "Trade" with another company who has not used up their allotment. Your friendly government bureaucrat will ascertain how many emissions your company or small business can emit. *(In my native country, this would mean that you have to haul out your checkbook!)* Everyone has to trade on an exchange. And Al Gore was going to own the exchange and get a commission on each and every trade. Billions in trading commissions! Now you know why he ruthlessly attacks every person who questions the evidence of global warming!

Anyway, Cap and Trade legislation had been jammed through the Democrat controlled House before the 2010 elections. But the Democrat controlled Senate, realizing this was political suicide, did not pass it. The day after the 2010 election Obama said: *"Cap-and-trade was just one way of skinning the cat; it was not the only way. It was a means, not an end. And I'm going to be looking for other means to address this problem."*[40]

On March 29, 2012, when everyone else was distracted by the U.S. Supreme Court hearings on ObamaCare; President Obama's EPA quietly released long-delayed regulations to apply global warming inspired rules never authorized by Congress to new coal-fired power plants. *(Note how Obama's EPA constantly exceeds its Constitutional mandate. Only Congress has the right to make laws. But the EPA regularly makes laws under the guise of "rule-making." What's a little violation of the Constitution among friends if the goal is to do what Obama deems to be "right?")* These rules will effectively block any new coal-fired power plants from being built in America, and a second round of related rules—expected after the 2012 election, of course—would shut down all existing coal-fired power plants. **In short, the coal industry will be crucified**!

Lisa Jackson and her EPA are job-killing machines and they don't care about the consequences of their actions. The EPA's new Maximum Achievable Control Technology (MACT) mandates require US power plants to cut the emissions of mercury from 29 tons a year to 5. Yet the EPA itself estimates that cutting even as much as 41 tons out of 106 tons "is unlikely to substantially affect total risk." For zero benefit, the EPA has issued one of the most expensive federal regulations ever. Of course, since the EPA is required to compare the cost and benefit of proposed regulations, the EPA (with great foresight) ensured that the proposed regulations would not incur any cost, because the cost of building a new coal-fired plant with MACT would be so prohibitive that no new coal fired plants would ever be built! Even the normally Democrat supporting Unions for Jobs and the Environment, an alliance of unions representing more than 3.2 million workers, has estimated that this needless regulation would jeopardize 251,000 jobs.

Tougher air quality rules from the Environmental Protection Agency are forcing some companies to choose between costly upgrades, closing older plants or building new power plants that can also run on cleaner-burning natural gas. The regulations would force coal energy plants to install giant scrubber-like materials inside smokestacks to capture and cleanse carbon particles before their atmospheric release. 81 gigawatts of existing generation are 'likely' or 'very likely' to be retired as a consequence of new EPA rules. That's nearly 8 percent of our installed capacity for electric generation and a retirement at that scale could have drastic consequences for many parts of our country, with brownouts and rolling blackouts a virtual certainty particularly in the industrial heartland. (*Those red states that refuse to vote for Obama deserve what they get! But remember, server farms cannot run with constant brownouts and rolling blackouts. Computers and servers will be destroyed without a stable source of electricity!!*)

A recent report from the Edison Electric Institute found that the Obama administration's air-quality policies alone could force the retirement of up to 90,000 megawatts of coal power, and require $200 billion in retrofits by 2020. The upgrade cost would fall on company employees and coal miners in the form of layoffs; as well as on businesses, which could expect to pay more for energy and have to raise the prices of their products; and on homeowners directly. [41] They will drain the disposable income of consumers and, most important, be a huge barrier to the creation of new manufacturing jobs. The result will be steeply higher electricity prices, lost jobs, and lower standards of living. An UBS stock analyst estimated the rates for power would rise from $126 per megawatt per day to $200. Another analyst predicted rates could go as high as $500. It is also possible the new rule would also apply to power plants that are modified, upgraded or even repaired. The added costs will pose significant hardships for hardworking Americans and be a barrier to companies contemplating building manufacturing facilities in the U.S.[42] *Remember our good friend Armendariz's theory? You don't have to be guilty in order to be punished!*

The Sierra Club rejoiced. It crowed that along with the 106 announced closures, 166 new plants **have been defeated** since 2002![43] *Take that, you electricity using retards!* 106 coal plants, 319 coal-fueled generating units totaling 42,895 megawatts, about 13 percent of the nation's coal fleet, have been announced closed nationwide since January 2010.[44] The Sierra Club claimed that this would prevent 2,042 premature deaths, 3,229 heart attacks and 33,053 asthma attacks each year and that altogether, these plants retiring will save about $15.6 billion in health care costs.[45] *(Don't ask me how they know it is 2042 premature deaths and not 2043. Or how they came up with the number of $15.6 billion saved in health care costs. I could just as easily say "A quarter of a million people are going to lose their jobs and there will be 2046 premature deaths caused by the stress of losing their jobs, their homes and getting divorced because of the Sierra Club and EPA rules." And I would be more accurate!!!)*

In 2012, New York Mayor Michael R. Bloomberg pledged to give the Sierra Club $50 million over four years if it can ensure by 2015 that a third of the nation's current coal plants are retired or slated for closure.[46] Coal is our cheapest fuel. If Mayor Bloomberg really cared about the American people, he would invest his $50 million in building cleaner burning coal plants in the U.S.A., wouldn't he? That way, he would achieve the environmentalist's goal and also ensure that America would not be dependent on Saudi oil. But the less coal we use, the more oil we have to buy from the Middle East. Mayor Bloomberg has joint investments with Prince bin-Talal of Saudi Arabia, which are so important that he has become an ardent supporter of the 9/11 Victory Mosque. I have no idea how much Bloomberg has invested in Middle East oil. But just as our media was very suspicious of Bush and Cheney and their oil connections when we went into Iraq; shouldn't our media ask Mayor Bloomberg about his oil connections and whether they are the motive for his absurdly generous "gift" of $50 million to ensure the destruction of our coal plants?

And what about the Sierra Club? What are they doing getting $50 million from Bloomberg to destroy coal while ignoring the birds being destroyed by Wind Farms?

Indiana is devastated. They get 95% of their electricity from coal.[47] Alcoa, which makes aluminum, of which a huge input cost is energy, is now building a plant in Saudi Arabia. Dow Chemical is doing the same thing"[48]

Ohio-based utility FirstEnergy recently announced it was going close six coal-fired power plants due to the costs associated with EPA regulations. The reduction in the supply of power is expected to almost double electricity prices.[49] In January 2012, Ohio based FirstEnergy Corporation said that six coal fired plants in Ohio, Pennsylvania and Maryland would be retired. All of those plans are due to be off line and shut down by September 1, 2012. In February 2012, it announced it will close three coal-fired power plants in West Virginia, Albright Power Station, Willow Island Power Station, and the Rivesville Power Station, by this fall. The company says 105 employees will be directly impacted. 660 megawatts and about 3% of FirstEnergy's total generation will be lost. In recent years, the plants served as "peaking facilities" and generated power during times of peak demand for power. The availability of these "peak demand" facilities keeps the cost of electricity low. The high cost to implement MACTS and other environmental rules is the reason these power plants are being retired."

American Electric Power (AEP), is another Ohio-based utility with a heavy reliance on coal. AEP said it will cost $6-$8 billion to comply with the EPA's rules and also to transition from coal to natural gas. The state has given the utility permission to recover these costs by raising its prices to the public. The plan also allows AEP to recover investments is solar power. And hardworking families and businesses will be forced to pay for Obama's energy policy.[50]

Pennsylvania is being hit hard: GenOn Energy Inc. plans to close five of its older coal-fired power plants in Pennsylvania over the next four years. These generate a total of 3,140 megawatts of electricity. The plants are in Portland, Shawville, Titus, New Castle and Elrama. Two plants in Ohio and one in New Jersey will also be closed. 315 people could lose their jobs.[51] The second set of plant closures will include 8 power plants, seven fired by coal, between June 2012 and May 2015.[52]

Illinois' second largest power generator, Midwest Generation, may abandon the state. Two Chicago coal-fired plants will close in the near future, Midwest Generation is reportedly considering closing each of its four other Illinois plants, and this could lead to more than 1,000 job losses and increased power prices.[53]

West Virginia has been devastated by a different set of EPA rules. In April 2010, the EPA issued new guidelines for companies seeking Clean Water Act permits for proposed surface coal mines, threatening not only to end surface coal mining in West Virginia but also to affect all forms of mining in the state. The EPA is also attacking coal mining, by trying to stop the technique known as mountaintop removal. Endless environmentalist lawsuits have lost in the courts, but the Obama EPA now claims that salt runoff from the process violates the Clean Water Act because it harms a short-lived insect (not an endangered species.) It has now proposed a rule that EPA Administrator Lisa Jackson concedes would effectively outlaw an industry that employs more than 15,000 miners in Appalachia.[54] West Virginia's then Democrat Gov. Joe Manchin sued the Obama administration in 2010 to overturn new federal rules on mountaintop removal mining because they usurped the authority of the state and the West Virginia Department of Environmental Protection.[55]

Texas has been attacked with yet another EPA rule: Then there's EPA's out-of-the-blue ruling last month, ordering Texas to cut emissions of sulfur dioxide by 47 percent. The draft version of the Cross State Air Pollution Rule had exempted the state entirely. The excuse for the change? A supposed need to slightly reduce emissions as monitored 500 miles away in Madison County, IL, a locale that meets the EPA air-quality standards in question. And the EPA only gave Texas just six months to comply, knowing it takes three years to build the necessary controls.

Particularly hard-hit will be Luminant, the largest merchant power producer in Texas, which relies on high-sulfur coal. It says curtailing plant and/or mine operations will be the only option to meet the EPA's unprecedented and impossible compliance timetable. Jonathan Gardner, a vice president of the International Brotherhood of Electrical Workers, warns that the rule directly threatens 1,500 employees at six different power plants across Texas.[56]

The Day of Reckoning is coming. The EPA has dangerously underestimated (or maybe not?) the impact of its unprecedented spate of rules on the reliability of the nation's electricity grid, because the announced retirements already exceed EPA's dubious low estimates. Existing coal-fired plants, even the old ones that don't run very often, play a major role in controlling costs because they keep the marginal costs down during peak periods."[57] Burning coal produces about 45% of electric generation, but nearly half of those coal plants haven't installed pollution controls to meet regulations, according to a Goldman Sachs analysis.[58]

Residential electricity prices are expected to spike by more than 10 percent beginning in 2015, with consumers paying between $150 and $330 a year more than this year, as coal plants, the least expensive producers of electricity, continue to close.

One Regional Transmission Organization, PJM Interconnection, an electric transmission system serving all or parts of Delaware, Illinois, Indiana, Kentucky, Maryland, Michigan, New Jersey, North Carolina, Ohio, Pennsylvania, Tennessee, Virginia, West Virginia and the District of Columbia; chooses the lowest-cost mix of power from bids offered by electricity producers fueled by coal, nuclear, wind, solar or natural gas, among others. It charges utilities $16 per megawatt-day in capacity payments based on the results of an auction held three years ago, in 2009. (A megawatt-day is about equivalent to the amount of electricity used by 330 homes in 24 hours.) Utilities pay the capacity charges regardless of who provides their electricity. On May 22, 2012, the auction for reserve capacity for 2013-2015 set the new price per megawatt-day at $136, 8 times higher than the price for the three years ended 2012. Goldman Sachs analysts estimate even higher figures, $220-$300 per MW-day at the next auction in 2015, or 14 times to 19 times this year's prices and roughly double the results of the May 22, 2012 auction.[59]

In the mid-Atlantic region, the new price was $167 per megawatt-day. For the northern Ohio region served by FirstEnergy, which had to close so many plants due to Obama's EPA regulations, the new price is $357 per megawatt-day for reserve capacity for 2013-2015, 21 times higher than the price for 2012.[60]

The Obama administration has a goal of 1.5 million electric cars by 2015, just when all these coal plants are shutting down. How exactly does Obama plan to generate enough electricity to meet *current* demand, let alone the increased demand as a million or more people plug their cars into the grid?[61]

Each Server Farm needs as much Electricity as a Small Town: 40% of all global energy production comes from coal. Computer and cell phone use is rising exponentially. All these gadgets need electricity. Personal computer data is now stored in the "Cloud." That romantic phrase is a euphemism for the fact that all data is now stored at Server Farms belonging to various big Internet companies. Google, Apple, Microsoft, Amazon and all big Internet companies have massive server farms. Data centers now consume about 1.3% of all global electricity, 277 terawatt-hours, per year. This exceeds the electricity use of dozens of countries, including Australia and Mexico![62]

Facebook disclosed in documents filed with the SEC that is stores more than 100 petabytes of information. (1 petabyte = 100 million gigabytes.) Just one of Apple's data centers in Prineville, Oregon draws 28 megawatts of power, the equivalent of a town of 28,000 people and is expected to grow to around 78MW or the equivalent of a town of 80,000 people when completed.[63] Google operates 11 data centers in six states and five foreign countries that require 260 megawatts of power, enough for 260,000 homes. Google is believed to have 24 server farms in the mid-west, and though it does not disclose locations or consumption, these farms must use at least as much as Apple and Microsoft's do.[64] Microsoft's facility near Chicago will need three electrical substations with a total capacity of 198 MW.[65]

If they were to rely on "green energy," Amazon has calculated that its 500,000 square foot facility would need about 6.5 square miles of solar panels (roughly 362 times the area of its facility!) Facebook's data center in Prineville would need a wind project covering about 14 million square meters, nearly 5.5 square miles, or about 3 times the size of New York City's Central Park.[66] Clearly, "green energy" can't power data farms.

All these high tech companies consume massive amounts of electricity. Once Obama shuts down the coal plants, where is the electricity going to come from?

(b) Of course, Obama is Crucifying Oil too. In 2008, the oil industry paid $37 million a day in royalties, over $13 billion a year to federal, state and other authorities.[67] Federal, state and local taxes related to the offshore oil and gas operations in the Gulf totaled $13 billion in 2009, according to NCPA[68]. The American Petroleum Institute estimates that we have U.S. resources to generate nearly 160,000 new, well-paying jobs and $1.7 trillion in revenues to federal, state, and local governments, with $1.3 trillion from offshore drilling alone. Obama seeks to further harm the oil and gas industry by removing what he calls "subsidies" but which are really depreciation deductions, the same as any other industries utilize when they write off the cost of capital investment. Businesses depreciate their machinery, their computers and a host of other items which have a limited life. The deductions the oil industry takes are no different. But Obama singles them out for special scorn and vituperation.

*It really disgusts me when Obama treats the American people like they are idiots who don't understand that depreciation deductions are ones which all businesses take; and asserts that they are "special tax write-offs for the oil industry." All Obama is doing is trying to extract more **Jizya,** or taxes, from one group of Americans. And as a bonus, he generates envy, anger and hostility among us. It disgusts me even more than the media never tells the public about this. But instead, allows Obama to pit one group of Americans, who work in the oil and gas industry, against the rest of us!*

Obama's 2012 budget calls for a $38.6 billion annual tax increase on oil and gas companies by eliminating their depletion deduction, which would hit Oklahoma, where 70,000 people are employed in oil and gas development, especially hard.[69] Oil and gas companies may continue to invest in exploration and development of our oil and gas resources, but they will have a lot less incentive to do so.

Oil companies pay an 18.75% royalty to the federal government on the oil produced on federal lands. Exxon Mobil, the biggest oil company, makes a profit of two cents per gallon of gasoline. Obama constantly sneers at "Fat Cat Oil Producers." But he does not tell you that taking into account both royalties and taxes, his federal government, together with the states and local municipalities, makes about 49.5 cents per gallon! In short, on a gallon of gas, Obama makes nearly 25 times as much money from oil as the oil companies do.[70] *(Yet another fact your media conceals from you!)*

In fact, if Obama really cared about us ordinary folks, he could waive the federal taxes on gasoline. That would bring the price of our gas down by over 35 cents a gallon!! Instead, Obama engages in class warfare, pitting the rich against the poor. And he constantly demonizes corporate America for doing what our free enterprise system wants them to do; and which his federal government is demonstrably unable to do. This is appropriate, I guess, for a union thug. But how is this appropriate for the President of the United States?

The Deepwater Horizon Oil spill provided Obama with the perfect opportunity to destroy oil production. It occurred 5000 feet down in the Gulf of Mexico in April 2010 and spilled for nearly 6 months before it was capped.[71] It caused damage to vast stretches of the Louisiana and Mississippi coastline and to three other gulf states. Immediately, Obama issued a moratorium on oil drilling in the gulf. A month later, he extended the moratorium for 6 more months. To justify this, he had his Czarina Carol Browner direct Ken Salazar to doctor a peer-reviewed report by seven oil experts. After they signed it, Salazar added two paragraphs to their report, to state that they recommended an immediate stoppage of drilling. *Anywhere else, this would be fraud, and the miscreants would be prosecuted. But this is Obama and his czar. They can, and do, do whatever they like; counting on the media to conceal what they are doing.*

In fact, the final report actually said a moratorium would do serious economic damage while accomplishing little in terms of safety.[72] The report had recommended that drilling be continued because one platform having a leak did not mean all platforms would have leaks. Also, floating oil platforms could not stand idle indefinitely "on moratorium" because the financing costs of the equipment was in the millions and they would have to move to other locations around the world to generate a return on investment and repay their loans. Furthermore, industry experts predicted that once they left, floating oil platforms would not return for 2 or more years. Ignoring the laws of economics and the advice of industry experts Obama persisted with a vindictive, but politically satisfying moratorium, and the rigs left, decimating the Gulf oil industry, exactly at a time when the Gulf states' economies were already reeling from the Oil Spill's effects on fisheries and tourism. Exactly as the experts had predicted, deep-sea drilling rigs owned by Laberde Marine, one of the leading deep water drilling companies, had to leave to Brazil to work for Petrobras, in which George Soros had a major financial interest.[73] And Obama gave Petrobras an Ex-Im Bank Loan at low interest rates. Having stopped all deep water drilling in the Gulf, Obama then went to Brazil, exhorted and praised them for their deep water drilling (in riskier circumstances than in the Gulf) and promised that we Americans would buy their oil![74]

Obama's original moratorium halted all deep water drilling and suspended drilling of 33 exploratory wells in the gulf. In July 2010, this was extended to include shallow water drilling in less than 500 feet.[75] District Judge Martin Feldman found that the moratorium was not justified and ordered that the drilling recommence.[76] But Obama has flouted the judge's ruling. He has issued only a few deep water drilling permits. And even today, is dragging out the approval process so no actual drilling can commence.[77]

Even prior to the Deepwater Horizon catastrophe, in 2009, Obama scrapped oil and gas leases in Utah, permanently banned drilling in ANWR and stopped offshore drilling in virtually all the coastal waters of the United States.

With oil at $100 a barrel, the lost opportunity equals $4.7 million in lost revenue each day, or $1.7 billion in 2009. In 2008, the offshore oil industry paid $237 million in rent, $8.3 billion in royalties and $9.4 billion for bids on new leases, totaling some $17.9 Billion. By comparison, in 2011, those numbers were $245 million in rent, $4 billion in royalties and just $979 million in lease bids, reduced to a total of $6.24 Billion. A recent study found that these moratoriums would cost the US over $2.36 Trillion through 2029.[78] *Again, as with coal, one must ask, why is Obama foregoing so much revenue to the Federal Government? A high school kid would know this is not the way to run a country. Why is the most brilliant man on earth doing this to our country?*

The Federal Government acts like a bunch of Thugs: Obama has made clear he can't stand profit making, especially by oil companies.[79] It's a case of trickle-down hate. When the BP oil spill took place, Ken Salazar promised that the Administration would "keep its boot on the throat" of energy giant British Petroleum until the oil gusher stopped, the spill was cleaned up and all damages paid for.[80] The old agency that regulated oil companies was deemed too friendly with the oil companies. In its place, three new agencies were created. And the Department of Interior officials seem to take sadistic pleasure in badgering oil companies. One new agency, the Office of Natural Resources Revenue (ONRR), headed by Gregory Gould, was created to levy untold millions of dollars in fines if companies don't kowtow to the new bureaucracy.[81] It now has a total of 600 employees. The agency's head Gould issued a mafia-like threat: "*If they cut corners, they could end up paying enough to quickly take care of the federal deficit*"

The fines levied on BP are truly enough to fund the national debt of quite a few countries. It has spent $14 Billion to stop the leak and clean up the spill. $6.5 Billion for an out-of-court settlement overseen by Ken Feinberg. $7.8 Billion in settlement between BP and thousands of residents and businesses along the Gulf of Mexico. Criminal environmental penalties could amount to $17-$40 Billion. Civil penalties could add another $20 Billion.[82]

As you can see, to get more money, Obama hires more regulators, who cost more money, so he hires yet more regulators to get more money. It is like bleeding the corporation with a thousand cuts. Taking more and more of its income to fund more and more intrusive regulations enforced by more and more regulators!! And you wonder why companies are not expanding their businesses and hiring more people?

(c) Obama will stop drilling in ANWR at all costs: The environmentalists say we should never drill in ANWR because of the potential environmental destruction, which will occur when oil is spilled over the vast swaths of Alaska. This must be recognized for what it is. It is just a way to prevent America from obtaining energy independence and make us more dependent on OPEC. Just consider the size of Alaska and the area where drilling will take place. Alaska has a landmass of 663,267 square miles or 424.5 Million acres. It is 3 times bigger than Texas.[83] ANWR alone has 19 million acres, an area bigger than Delaware. Oil drilling is only proposed for a tiny 2000-acre area, about the size of DC's Dulles Airport; approximately .0105% of the area of ANWR and 0.0004% of the area of Alaska. The drilling area is located in the coastal plains area. It is hundreds of miles away from, and thousands of feet below, the beautiful Brooks Range, which is (mis)used in photographs to prevent drilling. Oil would have to flow upwards to destroy these mountains! In fact, when oil drilling was first permitted in Prudhoe Bay, it actually led to an increase in the caribou population.[84] There is no possible way drilling in .0004% of Alaska can cause the kind of destruction the environmentalists claim they fear. The real reason to prevent drilling in ANWR is to make us more dependent on OPEC oil.

We all need to recognize that there is a game being played by Democrats and their environmentalist supporters to stop all drilling for every kind of oil and gas in America. **First, one regulates. Then, the other litigates.** Even though all environmental reviews were complete, Obama stopped Shell from drilling for oil in the Chukchi and Beaufort Sea areas of Alaska, even though the Gulf Oil spill took place in the Gulf of Mexico! He finally gave Shell a go ahead in 2011. Right on cue, some environmental coalition filed suit to stop drilling.[85] Between the Obama administration's stop and go permitting process and various environmental groups' lawsuits, drilling in ANWR has come to a complete halt. *Somewhere, an Arab Prince is smiling and buying up even more American businesses with the money he is making off us Americans!*

(d) Obama stops Americans from using Shale in Federal Land: America is blessed with vast shale formations that can produce an abundance of oil and natural gas. Shale gas now makes up 23% of US production. The **Bakken formation** centered on North Dakota is mostly on private land. And North Dakota is booming! It has the nation's lowest unemployment, less than 5%. Oil jobs are available at $140K per year![86] The **Marcellus shale formation** runs through northern Appalachia, Pennsylvania, West Virginia, New York and Ohio. A study by three Penn State University experts states that by 2013, shale will yield more than 40,000 new jobs in Pennsylvania alone, and by 2020 a quarter of a million jobs and inject more than $12 Billion into the state's economy![87]

But we are not exploiting the biggest shale deposit, which could bring us even greater economic stability. According to the government's own GAO, the biggest shale field, the **Green River shale formation** in Wyoming, Utah and Colorado, contains about 3 trillion barrels of oil of which over 50% is recoverable. And this amount is equal to the entire world's proven reserves and four times the proven reserves of Saudi Arabia! It would supply domestic oil consumption for more than 200 years. But Obama won't let us drill. 72% of Green River lies beneath federal lands managed by BLM and Obama has blocked drilling. Of course, you will remember from Part I of this book, that Obama has gifted over 21 million acres of public land for "green energy" projects that don't work!

In fact, Obama has put 97% of federal onshore lands and 97% of federal offshore lands off-limits to oil and gas drilling.[88] Remember that, the next time you hear Obama saying, *"We can't drill our way to energy independence."* It is a bald, two-faced lie! We can't drill our way to energy independence because Obama won't let us! Obama is doing all he can to prevent us from getting energy independent and from getting jobs for our people.

(e)   Armendariz Crucifies Fracking: Armendariz was the top EPA Administrator for Region VI, the major oil and gas-producing region of the Unites States. As Senator Inhofe said in his floor speech, *"The Obama Administration is fully engaged in an all-out war on hydraulic fracturing, and indeed all fossil fuels. . . . The EPA's "general philosophy" is to "crucify" and "make examples" of domestic energy producers so that other companies will fall in line with EPA's regulatory whims . . . Over the past year, the President has been going around the country pretending he's for an "all of the above" energy approach.* **But the truth is that the Obama—EPA has been fighting domestic energy production every step of the way and natural gas from shale is very much on the agency's chopping block."** [89]

Soon after Armendariz's speech in 2010 where he said he would "crucify" the first five he could find; the EPA targeted US natural gas producers in Pennsylvania, Texas and Wyoming. In all three of these cases, before investigations were complete, the EPA made headline-grabbing statements either insinuating or proclaiming that hydraulic fracturing was the cause of drinking water contamination. But in each case, EPA's comments were false and despite their best efforts, they were unable to find any sound scientific evidence to definitively demonstrate this link. The ultimate goal of these efforts is, of course, to strip states of their traditional authority to regulate hydraulic fracturing inside their borders and seize federal control over unconventional oil and gas development across this country. *That way, the Obama administration can have more control over devastating the development of America's vast domestic resources. And Obama can get closer to being our ruler and controlling everything in America! And this is one more way in which Obama is arrogating power and violating the 10th Amendment.*

In **Parker County, Texas**, Armendariz overturned a state decision that there was no contamination from hydraulic fracturing. He issued an EPA finding that the drinking water was being contaminated by hydraulic fracturing, issued a press release inciting public fear and anxiety and sent an email to his rabid anti-fracking friends, "we're about to make a lot of news . . . tune into Channel 8." These environmentalists had created a deceptive and fraudulent video purporting to show that the water discharged from fracking was causing the well water to catch fire. In fact, they had attached a hose to the well's gas vent, which vented naturally occurring gas. Two weeks later, in early 2011, the EPA filed suit against Range Resources demanding that they supply drinking water to the people in surrounding areas and pay $16,500 a day for each violation of the EPA order. In March 2012, just after Congress left for the Easter recess, and after Range Resources had spent time and money defending this lawsuit and filing an appeal, the EPA withdrew its case.

In **Pavilion, Wyoming**, the EPA did the same thing. It bypassed State findings, ignored 3 rounds of testing showing no contamination from hydraulic fracking and issued press releases indicating fracking was polluting the water. Later on, just as Congress was leaving for a recess, the EPA withdrew these findings. The EPA also continued to be recalcitrant and ignored Congressional demands for documents for months. Then, late the night before a congressional hearing, the EPA released 622 documents.

In **Dimock, Pennsylvania**, the EPA did worse. Both the State and the Federal EPA had declared the water safe to drink. One month later, the EPA reversed its position and declared the water unsafe to drink. But months later, on a Good Friday when no one was in town, it withdrew this finding hoping no one would notice it had backtracked!

Obama flies around the country on our dime, trying to take credit for the prosperity brought about by increased oil and gas production. But as you can see, it just is not true. He has blocked production at every turn. Since 2008, Obama has blocked drilling for oil from shale. 93% of the operating shale oil and gas wells in the US are located in private and state lands, not on Federal land. According to a report by the nonpartisan Congressional Research Service, Natural gas production in Federal lands is down 17% since 2008. And about 96% of the increase in oil and gas production also took place on private and State lands and not on Federal lands.[90]

Canada is already producing gas by fracking. Already in British Columbia there are hundreds of shale gas wells at work. Quebec, particularly in the St. Lawrence Valley between Montreal and Quebec City, is the next mother lode, according to companies exploring here. Estimates go from 25 to as high as 50 trillion cubic feet of gas. At the high end, that's enough to heat 15 million homes for 50 years.[91]

Even the Chinese Government shows more care for its people. It goes to unstable places like Nigeria and Libya in its attempts to drill for oil. It is even in Cuba, drilling for oil offshore, just adjacent to American territorial waters. *Ask yourself, why Obama is preventing us from drilling in our own country? The only possible explanation is that he is doing this deliberately. To further* **Stealth Jihad** *against us, make us* **Dhimmis or slaves**, *reduce us to a state of penury, make us dependent on him and assert his rule over us.*

(f) Blocking the Keystone Pipeline: The Keystone Pipeline would run 2,147 miles from Hardisty, Alberta to Gulf Coast refineries in Texas. One segment, opened in 2010, already runs from Canada to Illinois and cross-country permits were approved.[92] The Keystone XL extension was to go from Alberta to a major oil hub in Cushing, Oklahoma and from there to Texas.[93] States had the authority to issue all permits. Federal approval was required only for the segment that crossed from Canada to America. The State Department, which has the authority to grant the permission, had granted it in 2009, after four years of state, federal and local review and approvals.

There are already about 200,000 miles of similar pipeline in America which have functioned perfectly well all these years. And TransCanada, which was building Keystone XL, had been building pipeline in North America for more than 40 years. It had added further redundancies to Keystone XL to ensure there would be no leaks. This pipeline was going to move 700,000 barrels of oil per day from Canada, going through more than half a dozen states, creating jobs and contributing to local tax bases. All told, hundreds of thousands of jobs would have been produced. It was projected to provide over $800 million in state and local taxes and more than $20 Billion in new spending. In short, it would be a great boon for our economy.

In July 2010, the EPA barged in and asserted its authority, claimed the State Department's analysis was faulty, that Keystone XL work must be stopped and that approvals needed further study. Environmentalists began a massive campaign to stop the project on the grounds the pipeline would pollute water supplies and harm migratory birds.[94] In 2011, Obama shut down the project.

First, note the compete hypocrisy of the environmentalists. Over 200,000 miles of pipeline are already in operation without problems, and yet the Sierra Club complains vigorously about the Keystone XL pipeline and claims it could harm migratory birds. How? By jumping up and biting the birds? Meanwhile, they are silent when Democrat-controlled wind farms decimate birds, including various endangered species. Who funds these environmentalists? Why, Mayor Bloomberg and his $50 million to destroy coal, for one. The other funder? You, the taxpayer! Environmentalists are able to sue under the Equal Access to Justice Act (EAJA), which President Carter signed into law in 1980. The intent was to help the little guy stand up to federal agencies. But Environmental groups are using this law to sue very aggressively under the Clean Water Act, Clean Air Act and the Endangered Species Act. Every time they sue, they are collecting costs and fees as high as $750 an hour. So, of course, they keep suing to collect more money.

In late May 2012, an environmental group sued to "protect" the "endangered" sage grouse all across its former range, 155 million acres in 11 Western states; and particularly to restrict oil, gas and ranching over a vast area of federal land in Sublette County, Wyoming, which contains two of America's largest producing natural gas deposits. The EPA's endangered species list is not peer reviewed. They list as "endangered" a species that could be found in plenty in a neighboring area. They divide species into sub-species and then claim that we cannot drill where the sub-species is found. Frequently, their designation is the product of studies posted online by environmental groups, with whom they work in concert; or authored by the federal workers themselves. 41% of the authors in the sage grouse case were federal workers. The editor himself had authored one-third of the papers. Just so you know how serious and scholarly a study this was, I will quote from their expert, *"The greater sage grouse is one stochastic, catastrophic event away from extirpation in Sublette County."* [95] After that extirpation of the English language, how can a Judge do anything but ban all human activity anywhere near the sage grouse? And award the environmentalists $750 an hour for all their hard work?

I seriously doubt the government actually scrutinizes the invoices of the Sierra Club to ensure they are billing us correctly and not inflating their bills. It is their friends who occupy the EPA. So, it is really another money machine. Taxpayer money is paid out by pro-environmentalist EPA staff to environmentalists. And when the money runs dry, Obama jets across the country shouting, *"Everybody must pay their fair share!! More Jizya!! More taxes!!"* And you, who just lost your job in the oil industry or related industry, must fork out more of your wife's hard earned money to pay more taxes!! And the federal government is completely unable to account for how much it is paying out to Environmentalists. [96] Actually, Obama and his federal government are unable to account for anything, not the billions he spent on TARP and Stimulus and not even the income tax he collects. Why should he care? Obama and his government are not actually paying anything. Who pays? You do, through those taxes that Obama is so fond of collecting!!

Second, note the beautifully choreographed dance here. First, EPA issues some regulation or withdraws some approval. Next, environmentalists make a hue and cry. Next, the media amplifies the ruckus. Finally, Obama, who orchestrates all of this, gets to do what he wants; namely, to shut down the project that would have brought employment and prosperity to a great many Americans.

Canada is now exploring a pipeline to take its oil to its west coast and then ship it to China. China, unlike Obama, cares about its economy and is negotiating to buy that oil. The American people, realizing this was a great opportunity that we were losing, began complaining. Obama, realizing he would be losing votes over his decision, reversed course. But he did not approve of the Canada-America segment in the north, the only section over which he had any control. Instead, he went south to Cushing, Oklahoma, where his approval was not needed. *(He thinks Americans are so stupid that they don't know the north from the south of their own country!! And he is counting on the media to obfuscate what he is doing!)* There, in front of a crowd of hundreds, he thundered that he had "directed" his administration "to expedite the project, cut through the red tape, break through the bureaucratic hurdles and make this project a priority, to go ahead and get it done!"[97]

After this, can anybody believe anything that Obama says?

He has banned offshore drilling in the Gulf—an unconstitutional violation of a court order to lift the ban. He has extended this "moratorium on offshore drilling in the Gulf" to Alaska. His EPA has taken away previously granted authority for coal mining. His EPA says all coal production will damage the environment and so seeks to put a "Cap and Tax" law into effect without authorization from Congress. Obama has put an end to offshore drilling, crippled the Gulf of Mexico oil industry, prohibited ANWR development and other Arctic exploration projects, and now purports to be "worried" that fracturing rocks with high-pressure water will "harm the environment" and so seeks to stop oil shale extraction from the Marcellus Oil Shale Formation.[98] He and his government own 700 million acres of federal land[99] and he has put 97% of federal land off limits to energy exploration. He has also shut down the Keystone XL pipeline.

His EPA passes a rule here, a regulation there. Obama does not care that each rule and regulation results in lay-offs of 70,000, 100,000 people. He does not care that businesses have to close down. He does not care that our electricity prices skyrocket. He does not care that if we follow his rules, we will not have the capacity to meet future demand for electricity, especially for our server farms. And that if our server farms cannot operate, we cannot use our computers and all production in this country will grind to a halt. All he cares for is that our country gets poorer and more vulnerable to attack.

Obama is his name. Stealth Jihad is his game!!

Chapter 13

Saul Alinksy's Rules in Action:
Pick the target, freeze it, personalize it, polarize it.

Obama has ruled over us with an iron fist. His administration is easily the most corrupt ever and the most vicious. *Remember what I told you about Socialist governments? If you belong to the party in power, you can do anything. If you don't you are out of luck.* Sure enough wherever Republicans are to be found, Obama has singled out their industries and their jobs for destruction. You saw that in how he has handled our traditional energy industries. And you will see it below in the way he has handled the auto industry. And he does not care a whit about the hundreds of thousands of American people he has put out of work.

We have less jobs than when he took office. He is fudging the jobs numbers to try to jimmy the unemployment rate down to 8%. But if you look at the numbers, you know his economy is tanking. Our GDP rose only 1.9% in the 1st quarter of 2012. 44.7 million people are now on food stamps.[1] 6.7% of Americans are living in extreme poverty and this is an all-time high.[2] The number of Americans living below the poverty line has increased by 10 million.[3] 25 Million Americans are unemployed or underemployed. The U6 unemployment rate, counting unemployed, underemployed and discouraged workers, is still 15.2%. The unemployment rate with the full measure of discouraged workers is about 23%, which is depression level unemployment.

Blacks have suffered the most. Their unemployment rate has been over 15-1/2% for the entire 3-1/2 years Obama was in office. And black teenage unemployment is 40%. Hispanic unemployment is 11% and their youth unemployment rate is 25%. There are 6 million less jobs than when Obama started office.[4] The number of weeks it takes to find employment is, on average, at an all-time high of 45+ weeks.[5] There are 4.5 million long-term (6 months or more) unemployed workers now, up from 2.6 million when Obama took office.[6] At least in part this is because now almost 1 in 3 jobs require a license or some form of government permission.[7] Another reason is that Obama's economic policies, his constant verbal abuse and endless sneering at private industry have resulted in a lack of confidence among business people. Only 23% of American corporations plan to hire more employees in 2012.[8]

Our economy cannot improve without improvement in the housing sector. But Obama's record on this is dismal. Home sales hit an all-time low during 2011.[9] Nearly one-third of all mortgages are under water. This increased from 31/1% in fourth quarter 2011 to 31.4% in the first quarter 2012. Americans owe $1.2 trillion more than their homes are worth. Underwater homeowners in Los Angeles, Orange, Riverside, San Bernardino, Ventura and San Diego counties were a staggering $138.9 billion deep in negative equity at the end of the first quarter.[10] Nevada has the highest percentage of such homeowners, with 67%, followed by Arizona with 52% and then Georgia, Florida and Michigan. In Los Angeles County, 32% of homeowners are underwater, compared with a 25% in Orange County and 53% in San Bernardino County. High unemployment and economic instability could fuel more delinquencies and foreclosures.[11] Obama has purportedly tried to help homeowners refinance, but none of his programs have worked. The most recent, the Home Affordable Refinance Program won't work either. There is too little money in the program; the program only helps on the interest rate adjustment, not on any principal reduction; and it comes too late to be of any real help, because prices have fallen even lower since he took office.[12]

Remember what I told you about Socialists in my native country? They partied on, making themselves rich; forcing their political opponents into poverty; and not caring a whit about the poor, until it came time to have elections. Then, they suddenly announced their true love for the poor and proposed new programs for the poor, new rations of rice and sugar and demonized "the rich."

True to form, Obama will propose yet another housing or jobs program come election time. And he will blame the greedy bankers yet again. And hope that gullible people will believe him. The bottom line is that Obama has never held a private sector job in his life. He is totally inexperienced in any form of management. His style of management includes no encouragement and no cooperation whatsoever. Instead, he sneers and jeers at private industry. He does not know how to manage an economy. This, coupled with his political desire to have us all poor and dependent on him, makes economic recovery impossible for this country as long as it has Obama as its leader.

Excuses, Excuses. How has Obama helped this nation? Even he cannot say. All he has is blame and excuses. "This was all Bush's fault." Now that we are fed up hearing this, he uses different wording but still makes the same excuse, "I inherited the worst depression ever." Unspoken is, "And I deserve another chance to clean up the mess I inherited." Inherited from whom? Bush, of course! So, 3-1/2 years later, it is still Bush's fault. But, as I point out below, Obama tried what he claimed would work. But, after nearly a Trillion dollars spent on TARP and Stimulus and what not, all his proposals have failed. Are we supposed go deeper into debt to keep spending, and keep suffering from lack of jobs, just to give him another 4 years to keep blaming Bush and trying out the same things that did not work before?

He has sprinkled our money around like it was candy. $700 billion **for the Troubled Asset Relief Program (TARP)** to help financial institutions out of the mortgage crisis.[13] Then a month after taking office, Obama hustled congress into passing his **$789 billion Stimulus Bill** by promising that if it were passed unemployment could go no higher than 8%. *Remember, this was for shovel-ready jobs, fixing roads and bridges? How can we forget? Half-finished construction on our highways with those $30,000 dollar, bright neon orange signs telling us all this was done by the Stimulus program will always remind us!!*

Obama assured us that his stimulus bill would create or save a million jobs; but he was claiming as fact what could never have been more than a wild (and highly improbable) guess, and his more recent attempts to justify that guess have been fraudulent.[14] They have jobs created, jobs saved, and now they've added a new category: "Lives touched by the stimulus."[15] But, jobs were not his priority. As you saw in Part I, a large part of this money went to his cronies for Green Energy projects that didn't work.

Then he spent $200 billion for TALF to spur the market in securities, the auto bailout, or other bailouts of pension plans, States and municipal debt. All those institutions are still in trouble after all those bailouts and all that money spent!!

U.S. taxpayers are still owed nearly $133 billion that companies haven't repaid from the financial bailout, according to a quarterly Special Inspector General Troubled Asset Relief Program (SIGTARP) report. The report also states that as of December 31, 2011, the Treasury has "written off $4.2 billion and realized losses of $7.8 billion that the taxpayer will never get back," and that it "predicts losses on other TARP investments."[16]

Next, Obama tried the Cash for Clunkers Program. A clunker is a car which gets 15 mpg or less. A fuel-efficient car gets 25 mpg or more. At around an average 12,000 miles per year that is 320 gallons saved per car. With 700,000 vehicles participating, that was 224 million gallons per year @ $3 per gallon or $672 million per year saved. In short, Obama spent $ 3 Billion to save $375 million. In addition, the dealers were required to pour sand into the gas tank of the clunkers they took in, to make them inoperable. It was more important to prevent "global warming" than to allow some poor farm worker or student to buy and drive that clunker.[17]

Our Debt has Quadrupled. Since Obama got into office, Obama has run up $6 Trillion in federal debt in three years; while the 43 previous Presidents had run up only $10 Trillion in debt in all the previous 233 years of our country's existence.[18] Yet, he still shamelessly blames Bush. And where was he when Bush was supposedly single handedly running up that debt? Right in the U.S. Senate, cheering on Harry Reid/Nancy Pelosi's Democrat proposals for spending!! If Obama wanted to spend less while Bush was in office, he could have voted against those spending bills!!

The major auto companies were going bankrupt because they could not compete while paying their workers' extremely high wages, health care and pensions. The Bush Administration and Treasury Secretary Henry Paulson decided to use $17.4 billion of TARP funds to keep the auto companies afloat. The Obama administration increased that to $49.1 Billion.[19]

GM and Chrysler were major beneficiaries of these funds. At the time of the bailout, GM had $82 billion in assets and was $172.8 billion in debt.[20] There were 202,000 workers in GM plants all over the world.

There was that "Jobs Bank," a large pool of thousands of furloughed workers who received pay and benefits, but didn't work. GM factories were required to keep sufficient staff on their payrolls to operate at 80% of capacity, whether or not they needed to produce automobiles. Various union work rules guaranteed further inefficiencies. The average worker pay in union shops was $70 per hour while autoworkers in the right-to-work states got $45 an hour.[21] Pension obligations alone added $1,600 per vehicle in additional legacy costs (i.e., the costs paid to retired workers who had nothing to do with making automobiles any more).[22] From 2000 to 2005, GM had lost 74% of its market share, in part because of its overwhelming labor, pension and healthcare costs which increased the price of its vehicles; but also because it was hamstrung by government CAFÉ standards which required it to produce low fuel mileage small cars that had low market demand, low per vehicle prices and low margins; while it would have preferred to manufacture SUV's which were its most profitable item. It is not surprising that GM and Chrysler were bankrupt.

Legal bankruptcy proceedings have very structured rules that everyone must follow. One factor that makes our American economy so resilient is a strong bankruptcy system that allows failed companies to start over by declaring bankruptcy, but also provides a clear set of rules that reassure various creditors as to where they stand in the pecking order when a business goes bankrupt. Trillions of dollars are invested every year based on the reliance of creditors on the sanctity of these rules and the certainty of that pecking order. One of the other things the US prides itself on is that it is a country that abides by the rule of law. In other words, if you have a legal right, including a contractual right, then how that right is handled will be dictated by what the law provides. It used to be that the rule of law was one of the things that proudly distinguished us from Socialist/Communist countries, where their government frequently arbitrarily changes the rules to favor its own supporters.

Our bankruptcy laws have clear rules that dictate how the assets of a bankrupt company are allocated among its various stakeholders. First, the bankrupt corporation's assets are distributed to the secured creditors to the extent of their security interest. Secured creditors have a security interest, or lien, in a specific item, like a piece of equipment that they helped pay for. The secured creditor retains a security interest in that asset, just like your dealer holds the pink slip to your car until you pay off your loan. Or like the bank holds a security interest in your home, if you take money out on a home equity line and use the money to buy other items or fix up your home.

Next, the assets are distributed to unsecured creditors; like bondholders who have loaned money but are not secured; suppliers who have supplied goods or services; and employees who have earned future benefits like a pension but are not secured. There are certain special priorities within this class of unsecured creditors (for example employees who have not been paid wages will have a limited priority for those unpaid wages). But in general, all unsecured creditors will be treated equally, so that, if there are $100 million of unsecured creditor claims and only $10 million of assets left for the unsecured creditors; then each unsecured creditor should get $0.10 per dollar owed to the unsecured creditor.

Then, finally, if there is anything left, the shareholders are paid, also in order, according to what their contractual rights are, so preferred stockholders will get a distribution of assets before common stockholders.

As I told you in my Preface, this order is not followed in Third World socialist countries. The spoils of the bankrupt corporation are distributed as the country's political leaders think fit. In fact, there is one instance I still remember from my childhood. Because the CEO of the company was a member of the opposition political party, the union constantly went on strike against the company, more often than not unlawfully. These unpredictable and debilitating strikes caused a great deterioration in the quality of the company's products and services and increased expenses greatly. The union was protected by the government and it finally brought the corporation down. My native country did not have a strong bankruptcy code or a strong tradition of the rule of law. Once the company was on its knees, the government stepped in and handed over the company to the union leaders!! Compensation to the owners was an IOU, to be paid whenever the government and the union got around to it. But this is America. This cannot happen here, can it? . . . It did!

In the Auto company bailouts, Obama made a complete mockery of the Bankruptcy laws. And he violated our Constitution's requirement

that our government not impair the obligations of contracts. He played politics with GM and Chrysler. And everything he did, he did for those who had voted for him, particularly the unions. In fact, it would be accurate to say Obama saved the unions, not GM.

Obama purported to do a pre-packaged bankruptcy, meaning the terms of the bankruptcy would be settled privately by Obama, the auto union leaders and the creditors. Then, they would simply go in front of a judge as a formality. Through the course of GM's struggles in late 2008 and early 2009, the Treasury provided GM with $49.5 billion to help it through its stay afloat. Once GM and Chrysler went into bankruptcy, Obama, through his Czar, Steven Rattner totally disregarded the rules of our Bankruptcy Code. They decided who the winners and the losers would be and bullied and intimidated the executives, creditors and stockholders of GM and Chrysler to achieve the desired result,.

There was not even a pretense of treating people equally and fairly. Obama claims that he saved the US auto industry, but that's not really true. He saved the UAW. GM and Chrysler could have passed through the normal bankruptcy process, without Obama, but the UAW would have paid a price. They could have negotiated reduced wages and benefits just like the airline worker in the various airline bankruptcies and the steelworkers in various steel industry bankruptcies have done. And GM and Chrysler would have survived.

First thing, he fired GM CEO Rick Waggoner and wiped out GM's debts to anyone other than the UAW: GM's $54 billion debt to creditors was effectively reduced to $15.6 billion. Common shareholders were wiped out.[23] All GM debt to Delphi, a former GM owned company and a current parts supplier, was also wiped out. 20,000 white-collar workers at Delphi lost all their health and life insurance benefits and retained only 30% of their pensions. These pensions were dumped onto the taxpayer via the Pension Benefit Guarantee Corporation.[24]

Inexplicably, Delphi's UAW pensioners were given $1 Billion of GM's bailout funds in the bankruptcy proceeding, even though the new GM had no obligation to support Delphi's pensions.[25] Delphi's salaried retirees who saw their pension benefits evaporate after the GM bankruptcy are now suing the US Treasury, the Auto Task Force,

Treasury Secretary Tim Geithner, and ex-Auto Task Force heads, Steve Rattner and Ron Bloom. The first hearing against the Treasury Dept. and others occurred in August 2011. The basis of the suit is that the Obama Administration wrongfully used taxpayer dollars to pick winners and losers in the GM bankruptcy.[26]

Next, Obama forced GM and Chrysler to close down 700 dealerships, many of them the most productive dealers. Many of them protested they were being singled out because they had Republican owners or had made contributions to the Republican Party. They said they had been excellent partners with GM for decades. They tried to show they had been good corporate citizens, helping their cities. But nothing worked. They were shut down. The vast majority of the dealerships closed down were in rural counties. Obama had lost the nation's 1300 rural counties by nearly 80%. Obama won the inner city votes. And inner city minority and women owned dealerships were left open. In short, Obama picked the winners and the losers, and eliminated tens of thousands of jobs while he was at it.

The administration's own Inspector General Neil Barofsky demonstrated that Obama had acted out of racial bias. According to him, the White House Auto Industry Task Force and the Treasury Department "Auto Team" had no basis for ordering the expedited car dealership closure schedules. The Auto Team leader, Ron Bloom, a leftist union lawyer, admitted that there was no need to close the dealerships; that GM did not benefit at all. But that Obama had insisted on "shared sacrifice."[27] They discounted counter-testimony from auto industry officials that removing profitable dealerships from the network would actually cost GM money and that closing dealerships in an environment already disrupted by the recession could result in an even greater crisis in sales.[28] Barofsky found that "at a time when the country was experiencing the worst economic downturn in generations and the government was asking its taxpayers to support a $787 billion stimulus package designed primarily to preserve jobs, Treasury made a series of decisions that may have substantially contributed to the accelerated shuttering of thousands of small businesses and thereby potentially adding tens of thousands of workers to the already lengthy unemployment rolls; all based on a theory and without sufficient consideration of the decisions' broader economic impact."[29] But these were entrepreneurial businesses and private sector white-collar jobs, not the protected union and government sector jobs that the Obama regime wants to protect.

Post-bankruptcy, Obama arranged for GM to get a $45 billion business loss tax credit: Under our Bankruptcy Code and Internal Revenue Code, business loss tax credits are wiped out in a bankruptcy. How inconvenient. Obama had his IRS open up a new loophole and issue a series of notices in which it announced that the section 382 tax loss carry forward provisions of the bankruptcy law, which prevented carry forwards, did not apply to the GM bankruptcy. This gave GM and the new owners of the surviving GM Company, a $45 billion business loss tax credit. This meant that the first $45 billion that GM earned would be tax free! In 2011, GM earned $7.5 billion in profits but paid nothing in taxes. *Can't you just hear it? Having exempted GM from paying taxes for the next 20 years, Obama will continue to chant, "More Taxes!! I need more Jizya!! More Taxes!! Everybody must pay their fair share!!"*

GM & Chrysler's VEBA's were given $21.2 billion more than they would have received if they were treated the same as other unsecured creditors. As I noted above, in bankruptcy, creditors on the same class are to be treated equally. At the time of bankruptcy, GM owed outside unsecured creditors $29.9 billion, for which they received 10% of the stock of "new" GM and warrants to purchase 15% more at preferred prices. GM also owed $20.6 billion to its VEBA (Voluntary Employee Beneficiary Association), as unsecured claims. But the union's VEBA's got 17.5% of new GM and $9 billion in preferred stock and debt obligations for $20.6 billion of unsecured claims. Based on GM's current stock price, the VEBA collected assets worth $17.8 billion-$12.2 billion more than if the administration had treated it like the other unsecured creditors. Chrysler's UAW got an even sweeter deal. While Chrysler's junior creditors recovered none of their $7 billion in claims, the VEBAs got almost 50% of the new Chrysler and a $4.6 billion promissory note earning 9% interest in return for only $8 billion in unsecured VEBA claims. Net loss to the taxpayer from the Chrysler bailouts, $9.2 Billion.[30]

GM & Chrysler workers were allowed to keep their higher labor costs of $56 an hour instead of the $47 per hour of all its competitors. The administration also insulated the UAW from most of the sacrifices that unions usually make in bankruptcy, all at taxpayer expense. Section 1113 of the Bankruptcy Code enables reorganizing companies to improve their post-bankruptcy competitiveness by renegotiating union contracts to competitive rates. Almost always in a serious industrial bankruptcy driven by high labor costs, the new company demands concessions in wages and benefits. But Obama made no such demand of the UAW in the GM and Chrysler bankruptcies. At GM. the UAW did accept sharp pay cuts, but only for new hires. They only made very modest concessions for their existing members, like eliminating the in excusable Jobs Bank. As a result, GM still has higher labor costs ($56 an hour) than any of its competitors, and GM workers still make 40% more than the average American manufacturing worker. Even Steven Rattner, now admits "We should have asked the UAW to do a bit more. We did not ask any UAW member to take a cut in their pay." So, even while Obama was bending over backwards for his union supporters, he could not even get this one concession out of them to help GM and Chrysler compete in global auto industry markets.

If not for Obama's favoritism to the UAW, the taxpayers would not have lost $23 billion. Obama's unconstitutional favoritism of the UAW cost the taxpayer $26.5 billion.[31] But Obama still goes around the country claiming that GM has paid back all that it borrowed. In fact, this too is a lie. GM has only paid back part of its borrowings from the government. Also, while GM now has public shareholders, its stock price is nowhere near what would be needed for the US taxpayer to recoup its investment. GM can no longer borrow from other sources because of the way it treated its creditors in bankruptcy. Its attempt to sell shares to the public was not that successful. The government still is short $15 billion of the money it put into GM, $15 billion of lost corporate taxes (with another $34 million to go) and still owns 33% of GM stock, which it will surely dispose of at a significant loss (but, of course, not until after the election).[32]

GM paid $332.5 million in bonuses even though it still owed the taxpayer tens of billions. Though it still owed money to the government, it paid bonuses of $182 million to 26,000 white-collar workers, many of whom earned more than $100,000 a year. And paid $332.5 million in profit sharing to its factory workers.[33] GM actually received a check from the IRS for $110 million. And GM will continue to get such a check for the next 20 years.[34] This will cost the Treasury about $15 billion in lost tax receipts and Obama will have to gallop around the country shouting. *"Jizya!! Taxes!! Everybody needs to pay their fair share!"*

Obama forced GM to make "green" cars, which nobody is buying. Obama did get GM to agree to some concessions, although whether those concessions are of any value to the US taxpayer is questionable. Obama required GM to agree to a tightening of the CAFÉ standard to 54.5 mpg by 2025. How that will be achieved is still a mystery to all. Even a 2 passenger smart car can only do 41 mpg. One significant way that has been done in the past is to reduce the weight of cars. The National Highway Safety Administration has estimated that for every 100 pounds reduced from a 3000 pound car; highway deaths would rise 5%.[35] But this did not deter Obama, and GM was required to build hybrids and small cars, which are unprofitable. Despite Obama's claim that GM's Chevy Volt is the best car ever, quite a few Volts caught fire after crash tests because of damage to its Lithium battery.[36] Even though it comes with a $7500 tax credit, sales are down, way down. And, thanks to a Bloomberg FOIA request, it has been discovered that the feds are buying up all the hybrids that Ford and GM cannot sell to anyone else.[37] And GE is also forcing its employees to buy the Volt. Those who do not, will not be reimbursed for their business expenses in running the car.[38] In short, Obama's "green" car program is yet another "green energy" failure.

Vicious and spiteful retaliation. The most cooperative and productive auto workers have been locked out of employment in the auto industry because they do not belong to the UAW. While Obama sought concessions from corporate GM to get it to toe the line on the government agenda, it missed every opportunity to put restraints on the UAW. Today, in June 2012, there is an uptick in auto manufacturing. Plants in the South are increasing their share of vehicle manufacturing in the U.S. to about 50%, yet none of the factories operated by the foreign automakers in the region has union workers and few are GM or Chrysler plants.[39] Virtually all of the Detroit union workers who were laid off can have their jobs back if they want them. But some of the most cooperative and productive autoworkers at GM have been locked out of employment in the auto industry because they do not belong to the UAW. The UAW struck a deal with GM that the Moraine, Ohio plant would be closed for good even though it was one of GM's most productive and cooperative factories. Furthermore, the UAW insisted that Moraine's 2500 laid off workers be barred from transferring to other plants, thus locking them out of the industry's rebound. The reason: Moraine's 2500 workers were not members of the UAW![40] So you see, Obama loves workers, but only if they belong to unions which give him contributions.

Bondholders were wiped out: Next, Obama informed the GM bondholders, which included some other companies' pension plans and also individual GM retirees, that were owed $7 of $27 billion of the outstanding debt, that their debt would essentially be wiped out, even though the UAW, which was owed $5.4 billion, was given 17% of GM.

Hedge Funds were identified as the Target, Frozen, Personalized and Demolished: When Obama also wiped out the bondholders in the Chrysler bankruptcy, there was some resistance to the arbitrary high-handedness with which it was done. The brilliant bankruptcy attorney, Thomas Lauria went all the way to the Supreme Court arguing that under the Bankruptcy Code, his clients, the bondholders, were entitled to priority in payment. But he was no match for brilliant Obama, who after all, was extensively schooled by his hero Saul Alinksy and his book *Rules for Radicals*. Obama went public criticizing, *identifying and targeting* some of the bondholders. He then publicly shamed them calling them evil "speculators" who didn't deserve to be paid back. It did not matter to Obama that many of the bondholders were former auto workers who had invested their entire savings in the auto companies, which used to be considered as safe as Treasury bonds. Obama picked just one group, hedge funds, which he could attack. And he made "Hedge Funds" the poster child for rich evildoers that were taking money that should go to "poor hard-working auto workers." Never mind that the power and money was going to himself, through his government, and his buddies the union leaders. *Pick the target, freeze it, personalize it, and polarize it—Rule 13, Rules for Radicals, Saul Alinksy.*[41] The political pressure brought on these bondholders by Obama was extraordinary. And, in true acolyte fashion, the media mafia picked up this theme and ran with it. Some bondholders claimed they had received death threats. All of them backed away from their lawsuit out of sheer terror. And Lauria found himself with no clients. [42]

"Pick the target, freeze it, personalize it, and polarize it" **is standard operating procedure for Obama**. And you will see him use it over and over again in the coming months. When he wants to get something done, he sneers and jeers at a particular person or segment of his opponents calling them names, "evil" "rich" "speculators trying to take money the poor workers should have." The media will play an indispensable role in augmenting and enhancing Obama's polarizing rhetoric, never even trying to present the opposing point of view. They never pointed out the tremendous conflict of interest involved in Obama giving himself and the union that helped elect him, a majority share of one of America's biggest companies; that his government was taking over one of the country's biggest businesses; or that the government was totally disregarding the law and the Constitution as it stole from the bondholders to give to the UAW. The media were truly a Greek chorus to Obama's lead. And the "target" of Obama's vituperation just disintegrated!

You have already seen Team Obama in action in 2008. During the last election, it was accusations that he was a "racist" that frightened McCain into ordering that no one could ever use Obama's Muslim middle name "Hussein" or make any personal criticism of Obama. McCain wanted only "policy" disagreements with Obama to be discussed. His advisors, who were obviously working for Obama, failed to tell McCain how he was supposed to discuss "policy disagreements" with Obama, who had never held a private sector job in his life, and who had never taken a position on any bill that had any hint of controversy to it, but rather, had voted "present." And so, McCain was neutralized. He was so boring, he couldn't get people to even show up at his campaign appearances.

It was McCain's running mate Sarah Palin who revived his campaign. Enthusiastic crowds came to see her. And it was she who bore the brunt of a barrage of non-stop attacks in an attempt to *"target it, freeze it, personalize it and polarize it."* No one in the press pointed out that making such vicious personal attacks on Palin amounted to a "War on Women." Allegations were made that her Down's syndrome child was actually her grandchild. In fact, it was the press itself that followed talking points of Team Obama in trying to make out Sarah Palin to be some sort of uneducated hick hustler who was stealing campaign cash to put herself in fancy designer clothes, suitable only for those high-flown Washington elites! *(Think Obama's buddies Sarah Jessica Parker, Anna Wintour.)* Some

Saturday Night woman was able to review that aging and failing show and make a name for herself simply by mocking and sneering at Sarah Palin. They will call it "jokes," but they never "joked" about Obama in that way. And who can ever forget Charles Gibson peering over his glasses while he challenged Palin about some phony Bush Doctrine that he conjured out of thin air so he could mock her for her ignorance of foreign affairs? Or that sneering "interview" of Palin that Katie Couric did? According to Couric, Palin was an uneducated hick because she did not seem to be reading the leftist newspapers!! 200 attorneys were flown into Alaska to dig up dirt on Palin. But no one bothered to go to Chicago to discover whether it was true that Obama was never a Professor at Chicago University School of Law, but merely an adjunct who taught a course on Saul Alinksy's radical tactics! Or tell us that "community organizer" was simply a Marxist agitator, who set up the poor to riot and hate the rich! Some Sleazoid actually moved in next door to Sarah Palin's house where he could observe her daughters through their bedroom windows. No one called upon Obama to "denounce" such disgusting behavior.

Right now, you can also see Obama in action. His acolytes call upon his opponent Romney to "denounce" Trump for saying he wants to see Obama's Birth Certificate. This is supposed to be "racist!" The media, of course, will not tell you that, if not for the fact that he was President, Obama could not even obtain the lowest level security clearance without producing his birth documents and explaining his close relationships with Communists, Socialists and Marxists who want to overthrow our Constitutional form of government. The media also will not tell you that Obama himself is already overthrowing our Constitutional form of government. Romney is also being called upon to "denounce" Rush Limbaugh, the one person who can sway 20 million or more conservatives into enthusiastically working for and voting for Romney.

Every person who supports Romney is under attack. The whole goal of these attacks on Romney supporters is to isolate Romney from all those who support him. Once Romney stands alone, it is easier to attack him and bring him down.

Romney himself is currently being subject to a series of Alinsky *"target it, personalize it, freeze it and polarize it"* attacks. Supposedly, what Romney did as head of Bain Capital, and even what Bain Capital did after Romney left it; is evil incarnate. Far, far worse than any other Hedge Fund that loans money to failing businesses and attempts to turn them around. Evil Romney personally fired every person who lost a job if a Bain Capital business failed, and took the worker's money and made himself rich.

Even Mrs. Romney was attacked by an Obama operative, Hillary Rosen had visited the White House 29 times, no doubt to plot campaign strategy. As Rosen sneered, Mrs. Romney staying home and bringing up 5 children amounted to her "never working a day in her life."[43] Did anyone in the media ever look into the value of what Michelle Obama did in the work force? Her leftist thesis at Princeton? Her performance as a lawyer at Sidley & Austin? How did she get that cushy job at the hospital? Why was she paid $365,000 a year when she no longer had a law license and when her husband was not yet running for office? And did she ever listen to any of those "sermons" by Reverend Wright that Obama never heard in all the 20 years they attended Jeremiah Wright's "church"? All out of bounds for the media, though they attack anything connected to Romney with impunity.

Worst of all is what Obama is doing to Romney's campaign donors. Remember Raila Odinga, the Muslim leader of Obama's Luo tribe in Kenya? He used to go to opponent's rallies, call them out and publicly humiliate them. In his strongholds, people who voted against his party were killed. Obama now uses those same Kenyan tactics in America. American politics have always been rough. But never this disgustingly low.

Exactly as his Luo tribesman and Muslim leader, Raila Odinga did in Kenya, Obama is now targeting his opponent's campaign supporters and donors in America. His aim is to vilify, coerce, bully and expose them to public ridicule, scorn, shame and rebuke. His campaign has publicly accused eight private citizens of *"betting against America"* and of having *"less-than-reputable"* records because they gave money to his opponents.[44] According to Obama's "Truth Team" 2012, *"quite a few have been on the wrong side of the law, others have made profits at the expense of so many Americans."* This, even though his own supporters, the Unions, Hollywood liberals and Dot-Com liberals are all given a free pass. Hollywood regularly takes its production abroad to cheap countries

343

and deprives American workers of jobs. But that is ok. All the Dot-Com liberals get their computers and smart phones manufactured in China or elsewhere. But that is ok too. But when one of Romney's supporters takes some business to Mexico, that is a *"less than reputable"* practice and *"they have profited at the expense of so many Americans!"*

The JournoList is working in concert with Obama. This method of operation was the same JournoList practice we discussed in Part I. Media Matters and John Podesta make a daily call with the White House operatives to get their instructions and follow up with conference calls to various liberal media sycophants. Then one, and then another hyena comes in for the kill. *Don't believe me? Just listen to Rush Limbaugh. He regularly plays montages of all the media, echoing each other, using almost the same words, as they go in for the kill against Republicans!* This is the politics of personal destruction at its very worst. The first people targeted by Obama were the **Koch Brothers**. They were evil! They owned interests in oil!

Then, it was a Super PAC, **Americans for Prosperity**. Just listen to the innuendo and the aspersions cast on this group *"You don't know if it's funded by a foreign-controlled corporation. You don't know if it's a big oil company, or a big bank. You don't know if it's an insurance company that wants to see some of the provisions in health reform repealed because it's good for their bottom line, even if it's not good for the American people."* No, it is not some low-level political hack saying these things. Would you believe this is the President of the United States?[45] If it wasn't Obama, the media would surely question these McCarthyite smear tactics, but because it is Obama, they cannot even see it.

Another attacked in classical Saul Alinsky fashion of *"Pick the target, freeze it, personalize it, and polarize it"* was **Frank VanderSloot**, CEO of a wellness products company in Idaho Falls, Idaho. Mr. VanderSloot gave $1 Million to a Super PAC that supports Romney. And all hell broke loose. A DC political operative went all the way to Idaho Falls to scrutinize Mr. VanderSloot's divorce records. His children were targeted for harassment. Their Facebook and Linked-In files were scoured for information. His customers were targeted with emails detailing purported wrongs Mr. VanderSloot committed. The biggest accusation was that he was '*litigious, combative and a bitter foe of the gay* *rights movement."* He lost a number of his customers.[46] Nixon's plumbers broke into the Democrat's offices looking for information about their campaign tactics. For this, Nixon was impeached. But falsely smearing a donor of Romney's, causing his to lose business and intimidating even the donor's children is ok, so long as the miscreant is Obama!! This is political intimidation at its worst. Third World Politics, right here in America.[47]

Presidents unlike Senators or Congressmen, represent all Americans. Their powers—to jail, to fine, to bankrupt—are so vast as to require restraint. Any president who targets a private citizen for his politics is de facto engaged in government intimidation and threats. This is not Presidential behavior. It is Mafia behavior. This is the man who controls the Justice Department (which can indict you and jail you), the SEC (which can fine you and take your business down), and the IRS (which can audit you and also destroy your business). When Obama threatens you, his message is clear: You made a mistake donating that money to my opponent.

Obama has targeted insurers, oil firms, and Wall Street, making it clear that those who oppose him will face political retribution. In the case of Mr. VanderSloot, he also faced economic retribution. Obama is now trying to require companies to list their political donations as a condition of bidding for government contracts. *What do you think? If you donate to Republicans or to conservative causes, will you get any government contracts from Obama? This is yet another way in which he uses taxpayer money to further his personal political interests.*

It makes me very sad to see the primitive and authoritarian politics of the Third World being replicated here. Mr. Obama is half Kenyan. Yet Americans gifted him with the Presidency of the United States. He has a responsibility to make sure that he does not bring Third World Politics into America.

Sending the IRS after little people: But instead, he is doing even worse. When he sends his goons after rich people, at least, they can afford the attorneys and accountants that are required to defend against attacks by the tax collectors. But Obama has totally politicized the IRS. It is now selectively targeting Tea Party Groups and the individuals that head them. The essence of a Tea Party is that it is a grass roots organization of ordinary people with no rich guys like George Soros backing them. Many of them are poor but proud Americans. They have every right to engage in the political process.

But Obama thinks otherwise. His IRS goons have gone after 80 conservative/constitutionalist groups, including 9/12 Project groups around the country. Just since the first of this year, Tea Party groups in Hawaii, Texas, Ohio, California, Kentucky, and Virginia report receiving inquiries from the IRS challenging their claim to non-profit status. All of them received IRS letters which all came from a single office of the IRS in Cincinnati, Ohio. This is the same IRS that had trouble bringing itself to take any action against left wing groups like ACORN!

A Kentucky Tea Party group sought tax-exemption and waited for 18 months. This group next heard from the IRS on February 14, 2012 in a letter containing 30 main questions with a total of 88 separate inquiries. The IRS letter demanded the schedule and contact of every event sponsored by the group, speaker's names and what the speaker said, and every written communication associated with the event. The letter demanded the names and personal information of every member and volunteer. Other questions in the letter demanded the names of donors and asked for the names of "board members or officers who have run or will run for office (including relatives)." Meantime, Media Matters, which has the identical form of tax exemption, regularly meets with the White House and with the liberal media to organize attacks on Republicans. They are totally partisan. But the IRS has no problem with their tax-exempt status!

The purpose of these IRS letters is plainly to silence the opposition voices as Obama runs for re-election and as the ObamaCare regulations roll out. Who in these groups is really ready to stand up to an IRS audit as the price of speaking out in opposition to ObamaCare? Even if the audit finds nothing amiss, the cost of defending against it could bankrupt an individual or small business. But many of them are quite poor. They simply cannot afford the cost of attorneys and accountants to defend them. So, if they are attacked, they will be compelled to withdraw from the political process.

As the political opponents of Obama are taken down one by one, who is left? Only those who support Obama. And what does that mean? We no longer have a democracy. We have a dictatorship!

Compliance with ObamaCare will be policed by the IRS. Last month, Obama's proposed federal budget added $1.1 Billion to the IRS budget to hire over 5000 new IRS agents to oversee the implementation of ObamaCare. These new unionized IRS agents are the front wave of suppression of opposition to Obama and ObamaCare. If ObamaCare were repealed, they would be out of a job.[48]

And so, as I told you when I started this chapter, the purpose of the regulator is to regulate you and torment you. Otherwise, he would lose his job. So, once you give the government more money, it expands and hires more regulators and you are cooked!!

In my native country, the Socialists and Communists simply put placards into the hands of poor workers and had them scream, "Down with the Rich!" In America, we seem to be on our way to doing the same thing! Whoever Romney picks as running mate will be subject to Alinsky's "target it, freeze it, personalize it and polarize it" treatment. And ***"Racist"*** *will be the epithet of choice in the coming election. Coming in a close second will be* ***"Rich!"***

For all you liberals out there, it will be fun to watch Obama take down his opponents. You will exclaim, "He violated the Constitution, but it was brilliant Politics!" But when there is no opposition left, will it be just as funs watching your country turn into a Dictatorship?

Chapter 14

Converting America into a Caliphate

What do you know about life in a Caliphate? Nothing really. I'll bet you think you don't have to worry because those dreadful laws that enforce "honor" killings of women and even young girls, child "marriages," killing of gays and pets and all those terrible things, will not apply to you as a regular American. First of all, if we become a Caliphate, those laws will apply to you. But there is another aspect of life in a Caliphate that you, as an American, cannot even comprehend: the total loss of your personal freedom.

Once you lose your personal Freedom, you have lost everything: Let's take another look at Mohamed Bouazizi of Tunisia. He was just an ordinary young man with a college degree who couldn't get a job, just like many people you know here in America. His father was dead, so he tried to support his family of seven by selling fresh produce from a cart, which he stationed outside public buildings where people gathered. His produce was obtained on credit, as was his cart. He earned about $76 a week. But he dreamed big. Someday, he would own an Isuzu mini truck and be able to buy his produce outright. You probably think you will have those wonderful food stamps cards, those disability payments, those welfare payments and all those goodies, so you will not have to do that. But, once everyone becomes poor and there are no jobs for anyone, who is going to pay the taxes to support your food stamp cards and other benefits? Nobody. And, if you are not already there, you will become like Mohamed Bouazizi, struggling to make ends meet.

Petty bureaucrats constantly harassed him with demands for payment of fines and bribes for this, that and the other thing. He even had to pay a bribe for the location of his cart. You think you wil not be harassed? How about those exorbitant fines you pay for your traffic tickets or for parking outside your house but too close to your own mailbox or even for parking at a meter for a few extra minutes? How about having to pay $12 a day to cross a bridge or $385 for a monthly train ticket to go to work in Manhattan? How about having your gas prices double because

State and Federal governments are taking nearly 30% of the price in taxes? How about having your sales taxes constantly rising? And your property taxes, your food prices, your heating oil prices, your electricity bill, your water bill and the price of just about everything else rising? How about all the constantly increasing regulations you have to follow when you try to run your small business? How about having the IRS come after you because you didn't vote for Obama?

Mohamed Bouazizi had no freedom and no hope for a better life. The last straw for him was the total disrespect shown to him by a policewoman who overturned his produce cart, breaking the cart and spilling the produce into the gutter. To show her total contempt for him, she also spat on him. You must understand, this was a woman disrespecting him, in a world where the man is king. And she spat on him, which is the worst possible insult in almost the whole world. He ran into the city hall to complain, but he was a little person, invisible, and the authorities didn't even bother to listen to him. Have you even tried to talk to the authorities that rule over you? Your local, State or Federal government? Are they listening to your concerns at all? At some time, you will reach a breaking point, just as Mohamed Bouazizi did. What he did was pour paint thinner over himself and set himself on fire.[1] What will you do?

Your life is cheap. The authorities have no concern for you. Take a look at what Eric Holder and his DOJ did on Fast and Furious.

Fast & Furious: The first thing we need to know about Fast and Furious, which put over 2000 AK-47 semi-automatic assault rifles in the hands of known Mexican drug dealers without any means of tracking them, is that Obama says it was Bush's fault! Bush did have a similar but much smaller and much more carefully constructed program called "Wide Receiver." Unlike Obama, Bush's ATF agents worked cooperatively with the Mexican law enforcement to try to build a case against the Mexican cartels. Bush sought to go after criminals. But Obama and Holder changed the objective. They wanted to go after American citizens and take away their Second Amendment Rights.[2] Obama's Fast and Furious was completely reckless. But Obama, who tells us with every breath that he despises Bush, says that on this matter, he copied Bush. In fact, this is not true. Obama hatched his scheme on his own. Someone high up in Eric Holder's DOJ authorized the ATF to instruct American gun dealers to disregard the law and sell about 2000 AK-47's to known Mexican drug dealers. The stated theory was that these guns would be traced to the Mexican drug cartels and then we would catch them. The only problem was that there were no electronic tracing components on the weapons and there was no surveillance as the drug dealers took the guns away, so there was never any possibility that we could catch the drug dealers.[3]

You need some background to understand why Obama and Holder hatched this plan. In 2008, the Supreme Court had held that individuals were entitled to use guns for protection and that this Second Amendment right to bear arms could not be infringed upon by the Federal Government. In July 2010, it overturned a gun control law in Chicago and held that this restriction also applied to the States.[4] The liberals were furious and fast!! Four days later, Chicago passed another gun control law. And this set off a media blitz of articles complaining about the lack of gun control and how the "gun lobby's obduracy" was increasing the danger to civilians;[5] and how the British hate guns.[6] Obama himself had decried the gun violence in Mexico and made the dubious claim that 90% of the guns used were being sold by American dealers. Even the Mexican President made similar allegations. Fast and Furious was put into action at this time. It is fairly obvious that once the ATF itself sold American AK-47's to the Cartels, the AK-47's the Cartel used would be American guns![7] The only possible reason for permitting these guns into the hands of the Mexican cartels was to accomplish a political goal by using the increased violence and the prevalence of American guns in Mexico as an excuse to justify tighter gun-control legislation.[8]

Everyone concerned knew that there would be many resulting civilian deaths, but obviously considered this acceptable. The only way these guns could ever have been tracked is if they were found at the scene of a crime or discovered during a sting operation. In fact, several hundred Mexican citizens have been killed. In addition, Border Patrol Agent, Brian Terry and ICE Agent Jamie Zapata were both killed by guns traced back to this program.[9]

Assistant AG Lanny Breuer headed the DOJ's criminal division at the time and sent Darrell Issa's committee a letter stating neither he nor Eric Holder knew anything about this program. But later,

Breuer's department admitted that Breuer did know about ATF gun running as far back as April 2010. And Darrel Issa's House Oversight Committee obtained copies of wiretap authorizations made in 2010 that demonstrated that senior officials of the DOJ did have knowledge of that gun-walking (a tactic whereby the ATF allows guns to be bought by suspected arms traffickers) was being used in Fast and Furious.[10] This scheme was funded by $10 million of Stimulus money and it was AG Eric Holder who requested the funds for this purpose.[11] Former acting ATF chief Kenneth Melson, who oversaw Fast and Furious, admitted that he reassigned every manager involved in the program after Congress commenced its investigation. Mr. Melson himself was later promoted to a comfortable "senior advisor" position in the DOJ.[12] The chief of the criminal division of the U.S. Attorney's office in Arizona, Patrick Cunningham, took the 5th Amendment and refused to testify as to anything other than his name and title to Rep. Issa's committee.[13] As we go to press, Rep. Issa's committee and the House has voted to hold Eric Holder in contempt. Holder has to provide additional documents to the House committee without prior agreement to end it's investigation. But we still do not know who authorized the ATF to provide AK-47's to the Mexican Drug cartels or when senior officials at Justice knew about the program. By invoking executive privilege on June 20, 2012, Obama has given credence to the belief that the stonewalling is a cover up to protect someone high up in the White House, who sought political gain by selling AK-47s to the Mexican Cartels to kill innocent civilians. *And as for you, little person, you now know that the Obama White House does not care who gets killed when it is pursuing its political goals.*

You think you have a Constitutional Right to Bear Arms? Think Again. And do not doubt for a minute that Obama intends to take away your Second Amendment Right to bear Arms. If he can't do it through Fast & Furious, then he is going to doit another way. He is strongly supporting an UN Arms Treaty Resolution that, once enacted, gives Obama an excuse to confiscate all "unauthorized" arms, create an international gun registry, and enact toucher licensing requirements.[92]

You think you have a constitutional right to equal protection under the law? Think again. The New Black Panther party is a virulently racist and anti-Semitic organization whose leaders have encouraged violence against whites, Jews and law enforcement officers.[14] They are a Muslim group, have close connections to Minister Farrakhan's Nation of Islam, and also to Ahmadinejad of Iran.[15] They are also the favored children of Obama and Eric Holder's DOJ.

The New Black Panthers, a Muslim, racist, anti-Semitic group, are a favored group: During the 2008 election three New Black Panthers, dressed in paramilitary black uniforms, with one of them brandishing a nightstick, stood outside a polling place, made racial threats and racial insults to voters, and made menacing and intimidating gestures, statement and movements directed at individuals who were present to aid voters.[16] Bartell Bull, a respected Democrat Civil Rights Attorney and publisher of the left-wing Village Voice, witnessed this. He heard one of them yell, *"You are about to be ruled by the black man, cracker!"* As Mr. Bull later testified, it was the most blatant form of voter intimidation he had ever seen. One of the three criminals was Jerry Jackson, a member of Philadelphia's 14th ward and a credentialed Democrat Party poll watcher. Minister King Samir Shabazz was the second. Malik Zulu Shabazz, the New Black Panther Party Chairman, was the third. Just after the election, Malik Shabazz acknowledged on Fox News that his activities were part of a nationwide effort.[17]

As one career DOJ attorney said, it was vital that they prevent the paramilitary style intimidation of voters in the future. In 2007, then Senator Obama had actually introduced a bill to protect Americans from voter intimidation. The DOJ brought suit against the three men. The defendants did not appear at trial and the judge was about to render a default judgment against them. Suddenly, a top political appointee at Justice, Thomas Perrelli, withdrew the case.[18] The only "penalty" was an injunction prohibiting the person from carrying the nightstick from carrying a weapon in a polling place in the future, and that, only until 2012.[19]

Two career DOJ attorneys testified before a Congressional Committee. Former voting chief of the Civil Rights Division, J. Christian Adams said political appointees were ordering DOJ officials to stop pursuing race-neutral enforcement of the Voting Rights Act. He further testified that 72% of DOJ attorneys self-identified as "liberal" and that it was likely that hostility towards race-neutral enforcement of the Voting Rights Act had always existed, but that under Obama is had grown into a full-fledged affirmative action discrimination in favor of blacks.[20]

When Eric Holder testified at a house oversight hearing, he asserted that the DOJ does not enforce the law in a race conscious way. But he defended what the New Black Panthers had done by saying *"When you compare to what people endure in the South in the 60's, . . . to compare to what happened in Philadelphia . . . which is inappropriate, I think does a great disservice to those who put their lives on the line, who risked all, **for my people**."* [21]

The New Black Panthers are an extremely violent gang. Malik Shabazz has threatened to burn down Detroit.[22] King Samir Shabazz asserts that *"he don't obey the white man's law."* He uses bullhorns to shout out that he hates white people. Every iota of a cracker, he hates them. He hates white dirty cracker whores.[23] He shouts, *"You want freedom? You're gonna have to kill some crackers! You're gonna have to kill some of their babies!" "I'm about the total destruction of white people. I'm about the total liberation of black people. I hate white people. I hate my enemy . . . The only thing the cracker understands is violence . . . The only thing the cracker understands is gunpowder. You got to take violence to violence."*[24] He also went on a series of racially charged radio rants, *"You should be thankful we're not running around here hanging crackers by nooses and all that kind of stuff—yet, yet, yet,"*[25] He also teaches "black survival" techniques to little kids, how to use guns, how to use a machete and how to disable or kill an opponent.[26] The New Black Panthers actually placed a bounty on George Zimmerman's head offering $10,000 for him "dead or alive."[27]

So, there you are. If you are black, Muslim, racist, anti-Semitic and are willing to stand around polling places dressed in paramilitary garb, intimidating whites with racial slurs and nightsticks; and spew violent racist language at whites and threaten to kill them and their babies; why then, you are one of Obama's and Holder's chosen people.

Knockout King: This lawlessness, condoned and even encouraged by the White House, has given rise to another phenomenon, "Knockout King." This "game" involves gangs of black youths who beat up elderly, Chinese or Korean or white people at random, punch them to the ground and leave their victims bruised, injured, brain damaged and sometimes dead.[28] Meantime, they film the attacks and post them on social networks.[29] There have been hundreds of episodes of racial violence that have taken place in more than 60 cities in the past three years.[30]

At the **Iowa State Fair**, according to a police officer, black youths came down on white people like a swarm of bees and attacked them. You can watch it here.[31] In **St. Louis, Missouri**, Police Chief Dan Isom told the Associated Press that the city had seen about 10 such attacks over the past 15 months. *"These individuals have absolutely no respect for human life,"* Mayor Francis Slay said.

In **Chicago,** there is an epidemic of black crime, which is being concealed by the press and by the police. An attack at a Chicago train station also sparked outrage.[32] But the media downplay these attacks. According to one news anchor, anyone who writes about the epidemic of racial violence in Chicago is an *"idiot"* who engages in *"meaningless . . . race baiting."* Another asks, *"Why do you care so much about the attackers' race? If you fear or dislike blacks, I suppose it would confirm your prejudice. But otherwise, it tells you nothing useful."* A third says she worries how reporting the race of the criminals *"will reflect on all the good black kids."* But, bottom line; there is an epidemic of racial crimes being committed by young black youths. After a Blues concert on June 9, 2012 a mob attack left a visitor with a broken jaw. Another mob attacked a man trying to protect his wife and left him with a concussion, fractured orbital bone, 2 cracked teeth and a cut over his left eye. The next night another mob attacked and beat a doctor at Northwestern, the second attack on a doctor in a couple of weeks. They went into a gay district beating assaulting, destroying and even knifing and posted the videos on line.[33] They congregate in gangs and go into subways looting and attacking. Then they come out onto the streets and attack whoever is around. They go back in and go on to emerge at another station. The police are unable to keep up with the mayhem.[34] North Beach had to be closed down on Memorial Day after a crowd of 1,000 blacks attacked beachgoers. That weekend in Chicago, 10 were killed and 40 were shot. The next weekend, 8 were killed and 40 wounded. Superintendent of Police Gary McCarthy first claimed that crime was down. Later, after a major riot of over 1,000 black people, the Superintendent acknowledged that there was a problem and he was able to identify who was responsible: . . . Sarah Palin! Because she supports the right to bear arms!![35]

In the 2011 **Wisconsin State Fair**, a mob of 80 to 100 black teenagers tore through the fairgrounds and the parking lot, beating white people at random. This was the second such incident in Wisconsin in just over a month. And it was repeated on the July 4th weekend. In August 2011, a group of 20 to 30 youths went on the rampage in **Philadelphia's Center City** leaving 59 people being beaten and some hospitalized. In late June 2012, in **Portland, Oregon**, 10-15 hoodie wearing black youths ran into a Nordstrom's, stole clothing and raced out of the store. This was one of at least four recent attacks by "flash mobs" of black youths. In April, 20 of them chased a white couple into a convenience store. In early June, a bigger crowd attacked an Albertson's grocery store. In January, a 14-year-old white girl was beaten by three black women while about a dozen other black people took videos, shouted racial epithets and encouraged the assault. In all these cases, even with video proof of the racial motivations of the miscreants, the district attorney has declined to file hate-crime charges.[36]

Philadelphia's black Mayor Nutter increased police patrols and moved up a weekend curfew on minors to 9.00 P.M. Parents would be subject to fines each time any of their children got caught violating the curfew. And to his credit, he was blunt. *"You have damaged your own race. . . . Take those God-darn hoodies down, especially in the summer. Pull up your pants up and buy a belt 'cause no one wants to see your underwear or the crack of your butt."*[37]

Contrast this to Obama, who jumped to conclusions about Latino George Zimmerman's shooting of Trayvon Martin and tried to gain political advantage for himself by inciting racial animosity. He informed the public that if he had a son, he would look like Trayvon Martin.[38] Newsweek actually planned a cover of Obama in a hoodie.[39] And Representative Bobby Rush tried to wear a hoodie to the House floor.[40] *God only knows why liberals encourage young black children to dress like hoodlums. If I had any influence, I would ask them to wear round wire-rimmed eyeglasses, so they would look like intellectuals!* Of course, playing the race card is Obama's main strategy. He has always associated himself with race baiters and anti-Semites like Jeremiah Wright, Jesse Jackson and Al Sharpton. And the main plank of race baiters is the politics of envy. Black people are being taught that the reason they are poor is because the whites stole from them and made themselves rich. The excuses made at a forum by Portland area commentators after the hoodie wearing kids stole from Nordstrom's are illustrative: *"Rich white high school students wait, and grow up to flash mob our economy and legally* *manipulate our Congress with unregulated lobbying. They are taught by their rich white parents that they are helping grow the economy through deregulation and small government." "Funny, the Oregonian does not report on the rich old white guys who flash mob and are hijacking our economy and schools."* [41] And blacks are obviously being taught that they should hate whites and envy them. **So, we come to the first plank of the Obama commandments:** *Envy your neighbor!*

Blacks remain mired in poverty: The sad irony of this is that Obama does not really care about blacks. He took away the opportunity scholarships that allowed blacks to escape from the dismal Washington D.C. schools. He has favored Teacher's unions over education for black children. In fact, he places his teacher unions over all children. His Administration has given classroom disrupters so many rights; they cannot be removed from classrooms. And it is the inner city black kids who are not given a proper education.[42] And it is blacks that bear the brunt of most of the evils of extreme poverty. 70% of black babies are born to fatherless families. Obama talks a good game about abortions. But he does nothing to help bring emotional stability and security to black families. He talks a good game about focusing like a laser on jobs, but he has done nothing to provide inner city youngsters with jobs. In fact, whenever someone suggests a special inner city tax benefit for businesses opening there, Obama panders to the unions and makes it so that only union workers will get those jobs and not the inner city teenagers who need them. Inner city black unemployment is over 40.5%[43] In fact, blacks are living in poverty and hopelessness in the inner city right now, just as they were when he came into office. Nothing has changed. A lot of Hope; but no Change.

Obama only protects black thugs like the New Black Panthers. And law-breakers like the SEIU thugs. But by keeping blacks poor and dependent and pointing fingers of blame at the "rich whites," Obama gets his votes.

OWS: Another group of Obama's supporters is Occupy Wall Street (OWS). These started out as protests by young people who were unable to get jobs. But, they were quickly taken over by others with a political agenda. Among their supporters, providing them with blankets, food, organizational support etc. are Obama, Joe Biden and Nancy Pelosi; unions, including the SEIU, and people from the disgraced organization

ACORN.[44] Other supporters are Communist Party USA, The American Nazi Party, Revolutionary Communist Party, Black Panthers, Nation of Islam's Louis Farrakhan, CAIR, Iran's Supreme Leader, the Ayatollah Khamenei, Hugo Chavez, Revolutionary Guards of Iran, the Government of North Korea, the Communist Party of China and Hezbollah.[45] Why do you think Obama does not denounce OWS or its supporters? Once you read this list, are you not shocked at the extent of foreign and Communist//Marxist/Muslim support for OWS?

Given who controls OWS, it is not surprising that they have become extremely violent. There have been extremely violent events throughout the country, almost all of which have been studiously ignored by Obama's media. *(Why do you think the media ignores these events?)* First, OWS posted home addresses, phone numbers and even salary details of thousands of police officers throughout the country in retaliation for having being evicted from their camps in city parks. While they were at it, they also posted the same information about the Florida Family Association members who led a boycott of the TV show "All-American Muslim."[46] This alone demonstrates the Muslim involvement in the OWS movement. In Seattle, the OWS threw bricks and bags of steel at the police.[47] In Manhattan, they dumped feces and urine in an ATM lobby and destroyed Zucotti Park.[48] In Los Angeles, they destroyed the park outside City Hall and threw a farmer's market, which had been operating for decades, out of business. Five OWS members were arrested in a plot to blow up a bridge in Cleveland.[49] And at the May 2012 NATO summit in Chicago, they rioted, smashed windows and created mayhem and also assaulted four police officers and stabbed one of them.[50] Radical activists are responsible for hundreds of serious crimes, including murder, assault, gang rape, arson, rioting, and robbery. These actions, which are being cheered on by communist terrorists and Obama buddies Bill Ayers and Bernadine Dohrn, are designed to foment civil unrest and prompt change.[51]

ACORN & Its Reincarnation: Obama has always worked very closely with ACORN, the largest radical group in America, with their strongest chapter in Chicago. In fact, Obama was their lawyer and, as a Community Organizer, he also trained their people to organize aggressive demonstrations. They are a very confrontational group, which launches aggressive campaigns of sit-ins and disruptions to achieve their goals.

For instance, 200 protestors stormed a Chicago City Council meeting during a living wage debate, pushing aside the metal detector and backing the police against the doors. In Baltimore, they sent four busloads of profanity-screaming protestors to the Mayor's home, terrifying his wife and kids.[52] It was Obama who brought the lawsuit to allow motor-voter registrations, which have resulted in massive election voter fraud. In his 2011 budget, Obama had set aside $4 Billion of taxpayer money for ACORN and similar organizations to push for the registration of Democrat voters.[53]

But, in 2009 activist James O'Keefe caught many ACORN employees from various different offices offering "helpful advice" to what they thought was a pedophile pimp about starting a brothel staffed with underage children and committing other crimes on video. Andrew Breitbart aired those videos. And there were a number of convictions of ACORN workers for voter fraud. Soon after, popular revulsion prompted Congress to cut off funding of ACORN and groups related to it.

But Obama has done an end run around Congressional prohibitions. *Remember I told you he has no regard for his coequal branch, Congress? He just disregards the Constitution and does what he pleases, exactly like a Muslim Dictator.* In June 2012, it was discovered that Obama had designated $445.6 million for a "foreclosure relief" program to be run by Joe McGavin, formerly of ACORN and of ACORN's successor, AHCOA (Affordable Housing Centers of America). (*Are you still wondering why you can't refinance your house?*) ACORN, working with the SEIU, is actively involved in OWS. ACORN continues its radical operations even today, but has merely morphed into many different corporations.[54]

Calling anyone who opposes him a Terrorist: In 2009, Obama's DHS issued a broad based "Threat Assessment" against all Tea Party Supporters, Christians, Right Wing "extremists" and "Disgruntled Military Veterans". Apparently, actual terrorists are not terrorists, but any person who opposes Obama's policies could be a terrorist![55] Obama issued a related "federal report" on July 4, 2012. Americans "suspicious of centralized federal authority, reverent of individual liberty and protecting their personal freedoms" are categorized as extreme right-wing terrorists. Also included are fundamental religious groups. But the word "Islam" appears only once in the report and the word "Muslim" does not appear at all! It is clear that Obama is targeting Christians and freedom loving people. And it is equally clear that he has no regard for our Constitution at all—How else can you explain his report which criminalizes virtually everything our Founding Fathers stood for?[93]

Remember the TSA: They are armed and authorized to take police action against you if you object to their highly intrusive searches. They can, and do, set off false alarms so they can do intrusive searches on persons, even Senators, who oppose Obama. As reported above, they can now stop you on highways, ports and even subways; in fact they can stop and search you anywhere. They know they are violating your Fourth Amendment rights, but they do not care.

Youth Brigades: Hitler knew that if you control the youth, you control the future. At first, it was voluntary. By 1941, it was mandatory. Obama thinks likewise. In 2009, when he had control of Congress, Obama created a Youth Brigade, with anyone receiving school loans being required to serve at least 3 months in "public service." It cost $5 Billion. It expressly violated the First Amendment because it forbade any religious activity, or any petitioning of the government. It steered funding for public service away from churches, neighbors and individuals and created a federal public service organization in which federal bureaucrats would decide what constituted "public service." But this program languished, possibly because of the great opposition to banning religious organizations and because it was obviously unconstitutional.

Now, we have discovered that student loan debt has risen 82% in the past 10 years, and the total amount owed, $1 trillion dollars, exceeds the public's credit card liabilities. Student loans have risen by 511% while disposable income has risen by only by 73 %. Obama's solution, issued by Executive Order, with no input from Congress, is to permit student debts to be forgiven if the student works in the public sector. And also, to limit repayment to 10% of the yearly adjusted income and forgive all loans after 20 years.[56] But, current law provides that, while other debts are forgiven in a bankruptcy, Student Loan debt to the Federal Government survives.

What all this means: if a student has incurred substantial Student Loan debt and wants to get his loan forgiven, he has to work in public service, but not for any religious organization. And he cannot even work for a private charitable organization unless Obama's government has blessed it as a "Federal Public Service." And to make sure private charitable organizations are wiped out, Obama has even proposed to wipe out the charitable deduction and thus many charitable organizations won't be able to afford to pay any wages at all. And voila! Obama's Youth Brigade has been revived.

Little Kids: You remember Hitler's youth cults and the "happy" songs they sang to their leader. And you will recall the disgust and horror you felt in 2008 when watching videos of various teachers creating an Obama cult, indoctrinating little children, even in public schools, and making them sing hymns to Obama. In case, you have forgotten, here are a few:

http://www.youtube.com/watch?v=FO3NBqT3LBc&feature=related
http://www.youtube.com/watch?v=ettl3zfLWus
http://www.youtube.com/watch?v=cdPSqL9_mfM&skipcontrinter=1

The Ultimate in Cult Creation—A New American Flag: This was posted at the Lake County Democratic Party Headquarters in Florida,[57] and it speaks for itself.

America's New Ruler

Media: Even the media is getting in on the act. You already know that there is nothing Mitt Romney or his Vice Presidential pick can do that will not be viciously attacked by Obama's media. But Martin Bashir of MSNBC has gone beyond the pale. He just showed a video of Mitt Romney's campaign bus being blown up repeatedly. He will say it was just a joke. But I say, given the violence demonstrated by Obama's supporters, he is recklessly inciting supporters of Obama to assassinate Romney.[58]

Not content with the army he has amassed, Obama seeks to increase it. Virtually everything the Obama and his Regulators and Czars do today is focused on one thing, and one thing only. How to get him re-elected.

Welfare Rolls have Quadrupled: In 3 years of the Obama administration, direct payments increased 32% climbing by $600 billion. 49% of Americans now live in a home where at least one person gets a federal benefit like welfare, social security, workers comp, unemployment, subsidized housing etc. This is a 44% increase from before Obama took office. 36 million (15% of all Americans) now get food stamps and this is 45% higher since Obama took office, twice as high as the average for the previous 40 years. People on Social Security Disability Jumped 10% in Obama's first 2 years. ObamaCare will add 15 million to Medicaid rolls and another 24 million Americans will receive subsidies to pay their health insurance. The cost for this new coverage will be $130 billion a year.[59]

Welfare has also been allowed to get completely out of hand. There is so much waste and fraud, one does not know where to begin. More than half of welfare recipients have been on the dole for more than 10 years. Remember the Clinton/Gingrich welfare reforms that limited the amount of time someone could stay on the welfare rolls? Not any more. So, once again, it is not a temporary fix for a poor person but rather, has become a way of life. And Trump believes there is massive fraud in the system.[60] How about the woman with 15 kids by 5 different fathers who complains, "someone gotta pay for this!" [61] Or the woman on welfare living in a million dollar lakefront home in suburban Seattle?[62] Or the people in Alexandra Pelosi's video report: the guy who thinks he is entitled to some of Obama's stash? Or the guy who has 5 children by 3 women whom he does not support, but thinks he is 'single got to mingle,' and says he is entitled to food stamps because his ancestors built this place? [63] Or the guy who has had 30 children by 11 different women. And nine of those children were born in the last three years, after Hatchett, who is something of a local celebrity, vowed, "I'm done!" He is paying approximately two dollars a month per child and he has just asked a judge to reduce his child support payments.[64] Are any of these people really happy? How about their children? Can any of them care for their kids as a parent should?

People are now so poor that 30,000 people turned out for a chance to get a Section 8 housing voucher in South Fulton, Atlanta (population 40,000) when there were less than 10% of those number in available vouchers. Police and 4 other departments had to turn out in riot gear to quell the crowd. 52 were injured and 20 had to be taken to hospital.[65] Yet, welfare and the various other subsidies are so out of hand that a savvy one-parent family of three making $14,500 a year (minimum wage) has more disposable income than a family making $60,000 a year. And that excludes benefits from Supplemental Security Income disability checks. America is now a country that punishes those middle-class people who not only try to work hard, but avoid scamming the system. [66]

The way we now run our welfaare system cannot possibly be the best way to care for the needy. This so-called safety net takes away all the drive of the people and all their self-respect. Giving them "credit cards" filled with money does not give them self-respect. Welfare also induces people to become cheats. And it is not fair to those who do work. Welfare only mires people in poverty, giving them just enough to live on at the borderline.

Knockout King and other such mayhem can only take place if the kids in question have not had any parenting. All the social workers, therapists, psychologists, counselors, defense attorneys, judges and even parole officers in the world can never make up to a child for the lack of a parent who loves them, cares for them and treats them like they are special and precious. Our welfare system, which encourages women to produce babies that they can't and won't care for is a cruelty beyond comprehension.

It is not love, care and compassion for the poor. It is a cynical ploy. In exchange for all this misery, there is only one huge benefit. Obama gets their votes! Come to think of it, as long as they are dependent on government assistance they will vote Democrat forever!

Giving Amnesty and work visas to Illegals while we have nearly 13 million unemployed,[67] [68] 6 million less jobs than when Obama started his term[69] and 44.7 million people on food stamps:[70] Congress had, for the past 10 years, refused to pass the Dream Act giving illegals Amnesty. Obama could have passed such a law when he had control of both houses of Congress in 2008-10, but he chose not to. In September 2011, Obama admitted that he couldn't act unilaterally: *"This notion I can somehow just change the laws unilaterally is just not true. We are doing everything we can administratively, but the fact of the matter is there are laws on the books that I have to enforce."*

In June 2012, facing what looks like defeat in the 2012 election, Obama reversed course. He granted amnesty to what he acknowledged were 800,000 illegals, *(though we all know it will be many, many more)* saying he would not enforce our immigration laws against a class of persons that had come here as children and graduated from high school or entered the military. Of course, this so-called discretionary enforcement, electing not to enforce immigration laws against various classes of individuals is totally unconstitutional. And it ignores the fact that we have nearly 13 million of our own people unemployed.[71] Obama does not (yet) have the authority to make and enact laws, if Congress has not passed them. But he did it anyway. His policy memo to Homeland Security directing non-enforcement of our immigration laws, is full of details of who can get it, what they have to do to get it, how they will only get a work visa and not a green card etc.

But you know Obama. "Tricky Dick" should be his name. Virtually everything he tells the American people has a little twist. You need to have a lawyer with you to parse and understand what he says, because nothing is at it seems. These illegals will never be free American citizens. If they were, they'd start living as free people and start becoming prosperous. Then, they would stop voting Democrat. So they will be kept in a sort of limbo. But he did order ICE to give any young person they catch a work visa. Rush Limbaugh said it best, "Catch, Release & Vote"[72]

Voter Fraud: Parallel to this is Eric Holder's attempt to prevent States from purging illegals, non-residents and dead people from their rolls. *Yes folks, surprise! None of these people are entitled to vote!* Every State that tries to prevent voter registration of ineligible people is sued by Holder's DOJ, including, most recently, Florida.[73] 900 dead people voted recently in South Carolina and, of course, Holder sued to keep them on the rolls.[74] The Pew Research center recently reported that there are over 1.4 million dead people on the voter rolls.[75] Since Obama comes from Chicago, where the dead vote regularly,[76] it is understandable that Obama does not want to discriminate against the dead. And it is Obama himself who worked to pass motor voter registration, same day registration and voting without an ID; all indispensable aids to voter fraud.

But Holder has taken this even further. He is also sung all states that are requiring an ID to vote.[77] This is America. You need an ID to get on a plane. To cash a check. To buy large items on your credit card. And so that your employer can use E-Verify to give you a job. But it is oh, so discriminatory to ask someone who is voting to produce an ID before he or she can vote! In fact, that brilliant Journalist, James O'Keefe actually arranged for a white guy to impersonate Eric Holder himself, to demonstrate how easy it is to commit voter fraud.[78]

I could have told you all this without the painstaking research by simply telling you an anecdote from my native land. One of my father's workers, a Muslim, once took a whole day off to vote, when legally, he was entitled to only a half day. Curious, I asked him why he needed a whole day. He looked me straight in the eye and told me, "So I could vote". He told me, with a little bit of a smile and a wink, that he voted for my father's party. And that he voted three times! Now I was really interested. I asked, "How did you do that?" "Simple," he replied. "My precinct boss has a register of all the voters, so we know who has gone to the Middle East and wont be voting. I simply went in there and gave the name of one of those guys. Each time, I dressed a little differently. One time, I wore a scarf around my head, like I had just come from the Mosque. Another time, I tied up my sarong above my knees. The third time, I removed the headscarf and went in pants." Still puzzled, I asked him, "But what did you do about the indelible ink on your finger which showed you had voted?" He looked at me pityingly, "Why, Missy. I just used the nail polish remover Missy uses!" So there, you can learn a lot from simple people, if only you will listen to them!! And don't nobody tell me Sri Lankans aren't as smart as Obama!

On a more serious note, this is why Obama and the Democrats are so in love with Illegals. It has nothing to do with farm workers and the price of our salad leaves. And they don't give a hoot about illegals taking the jobs of poor black youths of whom 40.5% are unemployed. The blacks have nowhere to go but to vote for Obama.

It has everything to do with votes. Illegals are poor and desperate. If Obama gives them some of his stash, they will love him forever. They are used to having no hope. Vote fraud, bribery and corruption is normal for them back home. They have no idea that if we flood the country with illegals, we will become just like the countries they came from. They usually have no education. And they have no idea that it is our Constitution and the rule of law that prevents this country from going the way of other Third World countries. And, because they go to pubic schools, they will never learn either.

They will gladly sing those hymns to Obama in exchange for some of Obama's stash. And if it requires them to join the SEIU, pay some of their income to Obama through the SEIU, use a little violence here, a little shouting on people's doorsteps with a bullhorn there? They'll do that too. **May I present to you, . . . The perfect Obama voter—The Illegal!!**

Remember what Obama said just before the 2008 election? In talking about his plans to double the size of the Peace Corps and nearly quadruple the size of AmeriCorps and the size of the nation's military services, he made this rather shocking and chilling pledge: "We cannot continue to rely on our military in order to achieve the national security objectives we've set. We've got to have a civilian national security force that's just as powerful, just as strong, just as well funded."[79]

And remember the techniques of the Muslim leader Raila Odinga, Obama's fellow Luo tribesman in Kenya, whom Obama campaigned for? He did everything he could to intimidate his opponents. He called them out and humiliated and shamed them. He set up one group against another. When he lost, his tribe went on the rampage, massacring

Christians and burning down over 600 churches, many with women and children inside them.

Now Obama has his "civilian army," comprising his TSA, his Union buddies, the New Black Panthers, OWS, SEIU, ACORN, his Youth Brigade and of course, his Media. All ready to support him. All, including Martin Bashir, with proven records of violence, incitement to violence and/or intimidation against opponents. What do you think will happen if we fail to re-elect him President?

© First-Amendment-Rights.com

Obama's Supporters Get Him Re-Elected

ObamaCare was always a complete Hoax. *If I say I'll pass the Making Americans Millionaires Act ("MAMA"), does this mean I am the perfect Mama who will make you a Millionaire?* Well, the Patient Protection and Affordable Care Act is a hoax, exactly like my MAMA. It has a great title, but that's about it.

First, we were told that millions of poor people were suffering because they had no health care and that ObamaCare would make health care available for everyone. This was a hoax. And, in typical attorney weasel fashion, Obama was speaking about health insurance, not health care. In fact, health care was always available for everyone, with or without insurance, because of the Emergency Medical Treatment and Active Labor Act of 1985.[80] Hospitals are required to treat everyone in America, as long as they go to the emergency room. Once there, they get their heart surgeries, their follow up care, their convalescent care, their physiotherapy, the whole enchilada. In fact, our healthcare costs so much precisely because people come here from all over the world and make use of our healthcare facilities "for free." *I know a number of foreigners, including family members of some maids and gardeners, who have come here on "vacation," but knowing they have a medical condition that requires treatment. They come here toting their medical records, say they have a "medical emergency," go to the hospital and then get first rate medical care involving procedures that cost ordinary Americans or their insurers tens of thousands of dollars. Don't believe me? Go sit in any emergency room and watch who comes in. Or get any emergency room doctor or nurse at a quiet moment and ask them.*

Second, Obama promised us that his ObamaCare would "bend the cost curve." For those of us who were stupid, he explained his ObamaCare would bring the cost of health care premiums down by $2,500 for the typical family. This was also untrue. He brought in his great intellectual giant, MIT economist Jonathan Gruber, who told us his "Gruber Microsimulation Model" demonstrated "for sure" that ObamaCare would reduce the cost of premiums to young people by 13% and to the old by 31%. This high sounding "Microsimulation Model" was used to batter down all opposition, the skittish Democrats and even a professional study done by PriceWaterhouseCooper, which projected those individual premiums would rise by 47%. Administration operatives sneered that the PWC study could not be given any credence because insurers had paid for it; while Gruber was touted by himself, and by the White House, as an independent analyst. In fact, Gruber was the major advisor to the White House, and also the single most influential advisor to the CBO, which scored the bill and assured Congress and the public that it would save money.

PriceWaterhouseCooper considered what Gruber had failed to take into account, the single most expensive item in ObamaCare—**guaranteed issue**, the requirement that insurers accept people with pre-existing conditions. It is obvious to anyone who has not gone to M.I.T. that when someone can get coverage at any time and wants to game the system, even if they have a terminal disease; that person is going to wait until he gets terminally sick before he starts paying premiums. This means only the really sick will pay. And no insurer can afford to provide treatment for a terminal disease when his pool of paying insured only comprises the very sick. The net result is that premiums will go up sharply.

The other factor which Gruber failed to analyze properly was that insurers were required to price insurance by **"community ratings"** standards; meaning the very old (who usually had health care costs 6 times that of young people), could only be charged 3 times the price charged to the young (and usually very healthy). What this did, thanks to the AARP lobby, was to shift the cost of insurance from the old to the young, who could least afford it. There was a small penalty of $95 per year if a person failed to get coverage. Again, if you didn't go to M.I.T., you would know that young people would pay the $95 per year, rather than the $4,940, which was the average premium in 2010.

Furthermore, ObamaCare assured the poor that they would receive help to acquire their coverage. As a consequence of these and other stupid regulatory mandates, in 2012, Colorado saw a 19% increase in premiums, and in late 2011, Minnesota saw a 29% increase and Wisconsin a 30% increase in premiums. And, of course, as jobs and the economy went south and even more individuals decided to opt out of coverage; the premiums went higher still, making them even less affordable. And the government will be required to provide even more assistance. And the taxpayers will be on the hook for billions upon billions of extra subsidies.[81]

Promising your "children" could stay on your policy until age 26: This was also a great political move. Obama promises and gets all the credit. The parents pay a much higher premium. Or the Business pays. Someone other than Obama pays extra premiums for the "child" who is covered.

Fourth, Obama and his Democrat allies in Congress promised us ObamaCare was a jobs bill that would produce 4 million jobs. In April 2009, Obama explained that ObamaCare was one of the five pillars of the economy, "If we don't invest now in a more affordable health care system," he said, "this economy simply won't grow at the pace it needs to in two or five or 10 years down the road."[82] As you have seen above, this too was pure fantasy. We have fewer jobs now that we had when Obama assumed office. Whenever a small business owner talks about jobs, one of the major fears he expresses is that his business will grow past the employee threshold where ObamaCare mandates will kick in, requiring his business to provide health insurance be cannot afford. So, he keeps the number of employees low and does not hire additional workers.

Obama also swore to us that "if you like your healthcare or your doctor, you can keep it." This was also untrue. As the ObamaCare regulations kick in, more and more businesses are dropping healthcare coverage because it is becoming too expensive. A survey by the House Ways & Means Committee of Fortune 500 companies covering nearly 6 million workers showed that even after paying a penalty of $2,000 per employee, the companies stand to save $26.6 billion in 2011 alone by dropping coverage and shifting employees to health insurance exchanges.[83] Another study found that nearly 50% of employees plan to drop coverage altogether or shift to handing employees vouchers to enable them to buy their own coverage.[84] White Castle has just discovered an ObamaCare provision that penalizes them $3,000 per employee if they do not pay at least 91.5% of the premiums. It had been providing health care for its employees since 1924. But it only paid between 70-90% of the premiums, so under ObamaCare, it would be subject to the $3,000 per employee penalty amounting to over 55% of its yearly net income. This has constrained its future business plans and stopped all new hiring. White Castle is now trying to figure out if it can continue to operate its restaurants.[85]

What this means is that your employer will kick you, little person, out of your insurance coverage. And your doctor will refuse to accept you if the only reimbursement he gets is the pittance paid by the government insurance exchanges. So, of course, you will not get to "keep your doctor" as Obama promised!

Finally, we discover the true cost and causes of rising premiums. About 20% of California's population, or 7 million people, including its massive numbers of illegals, are uninsured. Reimbursement by the federal and state programs is woefully inadequate. So the hospitals and doctors shift the cost to insured patients. California families pay as much as $1,400 each in additional annual premium to cover the cost of the uninsured. The LA Times laments that if ObamaCare were to be struck down, California would lose as much as $16 billion annually in new federal money.[86] Even while admitting facts such as the cost shifting that had been done, making medical insurance much more expensive for California's working population; nobody has counted how many illegals are availing themselves of free health care! But we get some glimpses of the true state of affairs. Over two thirds of all births in LA County were to illegal aliens. And health care for illegals costs $2.5 billion a year.[87]

ObamaCare taxes makers of health devices so that many of them are threatening to close down. As they realize the looming financial burden imposed upon them by ObamaCare, various States, unions, pension plans and businesses have prevailed upon HHS to issue over 1231 waivers from its provision.[88]

So, what do we have after ObamaCare was passed? The same illegals will be subsidized. (Rep. Joe Wilson was right). The same Americans who are poor will be subsidized; except there will now be many more poor who have to be subsidized. The only difference is that those who are working and now have coverage will lose it. And eventually, everyone will be forced into government run Health Exchanges. The plans offered through those exchanges will ration care. And we will have to admit Sarah Palin was right because rationing will lead to the Death Panels which will decide who should and who should not get care.

But what did Obama gain? He got to nationalize the Health Industry. He will control over 20% of the country's economy. He created 159 new bureaucracies, commissions and boards to "streamline and decrease the cost of Healthcare.[89] *If that many bureaucrats can streamline the cost of anything, then my MAMA will definitely make you a millionaire!* He also hired 5000 new IRS agents to enforce healthcare.[90] *So many revenue agents to torment you!* In 2003, as a State Senator, he told the AFL-CIO conference that he was a "proponent of a single-payer universal healthcare [plan]." He repeated this at a SEIU forum in March 2007, "There is going to be some transition process. I can envision [in] a decade out, or 15 years out." In 2009, he referred to his plan as the "Pubic Option."[91] As I have told you, Obama is so slippery, you need a lawyer by your side to understand what Obama is really saying. What he was saying was that he wanted to nationalize the Health Industry and, with his ObamaCare Mandates, control every person in the United States. And that is exactly what ObamaCare is going to do.

The Second Obama commandment, "Everyone Else must pay for Abortions for Everyone who wants one." And, as I told you earlier, because of ObamaCare, he gets to tell everyone what is going to be insured, and of course that will include abortions for anyone who wants one, and Obama will let you know whether or not you are entitled to exercise your conscience. Remember, he said that because over 75% of women used birth control pills, the Catholic Church ought to change their doctrine! If you are a church, you are free to follow your faith and pick a health care plan that excludes or limits coverage for contraceptives, abortifacients and abortions. But if you are a church run school, foster care agency, hospital, nursing home, your conscience will have to be exercised on Sunday only, and while you are at it you can ask for forgiveness, because your charitable institution will be paying for coverage for contraceptives, abortifacients and abortions. This, of course violates the rights of the 70% of Americans who oppose abortions. By seeking to compel Catholic Institutions to pay for abortions for all of their staff and their students, Obama grossly violated their constitutional right to Freedom of Religion. And when you consider that birth control pills cost only four dollars a month; it was clear that what Obama wanted to do was not merely to force the Church to pay for other people's birth control pills. He was forcing them to violate their religious convictions and obey his edicts. Why? Because he doesn't want us to have other Gods. He considers himself to be the personification of the First Commandment.

© GLENN MCCOY © 2012 Belleville News-Democrat.
**Obama, our New Founding Father, comes down from Mount Sinai
To tell us what our New Constitution will be.**

Chapter 15

Think about what you have just read and answer the Question

So who is this man Obama and what is he doing to our Country? In all that I have chronicled, did you see anything that suggests he loves this country and its institutions? He constantly denigrates and runs down this country. He apologizes for us all the time. He has talked a good game about loving the poor. But have you seen him actually do anything for them except make them dependent on him?

He has facilitated infiltration by Muslim Terrorists and the building of Wahhabi Mosques in the U.S.: He has violated the very essence of our country by keeping the borders open even though he knows that Islamic terrorists are infiltrating through this border. A country with no borders is not a country. He has subverted our Refugee Resettlement program and converted it into a program that imports the most violent *Jihadis,* the Somalis, into America. And he has resettled them in quiet peaceful little towns all over America, causing a huge amount of stress and strife to the American people living there. He has permitted gigantic mosques to be built all over America knowing these Mosques are the base from which Imams preach violent *Jihad* against America and the safe houses in which plots are hatched and resentment and hatred stoked. I am not saying all are like this, or that even a large percentage are the source of plots and attacks, but in an America where government is harassing at Jews and Christians, branding some terrorists and making it difficult for the religious institutions of the U.S. to continue their good works (e.g., ObamaCare mandates thrust upon the Catholic run schools, hospitals and so on) our President has never met a Muslim cause he did not like. He actively supported building the 9/11 Victory Mosque, knowing that Muslim prayers would sung 5 times a day over the souls of the 3000 people the Islamic terrorists themselves had slaughtered. Our Flight 93 memorial is designed as a gigantic open-air Mosque. He ordered all federal law enforcement to stop using the term "Islamic Terrorist," even while putting forward the Tea Party and various Christian organizations as Terrorist threats.

He has elevated Islam into the prime position in this country and denigrated Christianity: We can't even call the actual Muslim terrorists "terrorists." But he has issued a "threat assessment" that states Christians, right wing activists and returning veterans are all potential "terrorists." And his Army friends have banned the use of the term "God" in the army and denied or burdened the exercise of First Amendment Rights of free speech and of free exercise of religion by our soldiers. I have shown you how Islam is being given a superior position in America today.

He has advanced the Caliphate globally: He has furthered *Jihad* against Christians in Kenya and Nigeria. He has aided the overthrow of dictators in Libya and Egypt who were friendly to us; and done nothing against Dictators in Syria and Iran who are our enemies and whose overthrow would benefit us and our friends in the Middle East. While committing to the wars in Iraq and Afghanistan in the short term, to enable him to skate through to this year's election without embarrassment; his actions have ensured that we will lose the peace and in a few short years our good works and efforts to put both countries on firm and non-extremist footing will be like footprints on the beach, washed away by ocean waves. We had placed terrorists captured on the battlefield in Gitmo. Obama has released them to Iraq and Afghanistan. He has commenced negotiations with what he calls the "good" Muslim Brotherhood in Egypt, the "good" Taliban terrorists in Afghanistan and the "good" Al Quaeda in Iraq. He has demoralized our Armed Forces by forcing them to obey Rules of Engagement that ensure more of our soldiers will get killed; by demanding that they comply with civilian rules of evidence when they capture a terrorist on the battlefield and by forcing them to work subordinate to what he calls "our Afghani Partners," even when so many of our "partners" are killing our soldiers.

He has handed over our secrets to the enemy and compromised national security with his leaks: He has handed over our most vital defense secrets, the stealth helicopter and a super secret drone, to our enemies. And with his reckless leaks to puff up his own image, he has caused very serious harm to our soldiers, our sources in hostile countries and our partners and friends in allied countries. The Taliban shot down a helicopter with 31 Navy Seal Team 6 members within weeks after he leaked that it was Navy Seal Team 6 that killed Osama. Pakistan jailed the doctor who helped us identify Bin Laden. Israel was exposed as the partner who helped insert Stuxnet into Iran's computers. And he has even bragged that he personally selects and authorizes the assassination of people by using drones.

He has made us even more dependent on OPEC: He has crucified our vital fossil fuel industry, preventing us from obtaining our energy from oil, coal, deep sea drilling and even from fracking for oil and gas. Meanwhile he blows smoke in our eyes by boasting about how American oil and gas production is as high as it has ever been (through no effort of his). He has given 15 million acres of our federal land for "Green Energy" projects that don't work, while simultaneously preventing the oil and gas industry from drilling for oil on federal land. He has even shut down the construction of the Keystone XL oil project which would have brought us oil from a friendly country, Canada. Thus, he has ensured that we would always be dependent on OPEC oil.

He has destroyed our economy, terrorized our people and driven them into poverty: I have shown you how our middle class is vanishing and our poor remain poor. He keeps spending our money; giving grants, federal loan guarantees, tax exemptions, tax credits and all kinds of goodies to his cronies for projects that don't work. Many of these projects were already in financial trouble and no one else would have accepted the risk and lent their own money for these projects. But Obama has given our money to his cronies, and left us on the hook to pay off on loan guarantees. He has wasted billions on hiring more and more government bureaucrats who will vote for him, but who will keep regulating, fining and tormenting us. He keeps demanding taxes from all of us, exactly like a Muslim ruler would. He keeps sneering about the "Millionaires and Billionaires" who wont pay their fair share of *Jizya* or taxes to him. But he has remains silent about his American buddies to whom he gives even more of our money. He is also silent about his Middle Eastern buddies who are Millionaires and Billionaires and who do not share anything with their own poor Muslim populations. He is constantly attacking private business. He keeps changing the rules and creating a climate of complete uncertainty, so private business cannot grow or hire more workers. The attack on private business is relentless: ObamaCare (and the different thresholds for the number of employees at which employer mandates kick-in); the threat of tax hikes at the beginning of 2011; the threat of tax hikes at the beginning of 2013;

shutting down oil drilling in the Gulf and then shutting down all off-shore drilling; setting new and more stringent CAFÉ standards for the oil industry; shutting down the Keystone XL oil pipeline project; adding armies of auditors to the IRS; putting out thousands upon thousands of pages of regulations for ObamaCare and Dodd Frank; setting up the Consumer Finance Protection Bureau; enforcing Cap and Trade without authorization from Congress by regulating carbon dioxide emissions; regulating the coal industry out of existence; regulating coal fired electric power generation out of existence; and so on. And he has not cared a whit about the millions of people who are unemployed and/or are put out of employment because of his onerous regulations.

He had shredded the Constitution: Maybe he was spoiled by having an overwhelming majority in Congress, but his standard operating procedure has been to design legislation without input from even moderate Republicans, refuse to compromise to get support from Republicans and then do whatever he wants, as though he was our King, using some excuse like "*I need to do what is right,*" "*It is the right thing to do*" or "*We cannot wait*" in order to justify violating the Constitution. Difference of opinion is not respected. Opponents are belittled, vilified and even bullied, in some cases by the President himself, in others by his brown shirts and attack dogs, frequently with union backing, with so-called progressive community organizers and with news anchors, TV talk show hosts, columnists and bloggers from the media. He has used the vast power of the Executive Branch to **violate our Freedom of Speech** by bringing constant pressure to silence Fox News, Rush Limbaugh and a host of other conservative commentators; and by asserting his right to shut down the Internet. He has **violated the Takings Clause** in the GM and Chrysler bankruptcies by taking the property rights of the bondholders and favoring his UAW. He has **violated our Fourth Amendment's prohibitions against Search and Seizure** in the manner his TSA operates. By expanding the TSA's role into all places where the public gathers, the TSA now takes the lead in what used to be police procedures reserved to the states. Obama has thereby **violated the 10ᵗʰ Amendment.**

He has disregarded the Senate's role: In January 2012, he brazenly **disregarded the "Advice and Consent"** requirement of the Constitution by bypassing the Senate and purporting to make 4 "recess" appointments while the Senate was officially in session. Claiming that the Senate was not doing any real work and that he couldn't wait, Obama announced that he had to make the appointments *"for the good of the people,"* and that **he** had determined that the Senate was not in session. But the real story was a power play by Obama, deliberately disregarding the Senate to make appointments of controversial people to controversial posts. One appointment was Richard Cordray to the Consumer Financial Protection Bureau. The CFPB is one of those controversial creatures of Dodd-Frank, an agency with enormous powers to regulate consumer credit and essentially no oversight. The CFPB has full discretion to pass its rules with scant guidance from the Congress as it decides what it thinks is best. It has an automatic and substantial budget grant directly from the Fed, which is not subject to review by anyone. The Senate was holding up Cordray's appointment in large part because they wanted to add some oversight to the law. Neither Obama, nor Harry Reid, wanted any checks on the CFPB so there was a deadlock which Obama decided to skirt by disregarding the Constitution.

The NLRB is also an agency that Obama has used to make law by regulation and administrative action that has no basis in the statute that gives the agency its power. By making 3 phony recess appointments Obama was able to get the NLRB back into action. He was also able to appoint Craig Becker, a notoriously radical union (SEIU, of course) lawyer whose appointment was rejected by the Senate precisely because he is a firebrand who wants to extend the NLRB's power radically and turn it to favor unions and his nomination had just been withdrawn by the Obama administration one month earlier. Becker is a proponent of Card Check and an advocate of implementing Card Check administratively without legislative authority to do it. Card Check would deprive workers of a secret ballot in elections to certify a union. Since the "recess appointments" the NLRB was responsible for the shakedown of Boeing, forcing them to agree to concessions with their union at their Seattle, WA facilities to get the NLRB to withdraw an agency litigation challenging the decision by Boeing to open a new plant in South Carolina (a right to work state) as a wrongful labor practice. In fact, the very reason that the Senate stayed in session through Christmas and New Year's was to prevent recess appointments of these two agency heads. *Notice the childish behavior. This is a President of the United States, who has sworn to uphold our Constitution, ignoring it because "he couldn't wait!"* Think about it. Has any previous American

President disregarded and dishonored our Constitution in this way and to this extent? Of course not. But once you realize we have an American President who considers the Islamic *Shari'ah* law to be the Supreme Law and our Constitution subordinate to it; then violating our Constitution at every turn is no longer a problem for him!

He wont cooperate with the House: In Fast & Furious, AG Holder lied to Congress about when he found out about the gun walking scheme of the ATF, which was one of the most hare-brained operations ever, which led to the illegal transporting of 2000 automatic weapons into the hand of the Mexican drug cartel and which led to the death of two US law enforcement officers with the weapons. Congress is trying to do its constitutional duty of oversight and find out who ordered and supervised this disastrous program, which resulted in the death of two federal agents and hundreds of innocent Mexicans. Holder has been the foil, stalling a response for over a year and refusing to hand over subpoenaed documents to the House committee. After Holder lost a showdown with the House committee on Wednesday, June 20, 2012, Obama was flushed out and had to put forward a claim of executive privilege with respect to documents, which the White House purportedly never saw!

He has set up a Fourth Branch of Government: The CFPB will have enormous powers to regulate virtually every financial institution. It can regulate everything from providers of mortgages, education loans and payday loans to insured depository institutions and credit unions. The CFPB will operate outside the Budget. It will use the Federal Reserve's earnings to fund itself. So Congress will have no ability to restrict this agency's action by cutting off its money. And it will have no ability to carry out oversight of this agency. The Director's decisions cannot be challenged by the Federal Reserve or by Congress. Essentially, this sets up a fourth branch of government, all the better to regulate us. So, in addition to making an unconstitutional appointment, the law itself is unconstitutional.[1] He did the same thing when he gave amnesty to illegals by fiat, without waiting for Congress to act. He said *"Congress wont act. But it is the right thing to do"* Once again, claiming for himself, as our King, the right to ignore Congress. and pick and choose which of the laws he will enforce. He got ObamaCare passed on Christmas Eve by deceiving the people as to what it would do. ***In fact, this is standard operating procedure with Obama. He just goes ahead and***

does something he shouldn't do. And then he dares Congress to reverse it. If they try, then he castigates them politically.

He has taken over vast swaths of the American Economy: Through the CFPB, he will control all finances of the country. He took over a large sector of the country's economy by taking over GM and Chrysler. He took over 20% of our economy with his ObamaCare. Through his various Czars, Lisa Jackson, Carol Browner and Ken Salazar, he is taking over the entire fossil fuel industry. By humiliating and denigrating private industry, and by borrowing so much money for the federal government that there is none left for private industry, he is destroying the private industry. Soon, everything in this country will be owned by Obama and his federal government. Soon, all of us will become *Dhimmis*, slaves working to support Obama and his federal government workers.

He does not show any respect for the Supreme Court either: At his 2010 State of the Union address, Obama castigated the Supreme Court, sitting right in front of him, with the whole of Congress present and with the nation watching on National TV, for their *Citizen's United* decision, which gave rights to Unions and Corporations to spend money on elections. He was so abusive that many Justices have stopped attending the State of the Union address.[2] Unprecedented. Does this technique sound familiar? *Pick the target, identify it, freeze it, personalize it and polarize it.* And he has succeeded in politicizing and polarizing the Supreme Court into his supporters and those not his supporters! Now, believing that the Supreme Court will overturn Obamacare, he is attacking them once again. Referring to them as "unelected" he stated that he is "confident that the Supreme Court will not take what would be an unprecedented, extraordinary step of overturning a law that was passed by a strong majority of a democratically elected Congress." It was actually passed by a mere 218 to 212 vote in the House and a 60 to 40 vote in the Senate after an incredible amount of arm-twisting and horse-trading. [3] Once again, he used the full spectrum of attack: attacking the Supreme Court's intellect and motives and implicitly threatening adverse consequences of a decision that Obama did not like. The Alinsky tactics are in full display, with the ultimate position being one of politicization and polarization. Anyone who has a passing acquaintance with the Constitution knows the Supreme Court does not run for election. By calling them "unelected" Obama sought to reduce their authority and subject them to ridicule. Chief Justice Roberts is said to have been in favor of ruling ObamaCare unconstitutional; but suddenly ruled in favor of ObamaCare, I just wonder, what threats were used against him?

He is eliminating his opponent and his opponent's supporters by using Alinsky's rules, *Target it, Freeze it, Personalize it and Polarize it:* While every politician does attack his opponent, Obama has carried these attacks to an extreme and its hard to think of anyone who has so universally used this method while occupying the post of President. He has targeted his opponent's supporters for annihilation. He examines their divorce records. He examines the supporter's children's records and social media postings. His cohorts target the supporter's clients with scurrilous accusations about the supporter, thus causing him to lose business. Right now, Obama's operatives are stalking Republican Members of Congress, photographing them and their families in their homes and posting the information on social sites.[4] The idea is to suggest that Republicans are rich and to stoke envy and resentment against them. But, it also gives every crazy thug a clear message: Go to the Republican's home and threaten, or even attack, his wife and his children! Anyone who does anything to support Obama's opponent is subject to attack. The threat is clear: support Obama's opponent and you will pay a huge price. This is Mafia like. It is also exactly like the tactics used by Obama's fellow Luo tribesman, the Muslim leader Raila Odinga in Kenya when he was contesting against a Christian Mwai Kibaki. Obama has used exactly the same tactics and has brought Kenyan tribal politics to America!

Pitting One Group of Americans against another: Obama has been shameless in how he is pitting one group against another. Latinos (but really the direct pitch is to Mexicans) against others. Women who want abortions against others. But worst of all is how he has used blacks, whom Democrats have deliberately keep poor and dependent on Democrat largesse and whom Democrat teachers' unions have kept ignorant and unable to get good jobs. He keeps suggesting to them that it is whites who are preventing them from advancing economically. He has fostered envy and resentment among them. Clearly, he is planning to have them riot and destroy whole cities if he is not re-elected. As I have said before, the slogan for this election is not "Hope" or "Change." It will be "Racist!!"

Just look at how the race card has already been played in the 2012 election season. When Trayvon Martin was killed, Obama said "If I had a son, he would have looked like Trayvon." As you have seen, as a direct consequence of Obama's incitement of black anger; various whites have been attacked and taunted in many different cities. An American President should have been trying to calm racial tensions. Instead, this American President seems to support only those Blacks who behave like thugs. What about the rest of us? The perfectly decent Blacks who are victimized by those thugs? The other Americans? Wasn't he supposed to be the President of all of us?. But once you recognize how Muslim Rulers operate, you realize that Obama will only support those who are his supporters. The rest of us are mere serfs, to be used to further his goals and to be kept poor and dependent on him, our Ruler. Democrat surrogates also play the race card almost any time someone criticizes the President. The statement that Obama does not understand the private sector is called a racist attack. Criticism of the Obama extravagance in the White House is called a racist attack. Asking to see Obama's original Birth Certificate is a racist attack. Questioning Eric Holder is a racist attack. If the Supreme Court had struck down ObamaCare, there would surely have been enormous political pressure brought to bear on the Justices. And some would have said the court did it because they wanted to destroy the signature achievement of a black President. Perhaps the fear of political reprisals is what caused Chief Justice Roberts to change his mind. As I have said before, the slogan for this election is not "Hope" or "Change." It will be "Racist!!"

He has created a vast and violent Civilian Army, which is, even now, threatening violence and virtual civil war in our country: Obama behaves like a community organizer even as he serves as President. How many times has he jumped in with a polarizing remark? For a President, surprisingly often. Remember Henry Louis Gates? When the Cambridge police answered a call on a burglary, an exchange between Gates and the police officers ended with Gates getting himself arrested. Obama at a press conference first admitted: "Now, I've—I don't know, not having been there and not seeing all the facts, what role race played in that." But then he went on to give his opinion like he had been there: "I think it's fair to say, . . . that the Cambridge police acted stupidly in arresting somebody when there was already proof that they were in their own home. And number three, what I think we know separate and apart from this incident is that there is a long history in this country of African-Americans and Latinos being stopped by law enforcement disproportionately." Obama jumped to conclusions about the Trayvon Martin case and said that if he had a son, he would have looked like Trayvon with his hoodie. Obama's Justice Department had, and still has, an obvious affirmative action program of ignoring black voter intimidation and black "hate crimes." The example set by the federal government has spread to law enforcement in various states, which are also ignoring black on white crime. As a result, black youths are playing "Knockout King" and committing a huge number of crimes and creating mayhem in public places in over 60 cities. The New Black Panthers are being permitted to agitate openly for the murder of white people. OWS has been taken over by various communist groups and was responsible for major property damage and the stabbing of a cop in Chicago recently. Obama is still funding ACORN's reincarnations. Obama has given amnesty and work permits to illegals. Obama is using the student loan program and student debts to induce kids to join his youth brigades. Children are still being indoctrinated to sing hymns to Obama. Obama's face has replaced the stars in our American flag flying at the Democrat offices in Florida. The TSA is being trained to do illegal and intrusive searches at airports and at times it surely appears to be politically motivated. The right to conduct these searches has been expanded to virtually every kind of transportation in the country. The TSA has been provided with millions of boxes of hollow point bullets, Mine Resistant Ambush Protected vehicles and even weaponized drones. The FAA has cleared airspace for these drones to operate within the U.S. Obama has given himself the right to take over the Internet and the right to declare Martial law. He and his civilian army are ready to strike!

I asked you at the end of Part III, what would it be like if the Militant Islamists' wildest dreams came true. In this Part IV, I have shown you that Obama is the living embodiment of those dreams. The Media is hiding information from you. But after you have read this book, you can have no doubts:

Obama is turning America into a Caliphate, keeping us poor and in a state of slavery or *Dhimmitude* with his constant demands for more taxes or *Jizya*. Since he is doing all this stealthily, the only

conclusion one can draw is that he is waging a *Stealth Jihad* against this country.

When the JournoList and the Islamists start up with their usual carefully orchestrated barrage of criticisms and attacks, remember that when the National Park Service tells you to watch out for Grizzly Bears; it doesn't "hate" the bears. It is simply warning you. So it is with this book. There is no "hate" for Obama or for Militant Muslims. This book is just warning you.

There is a conflagration that is burning up our Constitution, our Freedom and our way of life. It is coming closer and closer to you and someone is shouting, *"Fire!"* But the JournoList, the Islamists and Obama will use their usual technique of finding one little thing wrong and inflating it to cast doubt on everything that has been said: *"It's all a bunch of lies and exaggerations!"* And they will castigate and threaten the messenger: *"This book is full of Hate."* *"She's just a liar! A bigot! And a racist!!"* *"She hates Obama because he is black!"* *"She hates Muslims!"* *"She is an Islamaphobe!"* *"She has insulted Islam!!"* And then they will soothe you with: *"You are too sophisticated to believe that quack."* And contradict themselves with: *"Besides, the fire is just burning your neighbors. It is nowhere near you!"*

Having read this book, how will you answer the burning question?

Will you believe Obama, the Islamists and the JournoList and wait in a trance until you and your country are burned to a crisp?
Or
Will you wake up and shout "Good God!! There really is a fire!" . . . ?

Epilogue

With the Election Just Around the Corner

It had started out great. Nobody could ask a single question about him. Not about his birth certificate, not his Presidency of Harvard Law Review, not even what, exactly, he did as a Community Organizer. Nobody could challenge him on anything as he consolidated power and went beyond all bounds set by existing laws. Disparate enforcement of voter laws, flouting immigration laws, giving AK 47's to Mexican Drug Lords, doing end runs around Congress, mocking the Supreme Court; no matter what he did, they couldn't touch him. If they tried, he'd bring out his great club: **"Racist!"** And that would shut them up.

But now, the Obama campaign was in big trouble. Whites, even the Independents, were offended at the pure racial animus Obama had shown towards them. Catholics were offended that he tried to tell their Bishops what their Doctrine should be. Christians were upset because he was denigrating Christians, coddling Muslims, allowing the Muslim Brotherhood to dictate that the FBI must stop calling Islamic Terrorists "Islamic Terrorists" and even allowing Muslim mobs to march around the country. His talk of Social Justice, where he said he would take from the rich and give to the poor, just like Jesus, was not working. Nobody believed he was a good Christian even though he made numerous visits to Churches. Nobody wanted an atheist as their leader, so that wasn't working either.

Small business owners were freaking out saying they couldn't make money with all the regulations he had imposed on them. All the workers in the Mid-Western and Southern states that had the Keystone XL pipeline and big oil, coal and gas industries were furious with him for preventing them from getting jobs. Regular folks were screaming because all their employers had cut them off from their healthcare saying it had become too expensive, and had blamed him for his ObamaCare regulations. The unemployed were offended that he had suddenly given work permits to 800,000, and possibly millions, of illegal aliens at a time when unemployment was actually around 16%. He kept saying it was

8%, but the unemployed knew better. He had had another fight with the Republicans for yet another extension of unemployment benefits, this time to 130 weeks, saying "the depression he had inherited" was far, far worse than he had every imagined it could be. But they laughed at him, asking why he had spent so many billions on "jobs bills" and yet been unable to produce the jobs.

The bankers were fed up with him demonizing the rich. "He takes our money and then stabs us in the back," some of them complained. Hollywood was demanding yet more tax breaks, which he could never get through Congress. "Just pass some regulation," they ordered. "Say that after all, it is good for the country!" But he couldn't do that. How was he to say he was for the poor if he gave special tax breaks to the rich? Even conservative black pastors and independents were upset with him over his support for gays. But he needed the money the rich gays in Hollywood could give him. His media had gone all out to make the usual "everybody does it" defense; saying that Republicans, and everybody in Congress, was as bad as he. But nobody was swallowing that either. And worst of all, the unions were threatening to withhold funding and Democrat Congressmen and Senators were refusing to attend his convention in North Carolina. How was he to be crowned King if people didn't attend the coronation?

Information about the Stuxnet computer virus, that it was SEAL Team 6 that took out Osama and that he, personally, controlled the "kill list" of drone strikes on terrorists had been leaked. But instead of thinking he was a strong, brave warrior, the people had just been disgusted at his administration's leaking of national security secrets and risking soldiers' lives. He had ordered a strike on Syria's Assad. His media had spoken glowingly about how he cared about freedom and poor downtrodden people around the world. But the American people had recognized that he had waited until the Muslim Brotherhood got control of the opposition in Syria. They knew that the Muslim Brotherhood were regular visitors to the White House. They had learned that the Muslim Brotherhood had subverted the Arab Spring, overruled the wishes of the students and gotten control of Egypt and worse, that one of their leaders was a Zawahiri and brother of Ayman Zawahiri, the current leader of Al Qaeda. And they had seen the parallels to Carter's deposing of the Shah of Iran and handing it over to the Mullahs, who had oppressed those Iranians for the thirty years since. No, none of this was working.

And that Romney fellow seemed to be made of Teflon. Nothing stuck to him. The attacks on the "rich" were obviously not working. That wife of his kept smiling, even when she was attacked. And his pollsters were telling him that women actually liked her and that they were sorry for her because of her M.S. And even after the Media Matters team attacked him ferociously, that VanderSloot fellow said he was going to give more money to Romney. And this was emboldening everyone else. And now Romney was collecting more cash that he did. And that Supreme Court kept ruling against him. Even allowing Super Pacs and saying States could not stop them. And his unions were broke because of their stupid notion they could beat Scott Walker in Wisconsin. And that Media Matters guy was coming unhinged—too much coke! And even those Evangelicals seemed to be working for Romney. And he couldn't remind them that Mormons were not really Christians and that they used to practice polygamy, because he knew Romney would point out his own Muslim father was a polygamist, and furthermore, had never married or even lived with his mother.

Thank God, his media team had promised to take out Rubio with insinuations he could not be the Vice President because he did not qualify as a "natural born" citizen. Rubio was dangerous. He was a minority too. Can't play the race card against him. He articulated Conservative ideas and made them appealing to everyone. And he was too handsome. He had done his best to remind the Mexicans that Rubio was Cuban and not really a Hispanic, like they were. The Latinas didn't care that he was Cuban. They just drooled over him. And he was able to speak to them in Spanish! And the whites loved him too. He spoke too well and he could unite the country. And Rubio was clearly so brilliant, he didn't even need a teleprompter!

His options were limited. He was going to have to deploy his civilian army. He'd order the SEIU to provide the buses and bullhorns and accompany those kids when they went on their wildings, which they quaintly called "flash mobs." Like they did in Chicago, he'd make his union thugs control the kids and send them out on the streets to terrorize the whites. Breaking a few plate glass windows was o.k. After all, they needed to express their rage! Looting Portland's Nordstrom's was o.k. too—that s.o.b. voted for Republicans! He'd get his OWS/SEIU mobs to start riots in all the big cities. And the Muslims to continue their protests in Dearborn and New York City. And he'd get the New Black Panthers to start marching down the main drag in the major cities, banging their drums and threatening the whites with death. And if they started looting and rioting? Well, he didn't ask them to do that. And how was he to stop them when they were so aggrieved with the way Blacks had been treated in America?

But no one in any one city would find out about the riots in the other major cities because he'd get his Media Matters to make sure there was a news blackout on all the riots, just as they did earlier in May and June. Sure, the right-wingers would find out through their media, and would try to spread the news. But he'd arrange for some news signal failures. He had given himself the power to cut off the Internet. And perhaps he'd get Limbaugh's show cut off from time to time. Or maybe, he'd organize his speeches at exactly the same time, 12-3 Eastern, so people would listen to him and not to Limbaugh. And then, there was that brilliant ploy to get Fox News off the air by targeting their advertisers. It had actually worked in some cities. Murdoch and Bin Talal were furious. But a guy's got to do what a guy's got to do. And just after the stores and the hotels repaired their plate glass windows, and repainted their facades, he'd send his guys in to trash them again. The Insurance guys would say they would not pay to repair the damages. And the rich guys would soon be begging for mercy.

Then, he'd get someone to say there was a terrorist threat and he would deploy his TSA. The TSA would go around the country, patting down the private parts of young women. And their parents would explode. Just like Armendariz, the TSA would order the local police to pick out 5 or more fathers at random and put them in jail for disturbing the peace. That would teach them and put them under control. He would make speeches blaming the "racist whites," the conservatives, the Tea Party madmen and the Islamophobic, extremist Christians for the bombs. Maybe, he'd just say it again, "Christians clinging to their guns and religion!" He'd divide the nation. He'd remind the gays that the Christians hated them. And the women that Limbaugh hated them. And his civilian armies would continue to march. And the police would be too terrified to come out to confront and control the mobs. They'd hang around at the periphery of the riots and arrest someone they found there. Soon, he would have the whole nation terrified of his mobs—his civilian army, as he lovingly called it.

His drift nets were working. Slowly, methodically, he was pulling them shut. And the people were trapped and terrified. Too late, they had finally realized that the drift nets were closing in on them. He would let it be known that only he could control the mobs, just as he did when the mobs went to the rich bankers' houses early in his term. And he'd get the moderates to say they should really vote for him because only he knew how to bring the country under control and unite everybody.

The rich guys who owned the buildings the mobs trashed would call and beg for mercy. They were in a state of siege. The owners were going crazy. They were losing money hand over fist. They'd soon be bankrupt. The insurers would not pay for the damages. The suppliers would not deliver. The customers would not come. And just like the staff in Portland's Nordstrom's, some of their staff were leaving their posts to go and hang out with the rioters. The rich guys would plead for mercy. They'd offer large campaign contributions if only he would call off the mobs. But money would not cut it this time. They'd better vote him in, or else.

And that Biden. He was starting to complain. Maybe, he'd switch to Hillary. But then, he'd have to deal with that double crossing husband of hers. What to do? What to do?

There was only one thing left to do. He'd go to plan B. Someone would set off a bomb. It would be discovered that the perp was a white guy, most likely mentally unstable or even insane. He would not be a Christian, a Tea Party member or even a Conservative. The perp's emails and computer records would show he was a liberal. But his TSA and FBI would confiscate and hide those. Those records didn't matter in Gabrielle Gifford's case. None of that would matter in this case either. He would call the perp a Christian, right wing terrorist. He'd say it was Sarah Palin and Limbaugh and the conservatives with their violent rhetoric that egged on the perp.

He'd play the race card like a drum. He'd go on TV denouncing the violence and the racial hatred, call all the whites racists and demand that the whites stop hating him because of his race. He'd demand TV time on all networks to make his speech and his speechwriters would put it all on the teleprompter for him. He would intone, with great sorrow, that he was compelled to use his newly granted powers, (granted by himself, of course), to declare Martial Law. That he had been compelled to call out the TSA and the National Guard. And that he was compelled to order a curfew to bring the violence under control. And that he would have to postpone the elections.

"Yes!" he exulted, pumping his fists in the air. "That should work!!"

Endnotes

TABLE OF CONTENTS

1   http://www.nytimes.com/2008/09/21/nyregion/21lirr.html?
    pagewanted=2&_r=1
1   http://www.americanthinker.com/2008/10/evidence_mounts_ayers_
    cowrote.html

Part I of VI—INTRODUCTION

2   http://onekit.enr-corp.com/1003946/
3   http://abcnews.go.com/Politics/BothSidesAllSides/story?
    id=2773754&page=1#.T8_9b44Z2S0
4   http://spectator.org/archives/2008/10/17/obama-couldnt-be-cleared
5   http://www.americanthinker.com/2009/03/michelle_obamas_
    patientdumping_1.html

Part I, Chapter 2—Media Trickery

1   http://www.newsrealblog.com/2010/08/08/the-top-5-journolists-and-
    their-3-big-media-conservative-apologists/
2   http://blog.beliefnet.com/roddreher/2010/07/the-outrageous-journolist-
    scandal.html
3   http://www.salon.com/2010/07/20/journolist_reverend_wright/
4   http://dailycaller.com/2010/07/20/documents-show-media-plotting-to-
    kill-stories-about-rev-jeremiah-wright/
5   http://dailycaller.com/2012/02/12/inside-media-matters-sources-memos-
    reveal-erratic-behavior-close-coordination-with-white-house-and-news-
    organizations/4/
6   http://americaswatchtower.com/2011/05/26/barney-frank-admits-he-
    got-his-boyfriend-a-job-at-fanny-mae/
7   http://www.newsrealblog.com/2010/07/22/journolist-sick-puppies-
    planned-attacks-on-sarah-palin-systematic-femisogyny-in-action/
8   http://frontpagemag.com/2011/02/18/islams-uncovered-meat-excuse-
    for-sexual-assault/

9   http://atlasshrugs2000.typepad.com/atlas_shrugs/2011/02/lara-logans-vicious-violent-gang-rape-medias-silencesanction.html

10 http://www.wnd.com/2012/02/the-rotten-banana-award-goes-to/

11 http://www.radaronline.com/exclusives/2011/05/report-antonio-banderas-rape-movie-shocks-cannes-audience

Part I, Chapter 3—Eligibility & Brilliance

1   http/::obamareleaseyourrecords.blogspot.com:

2   http://www.wnd.com/2012/05/bush-v-gore-judge-your-evidence-mr-obama/

3   http://www.wnd.com/2011/05/298545/

4   http://www.safeguardourconstitution.com/news/bannedarticle.html

5   http://lawprofessors.typepad.com/conlaw/2011/12/ninth-circuit-birthers-have-no-standing-to-challenge-obamas-presidency.html

6   http://www.sodahead.com/united-states/david-axelrod---gets-obamas-opponents-sealed-divorce-records-opened-up/question-2312341/

7   http://www.youtube.com/watch?v=8muZ1Pe9OAo

8   http://www.wnd.com/2012/04/obama-lawyer-birth-certificate-irrelevant-to-eligbility/

9   http://www.wnd.com/2012/04/obama-attorney-mickey-mouse-could-be-on-ballot/

10 http://godfatherpolitics.com/5733/obama-attorneys-desperation-leads-them-tell-florida-judge-he-not-democratic-nominee/

11 http://www.usdebtclock.org/

12 http://startthinkingright.wordpress.com/2011/07/28/who-spent-more-average-bush-vs-average-obama-spending-per-day-proves-obama-most-reckless-and-irresponsible-ever/

Part I, Chapter 4—Socialism

1   http://biggovernment.com/whall/2011/11/16/80-of-green-energy-loans-went-to-obamas-top-donors/

2   http://biggovernment.com/whall/2011/11/16/80-of-green-energy-loans-went-to-obamas-top-donors/

3   http://www.therightplanet.com/2012/01/icymi-cbs-this-morning-on-oversight-committee-efforts-breaking-news-on-more-problematic-doe-loan-guarantees/

4   http://www.therightplanet.com/2012/01/icymi-cbs-this-morning-on-oversight-committee-efforts-breaking-news-on-more-problematic-doe-loan-guarantees/

5   http://www.humanevents.com/article.php?id=46256&keywords=Solyndra

6   http://news.investors.com/Article.aspx?id=599308&p=1&ibdbot=1

7   http://www.businessweek.com/news/2011-10-31/beacon-power-backed-by-u-s-loan guarantees-files-bankruptcy.html

8   http://www.denverpost.com/breakingnews/ci_20065647

9   http://www.washingtontimes.com/news/2012/jan/26/obamas-crony-capitalism-667847839/

10   http://keionline.org/node/1314

11   http://www.humanevents.com/article.php?id=47088

12   http://www.humanevents.com/article.php?id=46761

13   http://www.lonerepublic.com/tag/spectrawatt/

14   http://www.lonerepublic.com/tag/spectrawatt/

15   http://www.washingtonpost.com/business/economy/government-subsidized-green-light-bulb-carries-costly-price-tag/2012/03/07/gIQAFxOD0R_story.html

16   http://www.theblaze.com/stories/university-professor-defends-federally-funded-humor-grant/

17   http://frontpagemag.com/2010/09/14/jaw-dropping-823200-of-your-tax-dollars-were-spent-as-a-%E2%80%9Cstimulus%E2%80%9D-to-teach-africans-to-wash-their-penises-after-sex/

18   jack.dolan@latimes.com

19   http://articles.latimes.com/2012/feb/05/local/la-me-solar-desert-20120205

20   http://hotair.com/archives/2008/11/02/obama-well-bankrupt-any-new-coal-plants/

21   http://www.americanthinker.com/blog/2012/03/kathleen_sebeliuss_war_on_green_algae_power.html#ixzz1q1DQtCDZ

22   http://www.sunflower.net/documents/20081011MotiontoLiftSupCourtStay.pdf

23   http://cjonline.com/news/legislature/2009-04-13/sebelius_vetoes_coal_bill

24   http://freebeacon.com/algae-alimony/

25   http://frontpagemag.com/2012/03/21/obamas-algae-racket/

26   http://www.washingtontimes.com/news/2012/jan/24/buffett-would-profit-keystone-cancellation/

27 http://frontpagemag.com/2010/06/22/soros-oil-spill-payoff/

28 http://www.questionsquestions.net/docs04/engdahl-soros.html

29 http://www.usasurvival.org/docs/LoudonrprtJones.pdf

30 http://www.glennbeck.com/content/articles/article/198/29967/

31 http://www.washingtontimes.com/news/2012/mar/15/epa-regulations-hamper-oil-gas- production-report/

32 http://www.newsrealblog.com/2011/04/08/wind-power-even-more-useless-than-you-thought/?utm_source=feedburner&utm_medium=feed&utm_campaign=Feed%3A+nrb-feature+%28NewsReal+Blog+»+Feature%29

33 http://news.investors.com/article/586069/201109261837/wind-powers-political-payoff.htm?p=full

34 http://www.outloudopinion.com/2010/03/12/the-big-wind-power-cover-up-3-12-10/

35 http://online.wsj.com/article/SB100014240529702037111045771990 64065156548.html

36 http://www.theblaze.com/stories/minnesota-taxpayers-stuck-paying-for-wind-they-cant-use-or-sell/

37 http://news.investors.com/article/602312/201202241858/massachusetts-mandates-wind-power-electricity-use.htm?p=full-

38 http://www.juandemariana.org/pdf/090327-employment-public-aid-renewable.pdf

39 http://www.washingtonpost.com/wp-dyn/content/article/2009/06/24/AR2009062403012.html

40 http://www.newsrealblog.com/2011/04/08/wind-power-even-more-useless-than-you-thought/?utm_source=feedburner&utm_medium=feed&utm_campaign=Feed%3A+nrb-feature+%28NewsReal+Blog+»+Feature%29

41 http://www.outloudopinion.com/2010/03/12/the-big-wind-power-cover-up-3-12-10/

42 http://www.outloudopinion.com/2010/03/12/the-big-wind-power-cover-up-3-12-10/

43 http://online.wsj.com/article/SB1000142405297020478180457726711 4294838328.html?KEYWORDS=Birds+destroyed+by+Wind+Farms

44 http://www.latimes.com/news/local/la-me-condor-radar2-20120528,0,2831784.story

45 http://www.newton.dep.anl.gov/natbltn/200-299/nb215.htm

46 http://online.wsj.com/article/SB1000142405297020478180457726711 4294838328.html?KEYWORDS=Birds+destroyed+by+Wind+Farms

47 http://www.washingtontimes.com/news/2012/may/18/team-obamas-war-on-bald-eagles/?page=all#pagebreak

48 http://www.washingtontimes.com/news/2012/may/18/team-obamas-war-on-bald-eagles/?page=all#pagebreak

Part I, Chapter 5— Religion

1 http://conservapedia.com/Barack_Hussein_Obama

2 http://www.google.com/imgres?imgurl=http://socialcapital.files.wordpress.com/2011/01/tunisia-cc-marcovdz.jp

3 http://frontpagemag.com/2012/01/06/muslim-persecution-of-christians-the-christmas-edition/

4 http://www.persecution.org/category/countries/middle-east/saudi-arabia/

5 http://www.newsrealblog.com/2011/03/25/muslims-burned-69-churches-in-ethiopia-thousands-of-christians-flee/

6 http://www.dailymail.co.uk/news/article-1377977/Former-Archbishop-Canterbury-Lord-Carey-says-Christian-cross-ban-outrageous.html#ixzz1pFNwVM1N

7 http://www.dailymail.co.uk/news/article-2072555/Ministers-won't-cross-ban-Christians-Ex-archbishop-condemns-illiberal-assault-faith.html#ixzz1pFOAaG3y

8 http://frontpagemag.com/author/claude-cartaginese/page/6/

9 http://www.telegraph.co.uk/motoring/news/8930168/Allowing-women-drivers-in-Saudi-Arabia-will-be-end-of-virginity.html

10 http://direland.typepad.com/direland/2005/10/shocking_new_ph.html (gays)

11 http://www.stonegateinstitute.org/2796/muslims-ban-dogs-europe

12 http://islamqa.com/en/ref/69840

13 http://infidelsarecool.com/

14 http://www.youtube.com/watch?v=LEUif1--r38

15 http://professional.wsj.com/article/SB1000142405270230370300457744772272937948382.html?mg=reno64-wsj

16 http://frontpagemag.com/2012/01/05/the-arab-spring-an-obituary/

17 http://www.youtube.com/watch?v=Dc3PzHKCVGM&feature=player_embedded#!

18 http://www.wnd.com/2008/09/74635/

19 http://www.danielpipes.org/comments/137991

20 http://www.youtube.com/watch?v=iuXxtg4M_z8

21 http://www.youtube.com/watch?v=tmC3IevZiik

22 http://www.youtube.com/watch?v=tmC3IevZiik

23 http://latimesblogs.latimes.com/washington/2009/05/obama-cancels-national-prayer-day-service.html

24 http://www.wnd.com/2010/09/204973/

25 http://www.youtube.com/watch?v=LvnNYNc7HSA&feature=related

26 http://www.rushlimbaugh.com/daily/2010/08/13/no_time_for_boy_scouts_but_iftar_dinner_makes_obama_s_schedule

27 http://www.politico.com/politico44/perm/0811/white_house_dinner_16bcb086-a896-469a-b25c-bebc1b87edf7.html

28 http://www.youtube.com/watch?v=zDmT6NRdSsM

29 http://www.jihadwatch.org/2011/08/obama-spreads-false-claim-that-thomas-jefferson-hosted-first-ramadan-iftar-dinner-at-white-house.html

30 http://latimesblogs.latimes.com/washington/2009/05/obama-cancels-national-prayer-day-service.html

31 http://online.wsj.com/article/SB10001424052970204136404577211128 0758375336.html

32 http://www.jillstanek.com/archives/2008/08/baipaobamamp3.html

33 http://www.jillstanek.com/29383467.wav

34 http://www.stonegateinstitute.org/2796/muslims-ban-dogs-europe

35 http://islamqa.com/en/ref/69840

36 http://www.jihadwatch.org/2010/11/hamas-linked-cair-tsa-may-only-search-around-muslim-womens-head-neck.html

37 http://www.jihadwatch.org/2010/11/hamas-linked-cair-tsa-may-only-search-around-muslim-womens-head-neck.html

38 http://liberatednow.blogspot.com/2012/01/believe-or-die.html

39 http://www.thedailybeast.com:articles:2012:02:08:twitter-aflame-with-fatwa-against-saudi-writer-hamza-kashgari.html

40 http://www.christianpost.com/news/iranian-pastor-youcef-nadarkhani-execution-order-may-have-been-issued-69992/

41 http://frontpagemag.com/2012/06/06/muslims-slaughter-convert-to-christianity-in-tunisia/

42 http://s.michellemalkin.com/wp/wp-content/uploads/2009/04/hsa-rightwing-extremism-09-04-07.pdf

43 http://frontpagemag.com/2011/12/12/its-not-workplace-violence-its-islam/

44 http://atlasshrugs2000.typepad.com/honor_killings/

45 http://www.mererhetoric.com/2007/09/24/photographs-to-help-explain-why-there-are-no-homosexuals-in-iran-content-warning-graphic-photos-updated-video-added/

46 http://frontpagemag.com/2012/01/06/muslim-persecution-of-christians-the-christmas-edition/

47 http://frontpagemag.com/2011/12/14/testifying-on-behalf-of-egypts-christians/

Part II, Chapter 1—Islam

1   http://www.adjunct.diodon349.com/Obama2/3_things_you_must_know_about_islam_video.htm,

2   http://frontpagemag.com/2012/02/07/the-high-price-of-telling-the-truth-about-islam/

3   http://www.jihadwatch.org/2012/03/raymond-ibrahim-saudi-grand-mufti-calls-for-destruction-of-all-churches-in-region.html

4   http://www.pjtv.com/?cmd=mpg&load=3660&mpid=111

5   http/::frontpagemag.com:2011:12:02:non-muslim-muslims-and-the-jihad-against-the-west:

6   http://www.pjtv.com/?cmd=mpg&load=3660&mpid=111

7   http://frontpagemag.com/2011/12/02/non-muslim-muslims-and-the-jihad-against-the-west/

8   http://www.frontpagemagazine.com

9   http://www.jihadwatch.org/

10 http://atlasshrugs.com

11 http://www.militantislammonitor.org/docs?type=1

12 http://barenakedislam.com/

13 http://www.adjunct.diodon349.com/Obama2/3_things_you_must_know_about_islam_video.htm

14 http://www.adjunct.diodon349.com/Obama2/3_things_you_must_know_about_islam_video.htm

15 http://islammonitor.org/index.php?id=4050&option=com_content

16 EE.W. Lane 0 An Arabic-English Lexicon (London, 1865), Book I Part II, Jizya, p. 422

17 http://archive.frontpagemag.com/readArticle.aspx?ARTID=5246

18 http://www.investigativeproject.org/2008/mansur-ignoring-muslim-on-muslim-violence

19 http://www.presstv.ir/detail/236558.html

20 http://www.nytimes.com/2012/05/22/opinion/no-model-for-muslim-democracy.html?_r=2

21 http://www.bbc.co.uk/news/world-asia-16675086

22 http://www.jihadwatch.org/2012/02/islamic-coup-in-maldives-members-of-new-presidents-cabinet-have-demanded-sharia-law.html

23 http://atlasshrugs2000.typepad.com/atlas_shrugs/2011/12/sharia-in-action-maldives-closes-hundreds-of-luxury-resort-spas-as-anti-islamic.ht

24 http://www.bbc.co.uk/news/world-asia-16675086

25 http://islammonitor.org/index.php?id=4050&option=com_content

26 http:/frontpagemag.com:2011:12:14:testifying-on-behalf-of-egypts-christians:

Part II, Chapter 2—Jihad in Europe

1 http://www.dailymail.co.uk/news/article-2041244/Polygamy-Investigation-Muslim-men-exploit-UK-benefits-system.html#ixzz1rEEwNkDr

2 http://www.dailymail.co.uk/news/article-2041244/Polygamy-Investigation-Muslim-men-exploit-UK-benefits-system.html

3 http://www.jihadwatch.org/2011/02/wilders-the-lights-are-going-out-all-over-europe.html

4 http://online.wsj.com/article/SB10001424052970204642604577213553613859184.html

5 http://pjmedia.com/blog/paid-to-plot-the-wests-demise/

Part II, Chapter 3—Europe as a Caliphate

1 http://www.newsrealblog.com/2011/02/12/geert-wilders-all-over-europe-the-lights-are-slowly-going-out-1/

2 http://www.pi-news.org/2010/02/hate-jews-fleeing-from-malmoe/

3 http://www.wvwnews.net/story.php?id=7178

4 http://direland.typepad.com/direland/2005/10/shocking_new_ph.html

5 http://www.stonegateinstitute.org/2367/european-muslim-no-go-zones

6 http://www.economist.com/node/18530069

7 http://www.wnd.com/2012/03/the-dark-side-of-europes-diversity/

8 http://www.italymag.co.uk/italy/politics/muslim-duomo-prayers-spur-action

9 http://www.youtube.com/watch?v=CY1RPnSThFM

10 http://frontpagemag.com/2011/10/31/veracity-mendacity-and-islam/2/

11   http://www.euro-islam.info/country-profiles/sweden/

12   http://frontpagemag.com/2010/06/21/when-sweden-surrendered/

13   http://pjmedia.com/blog/paid-to-plot-the-wests-demise/?singlepage=true

14   http://www.answeringmuslims.com/2012/03/swedish-democrats-plan-
      to-bribe.html

15   http://www.telegraph.co.uk/news/uknews/1574694/Bishop-warns-of-no-
      go-zones-for-non-Muslims.html

16   http://www.dailymail.co.uk/news/article-2019547/Anjem-Choudary-
      Islamic-extremists-set-Sharia-law-zones-UK-cities.html

17   http://www.dailymail.co.uk/news/article-2020382/You-entering-Sharia-
      law-Britain-As-Islamic-extremists-declare-Sharia-law-zone-London-
      suburb-worrying-social-moral-implications.html#ixzz1ljpx1KSs

18   http://frontpagemag.com/2011/07/29/sharia-controlled-zones-sweep-uk/

19   http://www.dailymail.co.uk/news/article-1386558/Tower-Hamlets-
      Taliban-Death-threats-women-gays-attacked-streets.html#ixzz1lSPTzji6

20   http://www.exfl.com/islamic-london/islamic-tower-hamlets-london.htm

21   http://www.exfl.com/islamic-london/islamic-tower-hamlets-london.htm

22   http://www.dailymail.co.uk/news/article-2019547/Anjem-Choudary-
      Islamic-extremists-set-Sharia-law-zones-UK-cities.html

23   http://theopinionator.typepad.com/my_weblog/2011/11/even-after-the-
      hiatus-ive-taken-from-this-blog-a-quick-review-of-the-current-newsfinds-
      rapes-committed-by-muslim-men-contin.html

24   http://theopinionator.typepad.com/my_weblog/2010/01/-muslim-gang-
      rapes-man-in-manchester-center.html

25   http://frontpagemag.com/2012/06/12/anarchy-in-the-uk/

26   http://menmedia.co.uk/manchestereveningnews/news/s/1478292_video-
      hyde-gang-victim-17-year-old-daniel-stringer-prince-relives-horror-of-
      race-hate-crime-attack

27   http://atlasshrugs2000.typepad.com/atlas_shrugs/2012/02/uk-muslim-
      gang-brutally-attack-17-year-old-infidel-police-treat-it-as-religious-hate-
      crime.html

28   http://creepingsharia.wordpress.com/2010/02/13/muslim-leaders-agree-
      death-for-gays/

29   http://frontpagemag.com/2011/10/28/oslos-epidemic-of-rape/

30   http://frontpagemag.com/2012/01/09/muslim-gangs-drug-and-rape-
      children-all-over-the-uk/print/

31   http://atlasshrugs2000.typepad.com/atlas_shrugs/2011/05/lara-logan-
      on-egypt-rape-for-an-extended-period-of-time-they-raped-me-with-their-
      hands-what-really-s.html

32 http://barenakedislam.com/2009/02/26/uk-muslims-scamming-the-system-to-support-several-wives/

33 http://pjmedia.com/blog/paid-to-plot-the-wests-demise/?singlepage=true

34 http://www.americanthinker

35 http://archive.frontpagemag.com/readArticle.aspx?ARTID=5246

36 http://endtimestoday.com/2011/03/13/norway-100-somali-muslim-families-arrested-for-welfare-fraud/

37 http://barenakedislam.com/2011/01/17/uk-easy-street-if-youre-a-typical-muslim-you-can-milk-the-taxpayers-for-400000-in-benefits/

38 http://barenakedislam.com/2011/01/29/uk-ten-muslim-immigrant-families-cost-taxpayers-1-5-million-per-year-in-just-housing-benefits/

39 http://www.dailymail.co.uk/news/article-1347297/Somali-250k-benefits-cheat-Ayan-Abdulle-described-Britain-land-easy-money.html

40 http://www.dailymail.co.uk/news/article-1028399/Muslim-extremist-Abu-Qatada-receive-8-000-incapacity-benefits-year--bad-back.html

41 http://pjmedia.com/blog/paid-to-plot-the-wests-demise/?singlepage=true

Part II, Chapter 4—Alien Cultural Practices

1 http://islamqa.com/en/ref/69840

2 http://www.stonegateinstitute.org/2796/muslims-ban-dogs-europe

3 http://www.brusselsjournal.com/node/396

4 http://www.nationalreview.com/articles/246269/imam-rauf-s-books-ibn-warraq?pg=2

5 http://en.wikipedia.org/wiki/Arab_slave_trade

6 http://www.foreignaffairs.com/articles/24579/ali-a-mazrui/black-africa-and-the-arabs

7 http://theopinionator.typepad.com/my_weblog/2009/05/whist-browsing-the-web-yesterday-i-viewedthe-arab-times-online-site-and-came-across-several-news-articles-about-the-rape-an.html

8 http://frontpagemag.com/2011/06/06/muslim-woman-seeks-to-revitalize-the-institution-of-sex-slavery/

9 http://www.reuters.com/article/2010/08/26/us-srilanka-maid-idUSTRE67P17420100826

10 http://digitaljournal.com/article/315149

11 http://frontpagemag.com/2011/11/09/in-britain-muslim-police-dont-have-to-defend-jews/

12   http://online.wsj.com/article/SB10001424053111190363560457647201
1907391364.html

13   http://www.foreignpolicy.com/articles/2011/12/16/
the_real_mohamed_bouazizi

14   http://online.wsj.com/article/SB10001424053111190363560457647201
1907391364.html

15   http://frontpagemag.com/2012/01/05/the-arab-spring-an-obituary/

16   http://frontpagemag.com/2012/01/06/muslim-persecution-of-christians-
the-christmas-edition/

17   http://frontpagemag.com/2011/12/21/iraq%e2%80%99s-christians-
near-extinction/

18   http/::frontpagemag.com:2011:12:14:testifying-on-behalf-of-egypts-
christians:

19   http://frontpagemag.com/2011/05/23/solving-poverty-the-islamic-way/

20   http://www.jihadwatch.org/2010/03/nigeria-authorities-look-the-other-
way-from-church-burnings.html

21   http://online.wsj.com/article/SB10001424052970204624204577177690
2128726344.html

22   http://atlasshrugs2000.typepad.com/atlas_shrugs/kenyas_
killing_fields/

23   http://atlasshrugs2000.typepad.com/atlas_shrugs/2008/01/
obama-islam-and.html

24   http/::www.newsrealblog.com:2010:08:20:coming-to-america-sharia-in-
britain-and-its-17000-honor-attacks-on-women-a-year:

25   http://frontpagemag.com/2010/12/22/getting-away-with-honor-murder/

26   http://www.youtube.com/watch?v=vOIbgd5qcrg&feature=related

27   http://atlasshrugs2000.typepad.com/honor_killings/

28   http://www.americanthinker.com/2011/01/honor_killing_in_america.
html

29   http://www.theblaze.com/stories/was-the-santa-claus-killers-christmas-
day-massacre-an-honor-killing

30   http://www.nydailynews.com/topics/Aasiya Hassan

31   http://www.sullivan-county.com/islam/mothers.htm

32   http://atlasshrugs2000.typepad.com/atlas_shrugs/2009/11/
noor-almaleki-is-dead.html

Part II, Chapter 5—Apostasy

1   file://localhost/.%20%20%20http/::www.salon.com:2004:11:24: vangogh_2:

2   http/::www.liveleak.com:view%3Fi=cba_1204288477

3   http://www.newsrealblog.com/2011/02/12/geert-wilders-all-over-europe-the-lights-are-slowly-going-out-1/

4   http://www.brusselsjournal.com/node/382

5   http://news.bbc.co.uk/2/hi/4684652.stm

6   http://frontpagemag.com/2011/01/26/decision-in-denmark/

7   http://www.meforum.org/3111/europe-islamists-free-speech

8   http://frontpagemag.com/2012/02/07/the-high-price-of-telling-the-truth-about-islam/

9   http://www.nydailynews.com/news/world/cleric-anwar-al-awlaki-puts-draw-mohammed-cartoonist-molly-norris-execution-hitlist-article1.464988#commentpostform

10   http://www.worldmag.com/articles/16412

11   http://www.islamophobiatoday.com/2011/03/21/pastor-terry-jones-oversees-quran-burning-in-florida-church/

12   http://www.examiner.com/afghanistan-headlines-in-national/gop-makes-political-hay-of-afghan-koran-burning-incident

13   http://www.worthynews.com/5740-outrage-over-us-military-bible-burnings-in-afghanistan

14   http://www.worthynews.com/5740-outrage-over-us-military-bible-burnings-in-afghanistan

Part II, Chapter 6—Question

1   http://frontpagemag.com/2012/06/06/muslims-slaughter-convert-to-christianity-in-/

2   http://liberatednow.blogspot.com/2012/01/believe-or-die.html

Part III, Chapter 1—9/11

1   http://www.infoplease.com/ipa/A0001454.html   Khalid

2   http://www.americanthinker.com/2008/09/mistress_of_disaster_jamie_gor.html

3   http://www.dailymail.co.uk/news/article-2035720/9/11-jumpers-America-wants-forget-victims-fell-Twin-Towers.html

4 http://www.youtube.com/watch?v=KrM0dAFsZ8k

5 http/::www.nysun.com:national:clinton-spars-with-petraeus-on-credibility:62426:

6 http://voices.washingtonpost.com/fact-checker/2007/09/general_betray_us.html

7 http://www.militantislammonitor.org/article/id/5142

8 http://www.werismyki.com/artcls/cross_gives_hope.htm

9 http://www.christianpost.com/news/atheists-want-cross-removed-from-ground-zero-museum-52837/

10 http://www.whitehouse.gov/the-press-office/2010/09/11/weekly-address-president-obama-commemorates-ninth-anniversary-september-

11 http://www.historyplace.com/speeches/fdr-infamy.htm

12 http://religion.blogs.cnn.com/2011/09/07/progressive-christians-join-controversy-over-excluding-clergy-at-911-event/

13 http://michellemalkin.com/2009/04/14/confirme-the-obama-dhs-hit-job-on-conservatives-is-real/

14 http://kleinonline.wnd.com/2011/08/29/obama-adviser-compared-u-s-christians-to-al-qaida-also-likened-feared-terror-group-to-jewish-totalitarians-in-israel/im

15 http://godfatherpolitics.com/5993/new-report-if-you-love-liberty-you-might-terrorist/#ixzz1zg2uX2V5

16 http://www.wired.com/dangerroom/2011/11/obama-islamophobia-review/

17 http://www.investigativeproject.org/3453/islamist-lobbies-washington-war-on-arab

18 http://www.politico.com/politico44/perm/0811/white_house_dinner_16bcb086-a896-469a-b25c-bebc1b87edf7.html

19 http/::www.allvoices.com:contributed-news:9846769-saudi-billionaire-about-to-build-worlds-tallest-tower

20 http://www.latimes.com/news/local/la-me-yoshino-20120108,0,4655194.column (Iraqis are older)

21 http://www.washingtonpost.com/wp-dyn/content/article/2010/06/18/AR2010061803760.html (rules of engagement)

22 http://frontpagemag.com/2012/01/03/a-radical-islamist-sheikh-surrenders-on-behalf-of-america/

Part III Chapter 2—TSA

1   http://frontpagemag.com/2011/12/30/five-easy-steps-to-end-
    islamophobia/
2   http://www.wnd.com/2012/01/381953/
3   http://frontpagemag.com/2011/12/30/five-easy-steps-to-end-
    islamophobia/
4   http://www.wnd.com/2008/07/69601/
5   http://www.businessinsider.com/us-immigration-agents-are-loading-
    up-on-as-many-as-450-million-new-rounds-of-ammo-2012-
    3#ixzz1qYZjYgXiHom
6   http://www.businessinsider.com/us-immigration-agents-are-loading-
    up-on-as-many-as-450-million-new-rounds-of-ammo-2012-
    3#ixzz1qYZjYgXiHom
7   http://www.infowars.com/obamas-latest-executive-order-martial-law-
    confiscation-of-private-property-and-forced-labor/
8   http://deskofbrian.com/2012/04/homeland-security-vehicles-on-the-
    move/
9   http://www.gopusa.com/theloft/2012/06/19/is-a-spy-drone-coming-to-a-
    town-near-you/?subscriber=1
10 http://times247.com/articles/kuhner-obama-authorizes-himself-to-
    declare-martial-law
11 http://www.whitehouse.gov/the-press-office/2012/03/16/executive-order-
    national-defense-resources-preparedness
12 http://articles.latimes.com/2011/oct/27/nation/la-na-us-drone-20111027
13 http://www.homelandsecuritynewswire.com/texas-county-police-buys-
    drone-can-carry-weapons
14 http://www.foxnews.com/us/2012/03/05/ap-source-holder-will-address-
    targeted-killings/
15 http/::www.youtube.com:watch%3Fv=nemphOb4bts
16 http://yesbuthowever.com/muslim-tsa-catholic-nun-5000117/
17 http://www.jihadwatch.org/2010/11/hamas-linked-cair-tsa-may-only-
    search-around-muslim-womens-head-neck.html
18 http://www.facebook.com/pages/Aaron-Tobey-Naked-
    Protest/193416467365300
19 http://www.debbieschlussel.com/wp-content/uploads/2011/07/
    rumsfeldtsa2.jpg
20 http://tpmdc.talkingpointsmemo.com/2012/01/rand-paul-your-tsa-
    machines-are-lying-to-you-america.php#more
21 http://www.latimes.com/news/local/la-me-tsa-screeners-
    20120426,0,4508192.story

22 http://www.dailymail.co.uk/news/article-2116881/TSA-subject-child-wheelchair-invasive-airport-security-tests-Chicago.html

23 http://rawjustice.com/2010/11/22/10-of-the-most-outrageous-tsa-horror-stories

24 http://www.foxnews.com/us/2011/06/26/dying-woman-undergoes-additional-tsa-security-screening-says-family/

25 http://overheadbin.msnbc.msn.com/_news/2011/12/03/9191260-85-year-old-woman-i-was-strip-searched-at-jfk

26 http://rawjustice.com/2010/11/22/10-of-the-most-outrageous-tsa-horror-stories

27 http://www.foxnews.com/us/2011/06/26/dying-woman-undergoes-additional-tsa-security-screening-says-family/

28 http://jenniferbrix.com/wp-content/uploads/2011/07/natural.jpg

29 http://brianekoenig.com/2011/10/tsa-agents-ypat-down-breast-cancer-survivor/

30 http://rawjustice.com/2010/11/22/10-of-the-most-outrageous-tsa-horror-stories

31 http://www.theblaze.com/stories/cair-tsa-can-only-pat-down-muslim-women%E2%80%99s-head-neck/

32 ttp://www.washingtontimes.com/news/2010/nov/17/terrorists-hiding-in-hijabs/

33 http://www.dailymail.co.uk/news/article-2106631/Fireman-Sam-creator-Dave-Jones-detained-

34 http://rawjustice.com/2010/11/22/10-of-the-most-outrageous-tsa-horror-stories/

35 https://www.rutherford.org/publications_resources/commentary_channel/cancer_causing_airport_scanners_enough_is_enough/

36 http://articles.latimes.com/2012/jun/10/business/la-fi-travel-briefcase-20120611

37 http://www.dailymail.co.uk/news/article-2087419/TSA-workers-wear-monitoring-devices-test-scanners-dangerous-levels-radiation.html#ixzz1nkysAoM0

38 http://::www.thedailybeast.com:articles:2010:10:30:airport-pat-downs-the-new-tsa-rules-are-a-mistake.html

39 http://www.wnd.com/2012/03/tsa-to-start-fondling-drivers-now-too/

40 http://thenewamerican.com/usnews/constitution/9455-tsa-stages-highway-searches-to-show-its-tennessee-valley-authority

41 http://www.nytimes.com/2012/04/27/us/court-rules-florida-governors-drug-testing-order-unconstitutional.html

42 http://jurist.org/paperchase/2010/02/federal-appeals-court-rules-inmate.php

43 http://www.latimes.com/news/nation/nationnow/la-na-pn-supreme-court-strip-search-20120402,0,4628756.story

44 http/::www.huffingtonpost.com:2010:05:06:ahmed-khalfan-ghailani-gu_n_566517.html

45 http://townhall.com/columnists/michellemalkin/2011/04/08/tsa_follies_see_spot_fail/page/full/

46 http://godfatherpolitics.com/6180/obama-signs-executive-order-giving-him-and-federal-government-control-of-all-forms-of-communication-under-any-circumstance/#ixzz20utWrWVu
   http://freedomoutpost.com/2012/07/obamas-executive-order-national-security-emergency-comm/

Part III, Chapter 3—Flight 93 Memorial, Victory Mosque

1 http://www.gatestoneinstitute.org/1496/mosques-on-sacred-sites-of-defeated-enemies

2 http://www.americanthinker.com/2010/07/the_mosques_of_war.html

3 http://i191.photobucket.com/albums/z36/AlecRawls/Advertisements%20contra%20the%20crescent%20mosque/Ad2-ItWasTerrible-9-3-10_1000pxJPG.jpg

4 http://i191.photobucket.com/albums/z36/AlecRawls/Advertisements contra the crescent mosque/Ad2-ItWasTerrible-9-3-10_1000pxJPG.jpg

5 http://creepingsharia.wordpress.com/2010/08/29/flight-93-memorial-mosque/

6 http://islam.about.com/od/muslimcountries/ig/Crescent-Moon-Flags/

7 http://www.hudson-ny.org/1526/cordoba-mosque-controversy

8 http://www.nationalreview.com/articles/246269/imam-rauf-s-books-ibn-warraq?pg=3

9 http://www.stonegateinstitute.org/1526/cordoba-mosque-controversy

10 http://pjmedia.com/blog/ground-zero-imam-i-dont-believe-in-religious-dialogue/

11 http://www.nationalreview.com/articles/246269/imam-rauf-s-books-ibn-warraq?pg=2

12 http://www.youtube.com/watch?v=je1xtkVMvqo (waled shoebat)

13 http://www.youtube.com/watch?v=aGUT6X6079s&feature=
    related 12A (waled shoebat)

14 http://ezinearticles.com/?The-Ground-Zero-Mosque---A-Waiter-and-
    $4.8-Million-Dollars&id=4848220

15 http://telchaination.blogspot.com/2011/10/mayor-bloombergs-
    partnership-with-anti.html

16 http://www.foxnews.com/opinion/2010/08/04/peter-ferrara-muslim-
    mosque-manhattan-constitution-saudi-arabia-synagogues/

Part III, Chapter 4—Jihad in America

1   http://undergod.procon.org/view.resource.php?resourceID=69

2   http://keyboardmilitia.com/wp-content/uploads/Colored_Patriots_of_
    American_Rev.pdf

3   http://www.christiananswers.net/q-wall/wal-g003.html

4   http://www.wnd.com/2003/08/20465/

5   http://godfatherpolitics.com/5979/california-considers-allowing-
    more-than-two-parents/http://townhall.com/columnists/
    johnstossel/2006/12/06/who_gives_to_charity/page/full/

6   http://www.onenewsnow.com/Election2008/Default.aspx?id=164320

7   http://articles.cnn.com/2009-10-28/politics/hate.crimes_1_crimes-gay-
    rights-human-rights-

8   http://www.afa.net/Detail.aspx?id=2147483743

9   http://frontpagemag.com/2012/06/27/american-muslims-stone-
    christians-in-dearborn-michigan/

10 http://godfatherpolitics.com/5979/california-considers-allowing-more-
    than-two-parents/

11 http://www.wnd.com/2012/07/has-the-normalizing-of-pedophilia-
    begun/

12 http://frontpagemag.com/2011/12/12/its-not-workplace-violence-its-
    islam/
    http://atlasshrugs2000.typepad.com/honor_killings/
    http://www.mererhetoric.com/2007/09/24/photographs-to-help-
    explain-why-there-are-no-homosexuals-in-iran-content-warning-graphic-
    photos-updated-video-added/
    http://frontpagemag.com/2012/01/06/muslim-persecution-of-christians-
    the-christmas-edition/

13 http://s.michellemalkin.com/wp/wp-content/uploads/2009/04/hsa-
    rightwing-extremism-09-04-07.pdf

14 http://godfatherpolitics.com/5993/new-report-if-you-love-liberty-you-might-terrorist/#ixzz1zg2uX2V5

15 http://www.usatoday.com/news/science/archaeology/2001-03-22-afghan-buddhas.htm

16 http://www.dailykos.com/story/2012/07/15/1107127/-Desecration-and-destruction-in-Timbuktu

17 http://www.wnd.com/2012/07/the-death-cult-hopes-to-destroy-pyramids/

18 : http://frontpagemag.com/2012/raymond-ibrahim/muslim-brotherhood-destroy-the-pyramids/

19 http://articles.latimes.com/2012/apr/24/local/la-me-solar-bones-20120424

20 http://www.nctimes.com/blogsnew/news/transportation/region-hearing-delayed-on-tribe-s-request-to-halt-construction/article_638ec5f2-5c2f-5698-8479-9aeff387d225.html

21 http://frontpagemag.com/2012/raymond-ibrahim/muslim-brotherhood-destroy-the-pyramids/

22 http://www.au.org/about/people/ayesha-n-khan

23 http://blogs.ocweekly.com/navelgazing/2010/12/prop_8_judge_married_to_aclu_l.php

24 http://www.prop8trialtracker.com/2012/02/07/breaking-proposition-8-ruled-unconstitutional-by-9th-circuit-panel/

25 http://www.law.cornell.edu/supct/html/historics/USSC_CR_0391_0367_ZS.html

26 http://www.law.cornell.edu/supct/html/historics/USSC_CR_0491_0397_ZS.html

27 http://www.soc.umn.edu/~samaha/cases/texas%20v%20johnson,%20transcript.htm

28 http://en.wikipedia.org/wiki/William_Kunstler

29 http://urbanlegends.about.com/library/bl_mexican_flag.htm

30 http://americanpatrol.com/RALLIES/JULY42000/July4stills-1.html

31 http://michellemalkin.com/2010/11/12/middle-schooler/

32 http://www.foxnews.com/us/2010/06/23/students-sue-removal-american-flag-t-shirts

33 http://chalcedon.edu/research/articles/ten-commandments-judge-beats-550000-lawsuit-judge-roy-moores-battle-for-god/

34 http://www.wnd.com/2012/05/aclu-christianity-has-no-place-on-school-board/

35 http://www.aclu.org/religion-belief/government-display-mt-soledad-cross-war-memorial-declared-unconstitutional-aclu-case

36 http://articles.latimes.com/2011/jan/05/local/la-me-cross-appeal-20110105

37 http://www.reuters.com/article/2012/06/25/us-usa-court-cross-idUSBRE85O0WJ20120625

38 http://www.christianpost.com/news/christian-attorneys-ask-high-court-to-stop-aclu-s-attack-on-mojave-desert-cross-39074/

39 http://www.secularnewsdaily.com/2010/04/us-supreme-court-mohave-cross-may-stand-on-public-land/

40 http://articles.cnn.com/2010-05-11/justice/mojave.cross.stolen_1_mojave-national-preserve-cross-national-park-service?_s=PM:CRIME

41 http://www.rifuture.org/a-cross-grows-in-providence.html

42   (See my book, Chapter 1 & 3, Part III)

43 http://www.wnd.com/2012/05/christian-messages-banned-in-buffalo/

44 http://www.wnd.com/2012/06/refuse-to-photograph-lesbians-get-fined-700

45 http://www.kentucky.com/2012/03/26/2127245/hands-on-originals-t-shirt-company.html#storylink=omni_popular%23wgt=pop

46 http://www.gopusa.com/theloft/2012/07/06/atheist-sues-restaurant-over-church-going-discount/?subscriber=1

47 http://www.wnd.com/2012/01/judge-says-following-christian-beliefs-wrong/

48 http://www.wnd.com/2012/03/christians-who-signed-petitions-investigated/

49 http://godfatherpolitics.com/5440/school-tells-christians-they-cant-proselytize-during-after-school-programs/

50 http://godfatherpolitics.com/5811/court-upholds-jail-fines-bible-study-host/

51 http://freedomoutpost.com/2012/07/man-jailed-fined-over-12k-for-having-home-bible-study/http://freedomoutpost.com/2012/07/man-jailed-fined-over-12k-for-having-home-bible-study/

52 http://www.washingtontimes.com/news/2011/feb/18/freedom-to-be-christian-but-banned-from-acting-chr/

53 http://www.cbn.com/cbnnews/us/2012/May/awmakers-Back-Christian-Students-at-Vanderbilt/

54 http://www.moonbattery.com/archives/2011/06/judge-threatens.html

55 http://www.wnd.com/index.php?fa=PAGE.view&pageId=206561

56 http://cranston.patch.com/articles/aclu-asks-for-xx-xxx-in-attorneys-fees-in-prayer-banner-suit

57 http://www.theblaze.com/stories/teen-atheist-wins-big-school-district-wont-appeal-ruling-to-take-down-prayer-banner/

58 http://www.heritage.org/issues/education/dc-opportunity-scholarship-program

59 http://godfatherpolitics.com/6033/the-koran-is-coming-to-a-public-school-near-you/

60 http://godfatherpolitics.com/5380/arabic-mandated-in-new-york-public-schools-is-a-step-toward-the-islamization-of-america/#ixzz20BQEU7AZ

61 http://www.wnd.com/?pageId=380317#ixzz1hPHtdU8R

62 https://www.mtholyoke.edu/offices/comm/csj/991008/madonna.html

63 http://www.nytimes.com/2010/12/11/arts/design/11ants.html?pagewanted=2&_r=2&sq=cotter%20wojnarowicz&st=cse&scp=1

64 http://www.wnd.com/2012/06/new-movie-jesus-is-product-of-mary-being-raped/

65 http://www.foxnews.com/us/2010/03/25/texas-town-cross-plays-gay-christ/#ixzz1JuuEMTEc

66 http://www.nytimes.com/2011/04/14/theater/theresa-rebecks-play-o-beautiful-at-university-of-delaware.html?_r=1&pagewanted=printchorus

67 http://www.glennbeck.com/content/articles/article/198/44300/

68 http://skinnyreporter.com/clericsbanned.html

69 http://www.wnd.com/?pageId=380317 - ixzz1hPHtdU8R (The ultimate guide to attacks from anti-Christmas Grinches)

70 http://campaign2012.washingtonexaminer.com/blogs/beltway-confidential/congressmen-cant-say-merry-christmas-mail/261466

71 http://www.christianpost.com/news/atheists-want-cross-removed-from-ground-zero-museum-52837/

72 http://www.jihadwatch.org/2011/10/justice-department-forces-school-district-to-pay-75000-to-teacher-who-demanded-time-off-for-hajj.html

73 See Chapter 8, Part IV of this book

74 http://frontpagemag.com/2012/jamie-glazov/american-muslims-stone-christians-in-dearborn-michigan-1/

75 http://www.wnd.com/2010/09/208929/

76 http://www.thegatewaypundit.com/2010/05/unbelievable-seniors-not-allowed-to-pray-before-meals-at-nursing-home/

77 http://www.nationalreview.com/articles/229479/abolishing-good-friday-dennis-prager

78 http://www.gopusa.com/theloft/2012/06/21/you-can-pray-just-not-to-jesus/?subscriber=1

79 http://www.wnd.com/?pageId=361461#ixzz1cDBa1EK0

Part III, Chapter 5—Jihad in America

1   http://www.google.com/search?q=mosques+in+USA&hl=en&client=safa
    ri&rls=en&prmd=ivns&tbm=isch&tbo=u&source=univ&sa=X&ei=Exm
    nTYXEJIG8sAOthaD6DA&ved=0CCMQsAQ&biw=1163&bih=959

2   http://www.foxnews.com/opinion/2010/08/04/peter-ferrara-muslim-
    mosque-manhattan-constitution-saudi-arabia-synagogues/

3   http://www.npr.org/2011/11/03/141945254/new-mosques-cropping-up-
    in-chicago-study-shows

4   http://atlasshrugs2000.typepad.com/atlas_shrugs/2011/12/study-
    shows-majority-of-us-mosques-repositories-of-sharia-jihad-muslim-
    brotherhood-literature-and-pr.html

5   http://www.nationalreview.com/corner/243008/government-confiscates-
    your-money-build-mosques-andy-mccarthy

6   http://www.cbn.com/cbnnews/us/2010/August/Mega-Mosque-Plans-
    Target-Americas-Heartland

7   http://www.cbn.com/cbnnews/world/2010/August/Stakelbeck-on-
    Terror-Show1/

8   http://www.wnd.com/2012/05/judge-shuts-down-mega-mosque-
    construction/

9   http://atlasshrugs2000.typepad.com/atlas_shrugs/2010/06/broadcasting-
    abd-blaring-the-call-to-prayer-in-nyc.html

10 http://www.campus-watch.org/survey.php/id/16

11 http://www.studentsforacademicfreedom.org/news/2735/
    nazis-in-the-ivory-tower

12 http://biggovernment.com/fgaffney/2010/04/03/connect-the-dots-on-
    cairs-foreign-funding-and-lobbying-at-cairobservatory-org/

13 http://cairunmasked.org/?page_id=1297

14 http://pjmedia.com/blog/the-muslim-student-associations-terror-
    problem/

15 http://www.militantislammonitor.org/article/id/2710 (Orens)

16 http://archive.frontpagemag.com/readArticle.aspx?ARTID=20378
    (pipes)

17 http://www.thedailybeast.com/articles/2010/09/15/marty-peretzs-
    muslim-comment-draws-fire-harvard-in-crossfire.html

18 http://articles.cnn.com/2001-10-11/us/rec.giuliani.prince_1_saudi-
    prince-alwaleed-bin-israeli-withdrawal-criminal-attack?_s=PM:US

19 http://www.freerepublic.com/focus/f-news/2445630/posts
    (Bin Talal & Obama and other investments)

20   http://www.washingtonpost.com/blogs/on-faith/post/the-madness-over-all-american-muslim/2011/12/16/gIQAquwtyO_blog.html (John Esposito)

21   http://online.wsj.com/article/SB10001424052748704131404575111761 1125872740.html (Gitmo attys)

22   http://michellemalkin.com/2009/08/21/aclugitmo-jihadi-lawyers-questioned-on-blowing-cia-officers-cover/

23   http://shariahinamericancourts.com/

24   http://latimesblogs.latimes.com/nationnow/2012/01/federal-appeals-court-blocks-oklahomas-ban-on-sharia-law.html

25   http://www.ca10.uscourts.gov/opinions/10/10-6273.pdf

26   http://barnhardt.biz/ 1/21/12htt

27   http://www.shariahfinancewatch.org/blog/

28   http://www.wnd.com/index.php?fa=PAGE.view&pageId=321169 (Delta)

29   http://www.freerepublic.com/focus/f-news/2445630/posts (Bin Talal & Obama and other investments)\

30   http://telchaination.blogspot.com/2011/10/mayor-bloombergs-partnership-with-anti.html (bloomberg)

31   http://www.cnn.com/2012/01/26/us/new-york-muslims-nypd-film/index.html (bloomberg shd fire police chief)

32   http://seattletimes.nwsource.com/html/nationworld/2017323569_jihadmovie25.html

33   http://www.nj.com/news/index.ssf/2012/03/civil_rights_groups_file_compl.html

34   http://frontpagemag.com/2012/06/15/everythings-coming-up-jihad/

35   http://www.npr.org/templates/story/story.php?storyId=129584557 (Bin Talal & Fox News)

36   http://www.indyposted.com/32384/saudi-prince-alwaleed-bin-talal-announces-arabic-news-channel-collaboration-with-fox-news/

37   http://www.militantislammonitor.org/article/id/1375 (bin Talal owns 5%, alters news)

38   http://www.indyposted.com/32384/saudi-prince-alwaleed-bin-talal-announces-arabic-news-channel-collaboration-with-fox-news/

39   http://atlasshrugs2000.typepad.com/atlas_shrugs/2008/08/obamas-benefact.html

40   http://www.youtube.com/watch?v=LEUif1--r38

41   http://www.youtube.com/watch?v=LEUif1--r38

42 http://articles.nydailynews.com/2009-04-03/news/17920879_1
    _michelle-obama-hug-elizabeth-garrett-anderson

43 http://cnsnews.com/news/article/us-contains-enough-oil-and-gas-
    reserves-fuel-country-decades-petroleum-institute-says

Part III, Chapter 6—Muslims are setting traps
Part III, Chapter 7—Question
Part IV, Chapter 1—Obama confuses us
Part IV, Chapter 2—Illegals at Border

1   http://reason.org/news/show/western-land-federal-devolution.
    %C2%A0

2   http://reason.org/news/show/western-land-federal-devolution.

3   http://www.kevinwebb22.com/september-11/fbi-homeland-security-
    confirmed-terrorists-entering-america-southern-borders

4   http://www.wnd.com/2012/01/381953/

5   http://www.freerepublic.com/focus/f-chat/2733609/posts

6   http://www.wnd.com/2010/05/156441/

7   http://www.leaderandtimes.com/index.php?option=com_content
    &view=article&id=2296:sign-warning-visitors-to-sonoran-desert-
    national-monument-to-watch-for-drug-and-human-trafficking-are-no-
    hoax&catid=12:local-news&Itemid=40

8   http://www.zimbio.com/Illegal+immigration/articles/iu4qhQGBZ-t/Ariz
    ona+Under+Siege+Americans+Banned+5+500

9   http://www.leaderandtimes.com/index.php?option=com_content
    &view=article&id=2296:sign-warning-visitors-to-sonoran-desert-
    national-monument-to-watch-for-drug-and-human-trafficking-are-no-
    hoax&catid=12:local-news&Itemid=40

10 http://www.wnd.com/2010/06/172121/

11 http://abcnews.go.com/Business/maywood-california-top-cities-
    overwhelmed-recession/story?id=11032953#.T_2UxI4Z2S0

12 http://www.politico.com/news/stories/1010/43199.html#
    ixzz1mshBXsTx

13 http://articles.latimes.com/2010/sep/02/nation/la-na-lawsuit-arpaio-
    20100903

14 http://thenewamerican.com/usnews/politics/3879-mexico-joins-suit-
    against-arizona-illegals-sue-rancher-for-civil-rights-violations

15 http://www.desertinvasion.us/video/videos.html

16 http://www.federalobserver.com/2011/02/27/the-truth-about-roger-barnett/
17 http://www.washingtontimes.com/news/2009/feb/9/16-illegals-sue-arizona-rancher/?page=all#pagebreak
18 http://www.freerepublic.com/focus/news/2519120/posts
19 http://www.norcalblogs.com/gate/2010/05/rape-trees-segment.php
20 http://frontpagemag.com/2012/02/17/obama%e2%80%99s-new-illegal-alien-czar/
21 http://latino.foxnews.com/latino/news/2012/03/13/feds-open-new-reform-minded-immigration-detention-center-in-texas/
22 http://www.examiner.com/county-political-buzz-in-san-diego/ice-detention-facilities-provide-luxuries-for-those-awaiting-deportation
23 http://www.examiner.com/county-political-buzz-in-san-diego/ice-detention-facilities-provide-luxuries-for-those-awaiting-deportation
24 http://frontpagemag.com/2012/02/17/obama%e2%80%99s-new-illegal-alien-czar/
25 http://teapartypatriots.ning.com/?showAddContent=1&xg_source=msg_wel_network

Part IV, Chapter 3—Somalis

1 http://www.cbn.com/cbnnews/566637.aspx
2 http://www.acf.hhs.gov/programs/orr/funding/cma.htm
3 http://refugeeresettlementwatch.wordpress.com/
4 http://www.freedomrings1776.com/2011/08/of-somali-refugees-pork-and-our.html
5 http://www.thesocialcontract.com/artman2/publish/tsc_21_1/tsc_21_1_walker_refugee.shtml:
6 http://www.freedomrings1776.com/2011/08/of-somali-refugees-pork-and-our.html
7 http://super-economy.blogspot.com/2010/09/dont-believe-hype-somali-immigration-to.html
   Super-Economy: Don't believe the hype: Somali immigration to Minnesota is a complete failure
8 http://barenakedislam.com/2011/06/22/minnesotastan-3-muslim-women-charged-with-attacking-key-witness-in-somali-muslim-white-child-prostitution-ring/somali-sex-trafficking-2010-11-9-12-10-0/
9 http://barenakedislam.com/2012/04/09/29-somali-muslims-indicted-for-kidnapping-raping-and-selling-underage-white-girls/

10 .http://atlasshrugs2000.typepad.com/atlas_shrugs/2011/07/somali-
    terror-group-linked-to-al-qaeda-recruited-21-young-muslms-in-
    minnesota.html:

11 http://atlasshrugs2000.typepad.com/atlas_shrugs/2011/07/somali-terror-
    group-linked-to-al-qaeda-recruited-21-young-muslms-in-minnesota.
    html:

12 http://atlasshrugs2000.typepad.com/atlas_shrugs/2009/07/muslims-in-
    minnesota-we-hate-gays-video-of-assault-.html

13 http://www.youtube.com/watch?v=bjcpo3KcHSI

14 http://bigjournalism.com/bcarroll/2010/03/10/if-muslims-gay-bash-in-
    san-francisco-do-they-make-a-sound/

15 http://www.wnd.com/2012/03/obama-fanatic-guilty-in-arpaio-death-
    threat/

16 feed://michellemalkin.com/search/malik+shabazz/feed/rss2/

17 http://www.theblaze.com/stories/you-get-what-you-deserve-white-boy-
    13-year-old-set-on-fire-in-horrific-racially-charged-attack/

18 http://frontpagemag.com/2012/04/26/justice-for-trayvon
    %e2%80%94with-bricks-and-bats/

19 http://www.wnd.com/2012/05/100-blacks-beat-white-couple-media-
    buries-attack/

20 http://www.faithfreedom.org/articles/op-ed/muslims-out-of-the-military-
    rep-rick-womick-of-tennessee-has-the-right-idea/

21 http://refugeeresettlementwatch.wordpress.com/2011/02/22/state-
    senator-takes-major-step-to-reform-refugee-program-in-tennessee/

22 http://www.warriorsfortruth.com/news-somalis-maine.html

23 http://www.telegraph.co.uk/news/uknews/5215413/Every-phone-call-
    email-or-website-visit-to-be-monitored.html

Part IV, Chapter 4—Kenya, Nigeria

1   http://www.canadafreepress.com/index.php/article/4353Senator Barack
    Obama in Kenya

2   http://atlasshrugs2000.typepad.com/atlas_shrugs/2008/01/
    obama-islam-and.html

3   http://www.guardian.co.uk/world/2008/jan/02/kenya

4   http://atlasshrugs2000.typepad.com/atlas_shrugs/2008/01/
    jihad-in-kenya.html

5   http://www.thedailybeast.com/newsweek/2006/09/10/
    walking-the-world-stage.html

6   http://atlasshrugs2000.typepad.com/atlas_shrugs/2008/01/
    obamas-oginga-o.html

7   7. http://www.nytimes.com/2008/02/24/opinion/24kristof.html

8   http://www.nytimes.com/2008/01/02/world/africa/02kenya.
    html?pagewanted=all

9   http://www.alternet.org/rss/breaking_news/393962/
    obama_urges_kenya_to_work_with_icc_inquiry/

10 http://www.capitalfm.co.ke/news/2012/01/kenyan-picked-to-head-local-
    al-qaeda-wing/1

11 http://www.stratfor.com/weekly/al-shabaabs-threat-kenya

12 http://www.pbs.org/frontlineworld/stories/colombia/images/map.swf

13 http://articles.latimes.com/2012/apr/25/world/la-fg-nigeria-
    billionaire-20120426

14 http://frontpagemag.com/2012/01/12/nigerias-coming-civil-war/

15 http://frontpagemag.com/2012/01/12/nigerias-coming-civil-war/

16 http://online.wsj.com/article/SB1000142405297020462420457717690
    2128726344.html?mod=WSJ_article_comments

17 http://frontpagemag.com/2012/01/12/nigerias-coming-civil-war/

18 http://online.wsj.com/article/SB1000142405297020462420457717690
    2128726344.html

19 http://frontpagemag.com/2012/01/12/nigerias-coming-civil-war/

20 http://online.wsj.com/article/SB1000142405297020462420457717690
    2128726344.html?mod=WSJ_article_comments

21 http://online.wsj.com/article/SB1000142405297020462420457717690
    2128726344.html?mod=WSJ_article_comments

22 http://online.wsj.com/article/SB1000142405297020462420457717690
    2128726344.html?mod=WSJ_article_comments

23 http://www.guardian.co.uk/world/2012/jan/27/boko-haram-nigeria-
    sharia-law

24 http://www.youtube.com/verify_age?next_url=/watch%3Fv%
    3DlUd0Vcs8Tm4

25 http://www.theblaze.com/stories/obama-admin-official-says-religion-is-
    not-driving-extreme-violence-in-nigeria-the-day-after-islamists-slaughter-
    40-christians/

26 http://frontpagemag.com/2012/06/13/the-obama-administration's-
    genocide-denial/

27 http://online.wsj.com/article/SB1000142405297020462420457717690
    2128726344.html?mod=WSJ_article_comments

28 http://atlasshrugs2000.typepad.com/atlas_shrugs/2012/01/muslim-army-trained-and-funded-in-saudi-arabia-fights-until-nigeria-establishes-sharia-law.html

Part IV, Chapter 5—Middle East

1   http://www.latimes.com/news/nationworld/world/la-fg-iran-nuclear-20120428,0,353079.story

2   http://www.jewishjournal.com/iranianamericanjews/item/is_obama_listening_to_the_people_of_irans_calls_for_help/

3   http://www.iranian.com/main/blog/dr-mansur-rastani/president-obama-you-undermined-2009-iranian-uprising.

4   http://online.wsj.com/article/SB10001424052970204770404577078160095550518.html

5   Rush Limbaugh archive December 8, 2011

6   http://www.csmonitor.com/World/Middle-East/2012/0424/Iran-s-cyber-prowess-Could-it-really-have-cracked-drone-codes

7   http://www.google.com/search?q=Egyptian+uprising&hl=en&rls=com.microsoft:*&rlz=1I7ADFA_enUS338&prmd=ivnsu&source=univ&tbm=nws&tbo=u&sa=X&ei=egCKT4a7M4uNigKKlZipCw&ved=0CCUQqAI

8   http://frontpagemag.com/2011/02/03/barack-obama-and-the-muslim-brotherhood/

9   http://frontpagemag.com/2012/02/29/why-is-obama-in-bed-with-the-muslim-brotherhood/

10 http://frontpagemag.com/2011/11/18/obama-administration-training-egyptian-islamists-for-elections/

11 http://frontpagemag.com/2012/02/16/the-muslim-brothers-get-paid-to-threaten-america/

12 http://edition.cnn.com/2012/01/26/world/africa/egypt-us-lahood/index.html

13 http://www.nationalreview.com/articles/295501/obama-funds-egyptian-government-andrew-c-mccarthy

14 http://www.politico.com/news/stories/0611/58094.html#ixzz1QouVzO8a

15 http://frontpagemag.com/2012/02/29/why-is-obama-in-bed-with-the-muslim-brotherhood/

16 http://times247.com/articles/obama-deputy-admits-hundreds-of-closed-door-meetings-with-cair#ixzz1xJDg6hey

17 http://frontpagemag.com/2012/05/10/jihad-comes-to-egypt/
18 http://en.wikipedia.org/wiki/Bombing_of_Libya_(1986)
19 http://frontpagemag.com/2011/03/30/obama-and-thought-control/
20 http://www.infowars.com/nigeria-fertile-ground-for-balkanization/
21 http://www.newsrealblog.com/2011/04/02/matt-lauer-suggests-arming-al-qaeda-shows-american-compassion-for-all/
22 http://blogs.the-american-interest.com/wrm/2011/12/08/butcher-assads-allies-hezbollah-steps-up-hamas-steps-out/
23 http://en.wikipedia.org/wiki/2011%E2%80%932012_Syrian_uprising

1 http://en.wikipedia.org/wiki/Iraq_Liberation_Act
2 http://conservapedia.com/Operation_Iraqi_Freedom
3 http://articles.cnn.com/2002-10-11/politics/iraq.us_1_biological-weapons-weapons-inspectors-iraq?_s=PM:ALLPOLITICS
4 http://news.investors.com/article/525657/201003051905/sos-and151-save-our-navy-seals.htm?Ntt=so-s-save-our-navy-seals
5 http://news.investors.com/article/531172/201004221901/free-all-the-seals-from-travesty.htm?Ntt=so-s-save-our-navy-seals&p=full
6 http://www.washingtontimes.com/news/2011/dec/16/senators-decry-transfer-terrorist-iraqi-government/
7 http://www.guardian.co.uk/world/2010/nov/11/iraq-powersharing-deal-break-deadlock
8 http://frontpagemag.com/2011/12/14/obamas-abandoning-iraq-roadshow/

Part IV, Chapter 6—Iraq

1 http://www.wnd.com/2009/12/118941/
2 http://www.nypost.com/p/news/international/burqa_clad_taliban_fighters_blast_y7wmSYXw766wwgv92NYZQP
3 http://www.washingtontimes.com/news/2009/nov/16/us-troops-battle-taliban-afghan-rules/?page=all
4 http://washingtonexaminer.com/news/world/2011/04/afghan-rules-engagement-force-us-soldiers-free-insurgents-caught-red-handed
5 http://americaswatchtower.com/2012/03/24/united-states-soldiers-may-need-search-warrants-to-conduct-night-raids-on-the-taliban-in-afghanistan-in-the-future/
6 http://en.wikipedia.org/wiki/We_shall_fight_on_the_beaches
7 http://wiki.answers.com/Q/What_is_the_literacy_rate_in_Afghanistan

8   http://frontpagemag.com/upload/pamphlets/ViolentOpp.pdf

9   http://www.rawa.org/temp/runews/2012/02/16/for-punishment-of-elder-s-misdeeds-afghan-girl-pays-the-price.html

10 http://frontpagemag.com/upload/pamphlets/ViolentOpp.pdf

11 http://abcnews.go.com/Blotter/stoning-afghanistan-graphic-video-execution-shows-talibans-growing/story?id=12770754#.T5y3ge0Z2S0

12 http://www.huffingtonpost.com/2012/03/01/buck-mckeon-afghanistan-security_n_1314959.htm

13 http://www.usatoday.com/news/world/afghanistan/story/2012-03-26/Afghanistan-troops-NATO/53778664/1?csp=34news

14 http://www.washingtonpost.com/wp-dyn/content/article/2010/06/18/AR2010061803760.html
    (rules of engagement)

15 http://abcnews.go.com/International/wireStory/nato-service-member-killed-southern-afghanistan-16226536?page=2#.T5uNnO0Z2S0

16 http://atlasshrugs2000.typepad.com/atlas_shrugs/2012/05/obamas-dod-not-reporting-afghan-attacks-on-american-troops.html

17 http://latimesblogs.latimes.com/world_now/2012/06/3-us-troops-among-dead-in-two-blasts-in-afghanistan.html

18 http://articles.cnn.com/2011-06-22/politics/afghanistan.troops.drawdown_1_afghanistan-drawdown-surge-forces-president-barack-obama?_s=PM:POLITICS

19 http://www.washingtontimes.com/news/2012/feb/23/obamas-burning-koran-apology/

20 http://frontpagemag.com/2012/02/27/obama-sharia-enforcer/

21 http://www.blackfive.net/main/2012/02/bible-burning-vs-koran-burning-in-afghanistan.html

22 http://frontpagemag.com/2012/04/09/clearing-the-way-for-the-taliban/

23 http://online.wsj.com/article/SB10001424052970204136404577209391708596680.html?mod=googlenews_wsj

24 http://theunjustmedia.com/Afghanistan/Statements/Jan12/Formal%20proclamation%20of%20Islamic%20Emirate's%20victory.htm]

25 http://www.rawa.org/rules.htm

26 http://www.cbsnews.com/2100-224_162-4631708.html

27 http://www.cbsnews.com/2100-224_162-4631708.html

28 http://www.usatoday.com/news/world/afghanistan/2010-05-27-afghanistan-girls_N.htm

29   http://www.theweek.co.uk/politics/12131/taliban-accused-gas-attack-girls-girls%E2%80%99-school

30   http://www.theweek.co.uk/politics/12131/taliban-accused-gas-attack-girls-girls%E2%80%99-school

31   http://frontpagemag.com/2012/04/20/the-taliban's-poisoning-of-afghan-schoolgirls/

Part IV, Chapter 7—Afghanistan

32   http://www.reuters.com/article/2012/04/17/us-afghanistan-women-idUSBRE83G0PZ20120417

33   http://abcnews.go.com/Blotter/top-secret-stealth-helicopter-program-revealed-osama-bin/story?id=135306

34   http://www.guardian.co.uk/world/2011/may/02/osama-bin-laden-killed-abbottabad-raid

35   http://www.sodahead.com/united-states/obama-did-not-take-out-bin-laden/question-2445277/

36   http://barenakedislam.com/2011/05/02/did-senior-militaryintelligence-officials-overrule-president-obama-regarding-mission-to-kill-osama-bin-laden/

37   http://www.dailymail.co.uk/news/article-2137636/Osama-bin-Laden-death-SEALs-slam-Obama-using-ammunition-bid-credit.html#ixzz1twqunhrY

38   http://www.nypost.com/p/news/international/real_story_of_team_charge_IHMzMvBw4Q7l6reGL20etJ#ixzz1twSXsCmt

39   http://www.cbsnews.com/8301-503544_162-20060581-503544.html

40   http://www.msnbc.msn.com/id/44043847/ns/world_news-south_and_central_asia/t/us-troops-mostly-elite-navy-seals-killed-afghanistan/#.T6Gr0u0Z2S0

41   http://atlasshrugs2000.typepad.com/atlas_shrugs/2012/05/obamas-epicfail-pakistani-doctor-who-led-us-to-bin-ladens-hideout-is-jailed-for-33-years-for-treason.html

42   http://www.wnd.com/2012/06/will-heads-roll-for-the-stuxnet-leak/

43   http://larouchepac.com/node/22996

44   http://www.foxnews.com/politics/2012/06/10/rep-king-leaks-came-from-white-house-obama-trying-to-be-like-john-wayne/#

Part IV, Chapter 8—U.S. Army

1   http://www.teaparty.org/article.php?id=2771
2   http://thehill.com/blogs/defcon-hill/marine-corps/217901-hunter-marine-should-not-be-punished-for-facebook-posts
3   http://charismanews.com/us/33289-air-force-bows-to-atheists-in-multiple-anti-christian-moves
4   http://frontpagemag.com/2012/05/09/a-tale-of-two-courtrooms/?utm_source=FrontPage+Magazine&utm_medium=email&utm_campaign=5142dbe223-Mailchimp_FrontPageMag
5   http://foxnewsinsider.com/2012/05/07/911-plotters-ksm-delay-court-proceedings-with-antics-like-making-paper-airplanes-reading-magazines-and-feigning-sleep/
6   http://www.nationalcenter.org/ChargeoftheLightBrigade.html
7   http://aclj.org/american-heritage/decision-expected-camp-pendleton-memorial-cross
8   http://www.theblaze.com/stories/air-force-bows-to-atheist-complaints-will-remove-bible-requirement-for-on-base-lodging/faith
9   http://www.afa.net/Detail.aspx?id=2147520533
10 http://www.christianexaminer.com/Articles/Articles%20May10/Art_May10_18.html
11 http://skinnyreporter.com/clericsbanned.html
12 http://rightsoup.com/nidal-hasans-powerpoint-on-islam-business-card-ignored-by-the-politically-correct/
13 http://michellemalkin.com/2009/04/14/confirme-the-obama-dhs-hit-job-on-conservatives-is-real/?loc=interstitialskip
14 http://frontpagemag.com/2012/02/03/domestic-jihad-victims-deserve-purple-heart/
15 http://www.wnd.com/2012/02/navy-sued-over-manipulation-of-gay-data/
16 http://www.washingtontimes.com/news/2011/mar/22/military-set-to-train-for-end-of-dont-ask/?page=all
17 http://www.wnd.com/2012/03/bill-to-let-chaplains-hold-biblical-view-of-gays/
18 http://www.thebody.com/content/art54293.html
19 http://townhall.com/tipsheet/guybenson/2012/01/10/reminder_obama_to_lay_off_80000_us_soldiers
20 http://www.humanevents.com/article.php?id=49819

21 http://shark-tank.net/2012/02/04/25210/

22 http://www.rushlimbaugh.com/daily/2012/04/27/
    obama_to_veto_gop_student_loan_fix

23 http://townhall.com/tipsheet/guybenson/2012/01/10/
    reminder_obama_to_lay_off_80000_us_soldiers

24 http://townhall.com/tipsheet/guybenson/2012/01/10/
    reminder_obama_to_lay_off_80000_us_soldiers

25 http://www.wnd.com/2008/07/69601/

Part IV, Chapter 9—State Workers

1   http://online.wsj.com/article/SB1000142405297020419070457702432
    1510926692.html

2   http://online.wsj.com/article/SB1000142405297020419070457702432
    1510926692.html

3   http://www.nypost.com/p/news/opinion/opedcolumnists/
    look_who_trying_to_buy_the_election_ZJlWcQjzLQk1NRt82zLrLP

4   http://www.anncoulter.com/cgi-local/printer_friendly.cgi?article=411

5   http://www.wsws.org/articles/2010/feb2010/unio-f03.shtml

6   http://www.aei.org/papers/economics/fiscal-policy/labor/comparing-
    federal-and-private-sector-compensation/

7   http://www.foxnews.com/us/2011/05/20/lifeguard-pay-200g-riles-
    california-beach-city/#ixzz1U6M7ZQSZ

8   http://www.latimes.com/news/local/bell/la-me-bell-loans-
    20100901,0,1653339.story

9   http://timelines.latimes.com/bell/

10 latimes.com/news/local/la-me-02-02-salaries-20110202,0,
    4441320.story

11 http://www.latimes.com/news/local/la-me-vernon-pensions-
    20120601,0,5371733.story

12 http//www.latimes.com/news/local/la-me-cudahy-raises-
    20120529,0,5495824.story

13 jack.dolan@latimes.com 4.19.2011

14 anthony.york@latimes.com

15 Life's tough for $144,000 garbage collectors http://www.wnd.com/?pageI
    d=253645#ixzz1BpvI2YXF

16 http://www.nytimes.com/2008/09/21/nyregion/21lirr.
    html?pagewanted=2&_r=1

17 http://www.nytimes.com/2008/09/21/nyregion/21lirr.
    html?pagewanted=2&_r=1

18 http://www.anncoulter.com/cgi-local/printer_friendly.cgi?article=413

19 http://www.newsmax.com/Newsfront/Republicans-public-
    pensions/2011/02/08/id/385400

20 http://online.wsj.com/article/SB100014240527487040179045754098 1
    3223662860.html

21 http://www.foxbusiness.com/industries/2012/06/13/jpmorgan-
    questionable-muni-call/

22 *RiShawn Biddle on 9.1.11 @ 6:08AM, American Spectator*

23 http://online.wsj.com/article/SB10001424052702303592404577362220
    551217352.html?KEYWORDS=Michael+Corkery

24 http://online.wsj.com/article/SB10001424052970203707504577011901
    934288534.html?KEYWORDS=Sharon+Terlep++Matthew+Dolan

25 http://www.latimes.com/news/opinion/commentary/la-oe-fritz-pension-
    reform-20110118,0,7987400.story

26 http://spectator.org/people/rishawn-biddle/all

27 http://online.wsj.com/article/SB10001424052748704398804575071591
    602878062.html

28 http://www.latimes.com/news/local/la-me-0711-san-bernardino-
    20120711,0,3350406,full.story

29 http://online.wsj.com/article/SB10001424052748704398804575071591
    602878062.html

30 http://online.wsj.com/article/SB10001424053111903520204576482122
    127596128.html

31 http://abcnews.go.com/Business/maywood-california-top-cities-
    overwhelmed-recession/story?id=11032953#.T_2UxI4Z2S0

32 http://www.usatoday.com/news/nation/story/2012-02-29/stockton-
    california-bankruptcy/53296106/1

33 http://www.latimes.com/news/local/la-california-cities-in-
    bankruptcy-20120702,0,2178927.photogallery

34 http://latimesblogs.latimes.com/lanow/2012/07/san-bernardino-
    bankruptcy-officials-knew-of-risks-for-years.html

35 http://online.wsj.com/article/SB10001424052748704398804575071591
    602878062.html

36 http://online.wsj.com/article/SB10001424053111903520204576482122
    127596128.html

37   http://www.usatoday.com/news/nation/story/2012-02-29/stockton-california-bankruptcy/53296106/1

38   http://www.latimes.com/news/opinion/commentary/la-oe-fritz-pension-reform-20110118,0,7987400.story

39   http://frontpagemag.com/2010/09/07/obamas-next-union-bailout/

Part IV, Chapter 10—Federal Workers

1   http://www.washingtontimes.com/news/2010/feb/2/burgeoning-federal-payroll-signals-return-of-big-g/?page=all

2   http://endoftheamericandream.com/archives/10-mind-blowing-facts-which-show-how-members-of-congress-and-federal-employees-are-living-the-high-life-at-our-expense

3   http://www.forbes.com/sites/nathanvardi/2012/04/24/americas-richest-counties/

4   http://www.bloomberg.com/news/2011-10-19/beltway-earnings-make-u-s-capital-richer-than-silicon-valley.html

5   http://www.washingtontimes.com/news/2011/may/31/77000-feds-paid-more-than-governors/?page=all

6   http://endoftheamericandream.com/archives/10-mind-blowing-facts-which-show-how-members-of-congress-and-federal-employees-are-living-the-high-life-at-our-expense

7   http://www.washingtontimes.com/news/2012/jan/30/cbo-says-federal-employees-rake-in-much-more-pay/?page=all#pagebreak

8   http://www.commentarymagazine.com/article/what-public-sector-unions-have-wrought/

9   http://money.cnn.com/2012/05/10/news/economy/postal-service-loss/

10   http://money.cnn.com/2012/03/05/news/economy/postal_service_loan/index.htm

11   http://www.fra.dot.gov/rpd/passenger/274.shtml

12   http://www.gsa.gov/portal/content/100735

13   http://en.wikipedia.org/wiki/General_Services_Administration

14   http://www.foxnews.com/opinion/2012/04/18/gsa-parties-not-secret-service-prostitutes-betray-public-trust/

15   http://www.washingtonpost.com/politics/competitive-bidding-drives-gsa-inquiry/2012/04/15/gIQA1ZGMKT_story.ht

16   http://www.youtube.com/watch?v=karcOeSOPbo&feature=related

Part IV, Chapter 11—Magic Mystery Money Machine

1   http://wiki.answers.com/Q/What_is_1_percent_of_1_trillion_dollars
2   http://www.save-a-patriot.org/files/view/whofed.html
3   http://www.tysknews.com/Depts/Taxes/fed_banking_fraud.htm
4   http://www.thefreemanonline.org/features/who-owns-the-fed/
5   http://www.prisonplanet.com/the-federal-reserve-made-16-trillion-in-secret-loans-to-their-bankster-friends.html
6   http://kingdomecon.wordpress.com/2012/04/17/why-the-fed-our-central-bank-operates-a-financial-ponzi-scheme/
7   http://kingdomecon.wordpress.com/2012/04/17/why-the-fed-our-central-bank-operates-a-financial-ponzi-scheme/
8   http://theeconomiccollapseblog.com/archives/have-you-heard-about-the-16-trillion-dollar-bailout-the-federal-reserve-handed-to-the-too-big-to-fail-banks
9   http://www.bloomberg.com/news/2011-11-28/secret-fed-loans-undisclosed-to-congress-gave-banks-13-billion-in-income.ht
10 http://www.moneynews.com/Headline/fed-debt-Treasury/2012/03/28/id/434106
11 http://cnsnews.com/news/article/china-has-divested-97-percent-its-holdings-us-treasury-bills
12 *http://www.federalreserve.gov/newsevents/press/other/20110110a.htm*
13 12 U.S.C. 531
14 http://www.tysknews.com/Depts/Taxes/fed_banking_fraud.htm
15 http://www.bloomberg.com/news/2011-11-28/secret-fed-loans-undisclosed-to-congress-gave-banks-13-billion-in-income.ht
16 http://frontporchpolitics.com/2012/06/federal-reserve-board-members-bailed-out-their-own-banks-for-4-trillion/
17 http://theeconomiccollapseblog.com/archives/have-you-heard-about-the-16-trillion-dollar-bailout-the-federal-reserve-handed-to-the-too-big-to-fail-banks
18 http://www.ronpaul.com/congress/legislation/audit-the-federal-reserve-fed-hr-459-s202/
19 http://www.prisonplanet.com/the-federal-reserve-made-16-trillion-in-secret-loans-to-their-bankster-friends.html
20 http://www.bloomberg.com/news/2010-12-01/taxpayer-risk-impossible-to-know-for-some-fed-financial-crisis-programs.html
21 http://escapetyranny.com/2011/04/02/bernankes-secret-exposed-foreign-banks-got-most-of-the-secret-cheap-money-from-the-fed/

22 http://uclafacultyassociation.blogspot.com/2010/12/calpers-calstrs-profited-from-feds-talf.html

23 <http://www.teaparty.org/view_email.php?id=1248>

24 http://www.rushlimbaugh.com/daily/2010/12/02/is_anything_real_trillions_in_secret_fed_payments_revealed

25 http://moraloutrage.wordpress.com/2011/08/31/federal-reserve-audit-reveals-trillions-in-secret-bailouts/

26 http://www.prisonplanet.com/the-federal-reserve-made-16-trillion-in-secret-loans-to-their-bankster-friends.html

27 http://www.globalresearch.ca/index.php?context=va&aid=10489

28 http://www.bloomberg.com/news/2012-05-11/jpmorgan-loses-2-billion-as-mistakes-trounce-hedges.html

29 http://online.wsj.com/article/SB100014240527023040703045773965114207920008.html

30 http://www.prisonplanet.com/the-federal-reserve-made-16-trillion-in-secret-loans-to-their-bankster-friends.html

31 http://www.nytimes.com/2010/12/02/business/economy/02fed.html?_r=1

32 http://theeconomiccollapseblog.com/archives/have-you-heard-about-the-16-trillion-dollar-bailout-the-federal-reserve-handed-to-the-too-big-to-fail-banks

33 http://moraloutrage.wordpress.com/2011/08/31/federal-reserve-audit-reveals-trillions-in-secret-bailouts/

34 http://sdishman-triple-espresso.blogspot.com/2011/04/federal-reserves-discount-window.html

35 http://www.nytimes.com/2010/12/02/business/economy/02fed.html?_r=1

36 http://www.nytimes.com/2010/12/02/business/economy/02fed.html?_r=1

37 http://www.nytimes.com/2010/12/02/business/economy/02fed.html?

38 ://www.nytimes.com/2010/12/02/business/economy/02fed.html?_r=1

39 http://www.economonitor.com/blog/2011/12/more-on-those-secret-federal-reserve-loans-to-banks/

40 tp://www.bloomberg.com/news/2010-12-01/taxpayer-risk-impossible-to-know-for-some-fed-financial-crisis

41 http://online.wsj.com/article/SB122428567636046459.html

42 http://articles.latimes.com/2008/oct/03/business/fi-moneyblog3

43 http://latimesblogs.latimes.com/money_co/2008/07/sen-charles-e-s.html

44 http://timeline.stlouisfed.org/index.cfm?p=timeline

45   http://online.wsj.com/article/SB122428567636046459.html

46   http://patrick-hinton.suite101.com/the-start-of-the-global-financial-
      crisis-2008-a88065

47   http://en.wikipedia.org/wiki/Barack_Obama_presidential
      _campaign,_2008

48   http://online.wsj.com/article/SB10001424052748704022804575041280
      125257648.html

49   http://online.wsj.com/article/SB10001424052748704022804575041280
      125257648.html

Part IV, Chapter 12—Crucifying Private Industry

1   http://www.washingtontimes.com/news/2012/may/15/obamas-plan-to-
      crucify-political-opponents/

2   http://scaredmonkeys.com/2010/02/03/12541/

3   http://miseryindex2008.blogspot.com/2008_10_12_archive.html

4   *http://abcnews.go.com/Blotter/story?id=5987363&page=1#.T6CV9u0Z2S0*

5   http://abcnews.go.com/Business/story?id=7142769&page=1#.
      T8MQT44Z2S0

6   http://www.washingtontimes.com/news/2012/may/11/bbts-john-allison-
      5-questions-with-decker/

7   http://cloud.frontpagemag.com/wp-content/uploads/2011/10/
      fanniemae.gif

8   http://cnsnews.com/news/article/former-clinton-official-paid-26-million-
      fannie-mae-taxpayer-bailout-now-obama-shortlist

9   http://townhall.com/columnists/michellemalkin/2011/05/27/
      barney_franks_friends_with_benefits/page/full/

10   http://cloud.frontpagemag.com/wp-content/uploads/2011/10/
      fanniemae.gif

11   http://www.opensecrets.org/news/2008/09/update-fannie-mae-and-
      freddie.html

12   http://michellemalkin.com/2010/09/24/how-privileged-democrats-pay-
      for-their-houses/

13   http://money.cnn.com/2012/05/09/news/companies/fannie-mae-
      earnings/index.htm

14   http://www.humanevents.com/article.php?id=48196

15   Http://www.theblaze.com/stories/millions-of-taxpayer-dollars-used-to-
      defend-freddie-and-fannie-execs-on-trial-for-fraud

16   http://money.cnn.com/2010/05/19/news/companies/SEIU_Bank_of_America_protest.fortune/
17   http://rightwingnews.com/barack-obama/huge-mob-of-seiu-goons-attacks-bankers-home/
18   ttp://www.tripadvisor.com/ShowUserReviews-g32279-d224779-r62200402-St_Regis_Monarch_Beach-Dana_Point_California.html
19   www.newwest.net/topic/article/tamarack_resort . . . bankruptcy/ . . . /L36/
20   www.litchfield-park.org › . . . › E-Services › E-Community Alert News
21   http://www.usatoday.com/travel/hotels/2009-03-05-foreclosed-hotels_N.htm
22   http://online.wsj.com/article/SB124719403598721375.html
23   http://www.usatoday.com/travel/hotels/2009-03-05-foreclosed-hotels_N.htm
24   en.wikipedia.org/wiki/Fontainebleau_Resort_Las_Vegas
25   www.hotelchatter.com/ . . . /A_Sneak_Peek_Inside_Aria_Resort_and_C . . .
26   http://frontpagemag.com/2012/04/30/our-marie-antoinette-president/
27   http://michellemalkin.com/2011/02/28/sacrifice/
28   http://washingtonexaminer.com/politics/washington-secrets/2012/02/michelles-ski-trip-marks-16-obama-vacations/294051
29   ttp://www.judicialwatch.org/corrupt-politicians-lists/washingtons-ten-most-wanted-corrupt-politicians-for-2011/
30   http://www.dailymail.co.uk/news/article-1325075/Obama-India-visit-Biggest-US-President-40-planes-6-armoured-cars.html
31   http://www.dnaindia.com/india/report_mumbai-luxury-hotels-booked-for-obama-s-visit_1456673
32   http://www.dnaindia.com/india/report_mumbai-luxury-hotels-booked-for-obama-s-visit_1456673
33   http://frontpagemag.com/2012/04/30/our-marie-antoinette-president/
34   http://www.theblaze.com/stories/why-is-the-story-about-malia-obama-vacationing-in-mexico-disappearing-from-the-web/
35   http://michellemalkin.com/2009/07/26/culture-of-corruption-czars-of-the-obama-underworld/
36   http://www.sfgate.com/cgi-bin/article.cgi?f=/c/a/2008/11/02/MNTL13SU6S.DTL
37   http://www.pressherald.com/opinion/u_s_-oil-gas-reserves-surpass-average-opec-nation_2011-02-25.html

38 http://www.pressherald.com/opinion/u_s_-oil-gas-reserves-surpass-average-opec-nation_2011-02-25.html

39 http://naturalresources.house.gov/Issues/Issue/?IssueID=56687

40 http://www.foxnews.com/opinion/2012/03/29/electric-rates-will-soar-now-that-obamas-epa-has-crushed-coal-fired-power/

41 http://www.nypost.com/p/news/opinion/opedcolumnists/obama_war_on_coal_zVrf0OxP4RcUfmymSsDcOJ

42 http://townhall.com/columnists/tomborelli/2012/02/08/obamas_war_on_coal_undermines_manufacturing_jobs/page/full/

43 http://thinkprogress.org/climate/2012/02/29/435012/dirty-aging-coal-plants-set-to-close/

44 http://www.chicagotribune.com/business/ct-biz-0517-rate-shock-20120517,0,5649803.story

45 http://thinkprogress.org/climate/2012/02/29/435012/dirty-aging-coal-plants-set-to-close/

46 http://www.washingtonpost.com/national/health-science/utilities-announce-closure-of-10-aging-power-plants-in-midwest-east/2012/02/29/gIQANSLEiR_story.html

47 http://dailycaller.com/2011/08/11/white-house-epa-ignore-small-business-admins-report-that-new-coal-regulations-will-kill-jobs-economy/#ixzz1vBx7ByyM

48 http://dailycaller.com/2011/08/11/white-house-epa-ignore-small-business-admins-report-that-new-coal-regulations-will-kill-jobs-economy/#ixzz1vBx7ByyM

49 http://townhall.com/columnists/tomborelli/2012/02/08/obamas_war_on_coal_undermines_manufacturing_jobs/page/full/

50 http://www.wvmetronews.com/index.cfm?func=displayfullstory&storyid=50837&type

51 http://www.cbsnews.com/8301-505245_162-57388567/5-pa-coal-fired-power-plants-to-close/

52 http://www.cbsnews.com/8301-505245_162-57388567/5-pa-coal-fired-power-plants-to-close/

53 http://www.huffingtonpost.com/2012/03/05/illinois-coal-plants-midw_n_1321336.html

54 ttp://www.washingtonpost.com/national/health-science/utilities-announce-closure-of-10-aging-power-plants-in-midwest-east/2012/02/29/gIQANSLEiR_story.html

55 http://www.nytimes.com/gwire/2010/10/06/06greenwire-wva-sues-obama-epa-over-mining-coal-regulation-48964.html

56 http://townhall.com/columnists/tomborelli/2012/02/08/
    obamas_war_on_coal_undermines_manufacturing_jobs/page/full/

57 http://www.washingtonpost.com/national/health-science/
    utilities-announce-closure-of-10-aging-power-plants-in-midwest-
    east/2012/02/29/gIQANSLEiR_story.html

58 http://www.chicagotribune.com/business/ct-biz-0517-rate-shock-
    20120517,0,5649803.story

59 http://www.chicagotribune.com/business/ct-biz-0517-rate-shock-
    20120517,0,5649803.story

60 http://www.foxnews.com/opinion/2012/05/22/obamas-war-on-coal-hits-
    your-electric-bill/

61 http://hotair.com/archives/2012/03/01/five-coal-fueled-power-plants-to-
    close-due-to-obama-administration-regulation/

62 http://online.wsj.com/article/SB100014240527023036105045774 2025
    1668850864.html?KEYWORDS=Renewable+energy+ca%27t+run+the
    +cloud

63 http://www.smartplanet.com/blog/smart-takes/how-much-energy-does-
    facebook-use-in-a-day/25620

64 http://www.googlefalle.com/googletrap/googletrap/index.php/
    2008/04/29/where-are-google's-server-farms/

65 http://www.economist.com/node/11413148

66 http://online.wsj.com/article/SB100014240527023036105045774 2025
    1668850864.html?KEYWORDS=Renewable+energy+ca%27t+run+the
    +cloud

67 http://frontpagemag.com/2010/11/03/bullying-oil-producers/

68 http://cnsnews.com/news/article/obama-administration-moratorium-oil-
    drilling-hurts-consumers-report-says

69 http://epw.senate.gov/public/index.cfm?FuseAction=Minority.
    Speeches&ContentRecord_id=ea800426-802a-23ad-4e25-9051360ff8fc

70 *http://cbl2988.hubpages.com/hub/The-Idiot-In-Chief-President-Obama*

71 http://en.wikipedia.org/wiki/Deepwater_Horizon_oil_spill

72 http://junkscience.com/2012/03/30/ibd-house-panel-says-obama-hides-
    ball-on-energy-truth/

73 http://frontpagemag.com/2010/06/22/soros-oil-spill-payoff/

74 <http://click.email.americansolutions.com/?qs=0bc4f760209f17ba97d00
    c5698ea38592138be4fa3b29e852b124e9e2cf43cee>,

75 http://www.cbsnews.com/2100-201_162-6670917.html

76 http://www.foxnews.com/politics/2010/06/22/federal-judge-blocks-
    obamas-offshore-drilling-moratorium-gulf-mexico/

77 http://cnsnews.com/news/article/obama-administration-moratorium-oil-drilling-hurts-consumers-report-says

78 http://cnsnews.com/news/article/obama-administration-moratorium-oil-drilling-hurts-consumers-report-says

79 http://www.foxnews.com/on-air/oreilly/transcript/president-obama-goes-attack-against-oil-companies

80 http://www.npr.org/blogs/thetwo-way/2010/05/obama_teams_tough_bp_talk_unde.html

81 The latest example involves a new agency created to levy untold millions of dollars in fines if companies don't kowtow to the new bureaucracy. The agency's head gave the tasteless warning: "If they cut corners they could end up paying enough to quickly take care of the federal deficit

82 http://online.wsj.com/article/SB100014240529702034586045772616403265111180.html

83 http://en.wikipedia.org/wiki/List_of_U.S._states_and_territories_by_area

84 http://www.cdfe.org/center-projects/energy/the-truth-about-anwr

85 http://online.wsj.com/article/SB1000142405270230387960457741052059464698.html?mod=googlenews_wsj

86 http://www.usatoday.com/news/nation/census/2011-03-16-north-dakota-census_N.htm

87 http://blog.heritage.org/2011/07/21/study-marcellus-shale-an-economic-godsend-for-pennsylvania/

88 http://news.investors.com/article/611380/201205141900/green-river-equal-to-worlds-oil-reserves-.htm?p=full

89 http://epw.senate.gov/public/index.cfm?FuseAction=Minority.Speeches&ContentRecord_id=ea800426-802a-23ad-4e25-9051360ff8fc

90 http://epw.senate.gov/public/index.cfm?FuseAction=Minority.Speeches&ContentRecord_id=ea800426-802a-23ad-4e25-9051360ff8fc

91 http://www.thestar.com/news/quebec/article/839794--quebec-between-a-rock-and-a-hard-place-on-gas-from-shale

92 http://en.wikipedia.org/wiki/Keystone_Pipeline#Keystone_Pipeline

93 http://www.mcphersonsentinel.com/news/x43408844/Keystone-pipeline-delivers-oil-to-NCRA

94 http://www.washingtontimes.com/news/2012/mar/21/pipeline-ruling-filled-with-politics/

95 http://www.washingtontimes.com/news/2012/may/31/killing-jobs-to-save-the-sage-grouse/

96 http://www.foxnews.com/politics/2012/05/08/environmental-groups-paid-millions-by-federal-agencies-sue-studies-show/?test=latestnews

97   http://cnsnews.com/news/article/obama-claims-credit-southern-end-
     keystone-pipeline

98   http://blog.energytomorrow.org/2010/11/addressing-
     hydraulic-fracturing-issues-one-by-one.html?gclid=CKHq_c-
     frKcCFQwFbAodN0kjCw

99   http://www.wnd.com/2012/04/obamas-secret-plan-to-seize-americans-
     land/

Part IV—Chapter 13: Saul Alinsky's Rules for Radicals

1   http://www.fns.usda.gov/pd/34snapmonthly.htm

2   http://theeconomiccollapseblog.com/archives/extreme-poverty-is-now-at-
     record-levels-19-statistics-about-the-poor-that-will-absolutely-astound-
     you

3   http://www.guardian.co.uk/business/2012/jan/11/poverty-america-likely-
     worse-report

4   http://www.forbes.com/sites/peterferrara/2012/01/12/the-worst-
     economic-recovery-since-the-great-depression/2/

5   http://research.stlouisfed.org/fred2/series/UEMPMEAN

6   http://www.bls.gov/news.release/pdf/empsit.pdf

7   http://times247.com/articles/almost-1-in-3-jobs-require-a-license

8   http://latimesblogs.latimes.com/money_co/2011/12/less-than-a-quarter-
     of-companies-to-hire-in-2012-careerbuilder.html

9   http://money.cnn.com/2012/01/26/real_estate/new_home_sales/index.
     htm?iid=HP_River

10   http://www.latimes.com/business/realestate/la-fi-negative-equity-
     20120524,0,985482.story

11   http://www.latimes.com/business/money/la-fi-mo-zillow-
     underwater-20120524,0,165710.story

12   http://swampland.time.com/2011/10/24/who-obamas-housing-plan-
     helps-most-hint-he-doesnt-own-his-home/

13   http://en.wikipedia.org/wiki/American_Recovery_and_
     Reinvestment_Act_of_2009

14   http://www.theblaze.com/stories/report-treasury-writes-off-billions-in-
     tarp-loans-watchdog-discovers-more-fraud/

15   July 29, 2010, GAO report, pages 26-28.

16   http://www.theblaze.com/stories/report-treasury-writes-off-billions-in-
     tarp-loans-watchdog-discovers-more-fraud/

17   http://www.atr.org/presidential-math-cash-clunkers-spent-billion-a3816

18 http://www.brillig.com/debt_clock/

19 http://en.wikipedia.org/wiki/Troubled_Asset_Relief_Program

20 http://en.wikipedia.org/wiki/General_Motors_Chapter_11
    _reorganization

21 http://gaanderson.hubpages.com/hub/Obama-General-Motors-GM-
    Tarp-Bailout-Untold-Details

22   http://frontpagemag.com/2012/02/01/obamas-auto-bailout-lies/

23 http://godfatherpolitics.com/4959/president-obama-stole-our-money-to-
    keep-general-motors-alive/

24 http://frontpagemag.com/2010/09/22/the-delphi-disaster-an-economic-
    horror-story-obama-won't-tell/

25 http://online.wsj.com/article_email/
    SB10001424052702303768104577462650268680454-
    lMyQjAxMTAyMDEwNDExNDQyWj.html#articleTabs=article

26 http://nlpc.org/stories/2011/07/25/gm-bankruptcy-fallout-delphi-
    retirees-suing-treasury-and-auto-task-force

27 *http://frontpagemag.com*/2010/07/23/obamas-dealergate/

28 http://www.americanthinker.com/2010/07/race_played_role_in_obama_
    car.html

29 *http://frontpagemag.com*/2010/07/23/obamas-dealergate/

30 http://online.wsj.com/article_email/
    SB10001424052702303768104577462650268680454-
    lMyQjAxMTAyMDEwNDExNDQyWj.html#articleTabs=article

31 http://www.forbes.com/sites/paulroderickgregory/2012/02/06/american-
    airlines-shows-the-corruption-of-obamas-gm-bailout/

32 http://times247.com/articles/gm-bails-on-taxpayers-in-favor-of-big-
    worker-bonuses

33 http://www.newser.com/story/140728/gm-to-spend-500m-on-worker-
    bonuses.html

34 http://www.foxnews.com/opinion/2012/05/18/what-gm-bailout-really-
    cost-american-taxpayers/

35 http://spectator.org/blog/2011/08/04/bodies-found-near-
    exploded-caf

36 http://www.forbes.com/sites/jimhenry/2011/12/12/chevy-volt-battery-
    fires-threaten-all-electric-ve/

37 http://online.wsj.com/article/business_world.html

38 http://gas2.org/2012/02/20/ge-forcing-employees-into-chevy-volts/

39 http://online.wsj.com/article_email/
    SB10001424052702303768104577462650268680454-
    lMyQjAxMTAyMDEwNDExNDQyWj.html#articleTabs=article

40 http://online.wsj.com/article/SB100014240527023041771045773071 8
    4099140656.html?mod=WSJ_hps_editorsPicks_1

41 http://www.alinskydefeater.com/Blog/2011/09/the-alinsky-tactics-rule-
    13-pick-the-target-freeze-it-personalize-it-and-polarize-it/

42 http://www.bloomberg.com/apps/news?pid=newsarchive&sid=af4lR7a4
    FXsM

43 http://www.theblaze.com/stories/dem-strategist-attacks-ann-romney-as-a-
    stay-at-home-mom-never-worked-a-day-in-her-life/

44 http://times247.com/articles/team-obama-names-private-citizens-who-
    donated-to-romney-camp

45 http://www.redstate.com/erick/2010/08/23/barack-obamas-attempted-
    character-assassinate-of-the-koch-industries/

46 http://online.wsj.com/article/SB10001424052702304723304577368 28
    0604524916.html

47 http://online.wsj.com/article/SB10001424052702304723304577368 28
    0604524916.html

48 http://www.humanevents.com/2012/03/02/obamas-irs-targets-tea-party/

Part IV—Chapter 14: Converting America into a Caliphate

1 http://www.foreignpolicy.com/articles/2011/12/16/
   the_real_mohamed_bouazizi

2 http://frontporchpolitics.com/2012/06/the-difference-between-wide-
   receiver-fast-and-furious/

3 http://www.washingtontimes.com/news/2012/jan/19/
   fast-and-furious-stinks/

4 http://www.nytimes.com/2010/06/29/us/29scotus.html

5 http://www.nytimes.com/2010/07/11/opinion/11sun1.html

6 http://www.columbiamissourian.com/stories/2010/07/22/column-little-
   gun-control-would-be-good-america/

7 http://legalinsurrection.com/2011/07/obama-sold-tracked-same-guns-to-
   cartels-he-hoped-to-ban-because-they-were-tracked-from-cartels/

8 http://www.washingtontimes.com/news/2011/dec/15/obamas-watergate-
   758295296/

9 http://godfatherpolitics.com/5495/fast-and-furious-knew-deaths-
   inevitable-but-acceptable/

10 http://www.washingtontimes.com/news/2012/jun/5/issa-fast-and-furious-documents-show-officials-had/

11 http://us2.campaign-archive2.com/?u=0c63abc741fff5c4813d80e0a&id=e575483008&e=25f099f85b

12 http://www.washingtontimes.com/news/2011/dec/15/obamas-watergate-758295296/

13 http://www.washingtontimes.com/news/2012/jan/20/federal-prosecutor-cites-fifth-fast-furious-probe/

14 http://www.splcenter.org/get-informed/intelligence-files/groups/new-black-panther-party

15 http://www.theblaze.com/stories/ahmadinejad-farrakhan-new-black-panthers-shocking-new-details-on-their-meeting-the-beast-alliance-that-was-forged/

16 http://professional.wsj.com/article/SB124451552193396877-email.html?mg=reno-wsj

17 http://professional.wsj.com/article/SB10001424052970203550604574361071968458430.html?mg=reno64-wsj

18 http://professional.wsj.com/article/SB10001424052748703559604576176381487078812.html?mg=reno64-wsj

19 http://professional.wsj.com/article/SB124451552193396877-email.html?mg=reno-wsj

20 http://www.newsrealblog.com/2010/10/01/barack-obama-and-eric-holders-affirmative-action-justice-department/

21 http://professional.wsj.com/article/SB10001424052748703559604576176381487078812.html?mg=reno64-wsj

22 http://www.myfoxdetroit.com/dpp/news/charlie_leduff/leduff-to-minister-malik-shabazz-burn-down-detroit-are-you-out-of-your-mind-20120227-msdk

23 http://www.youtube.com/watch?v=oBhzJnJIilI

24 http://michellemalkin.com/2010/07/09/whitewashing-black-racism/

25 http://www.theblaze.com/stories/new-black-panther-field-marshal-whites-should-be-thankful-were-not-hanging-crackers-by-nooses-yet-yet-yet/

26 http://www.youtube.com/watch?v=8h2n3vJo7Xo&feature=player_embedded#t=116s

27 http://frontpagemag.com/2012/04/16/a-death-bounty-and-an-attorney-general/?utm_source=FrontPage+Magazine&utm_medium=email&utm_campaign=b1e30dcf74-Mailchimp_FrontPageMag

28 http://www.dailymail.co.uk/news/article-2078484/Knockout -King-The-sickening-game-claiming-lives-country.html# ixzz1y5ZsyDdm

29 http://frontpagemag.com/2011/12/29/mall-mayhem-and-race-reality/

30 http://www.wnd.com/2012/06/black-mob-violence-hits-nordstroms/

31 http://www.youtube.com/watch?v=7qeMslmDBxY&feature=watch

32 http://www.dailymail.co.uk/news/article-2078484/Knockout-King-The-sickening-game-claiming-lives-country.html

33 http://www.wnd.com/2012/06/chicagos-unreported-race-war/

34 http://www.chicagonewsreport.com/2012/06/downtown-chicago-cops-outnumbered-by.html

35 http://www.wnd.com/2012/06/chicagos-unreported-race-war/

36 http://www.wnd.com/2012/06/black-mob-violence-hits-nordstroms/

37 http://frontpagemag.com/2011/08/10/weapons-of-mob-destruction-2/

38 http://www.huffingtonpost.com/2012/03/23/obama-trayvon-martin_n_1375083.html

39 http://www.theroot.com/blogs/tina-brown/newsweek-spiked-cover-obama-trayvon

40 http://www.washingtonpost.com/blogs/2chambers/post/rep-bobby-rush-wears-hoodie-on-house-floor-for-trayvon-martin/2012/03/28/gIQAlf8WgS_blog.html

41 http://www.wnd.com/2012/06/black-mob-violence-hits-nordstroms/

42 http://www.wnd.com/2012/03/obama-team-protects-black-thugs/

43 http://wherechangeobama.blogspot.com/2012/04/black-youth-unemployment-rate-increases.html

44 http://www.theblaze.com/stories/this-is-the-comprehensive-list-of-those-supporting-occupy-wall-st/

45 <http://pjmedia.com/zombie/2011/10/31/the-99-official-list-of-ows/>

46 http://www.washingtontimes.com/news/2011/dec/20/hackers-post-cops-personal-data-online/

47 ttp://www.theblaze.com/stories/new-video-seattle-cops-say-occupy-protesters-threw-bricks-and-bags-of-steel/

48 http://www.theblaze.com/stories/shock-video-ows-protester-caught-dumping-feces-in-atm-lobby/

49 http://www.therightperspective.org/2012/05/01/occupy-anarchists-arrested-in-terror-plot/#more-22292

50 http://frontporchpolitics.com/2012/06/romneys-campaign-bus-explodes-on-msnbc/

51 http://frontpagemag.com/2012/05/21/nonviolence-explodes-in-chicago/

52 http://www.nationalreview.com/blogs/print/224610

53 http://michellemalkin.com/2009/04/14/confirme-the-obama-dhs-hit-job-on-conservatives-is-real/?loc=interstitialskiphttp://www.washingtontimes.com/weblogs/watercooler/2010/feb/10/acorn-slated-get-nearly-4-billion-obamas-fiscal-20/

54 http://frontpagemag.com/2012/06/12/obama-gives-446-million-to-acorn-veteran/?utm_source=FrontPage+Magazine&utm_medium=email&utm_campaign=718c706201-Mailchimp_FrontPageMag

55 http://michellemalkin.com/2009/04/14/confirme-the-obama-dhs-hit-job-on-conservatives-is-real/?loc=interstitialskip

56 http://www.rushlimbaugh.com/daily/2011/10/27/obama_s_student_loan_fraud

57 http://usnews.msnbc.msn.com/_news/2012/03/15/10702389-obamas-image-on-american-flag-angers-vets

58 http://frontporchpolitics.com/2012/06/romneys-campaign-bus-explodes-on-msnbc/

59 http://news.investors.com/Article/598993/201201260805/entitlements-soar-under-president-obama.htm

60 http://www.humanevents.com/author/Adam-Tragone/

61 http://www.glennbeck.com/2011/12/02/homeless-woman-with-15-kids-someones-gotta-pay-for-this/

62 http://www.theblaze.com/stories/feds-raid-million-dollar-home-of-welfare-recipient-in-washington-st/

63 http://www.youtube.com/watch?v=0QlOWd2Afok&feature=related

64 http://www.latimes.com/news/nation/nationnow/la-na-nn-tennessee-man-has-30-kids-20120518,0,4036567.story

65 http://www.moonbattery.com/archives/2010/08/hope-change-flo.html

66 http://www.zerohedge.com/article/entitlement-america-head-household-making-minimum-wage-has-more-disposable-income-family-mak

67 http://www.fns.usda.gov/pd/34snapmonthly.htm

68 http://www.bls.gov/news.release/pdf/empsit.pdf

69 http://www.forbes.com/sites/peterferrara/2012/01/12/the-worst-economic-recovery-since-the-great-depression/2/

70 http://theeconomiccollapseblog.com/archives/extreme-poverty-is-now-at-record-levels-19-statistics-about-the-poor-that-will-absolutely-astound-you

71 http://www.bls.gov/news.release/pdf/empsit.pdf

72 http://www.rushlimbaugh.com/daily/2012/06/15/obama_amnesty_plan_catch_release_vote

73 http://godfatherpolitics.com/5653/how-the-election-is-being-rigged-before-you-vote/

74 http://www.wltx.com/news/article/167748/2/DMV-900-Dead-People-May-Have-Voted-

75 http://times247.com/articles/pew-center-1-8-million-dead-people-registered-to-vote

76 http://www.heritage.org/research/reports/2008/04/where-theres-smoke-theres-fire-100000-stolen-votes-in-chicago

77 ttp://www.rnla.org/pressreleases/PR-SouthCarolinavoterIDfinal.pdf

78 http://recursivedigressions.blogspot.com/2012/05/lets-impersonate-eric-holder-game.html

79 http://www.americanthinker.com/2008/07/obamas_civilian_national_secur.html

80 http://articles.latimes.com/2012/jun/18/nation/la-na-emergency-care-20120619

81 http://www.forbes.com/sites/aroy/2012/03/22/how-obamacare-dramatically-increases-the-cost-of-insurance-for-young-workers

82 http://washingtonexaminer.com/article/1349376

83 http://www.foxnews.com/politics/2012/05/01/employers-could-save-billions-by-dropping-workers-from-health-plans-report/

84 http://www.hartfordbusiness.com/apps/pbcs.dll/article?AID=/20120619/NEWS01/120619780

85 www.rightwingnews.com/liberals/obamacare-a-threat-to-white-castle-and-ihop-this-time-it's-personal/

86 http://www.latimes.com/business/la-fi-supreme-healthcare-calif-20120620,0,1852327.story

87 http://www.cis.org/articles/2004/fiscalexec.html

88 http://bcfoley.blogspot.com/2012/01/final-obamacare-waiver-count-1231.html

89 http://www.saveyourrights.com/government-control/the-new-labyrinthine-bureaucracy-of-obamacare-159-new-ones-to-streamline-and-decrease-cost-of-healthcare/

90 http://www.rushlimbaugh.com/daily/2012/04/10/what_does_the_irs_know_about_obamacare_that_we_don_t

91 http://frontpagemag.com/2009/12/23/the-communists-behind-obama%e2%80%99s-health-care-goal

92 http://www.forbes.com/sites/larrybell/2011/06/07/u-n-agreement-should-have-all-gun-owners-up-in-arms/

93 http://godfatherpolitics.com/5993/new-report-if-you-love-liberty-you-might-terrorist/#ixzz1zg2uX2V5

Part IV—Chapter 15

1 http://frontpagemag.com/2012/01/10/obamas-assault-on-separation-of-powers/

2 http://blog.heritage.org/2010/01/28/the-truth-about-president-obama-and-citizens-united/

3 http://www.washingtontimes.com/news/2012/apr/3/obama-flunks-constitutional-law/

4 http://www.washingtontimes.com/news/2012/jul/12/democratic-stalkers/

Disclaimer:

Statements made in this book have been backed up by 48 pages of end notes referring you to the source material. These end notes were very carefully checked again just prior to going to press. Some of them had already been removed from their web sites and were replaced. Others may be removed later on, after the book is published. When a particularly illustrative citation is missing, you have a choice to make: Either this author was making up citations or interested parties removed the citation so you couldn't read it and inform yourself. I leave it to your good sense to figure out which it is . . . . R

The Price of Freedom is Eternal Vigilance

-Thomas Jefferson

Rohini DeSilva is a Christian and a Tea Party supporter who admires Andrew Breitbart, Glen Beck, and Rush Limbaugh for their strong advocacy of Conservative principles.

She grew up in Sri Lanka as Socialists acquired power, became rich, denied citizens their freedom and obliterated private businesses with taxes and regulations. She has a Fellowship in Music and a BFA in Interior Design. She graduated from Columbia Law School with honors and learned that our Constitution prevents the government from infringing on our individual liberty; before Marxist Professors distorted it to assert the government had power over everyone and everything.

She brings her unique perspective, analytical skills and meticulous research to warn the American people that we face a great threat from the vile brew of Socialism and Militant Islam that Obama is thrusting upon us; to remind them that we have freedoms that everyone else yearns to have; and that we need to be eternally vigilant lest our freedoms be taken away.